Also by Carey McWilliams

Ambrose Bierce: A Biography
Louis Adamic and Shadow-America
Factories in the Field
Ill Fares the Land
Brothers Under the Skin
Prejudice: Japanese-Americans: Symbol of Racial Intolerance
Southern California Country: An Island on the Land
A Mask for Privilege: Anti-Semitism in America
North from Mexico: The Spanish-Speaking People of the United States
California: The Great Exception
Rocky Mountain Cities
Witch Hunt: The Revival of Heresy
The California Revolution
Dictionary of American Biography (contributor)
While You Were Gone: A Report on Wartime Life in the United States, edited
   by Jack Goodman, contains a chapter by Carey McWilliams entitled
   "What We Did About Racial Minorities."

by Carey McWilliams

The Education of
Carey McWilliams

Education is that which remains after
one has forgotten all one has learned.
— Sir Lewis Namier

SIMON AND SCHUSTER
NEW YORK

COPYRIGHT © 1978, 1979 BY CAREY MCWILLIAMS
ALL RIGHTS RESERVED
INCLUDING THE RIGHT OF REPRODUCTION
IN WHOLE OR IN PART IN ANY FORM
PUBLISHED BY SIMON AND SCHUSTER
A DIVISION OF GULF & WESTERN CORPORATION
SIMON & SCHUSTER BUILDING
ROCKEFELLER CENTER
1230 AVENUE OF THE AMERICAS
NEW YORK, NEW YORK 10020
DESIGNED BY IRVING PERKINS
MANUFACTURED IN THE UNITED STATES OF AMERICA
PRINTED AND BOUND BY FAIRFIELD GRAPHICS, INC.
1 2 3 4 5 6 7 8 9 10

LIBRARY OF CONGRESS CATALOGING IN PUBLICATION DATA

MCWILLIAMS, CAREY, 1905–
    THE EDUCATION OF CAREY MCWILLIAMS.

    BIBLIOGRAPHY: P.
    INCLUDES INDEX.
    1. MCWILLIAMS, CAREY, 1905-   2. JOURNALISTS-
UNITED STATES—BIOGRAPHY.   I. TITLE.
PN4874.M475A33   070.4'092'4 [B]   78-31675

ISBN 0-671-22876-5

Portions of this manuscript appeared in *Westways,* in
Gambit (the publication of Station KCET in Los Angeles), and in *Working Papers* in a different form but
are used here with the permission of the editors. I am
indebted also to the editors of Doubleday & Company, Inc., for permission to quote from America in
Our Time by Godfrey Hodgson, copyright © 1976
by Godfrey Hodgson.

Dedicated to Iris

How many loved your moments of glad grace,
And loved your beauty with love false or true,
But one man loved the pilgrim soul in you,
And loved the sorrows of your changing face.

W. B. YEATS

CONTENTS

ACKNOWLEDGMENTS   12

PREFACE   13

BOOK I

CHAPTER I.   *HYBRID HERITAGE*   19
                1. The Missouri Kinfolk   19
                2. The Immigrant Connection   22
                3. The Oatley Sisters   23

CHAPTER II.   *GROWING UP IN STEAMBOAT*   27
                1. Boom, Then Bust   27
                2. The Missouri Greenhorn   28
                3. End of a World   33

CHAPTER III.   *THE REBELLION OF THE TWENTIES*   39
                1. The New Generation   39
                2. The Discovery of Los Angeles   42
                3. The Mencken Contingent   50
                4. From Mencken to Bierce   55
                5. Bierce's "Gilded Age"   58

CHAPTER IV.   *THE SURGING THIRTIES*   64
                1. The Politics of Social Protest 67
                2. Factories in the Field   74
                3. "Organize!"   81
                4. The Life and Times of Willie Bioff 86
                5. The Antifascist Phase   92
                6. The Ordeal of Humphrey Cobb   95

CHAPTER V.   *THE WAR YEARS*   98
                1. The Racial Revolution   98
                2. "Relocating" the Japanese   101

3. *The Sleepy Lagoon Case*   108
4. *The 1943 Riots*   112

CHAPTER VI.   *THE COMING OF THE COLD WAR*   116
1. *First Signs and Portents*   116
2. *The Domestic Cold War*   119
3. *The Wallace Movement*   127
4. *"The Capital of Anti-Semitism"*   130
5. *The Hollywood Ten*   135

BOOK II

CHAPTER VII.   *THE KIRCHWEY YEARS*   143
1. *"How Free is Free?"*   146
2. *The Greenberg Incident*   149
3. *The Cultural Cold War*   151
4. *Notes on McCarthyism*   158
5. *This Newfangled Treason*   165
6. *Cold War Casualties*   173
     Death of a Scholar   174
     Death of an Immigrant   176
     Death of an Actor   180
     The "Exile" of Edgar Snow   182
7. *"Watch the closing doors."*   185

CHAPTER VIII.   *THE KIRSTEIN YEARS*   193
1. *The Great American Barbecue*   195
2. *Civil Rights: In Perspective*   204
3. *The Revival of Muckraking*   213
4. *The Peace Movement: First Phase*   221
5. *The Bay of Pigs*   227
6. *Speaking of Scoops*   232
7. *Notes on Contributors*   235
     Presenting Jacob Bronowski   239
     Introducing the Revisionists   243
     Reporting the Counterculture   246
8. *The Persistent Right*   250
9. *The Camouflage War*   256

CHAPTER IX.   *THE STORROW YEARS*   261
1. *The Vietnam Decade*   264
2. *Johnson's Dirty War*   268
3. *The Emergence of a Challenge*   273
4. *Nixon's War*   285
5 *Covering Up the Cover-up*   299
6. *The Cold War Trap*   310

The Education of Carey McWilliams   11

NOTES   325

SELECTED BIBLIOGRAPHY   332

INDEX   345

ACKNOWLEDGMENTS

I am indebted to *Nation* publishers George Kirstein and his successors James and Linda Storrow and Gifford Phillips for their help and continued loyalty. My former colleagues at THE NATION, including Robert Sherrill, Fred J. Cook and Frank Donner, have been most helpful. My boyhood friend John Rolfe Burroughs and my brother, Casley McWilliams, were indispensable sources on the chapter "Growing Up in Steamboat," as was F. R. Carpenter of Hayden, Colorado. Mrs. Fred Trosper supplied useful facts and details on the Casley family. I should also like to acknowledge a special debt to the late Loren Miller, author of *The Petitioners: The Story of the Supreme Court of the United States and the Negro* (1966), who was my friend and counselor on racial issues from the early 1930s until his death. Dan Biderman and Clay Steinman were of assistance on the history of the trade union movement in Hollywood. And my thanks to Mr. and Mrs. W. H. Ferry, Bernard Rapoport, F. Palmer Weber, Mr. and Mrs. Ralph Shikes, Victor Rabinowitz, Leonard Boudin and Joseph Crown for their encouragement. As always I am deeply indebted to Joseph and Mary Aidlin for their steadfast friendship over many years and their invaluable counsel. And I cannot adequately express the debt I owe my wife, Iris Dornfeld, and my sons, Wilson Carey McWilliams and Jerry Ross McWilliams, for their patient tolerance of my often quirky ways and their undeviating support through some rough and troubled times.

C. McW.

PREFACE

In only the most limited sense is this an autobiographical narrative. I am much too discreet to write about my private life, and besides I lack the temperament even if that were my intention, which it is not. Nor have I sought to give a full account of my editorship of *The Nation;* that is another story, for another time. Here I deal only with important political aspects of the experience, with some asides on editorial problems and a few of the uncounted contributors I came to know over the quarter of a century I edited the magazine. Nor have I set out to write a history of the period these pages cover. I am not—repeat *not*—an historian, nor do I need to be reminded of the perils of posing as one. What follows is "personal history," or, more accurately, a personal political memoir, not so much of the times as of important phases of the politics of the times. More by chance than design I was an active participant in *some*—by no means all—of the critically important political movements and controversies of the period extending roughly from the 1929 crash, and even a bit earlier in an introductory sense, to the ouster of Richard Nixon from the White House and the withdrawal of the last U.S. troops from Vietnam on April 29, 1975. Most of the first three decades of this period were spent in California, where, ineluctably, I got caught up in some of the liveliest political action of those years. During most of the final three decades, I was even more closely and continuously involved in left-radical-liberal politics as editor of *The Nation.* In the pages that follow I have sought to convey some measure of my feelings and perceptions, past and present, about the evolving and disappearing "worlds" of this period.

The Henry Adams "education" format is well suited to this purpose. It enabled Adams, as Ross Lincoln Miller has written, to establish a style of inquiry which put him in touch with a world for which his education had not prepared him; it was a way of integrating his mind and his actions. He set out to contrast his boyhood experiences, what he called his "pastoral" education, and his formal or "accidental" education, with the experience, the real education, to which he was later exposed through the interaction of history and politics. My early experiences were more truly "pastoral" than his, and my formal or "accidental" education far more irrelevant than he found his to be. What Adams sought to do was to remove the tension between experience and idealism, or, stated another way, "to come to terms with a world whose logic escaped him." In this sense, as Miller notes, *The Education of Henry Adams* is "like a Chinese joke in that the point lies only in the telling." [1]

Of recent years historians have pointed to the atrophy of historical consciousness. Some writers, Lillian Hellman is one, complain that "we are a people who do not remember much," while others have said that history has little meaning for the "now" generation. Irving Howe, for example, has playfully observed that both of his children have "an historical imagination. They can think back as far as me!" Our various "worlds" have come and gone at such an accelerating clip that we have lost the "feel" of events, movements, and controversies that took place "only yesterday." Yet it is still true, as E. H. Carr pointed out, that "history is past politics and politics present history." Personal history is one means by which the politics of the recent past can be made relevant to present history. Just as Adams sought to ease the tension between experience—his real education—and his idealism, so I have sought a similar accommodation. In the pages that follow I explain how an early idealism has survived some punishing and bitter experiences through fusion with a radical view of the politics and history of the last half century.

A final comment. By my idiosyncratic reckoning I have known five "worlds": the one I grew up in as a boy on a cattle ranch in northwestern Colorado; the world of the 1920s, which I explored as an "expatriate" in Los Angeles; the surging world of the 1930s, which, as one might expect, was a bit more tempestuous in California than elsewhere; the exciting "world" of the war years with the promise of a postwar "peace" that never came; and the thirty-year phase of the Cold War that coincided with my years at *The Nation*. Essentially, Book I deals with my years in California (1921–51), Book II with *The Nation* involvement. Logically Chapter VI, on the inception of the Cold War, belongs in Book II, but it is included in the first section because of the California setting. Book II divides into three decades during each of which I served under a different publisher at *The Nation*. "The Kirchwey Years," 1945–55, marked the inception of the Cold War and the rise of McCarthyism; "The Kirstein Years," 1955–65, the middle years of the Cold War; and "The Storrow Years," 1965–75, the period from the escalation of the war in Vietnam to its inglorious finale.

BOOK I

CHAPTER I

HYBRID HERITAGE

1. THE MISSOURI KINFOLK

In late spring, 1975, the United States Supreme Court—Justice Douglas dissenting—upheld the will of Homer McWilliams of Kansas City, who had departed this life on January 3, 1966. The will left virtually the entire estate, appraised at more than $11 million, in trust to Protestant Christian hospitals of Jackson County, Missouri, operated and maintained for the care of patients born of white parents in the United States. The litigation, which had been pending for a decade, had been initiated by the trustee to test the will's validity. Named as parties were certain hospitals in the community and four "next of kin," including my brother, Casley, and myself. Although the will obviously discriminated against blacks, Jews, Catholics, and persons not born in this country, it was upheld. As one of the lawyers remarked, "I guess the decision means that a man still can have a say about where his money is spent even after he is dead. Whether or not we agree with his thoughts, it was still his money." The trial judge was less considerate: "The testator's will might well have furnished a charter for the Ku Klux Klan. Every prevalent prejudice of the era in which it was written was expressed."[1]

But this is a bit unfair. Cousin Homer, who never married and had no direct descendants, had reason to be grateful to the beneficiaries of his oddly worded will. On January 21, 1947, eighty years of age, he entered Trinity Lutheran Hospital following a

traffic accident, and he remained there until his death nineteen
years later. For nearly two decades he kept three shifts of nurses in
attendance, at a cost of $300,000, and his meals and his private
room overlooking Penn Valley were said to have cost another
$200,000. Obviously he had reason to reward the hospital and its
sister institutions for having provided excellent medical care and
attention. But where had he acquired this "thing" about blacks,
Jews, Catholics, and the foreign-born?

An only child, he was born in Chillicothe, Missouri, July 18,
1867. His father had made a fortune by buying mules, once important in time of war, and selling them to the Union Army during
the Civil War. The fortune had been wisely invested in Kansas City
real estate which the son shrewdly managed. An accident in early
childhood left Cousin Homer with a stiff left leg; he always walked
with a limp and carried a cane. The gimpy leg had important
psychological consequences: because of it he professed to believe
that women were interested only in his wealth. Obviously the fact
that the local press referred to him for years as "the richest single
man in Kansas City" did not make him less attractive to women,
but the bit about the lame leg was a put-on. He was tall, handsome,
and could be quite charming. My father, born a year earlier, was
perhaps his one close friend. As young men they saw a great deal
of each other before my father "went west" to Colorado, and the
friendship persisted. Cousin Homer would usually spend a few
weeks each summer in Colorado and was often a guest at our
ranch. I do not remember him sounding off about blacks, Jews,
Catholics or the foreign-born, but he was not the type that "sounds
off" about anything. It was clear, however, that these groups were
not on his list of favorite peoples. Not surprisingly, he shared the
social biases of the rich of his time and place. He also shared the
same family or tribal background as my father.

The McWilliams clan were Scotch-Irish Protestants who had
been settled in Northern Ireland by Oliver Cromwell, a very remote ancestor by way of the Cromwell-Cleveland-McWilliams connection. The McWilliams and Cleveland families were part of the
Scotch-Irish influx from Northern Ireland that settled in North
Carolina and Virginia in pre-Revolutionary times. One of my
ancestors, John McWilliams, married Elizabeth Cleveland—Grover
Cleveland was part of her tribe—and the couple migrated from
Virginia to Berea, Kentucky, via the Cumberland Gap. They had
three sons and four daughters, and the original homestead is still
owned and farmed by latter-day descendants. Since the farm was
too small to support the sons and daughters and their children, my
grandfather, Samuel McWilliams, decided to move on to Missouri

and settled near Plattsburg, in Clinton County, not many miles from Kansas City, perhaps because other members of the family had settled in the same general area.

Originally, of course, the family were Presbyterians, but my grandfather joined the Baptist Church—the "hard-shell" variety— about the time of the Kentucky to Missouri migration. In Missouri, he married my grandmother, Nancy McCorkle, of the same Scotch-Irish stock. Shortly after their marriage in the autumn of 1860 he was commissioned a captain in the Confederate Army, and he took part in the battles of Wilson's Creek (near Springfield), and Lexington, where his company was nearly destroyed. When he returned to his farm to enlist new recruits in the fall of 1861, he saw his daughter—the firstborn—for the first time. A day or two later he was arrested by Union troops and given a nine-month prison sentence. "Captain Sam," as he was always known, was a Gothic American type: bearded, cantankerous, opinionated (he was said to know more things for certain than any man in Clinton County), dour, and obstinate. Nominally a "hard-shell" Baptist, he seldom attended church, and he disagreed with everyone about religion. He was, of course, a Democrat. He owned one slave, a farm hand, who was given his freedom before the end of the war. At what would today be regarded as an early age, "Captain Sam" rented out his farm and moved into the town of Plattsburg, where he and my grandmother, a jolly pixy type, lived out their days.

As these notes suggest, the McWilliams family tradition was Protestant, Democratic (in the partisan sense), and definitely if not passionately Southern (Missouri being a border state). I do not doubt that the tradition included a fairly strong bias against Catholics, Jews, blacks, and the foreign-born, in relatively that order. Originally my father no doubt shared these biases, but they quickly ceased to have much meaning for him in northwestern Colorado. For Homer, however, they remained meaningful; with him tribal biases were reinforced by class biases. He was born rich, my father was not.

In May, 1944, I was invited to address the Missouri State Conference of Social Work at its annual meeting in Kansas City's Civic Auditorium on the subject of racial discrimination. *Brothers Under the Skin,* which deals with racial minorities, had been published in 1943, while *Prejudice,* an account of the mass evacuation of the West Coast Japanese Americans, had been announced for publication that fall. As I was about to be introduced, I noticed a tall, distinguished-looking figure limping down the center aisle with the aid of a cane. He came as far forward as he could and settled down in an aisle seat about ten rows from the platform. It was, of course,

Cousin Homer. There he sat, hands folded on the cane, eyes riveted on me. I am sure he disagreed with every word I said. The next day I called at his tiny crowded office where he sat at an enormous rolltop desk and we had a fine time chatting about the family, his visits to the ranch, and other matters. Not a word was said about race or minorities or the talk I had given the day before.

So much for the Missouri kinfolk.

2. *THE IMMIGRANT CONNECTION*

My mother's parents were both immigrants with Catholic backgrounds. My maternal grandmother was born in Hamburg, Germany, August 18, 1843, and came to this country at the age of twelve, speaking not a word of English. My maternal grandfather, known as Paul Casley, an only child, was born in Plattsburgh, New York, October 20, 1844, the son of French-Canadian Catholic parents. His father, Paul Castongue, a carpenter and log cutter, had moved from Montreal to upstate New York in the 1830s and later settled in Wisconsin. When Paul Castongue first arrived in the states, he spoke scarcely a word of English, and neighbors, friends, and associates had difficulty pronouncing and spelling his name. So he became known, variously, as Castley, Cassily, and Casltey but finally settled on Casley as his new American monicker. My grandfather had been christened Paul Octave de Laval Castonguay (that spelling was used) but was always known as Paul Casley.

When the Civil War broke out, the Casley family was living in Wisconsin. There, on August 15, 1862, my grandfather enlisted in Company A of the Twenty-seventh Wisconsin Regiment for a term of three years. He is described in the certificate of service as eighteen years of age—which may account for the fact that he served as a drummer boy—with hazel eyes, auburn hair, light complexion, five feet five inches tall, by occupation a farmer. He was mustered out of the service at Brownsville, Texas, on August 4, 1865, and a few months later he married my grandmother. Both maternal grandparents died when I was quite young, and I have few memories of them.

Paul Casley was a small feisty man, an enthusiastic member of the Elks fraternal order, long active in the Grand Army of the Republic, and a vociferous and extremely partisan Republican. Through his G.A.R. and Republican connections, he acquired a position with the Postal Service and in later life served as a railroad postal clerk on the Denver & Rio Grande line operating out of

Denver. In class terms, my maternal grandparents were lower middle class, frugal, hard-working, "respectable." Since their immigration their Catholicism had become somewhat attenuated and so, too, had their ethnic ties. My grandmother spoke some German, my grandfather a little French.

I can imagine no two couples more dissimilar than my paternal and maternal grandparents. If they had ever met, I don't know what they would have had to talk about except the weather and the family connection. All of the Casleys were Republicans, all of the McWilliamses were Democrats. One family had strong ties with the North, the other with the South. "Captain Sam" and wife were native-born Protestants of pre-Revolutionary stock; Paul Casley and wife were Catholic immigrants. The two sets of grandparents were equally conservative; in neither family was there a suggestion of "populism" or of "progressive," much less "radical," thought. Few members of either family could be accused of harboring "intellectual" interests. Of the two lines, the McWilliams influence was the stronger, if only because the Casley grandparents died before I had a chance to know them, and their children lived far from us in widely scattered locations. But there was one vivid exception: my uncle Vernon Casley and his colorful wife, Lottie—one of the queens of the Klondike—both of whom occupy a special niche in my affections.

3. THE OATLEY SISTERS

My Uncle Vern—he was christened Vernon Durwood Lafayette Casley—the youngest member of the Casley tribe, was a happy-go-lucky, kindly man for whom I have nothing but fond memories. At an early age he had run away from home and was living in Northern California when word came that gold had been discovered in Alaska. He was never cut out to be a prospector—the rough outdoor life was not to his taste—or a miner, since he disliked hard work of any kind. I have never known anyone who enjoyed a good time more than he did. So when he got to Alaska, as he soon did, he made his living playing a mandolin and a guitar in saloons and dance halls and, later, as a dealer at the gambling tables. In this way he came to know Lottie Oatley.

Lottie and Polly Oatley were daughters of a pair of British music-hall entertainers. Talented, attractive, spirited, and beautiful, "the Oatley Sisters," as they were billed from early childhood on, had been raised in theaters, music halls, and cheap hotels. They never went to school; they never lived in a "home." From the time

they could toddle the sisters had been trained as "child entertainers," billed, managed, and exploited by their parents. As they
grew older the Oatley sisters sang and danced together, performed
solo bits, and took part in incredibly corny skits, including a fake
"Uncle Tom's Cabin" in which Lottie played the part of Little Eva.

The sisters, who had crisscrossed the country several times with
their parents, happened to be appearing in San Francisco when
word came that gold had been discovered in Alaska. Opportunists
as always, the Oatleys left immediately for the Klondike. The most
direct route at the time was across Chilkoot Pass via Skagway and
then, when spring came, down the Yukon River by boat to Dawson.
In that first great burst of enthusiasm, some 22,000 gold-seekers
climbed Chilkoot Pass, including the four Oatleys, who became
famous in Klondike history for having brought the first piano over
the pass. In mid-June of that first year, the Oatleys and their piano
were loaded on Captain Goddard's little steamboat which was conveyed through some of the more dangerous gorges and rapids en
route to Dawson.

In 1898 Dawson was crawling with homeless men looking for
gold; overnight it had become the largest Canadian city west of
Winnipeg. There were, of course, few women. But of saloons and
dance halls there were many. One of these was the Bank Saloon,
whence, writes Pierre Berton in *The Klondike Fever* (1958), came

> the wheezing sound of a portable organ and the light tap of
> dancing feet. The crowd flowed toward it nightly, for here the
> Oatley sisters, two pretty, petite girls, danced and entertained
> on a rough platform while a big pompadoured German made
> music for them. After twenty dances with the customers at a
> dollar a dance, the sisters stopped for breath and sang senti-
> mental songs, and as their clear, bell-like voices piped in two-
> part harmony in the bright evening air, a hush fell over the
> throng clustered about the little stand. They sang "Break the
> News to Mother," and they sang "A Bird in a Gilded Cage,"
> and they sang "I Love Her, Yes I Love Her Just the Same."
> And as they sang, each man fell silent, alone with his thoughts;
> and the sound of the organ and the words of the familiar songs
> brought tears to many eyes. "A lot of those songs are graven
> on the walls of my memory," Bert Parker wrote fifty years
> later. "I stood there with my mouth open, listening to the Oat-
> ley sisters sing those sad ballads. I never knew them personally
> and didn't have enough money in those days to get near
> enough to get a good look at them. But they sure helped me to
> put many a lonesome night behind me."

And occasionally the sisters sang for charities. Among my Aunt Lottie's effects I found a letter dated September 21, 1898, addressed to "Misses: The Oatley Sisters, Dawson, Y. T.," thanking them for having donated the proceeds of a "sacred concert" in the amount of $259.50 to Dawson's two hospitals, St. Mary's and the Good Samaritan.

Perhaps the most flamboyant character then in Dawson was "Nigger Jim" Daugherty, a blond giant of a man, who was called "Nigger Jim" not because of his color but for his soft Missouri accent and his fondness for spirituals, which he liked to sing accompanying himself on the banjo. On arriving in the Klondike in 1894, before the big rush, he had staked out some valuable claims; one sold for $360,000, enough, reports Berton, to purchase two dance halls for the singing Oatley Sisters, one of whom, Lottie, he soon married. A big man seldom seen without a cigar in his mouth and a huge Stetson hat on his head, he went in for flashy diamond rings and stickpins. He was instantly taken with Lottie Oatley, who was instantly taken with his wealth and lavish spending. To impress her he would stand at the bar of the Pavilion or the Bank Saloon and drink the best vintage champagne until dawn. Berton reports that he once drank all the champagne in Skagway and then chartered a steamer to go to Juneau, a hundred miles down the coast, for a fresh supply. His generosity was a byword. Once he had been robbed of twenty thousand dollars. "A friend captured the thief, and as a reward Jim bought him a saloon." His name is linked with a famous Klondike incident, "the Nigger Jim Stampede." Word got around that he had quietly staked out a claim in a remote part of the territory, and everyone was sure that he knew what he was doing. So in the dead of winter hundreds of claim-seekers stampeded to the new field, which proved to be a bust. At the Tivoli saloon they made up a topical song about the stampede which contained this couplet:

> *Nigger Jim just wanted to know*
> *If a fresh cheechako could outrun a sourdough.*

As for Jim, writes Berton, he sat in a box with Lottie Oatley beside him and laughed and applauded while the champagne ran as swiftly "as the water in the sluiceboxes on El Dorado."

But Nigger Jim's drinking and wastrel ways proved too much for Lottie Oatley, who was tough and realistic in all matters in which money was involved. Although she had spent most of her life in saloons and dance halls, she rarely took a drink. In one of the Dawson saloons in which she performed, she met Vernon Casley, and not long after that first meeting she divorced Nigger Jim and married my uncle. Once the Klondike fever began to abate, the two of them took a small troupe of players to China, where they entertained in the port cities for some years. Later they returned to Prince Rupert, British Columbia, where they operated the Empress Hotel until moving to Hollywood in 1920. After my father's death, my mother and her two sons joined them there.

In my youthful eyes, my uncle and his wife were storybook romantics, what with their travels, theatrical backgrounds, and adventures in the Far North. When my uncle visited Denver, he invariably took us to the best restaurants, bought box seats at the theaters, and entertained us royally at Elitch's Gardens. Once Lottie and Vern spent several weeks with us at the ranch, and I remember staring in awe at my aunt's magnificent jewels: rings, brooches, earrings, necklaces, and assorted pins and pendants. Her motto, often voiced, was: "If you got 'em, wear 'em," which she did, wherever she went, whatever she did. She and my uncle were not at all middle-class Main Street types: they were "outsiders," exotics. They slept late, drank beer in the morning, scorned middle-class conventions, and laughed at the prevailing pieties.

With such a comically mixed background it is not surprising that I never identified with any specific ethnic or religious group. I am neither a WASP nor an ethnic but a hybrid, a maverick without a pedigree. At an early age I got used to writing "non-church" or "unaffiliated" or "mixed origins" in filling out questionnaires. Anyone with a background as mixed as mine might be expected to feel a bit of an outcast in today's America, in which ethnic backgrounds and "roots" have acquired a new significance. But I have no such feeling. In fact, I am rather proud of my hybrid inheritance and would not have it otherwise. But I cannot see that tribal loyalties or immediate family influences had anything to do with shaping my political convictions. Both my father and my mother, and their parents, were quite conservative in political outlook and held conventional views on religious and social issues. My Uncle Vern and his wife were highly unconventional types but conservatives by temperament; they had no interest in books, ideas or politics. Far more important than family influences were the early years I spent on a cattle ranch in Colorado. For quite logically it is on frontiers, as Lionel Trilling (the urban sophisticate) once pointed out, where the tags and identifications have been discarded or never recognized, that a sense of justice and equality often emerges.[2]

CHAPTER **II**

GROWING UP IN STEAMBOAT

Most American radicals of my generation came of age politically in the Depression years. I was a decade ahead of them: I got my comeuppance in the ways of laissez-faire capitalism in the wake of World War I. The experience made me a premature skeptic and a rebel and permanently impaired my confidence in "the system." It also turned my life upside down. My father died, the family fortune vanished, and my mother and her two sons became migrants, not "dusted" or "blown" off the land but unceremoniously booted off by the demise of the range-cattle industry that came in 1919. For Henry Adams, the appearance of the new Cunard liners in Boston Harbor and the first telegraphic messages announcing the nomination of Polk and Clay marked the end of the "pastoral" phase of his education. The crash in the cattle market marked the end of mine. It destroyed the first of the several "worlds" I have known and changed the course of my life. In a wholly unexpected turn of events, I found myself a nearly penniless "expatriate" in Southern California, just as the fantastic boom of the 1920s was beginning to gather momentum.

1. BOOM, THEN BUST

The sudden end of the wartime cattle boom brought to a dramatic close a significant phase of Western history. From beginnings in Texas and the Southwest, the cattle frontier moved north through Oklahoma and Kansas to Wyoming and Montana. An abundance of free grazing lands was the magnet that drew it northward. During the early cattle drives to Wyoming and Montana, northwestern Colorado had been bypassed because of its relative inaccessibility; it was on the wrong side—the western slope—of the Rockies. But there in a vast 150-mile diagonal stretch of country that tilted westward to the Utah border, the familiar drama of the cattle frontier was reenacted for the last time.

The reenactment was short-lived—less than a generation—but a good show while it lasted, complete with saloons, whorehouses, tough sheriffs, stagecoach lines, bandits and outlaws (Butch Cassidy had a hideaway in these parts,) hired gunmen (Tom Horn), cattle rustlers galore, and such legendary figures as Queen Ann Bassett of Brown's Park, where overland cattle drives paused before moving on to California only to have their herds sharply diminished by resident rustlers. The Colorado historian John Rolfe Burroughs—a boyhood friend; our fathers were in business together—thus describes the final boom in the range-cattle industry that began once the Moffat rail line was completed to Steamboat Springs in 1908:

> For the next several years, more cattle went to market from Steamboat Springs stockyards than any other shipping point in the United States. Decades after the range cattle business elsewhere was little more than a memory, Steamboat Springs and its neighbor, Craig, forty miles to the west, were roaring cowtowns serving a region larger in extent than Massachusetts, Connecticut, Rhode Island, and Delaware combined. In an area bounded on the north by the Colorado-Wyoming state line, on the south by the White River watershed, on the east by the Continental Divide, and on the west by the impassable canyons of the Green River, there belatedly occurred in microcosm everything that had characterized the vast range-cattle industry at an earlier date.[1]

But by 1919 the open-range cattle industry was *kaput* and this last frontier had vanished.

2. *THE MISSOURI GREENHORN*

Born in Plattsburg, Missouri, May 23, 1865, christened Jeremiah Newby McWilliams, my father was always known as Jerry; the only use he ever made of his middle name was to designate the special railroad stop at our ranch "Newby," Colorado. As a young man, restless and ambitious, he soon left Plattsburg for Kansas City, where he got a job as salesman in a men's-clothing store. It was then that he and Cousin Homer became great friends; a year apart in age, they "ran around together." But at age twenty-one, my father became afflicted with "lung trouble," for which the popular remedy of the day was to "go west." So with five thousand dollars borrowed from relatives, he set out in 1886 for Steamboat Springs, Colorado, where he had been told a new town was in the making.

In those days one went from Denver to Wolcott on the Denver & Rio Grande and then by Concord stagecoaches to Steamboat, some eighty miles distant, via beautiful Egeria Park. The awesome scenery en route must have enormously impressed my father, fresh from the Missouri flatlands and a greenhorn of greenhorns. Indeed, he never managed to shed the label. He neither smoked nor drank, although he would take a glass of wine on special occasions. In Western eyes, he remained an irredeemable square because he refused to opt for the life style of the cowhand. Cowboys are style-obsessed: reins must be narrow and made of buckskin; ropes must be coiled just so; spurs must have the right kind of rowels; stirrups must not be too broad. To them my father was a comic figure. He wore flat-heeled boots; his saddle had a flat pommel; he did not use spurs. His broad-brimmed black hat might have been worn by a Mormon preacher. Most of the time, even on roundups, he wore a business coat and vest with high celluloid collar and tie (he was still that salesman in the men's-clothing store). If he tried to rope a steer, he usually ended up roping himself. He would not permit liquor or guns (except under lock and key) on any of his ranch properties. But if his cowhands and his two sons were endlessly amused by the figure he cut at the ranch—and they were—they had great respect for his phenomenal knowledge of livestock, cattle and horses alike, weight, age, state of health, and approximate sales value. Cowhands liked him but found it difficult to communicate; he was usually preoccupied and never much of a talker.

In 1886 the town of Steamboat Springs consisted of a livery stable, a stagecoach inn, a blacksmith shop, four saloons, and a general store, the New York Emporium (with a ridiculous false front), which my father proceeded to buy. As late as 1903 the town's population numbered only about three hundred. The site had attracted the attention of early-day trappers and explorers because of the number and diversity of its mineral springs. Some of these were of the warm-water variety in which it was possible to boil an egg in winter. One, across the Yampa River from the town, emitted the *chug-chug* sound of a steamboat, which could be heard for miles around; later, a railroad cut in the side of the mountain near the spring made the *chug* barely audible. In time the warm springs were developed as a community facility with outdoor and indoor pools and private baths.

West of Steamboat, which is about 175 miles from Denver "as the crow flies," are the semiarid big-sky sagebrush lands around Hayden and Craig where some of the largest cattle operators once had their headquarters. One of the most famous of these outfits was the Two Circle Bar Ranch owned by the Cary family, a huge spread with twenty-five or thirty cowhands. The Carys were friends and patrons of my father, as were the heads of the legendary Carey cattle dynasty in Wyoming. John Cary, one of Colorado's best-known Democrats, served in the State Senate for many years; my father was his successor. I was supposed to be named after the Cary tribe, but that presented a bit of a problem: the Careys, unrelated to the Carys, were also friends and patrons. But since their domain was in Wyoming, my father concluded that it would be less confusing if I were named "Carey" rather than "Cary." The logic escapes me, but so it came to be.

Cattle ranching in the upper Yampa region around Steamboat assumed quite a different pattern than in the big-sky areas farther west. The mountains are steeper (the Continental Divide is the eastern boundary), the foothills abbreviated. There are sharply defined small valleys and parks with swiftly flowing "white water" streams. The precipitation is much heavier than in areas farther west; the snowfall averages—or did—160 inches. Beautiful timothy-and-clover meadows produced an abundance of hay, but the ranches, mostly of eighty or 160 acres, could not support many cattle. A few large operators, principally my father, would buy the surplus hay and livestock. During the long winters cattle had to be fed on feedlots in the snowbound pastures. In late spring, they would be driven twenty miles west and turned loose to forage for themselves. This was sagebrush country; with less snow, the grass appeared sooner and it was a good place for cows to calve. In an early summer roundup the calves would be branded and ear-marked, and the males castrated. The herds would then be driven back to the Yampa Valley and up into the forest reserves and mountain parks of the Continental Divide. For years my father kept a camp at Rabbit Ears Pass (elevation 10,719 feet), which served as a base of operations. In late summer, fat and wild as deers, the cattle would be rounded up again and driven down to the valley, where the two- and three-year-old steers would be cut out and shipped to the Denver market.

For years this was the basic pattern: primarily a business of raising cows and selling steers as beef. But with the wartime boom that began in 1914, the large operators, including my father, began to buy thousands of yearling steers in New Mexico and Arizona, where drought and overgrazing had created a buyer's market. These wild and skinny longhorns would then be shipped to northwestern Colorado, branded and dehorned, fattened for a year or so, and sold on a steadily, often sharply rising market. A great business while it lasted; one season we ran seventeen thousand head of cattle on the open range.

My father, the Missouri greenhorn, was more or less forced into the cattle business. Soon after he purchased it, the New York Emporium failed. Somehow he managed to get a line of credit in Denver which enabled him to drive a herd of cattle in from Wyoming. Over the years his cattle operations steadily expanded; he also carried on an active real-estate and loan business, principally buying and selling ranches.

At the opening of the fall school term in 1895, my mother, age twenty-one, arrived in Steamboat from Denver to be the new teacher. On February 3, before her first term was finished, she married my father: pretty young schoolteachers did not remain single long in northwestern Colorado. In the winter months we usually lived in Steamboat—the schools were there—but in early spring we would move to my father's Mesa Ranch, five miles from town, with its three barns, bunkhouse, guest house, family residence, and sundry sheds, granaries, corrals, etc., where we would remain until middle or late November. After my father was elected to the State Senate, we spent our winters in Denver.

Around the turn of the century, David H. Moffat, the Denver financier, decided to build a new rail line across the Continental Divide, thus ending the isolation of northwestern Colorado and, it was hoped, giving Denver a direct link with Salt Lake City. Moffat was sixty-three years of age, at the peak of a successful career, when he made his momentous decision to "cross the Rockies." It took two years to build the line as far as Corona, the "Top of the World" station at the crest of the Divide, elevation 11,666 feet, but only sixty-five miles from Denver. It took four more years to extend it to Steamboat Springs, where the first train puffed into the station on December 13, 1908. It had cost $14 million, or better than $75,000 a mile, and was, at the time, the highest full-gauge railroad in the world. Some years later it was extended to Craig, 230 miles from Denver, but it got no farther; Moffat's dream of a through line was never realized. (In the State Senate, my father helped initiate legislation which finally made it possible, years later, to construct the six-mile-long Moffat Tunnel, which was opened on February 18, 1927.)

Word that such a fantastic rail line was being built over the most dramatically beautiful part of the Continental Divide stimulated interest in northwestern Colorado. The local Steamboat newspaper reported that my father had sold forty-one ranches in 1901. It also noted that he had just purchased "one of the swellest rubber-tired buggies ever to reach Routt County," its color "fast red." A new bathhouse was completed in 1909; the 100-room Cabin Hotel, quite fancy for a small town, was opened in 1910. Charlotte Perry and Portia Mansfield opened their famous summer dance school in 1914. Wealthy families from the Middle West began to buy summer residences in the region. But cattlemen were the principal beneficiaries of the new line; cattle could now be shipped directly to the Denver stockyards by rail in from nine to ten hours. Previously they had to be driven to rail points in Wyoming or across the range to Denver.

Important events often come unannounced, on tiptoe. So it was in the autumn of 1913 when Carl Howelsen, a Norwegian ski instructor, visited Steamboat Springs for the first time and decided it would make an ideal ski resort. The Cabin Hotel had been built and the railroad had arrived from Denver, so his visit was well timed. The first winter carnival was staged in 1914. As kids we knew nothing of skis; sleds and snowshoes, yes, skis, no. And there was too much snow for skating. But Howelsen soon had us practicing jumps and downhill runs. It was quite remarkable, in fact, how quickly skiing caught on. Today, of course, Steamboat has become "the St. Moritz of the West," with fifty or sixty fine ski runs, condominiums, chalet-type rentals, shopping centers, restaurants, bars, and hotels. At Storm Mountain the slopes are ideal, the wind patterns perfect, and there is usually an abundance of snow. It has been renamed Mount Werner in honor of Bud Werner, the first American skier to win a great reputation in Europe; he was killed at St. Moritz in 1966 when overtaken by an avalanche. The Werners bought my father's Mesa Ranch after his death. For years Storm Mountain—Mount Werner—was a source of keen annoyance to him: he could think of nothing that might be done with it to turn a profit!

Growing up in such an extravagantly beautiful, long-isolated, sparsely settled mountain paradise induced in me, as a youngster, a strange sense of timelessness. The steep slopes of the Continental Divide seemed so close you felt you could reach out and touch them. The Flat Top Wilderness area had such harsh and rugged contours, the mountain lakes, parks and streams such pristine purity, that one had a feeling the region had always been like this and would never change. It never occurred to me to contrast the geological age of the region with the age of the settlements. The mountains were millions of years old; the settlements dated from 1875 or thereabouts. To me the settlements seemed as timeless, as resistant to change, as the landscape. So when this very special pastoral "world" of the open-range cattle industry suddenly and dramatically collapsed, the shock was the greater for being wholly unanticipated. I learned once and for all that social structures are transitory and that even a mountain can change in meaning and appearance—witness what has happened to Mount Werner.

3. *END OF A WORLD*

My parents were enormously hard-working, practical, energetic, no-nonsense types. They were deeply devoted to their two sons, and we knew it, but nothing much was said on the subject; any audible or visible show of affection was regarded somehow as bad form. They were devoted to each other too, but there was seldom any show of affection between them. My mother was a warm, friendly, kindly person; my father was no less friendly but often self-absorbed and less responsive. Neither was addicted to the punishment syndrome. Perhaps their greatest virtue as parents was that they let us lead relatively unsupervised lives. Neither had time to "play" with us or to keep a close eye on our activities. But there was little need for that. We might be frost-bitten or break a leg, but external social hazards were virtually nonexistent.

Each of us had regular chores and assignments. We worked as hard as any of the cowhands, riding range, mending fence, taking part in cattle drives and roundups, haying, milking cows. But it was all so much a part of an established way of life that it did not seem like work performed under orders or compulsion. The tasks we performed were varied, spiced with danger, and, for all the physical rigors, inherently interesting and often fun. Besides, we liked the outdoors and doted on the cowhands. My father bought me a buckskin pony and a cowboy outfit, with white angora chaps, boots, spurs, saddle, and Stetson hat, when I was still so young I had to mount Buck from the steps of a ladder or by standing on a barrel. Like my brother, I was given a string of horses at age twelve or thirteen—Tramp, Navajo, Dick, and Buttons. Each cowhand was responsible for his string: he had to see that they were properly shod and currycombed, their manes trimmed, and their tails stylishly plucked. Cowhands talk more about horses than they do about women. The characteristics of every horse in our large "cavvy" were well known and endlessly discussed. Bucking horses from northwestern Colorado, with such names as Pin-Ears, Carrie Nation, and General Pershing, frequently won top prizes at the Cheyenne rodeo. They were known by name to every cowhand in the region, and the betting on whether they could or could not be ridden was often feverish.

On the ranch my brother, three years my senior, and I spent more time in the company of cowhands than we did with our parents. I often wondered what they would have thought had they been able to listen in on the wonderful bunkhouse talk to which we were exposed when, on an idle day, the cowhands would compete in telling tall tales of rowdy adventures in saloons, long binges in Denver, and visits to whorehouses. The bawdier the tales, the more fascinating we found them, and the profanity was invariably superb. The cowhands I knew were a happy-go-lucky lot, romantic, stoical, hardbitten physical types, with a marvelous sense of humor. I found them highly entertaining, aped their ways, and learned to curse as well as they did. Although their manners were rough and their talk was salacious, I cannot say that long association with them did me any harm.

Steamboat Springs, in one respect at least, did not resemble the fabled Western cow towns. At an early date, saloons and whorehouses were compelled to relocate on the south bank of the Yampa River in a community known, inevitably, as Brooklyn. Since the ball park and the rodeo grounds were also on that side of the river, Brooklyn became a kind of sporting center for the region. It had half a dozen saloons, a grandstand, a few cheap hotels, and three or four houses of prostitution. The madams, some nicknamed after famous bucking horses, were local celebrities, known far and wide, the subject of many bunkhouse tales. Generally they kept well to their side of the river, but at rodeo time they would appear in stylish blue corduroy riding costumes with fancy blouses and gay bonnets and, on handsome saddle horses, would parade back and forth in front of the grandstand, much to the annoyance of the very proper Steamboat housewives.

When I first started to ride to school from the ranch, my mother carefully instructed me to use the "valley" road, which did not go through Brooklyn. I would dutifully do as told in the mornings, since there was little to observe in Brooklyn in the early hours. But on returning in late afternoon, I invariably took the forbidden "hill" road. After racing across the bridge, I would slow my horse to a plodding walk while I glanced through swinging saloon doors, examined occasional drunks asleep on the wooden sidewalks, or furtively looked up at curtained windows from which, now and then, a friendly lady would smile and wave. In 1918, the night before statewide Prohibition went into effect, most of Brooklyn went up in flames. I was having dinner with friends at a Steamboat restaurant, and everyone rushed out into the street to watch the gorgeous night sight of Brooklyn burning across the river. None of us realized just then that the range-cattle industry was also about to go up in smoke.

In winter we always went to Denver at "Stock Show Time," a big event in the lives of cattlemen and their families. While the women did a year's shopping in the department stores, the men would gossip in the hotel lobbies and attend to business at the stock-yards. In the evenings the families would attend the stock show to see Miss Lulu Long drive her fine horses or Wild Bill Cody perform; or they would visit the Orpheum, Broadway, or Denham theater. En route to Denver, the train would usually be stalled for hours in the mile-long snowshed at Corona; as winds howled and engines hissed steam, bored and weary parents tried to keep an eye on unruly kids rampaging up and down the aisles. If the weather was clear, one could look down the Devil's Causeway, a sheer drop of some six thousand feet, as the train finally pulled out of the snowshed. But the winter trips were worth the hazards and hardships: Stock Show Time was the high point of the year. The Christmas glitter, the bright lights, the wintertime background, made Denver seem like a fairyland city. The lobbies of the Brown Palace, Shirley-Savoy, Albany, and Kenmark hotels were crowded with visitors, as were the Tabor Opera House and the theaters and restaurants, and the stately mansions of the mining tycoons on Capitol Hill gave the city an air of elegance and splendor.

The population of Steamboat, and the surrounding area, was made up of all kinds of people. I remember one or two families that may have been Jewish but were not known as such; there was no synagogue, and the word "Jew" had only Biblical connotations to me until I entered prep school in Denver. My father once had a black chuckwagon cook, a delightful and popular black couple were in charge of the community baths, and an ancient black lady, a particular favorite of mine whose name was Tennessee Carolee Wagner, took in laundry. I can remember no other blacks. There was one Mexican-American family. Indians had been known to live in northwestern Colorado and to visit it from time to time but not in large numbers. After the Meeker Massacre (1879) the remaining Utes were settled on reservations. We were not aware, when I was growing up, of anything remotely resembling an Indian presence.

Of Orientals there were none. Most of the townspeople and ranchers were a mixed bag in terms of education, origins, and backgrounds. It was not considered good form to inquire too closely into a person's background or antecedents, so I never really knew where some of our friends came from and I could not have cared less. A nearly universal social democracy prevailed. Only in the coal-mining towns of Oak Creek and Mount Harris, which came into being with the completion of the railroad, could ethnic enclaves be found; most of the miners were recent European immigrants.

It is hardly necessary to say that I did not grow up in an intellectual household. My father glanced at local newspapers and occasionally read the Denver papers. But I have few memories of seeing him with a book in his hand. My mother, a high-school graduate, always subscribed to one or more popular magazines and liked to read but found little time for it. At the ranch we had a small bookcase which contained the collected works of Dickens and Sir Walter Scott, quite a number of popular novels by writers such as Rider Haggard, Winston Churchill (not, of course, Sir Winston), and Irving Bachellor, a large number of popular Western novels by B. M. Bower, Owen Wister, William MacLeod Raine and others, some of George Eliot's novels, a dog-eared copy of *Quo Vadis,* and several anthologies of British and American poetry. I do not know how I came to be an avid reader at an early age, but I did. My first published writing was a letter in the *Rocky Mountain News* taking the editors to task for having mistakenly published one of Arthur Henry Clough's poems under another poet's name.

My father was a traditional Democrat, my mother a traditional Republican. Both were quite conservative; it was not a household in which political discussion reverberated or one in which religious arguments got out of hand. I am sure my parents thought of themselves as "Christians," but they were not members of any particular denomination and seldom attended church services. Each year my father contributed an equal amount to the various churches of the community, including the Catholic church. While he thought it might do "the boys" some good to attend a Sunday school of their choice, he was not insistent about it. Nor was my mother. The Western experience had severed whatever church ties they had before coming to northwestern Colorado.

After my father's election to the State Senate we spent the winter months in Denver, where I was enrolled, along with my brother, in the Wolfe Hall Military Academy, located near the old Lawrence Phipps mansion on Colfax Avenue close to Miss Wolcott's School for Girls. Wolfe Hall was run by Episcopalian ministers under church auspices. My father did not think my brother and I were sufficiently sophisticated to enter Denver public schools; his friends in the State Senate and at the Denver Club convinced him that Wolfe Hall was the place for us. It should have been a good school—it was expensive—but good it was not. I spent as much time as I could exploring the State Capitol, listening to Senate debates, reading in the largely deserted State Library, and bicycling through Cheesman Park. Because of my father's last illness—he insisted on returning to the ranch in the dead of winter—I graduated from Steamboat Springs High School on May 26, 1921, took the part of "Lord Algernon, straight from England" in a play, *The Dream That Came True,* by an unnamed playwright, delivered a feverishly patriotic class oration on the inevitable postwar theme "Lest We Forget," and won a scholarship to the University of Denver.

Long before his death my father had become, in the words of John Rolfe Burroughs, "Routt County's leading citizen, Northwestern Colorado's State Senator, and one of its wealthiest men" (a bank statement of January 4, 1919, which Burroughs unearthed, indicates that he then enjoyed a net worth of $250,000).

> There were no laws governing the situation, and in addition, people were reconciled to Jerry McWilliams doing pretty much as he pleased. . . . As long as he stuck to cows, he did all right. Then the war came along, and in company with other cattlemen, he commenced speculating in steers and, for a time, did famously. . . . But the economic debacle which followed in the wake of the war caught Jerry McWilliams, along with practically every other cattleman in Northwestern Colorado, with a big inventory of high-cost cattle.[2]

During the war years the German Navy had kept Argentine beef off the booming domestic market, but once the blockade was lifted the boom collapsed even more suddenly than it began and the big cattle empires went down like a row of tenpins.

On December 17, 1919, the Steamboat *Pilot* carried a front-page story headlined: "Senator McWilliams Seriously Ill." In his history, Burroughs provides the final footnote: "For years on end Jerry McWilliams had driven himself unmercifully—with enthusiasm, it is true, but, nevertheless, driven himself. The dynamo had finally run down, and he passed away on Feb. 3, 1921, precisely twenty-six years to the day after he married Hattie Casley." His will, written before the debacle, contained "A Last Word to My Sons" which reads: "Do not speculate or seek to get rich too quickly. Be patient, be morally right, keep a clear conscience and good company, although you may die a pauper be honorable in all things."

The irony is, of course, that it was his effort to get rich too quickly that proved to be his undoing. But then, how could he be expected to know that an idiotic war launched thousands of miles distant in Europe would destroy almost literally overnight the "world" that was his proudest achievement, that he had labored so long and so hard to create? Of this war, Henry James wrote that it was "a thing that so gives away the whole long age during which we have supposed the world to be, with whatever abatement, gradually bettering, that to have to take it all now for what the treacherous years were all the while really making for and *meaning* is too tragic for any words."

CHAPTER **III**

THE REBELLION OF THE TWENTIES

A writer is born in a decade and not in a year.
—James Thurber

1. THE NEW GENERATION

No shared experience is more fundamental than membership in the same generation. "You belong to it, too," wrote Thomas Wolfe, "you came along at the same time. You can't get away from it. You're part of it whether you want to be or not."[1] But a political generation is not a biological generation. A new political generation surfaces when the best and brightest suddenly find the prevailing culture insufferable and rebel against it. This happens less frequently than we imagine and at irregular intervals; the span of a political generation is usually not more than ten to fifteen years.

The new political generation of the 1920s was neatly packaged: it began with the armistice and closed with the 1929 crash. Because it included a relatively large expatriate contingent, it has been tagged as "lost," uncommitted, decadent. In Scott Fitzgerald's view, it had "no interest in politics at all . . . life . . . was largely a personal matter."[2] In a sense he was right, but the cultural rebellion of the 1920s was a necessary first step to the radical criticism of the 1930s. Before politics could be taken seriously, things had to be called by their right names, tribal pieties reexamined, and conventional values compared with contemporary realities. The 1920s, as Loren Baritz points out, were "a kind of parenthesis in historical time."[3]

With me the cultural rebellion of the decade dates from publication of *This Side of Paradise,* which I first read while riding in the caboose of a cattle train between Steamboat Springs and Denver the year before I enrolled in the university. I had difficulty then and later in understanding why it made such a deep impression, for it is not a great novel. In the late 1920s I tried to define the reasons in a magazine article which drew a note from Fitzgerald in which he said—as he had to others—"You liked *This Side of Paradise* because it was written in depression or despair." Perhaps; but I was not in a state of depression or despair: I was rebellious. The book was like a breath of fresh air. Just to be able to say, "why, that's how I feel!" was in itself a liberating experience. The conventional literary culture was stuffy, boring, and empty; it invited rebellion.

As the decade dawned, John Maynard Keynes sensed what it would be like politically: "We are at the dead season of our fortune. . . . The true voice of the new generation has not spoken and the silent opinion has not yet formed."[4] In this country it was not a question of exhausted energies, as it was in Europe, but of the sudden and brutal eclipse of high hopes. Great wars, Denis Brogan once observed, are always supposed to purify life, morals and character at the beginning and have never done so at the end. American intellectuals had reason to be turned off by the rhetoric and idealism of Woodrow Wilson. Disclosure of the "secret treaties," the stupid mishandling of relations with Russia, and the harsh and unrealistic terms imposed on Germany made a mockery of the Fourteen Points and assured, as we now know, the rebirth of German militarism under the Nazis and the rise of Italian fascism. American intellectuals may not have realized that this country's involvement in World War I, and the aftermath of that war, had made a second world war more or less inevitable, but a sense of disillusionment and betrayal was nearly universal. Nor were they enthralled by domestic politics. The short but savage "red scare" of 1919–20 put a damper on "radical" activities and kept labor on the defensive.

Even so, the La Follette–Wheeler campaign, largely based on unrest in the Midwest farm states, registered a significant protest in 1924. With little organization and meager funds (perhaps not more than $250,000 in all), the La Follette–Wheeler ticket polled 4,822,319 votes, which represented seventeen percent of the total popular vote by comparison with twenty-nine percent received by John W. Davis, the Democratic nominee. But the La Follette protest—brief, premonitory, a hint of things to come—did not arouse much enthusiasm among intellectuals, although it was strongly supported by *The Nation* and its editor, Oswald Garrison Villard. Conceivably the movement might have survived but for the death of La Follette on June 18, 1925. With his death and the surge of "prosperity" that came with the Coolidge years, American politics became increasingly silly and fatuous. Momentous issues shaping up on the world stage went unnoticed and undebated. The liveliest domestic issues were Prohibition, evolution (the fundamentalist controversy and the Scopes trial in Tennessee) and the threat which "reds," Catholics, Jews, and "foreigners" (immigrants)—"the new barbarians" they were called in a book of that title by Wilbur Cortez Abbott published in 1925 (even John Jay Chapman got caught up in this senseless agitation)—were thought to pose to the values of an older, largely rural, predominantly Protestant culture and society.[5] The "Jazz Age" certainly did not lack for noise, commotion, and clashing opinions on cultural and social issues, but its politics—note an exception for the La Follette protest—remained sluggish and irrelevant. Nevertheless, a new note was emerging in American writing that foreshadowed a significant change in perception. In varying ways, *The Great Gatsby, An American Tragedy,* and *Arrowsmith,* all published in 1925, reflect a sharply critical attitude toward the "American Dream" in its contemporary manifestations. Hadn't Fitzgerald spoken in *Gatsby* of "the green light, the orgiastic future, that year by year recedes before us"?

I was not old enough to have served in World War I and was a bit too young to qualify as a full-fledged member of the "lost generation." But the romantic and rebellious mood of *This Side of Paradise* had invaded the campus in my freshman year, and the cultural rebellion was in full swing. Campus intellectuals did not venerate Stuart P. Sherman or Irving Babbitt and enjoyed baiting professors who did. *The Smart Set* was held in high esteem; we read the books that Mencken praised and had only a slight interest in politics. Most of our energies went into extracurricular activities and high jinks. It was a lively time, the setting was beautiful, and we made the most of it.

I was on my own for the first time, at the ripe age of sixteen, with a small allowance and a Ford sedan. My father was dead, my mother had gone to live in Los Angeles, and my brother was at the ranch assisting in the liquidation of my father's tangled affairs. Scott Fitzgerald once said that the Jazz Age actually peaked as early as 1922. It did for me. A few days after a disastrous St. Patrick's Day spree, I boarded a train for Los Angeles, my scholarship canceled, an indignant dismissal notice in my pocket. I was about to become an "expatriate" but in Southern California, not in Europe.

2. *THE DISCOVERY OF LOS ANGELES*

Coming to, so to speak, in Los Angeles in the spring of 1922, after that brief season of fun and frolic in Denver, was a jarring and, for a time, painful experience. Suddenly I found myself in a strange new city that was changing every hour on the hour; I was broke, without prospects or connections, and with essentially one skill: I could type. But I soon got a job in the business office of the Los Angeles *Times,* and there I stayed—for seven years. Fortunately I was able to arrange a work schedule which permitted me to hold what was in effect a full-time job by working afternoons, weekends, and a portion of the early night shift. So I was able to attend the University of Southern California, first Liberal Arts and then the Law School, from which I graduated in 1927.

For an informal but revealing "education" in the ways of laissez-faire capitalism, I had come to the right place at precisely the right time. In the Southern California of the 1920s, the whole saga of frontier growth and westward expansion, the storybook version of the American Dream, was given its penultimate staging in a semitropical setting at the western edge of the continent. Concentrated in time and space, the reenactment accelerated at such a pace that it attracted worldwide interest and attention. The various phases of economic development—pastoral, agricultural, "cottage" industries, industrialization, urbanization, postindustrial—came in such rapid succession that the region's growth seemed staged or contrived, like an outdoor pageant or a motion picture being shot on location.

The Great Los Angeles Boom of the 1920s was just getting under way when I arrived. Other great cities—London, Paris, Constantinople, Athens, Cairo, Peking, Moscow, Tokyo, New York—had evolved as historic entities over long periods of time. Los Angeles emerged out of nowhere, without much of a past. The first hundred years were a kind of prehistory in which it moved from pueblo to cow town to hick town at a leisurely pace. San Francisco was a famous city from the moment gold was discovered, but Los Angeles slumbered on for decades. Then suddenly, beginning in the 1920s, it achieved great-city status through a process of forced growth based on booster tactics and self-promotion. Initially growth was stimulated by luring latter-day "pioneers" seeking low-cost retirement in pleasant circumstances, to a new kind of "frontier" where the sun shone most of the time and winter was another name for summer. But residential expansion required water, which was in short supply. So, using control of limited water resources as a key pressure, the city extended its domain; outlying communities were forced to merge with Los Angeles or face annexation. In the process, highly productive orchards, citrus groves and produce fields had to make way for unplanned and often jerry-built subdivisions, and much of the beauty and charm of the region was lost or impaired.

The first major step in the city's "water imperialism" was its raid on the water resources of Owens Valley, some 230 miles distant, carried out by a series of maneuvers (given fictional treatment in Robert Towne's film *Chinatown*), some of which were tainted with force, fraud, and deception. The desecration of this beautiful valley on the east side of the High Sierras was justified in terms of "the greatest good for the greatest number," which turned out to mean maximum quick profits for the promoters of Greater Los Angeles. Then, as the Los Angeles area continued to expand—hundreds of subdivisions were spawned between 1922 and 1928—more water was needed for *future* growth, so the city reached out to tap Colorado River supplies and, later, began to draw water from the Central Valley, with far-ranging consequences.

As the boom of the 1920s gained momentum, the new media—radio and motion pictures—projected an image of Los Angeles that attracted worldwide attention. Aggressive national advertising and promotion campaigns drew more and more people to the region. The accelerating influx was "good for business," since it stimulated the growth of industry and kept wages low. The expansion of the motion picture industry and the discovery of important oil fields helped fuel the boom, as did the opening of new industries; the first tire-manufacturing plants, for example, date from 1919. After 1915 auto travel to California increased as thousands of tourists and visitors swept into the region, including many Middle Western farm families that had decided to rent or sell their farms and move west. The growth of the state societies—a unique Southern California phenomenon—accurately mirrored this significant shift in population. Some of the societies had huge memberships; the annual picnic of the Iowa Society, usually held in Long Beach, seldom failed to attract thousands of transplanted Iowans. In retrospect, the spectacular growth of the region can be seen as the first phase in the development of what is now known as the Sun Belt.

As luck would have it, I had gone to work for the institution that more than any other was responsible for the phenomenal growth of Southern California. General Harrison Gray Otis, publisher of the Los Angeles *Times*, had been the moving force in the city's first boom at the turn of the century. The second, that of the 1920s, was masterminded by his son-in-law, Harry Chandler, who succeeded him as publisher. From the time he stepped into the shoes of General Otis until his death in 1944, Harry Chandler was, beyond all doubt, the city and the region's most influential resident. He was the generalissimo of the forces that engineered the great postwar boom. As part of its expansionist strategy, the *Times* would publish any and all kinds of advertising and then worry about collecting for it. So those of us in the legal and credit departments engaged in a round-the-clock feud with an army of deadbeats, con men, fly-by-night promoters, "business opportunity" crooks, bad-check artists, noisy tent-style evangelists, proprietors of cheap dance halls, flashy oil promoters of the C. C. Julian type, and not a few realtors who later became civic leaders and multimillionaires, all desperate for advertising but usually unable or unwilling to pay for it. What water was to the region, advertising space in the *Times* was to them.

For a time I had responsibility for accounts in the old dilapidated Music and Arts Building, a relic of the boom of the 1880s, located a block or so from the *Times*. Its "studios" housed a constantly changing swarm of voice teachers, "masseurs," swamis, mind readers, graphologists, yogis, ballet dancers, faith healers, spiritualists, fake publishers, dubious literary and theatrical agents, so-called talent scouts, and other exotic types drawn from the ends of the earth to the "bright spot" that was Los Angeles: the new city of the future. This battered hulk of a building, with its wide corridors which made bizarre twists and turns, might have been fairly described as a museum of two-bit predators out to con the ignorant and fleece the innocent. Indeed, few vantage points offered such an excellent close-up view as my work provided of the armies of men and women on the make who had surged into Los Angeles in search of fame, fortune, easy money, and instant success. Of course, this view was somewhat distorted—it focused on the seamy side of the boom—but it strongly reinforced my misgivings about the "prosperity" of the Harding-Coolidge-Hoover years. How could a society be truly prosperous that spawned such a vicious economic underworld, that despite appearances caused so much unadvertised hardship and unreported financial loss? Nathanael West's *The Day of the Locust* (first published in May, 1939) offers a classic picture of the "underside" of Hollywood and the motion picture industry—the American Dream in disarray—but the counterpart could be found in most phases of the region's mushroom development; the surface was bright and pleasing, but the nether side was often dark and ugly.

To say that my first reactions to Los Angeles were negative would be a gross understatement. I loathed the place. It lacked form and identity; there was no center. By contrast to its never-ending spread and sprawl, Denver was a beautifully structured small city. Those rows of rococo mansions on Capitol Hill stood as monuments to the fortunes in silver and gold made in Cripple Creek and Leadville; they reflected pride, position, wealth. The elegant ladies who buzzed around the city in the winter months in handsome electric coupés knew exactly who they were and what they represented and so did everyone else. But Los Angeles was a city of strangers, of milling marauders staring at one another without a glint of recognition. There were never many "first families," in the historic sense, and tidal waves of newcomers had pushed most of them into the background so that civic leadership was up for grabs.

To Louis Adamic, Los Angeles in the 1920s was the "Enormous Village," and that about describes it, a village in outlook, civic feeling, and even appearance. Westwood was yet to be; in the spring, after the rains, the area between La Brea and Beverly Hills would be ablaze with wild mustard growing in what were then open fields. Hollywood was still a village and San Fernando Valley largely undeveloped. On my first night in Los Angeles I attended a benefit concert staged by motion picture stars in a circus tent on a vacant lot at Sunset and Vine. The affair exuded the atmosphere of a small-town shindig; I remember that the actor Wallace Reid played a strident trombone solo. The city's best-known residents in 1922 were Aimee Semple McPherson,[6] who was to open Angelus Temple in 1923, and the Reverend Robert Shuler, a hellfire-and-brimstone parson with a large radio following. Aimee opted for love and kindness, while Shuler flayed fornicators and other sinners. Protestant fundamentalism was the dominant religious force; Catholics were a largely unnoticed constituency with little political clout; and the Jewish influx was just starting. Revivalism went hand in hand with comically corrupt boom-town politics. Social organization was rudimentary; Los Angeles, in the 1920s, had the finest murders ever, from Clara Phillips and her not-so-gentle hammer to the Black Dahlia and William Desmond Taylor cases. Slight wonder, then, that it should have inspired some of the best private-eye fiction. The city had more newspapers then than now, but even so the press could not keep up with the crazy pace of events. As the columnist Lee Shippey once remarked, in Los Angeles "tomorrow isn't another day, it's another town." It surely was in the 1920s.

Gradually I began to acquire a relish for this strange new scene.

Long before the end of the decade, I came to feel that I had a ringside seat at a year-round circus. As more and more visitors felt a compulsion to jot down their impressions for the folks back home, the fame of Los Angeles spread far and wide. The new world of motion pictures attracted universal interest. Then, too, the city became a source of marvelous news stories for the national and world press: the disappearance of Sister Aimee, the gaudy murders, and the tribulations of Fatty Arbuckle, Charles Chaplin, and Mabel Normand. Still later, of course, the spectacular increase in wealth, power, and population invited a new and more serious interest. The flow of visitors—and investors—was stepped up. More and more Americans had been to Southern California or were planning a visit or had a cousin who lived there. By the end of the decade, Los Angeles was perhaps the most highly publicized, talked about, city in the world. It was a "now" city that piqued curiosity and interest, a city without a past whose emergence coincided with new modes of transportation (the automobile and the airplane) and new forms of communication (motion pictures and radio); it was, in fact, destined to become the media capital of the world. The effect of this upsurge of interest and attention was to create a growing market for "L.A." stories which those of us who were just beginning to write were only too happy to supply.

The range of interesting subject matter was fantastic. It was in Southern California that I first acquired a reporter's interest in religious cults and occult movements. The "psychic" world was even fruitier then than it is today. I found it impossible to keep track of the new cults, occult sciences, and religions. In the words of Annie Besant, who had settled in Ojai in 1926, Southern California had "an incomparable multiplicity and diversity of faiths." In that year Los Angeles had seven separate churches of the American Theosophical Association and twenty-nine affiliates of the National Spiritualists Association. Hamlin Garland, the distinguished American novelist, and his circle of friends were then receiving nightly messages, or so they thought, from Henry James, Sir Arthur Conan Doyle, Dwight L. Moody, and Walt Whitman. I interviewed Garland—a handsome grandfatherly type with snow-white hair—a number of times and often took long walks with him in Griffith Park.

In the 1920s, Francis Grierson, author of *The Valley of Shadows* (1909), a book about Illinois on the eve of the Lincoln–Douglas debates that had drawn high praise from Edmund Wilson, Theodore Spencer, Bernard de Voto, and Van Wyck Brooks, came to live in Los Angeles and aroused much local interest with his piano improvisations and "messages" from the dead. Zona Gale, Edwin

Markham, Sara Teasdale, Mary Austin, and others were fascinated by his personality, interested in his writings, and tried to help him. I found him to be a most intriguing figure, part genius, part faker. As Van Wyck Brooks once said, he was "a strange fish, quite unlike anything in American literature." After a distinguished career in Europe as a concert pianist, appearing at court circles from Moscow to London, Grierson had helped make San Diego a center for psychic and occult phenomena in the late 1880s but was soon forced to leave under a cloud of scandal. Among his books was *Psycho-Phone Messages,* which created quite a stir when published in Los Angeles in 1921. At a concert which Zona Gale arranged for him in 1927, he suddenly slumped over the keyboard, quite dead. So far as I could learn, none of his devotees received psycho-phone messages from him. Even Upton Sinclair got caught up in the Los Angeles enthusiasm of those years for "vibration messages" and wrote a book about them: *Mental Radio* (1930). In such a lush setting, I soon began to tap the abundant supply of fascinating characters and lively subjects for magazine articles. At first I contributed to California magazines, of which there were a surprising number in those days—*The Overland Monthly, The Argonaut, The Dumbook, Hesperian, Game and Gossip, Sports and Vanities,* San Francisco *Review,* and *Saturday Night*—and then began to write articles and reviews for the Los Angeles *Times,* the San Diego *Union,* and national publications.

But I had other and better reasons for being pleased that I had come to live in Los Angeles. I soon came to know an interesting group of intellectuals: painters, writers, bookmen, designers, architects, and journalists, most of whom had arrived in Southern California at about the same time I did. In sober fact, we became the first "bohemians" of modern Los Angeles. Included were Jake Zeitlin, the bookdealer; Paul Jordan Smith, literary editor of the Los Angeles *Times;* Arthur Millier, its art critic; Phil Townsend Hanna, editor of *Westways;* Will Connell, the photographer; Lloyd Wright, the son of Frank Lloyd Wright; Merle Armitage, the impresario; Hildegarde Flanner, a fine poet; Kem Weber, the designer; Louis Adamic; Herbert Klein, the journalist and author; José Rodriguez, the musicologist and radio commentator; S. MacDonald Wright, the painter (brother of Willard Huntington Wright, "S. S. Van Dine"); Lawrence Clark Powell, librarian and critic; Duncan Aikman, then West Coast correspondent for the Baltimore *Sun;* the architects Richard Neutra, R. W. Schindler and Harwell Harris; Ward Ritchie, the printer; and others. I became indebted to this group for many insights about Southern California, its culture, history and folkways. For a time some of us published *Opinion,* one of the better little magazines of the period, which we usually put together at dinner meetings at René and Jean's French restaurant, where you could get a good meal for seventy-five cents. Also some of us formed Primavera Press, which brought out quite an interesting list of first-rate books, mostly about California. The nascent bohemia of Los Angeles was hardly comparable to the Left Bank in Paris or New York's Greenwich Village, but even so we managed to strike a few sparks.

As a young lawyer with literary interests I was a sucker for fine bookshops, of which there were not too many in Los Angeles in the 1920s. As part of my coverage of the local "literary scene" for the weekly *Saturday Night,* I met a young poet from Texas, Jake Zeitlin, shortly after his arrival in Los Angeles in 1925. At that time he managed to eke out a living, of a sort, by peddling rare books. We became great friends, and a few years later I helped him organize the first of several bookstores—At the Sign of the Grasshopper it was called—near the Los Angeles Public Library; later he had a shop around the corner on West Sixth Street designed by Lloyd Wright, and later one near Westlake Park. Today Jake is California's dean of rare-book dealers, and his Red Barn bookstore on La Cienaga Boulevard is world-famous. You never knew just whom you might meet in Jake's shops: Aldous Huxley, Hugh Walpole, Edward Weston, D. H. Lawrence, or some young poet who had just hitchhiked his way to Los Angeles.

At about the same time, I also met Stanley Rose, another Texan. A country boy from Matador, Texas, Stanley had run away from home to enlist in the Army in World War I. At the war's end he cleverly feigned mysterious psychiatric disorders and managed to spend a year or more in a delightful facility near Stanford University, where he acquired a taste for reading and a fondness for books. He too peddled books for a time in Los Angeles, primarily risqué items which he hawked in the studios. As with Jake, I lent Stanley a hand in organizing the two stores he operated, one on Vine near Hollywood Boulevard, the other next door to Musso-Frank's restaurant. Both were favorite meeting places for writers: Bill Saroyan, George Milburn, Erskine Caldwell, Louis Adamic, William Faulkner, Nathanael West, Frank Fenton (*A Place in the Sun*), John Fante, Jo Pagano, Jim Tully, Owen Francis, and others, and also for actors and directors. Both shops were hangouts for Hollywood writers and artists (many painters)—"intellectuals," if you will—in much the same way that Jake's shops were in downtown Los Angeles.

Stanley was a superb storyteller and a very funny man whose generosity was proverbial. In the late afternoons, as he began to warm up for the evening with a few drinks, he would hold court in the store, entertaining whoever happened to drop in, and the performance would invariably continue into the early morning hours in the back room at Musso's. At one time Stanley had been part owner of the Satyr Book Store on Vine Street. His two associates in this enterprise managed to induce him to take the rap for a pornographic item the three of them had published in violation of the copyright. The two associates were married; Stanley was not; and, besides, they glibly assured him that a jail sentence would not be imposed. Always amiable, Stanley entered a plea of guilty, drew sixty days in the cooler, and promptly sent for me. I arranged to secure his release and induced his associates to buy out his interest. The two of us then organized the first of his bookstores, directly opposite the Satyr shop on Vine Street. After a few drinks, Stanley would now and then emerge from the store and, to the amusement of his customers, swagger to the curb, shake his fist at his two former associates across the street, and hurl eloquent Texas curses at them. Uneducated but of great native charm, he was forever being lured on expensive hunting and fishing trips by wealthy actors, writers and directors on their promises to buy large libraries of books, which of course they never did; they merely wanted him along as court jester. Stanley dressed like a Hollywood swell, spoke like the Texas farm boy he never ceased to be, and carried on as Hollywood's unrivaled entertainer and easiest touch until his death in 1954. We were close friends during all the years he held court in the two bookshops which have long since become part of the legend of Hollywood.

Like other "bohemian" intellectuals, I had little active interest in politics in the 1920s. I kept inveighing, in my diary, against "a crazy money-mad world, formless and chaotic" which, paraphrasing La Fontaine, was endurable only to those of stout stomach and a sinful heart. I had only the most limited contact with any "left" politics, although some of the newspaper and magazine pieces I wrote were often rebellious in tone and content. In 1924 I met Upton Sinclair for the first time and wrote a piece about him which reflected my admiration. But there was not much of a socialist movement in Los Angeles in the 1920s; an earlier prewar movement, which had shown surprising strength, had been crushed after the dynamiting of the Los Angeles *Times* on October 1, 1910. Shortly after I came to Los Angeles, Sinclair had tried to address an outdoor meeting of striking longshoremen at Liberty Hills in San Pedro and had been arrested along with several hundred people. All he had managed to say before being arrested was, "This is a delightful climate . . ." But by then, 1923, the open-shop movement was in full swing and organized labor throughout California was on the defensive. On August 23, 1927, I had lunch with Sinclair in a huge dank, dreary, nearly empty cafeteria in Long Beach where Upton was then living, the day Sacco and Vanzetti were executed. I can still see the huge ominous headline: "Sacco and Vanzetti To Die!" I was supposed to interview Sinclair about his novel *Oil,* which had just been published, but we spent the entire afternoon talking about the executions in Boston. At the time I was more concerned with the literary ferment of the 1920s than with politics or causes, although I never doubted the innocence of the two anarchists. But listening to Upton gave me an uneasy feeling that the executions had a deeper and graver significance than most Americans realized.

The university or "formal" phase of my education, which proved to be largely irrelevant, was concluded in 1927. I was not well matched to the kind of institution I attended. The University of Southern California was then as it is today a famous football factory, and I did not play football. But I cannot say that the time I spent there did me any harm and I have fond memories of the place. I wrote editorials for the *Daily Trojan,* which were sassy enough to keep the editor in hot water most of the time, and edited the college literary magazine. But this phase of my education failed to provide much by way of guidance to the "world" of the 1920s which was soon to be snuffed out. Of more lasting impact were my explorations of the Southern California milieu and the emerging new city of Los Angeles, the influence of rebel writers of the period, and the more or less chance discovery of the "outsider" or "maverick" strain in American letters represented by Ambrose Bierce. A major influence in this informal or accidental phase of my "education" was H. L. Mencken.

3. *THE MENCKEN CONTINGENT*

H. L. Mencken was so much a part of the cultural revolt of the 1920s that he is often thought of as a man of the decade. But he belonged to an earlier generation. He was forty years of age when the twenties dawned; his career as a journalist dated from 1899. His values and outlook had been shaped by forces and influences operating around the turn of the century. "My basic ideas," he once wrote me, "go back to my early environment, and also show certain hereditary influences"—a reference to his third-generation German immigrant status. Basically Mencken was quite conservative. He came from a solid middle-class background. He had no quarrel with the Protestant ethic. He baited the "booboisie," not the bourgeoisie. Yet he was always an outsider, a cultural maverick. His background had been the noisy newsroom, not the quiet campus. He instinctively identified with the native tradition of dissent, with such maverick and outlaw figures as Poe, Twain and Bierce. "It is almost as safe to assume," he once wrote, "that an artist of any dignity is against his country . . . as it is to assume that the country is against the artist."

By his own lights, he was a consistent libertarian but never a liberal. He opposed the hounding of radicals and insisted on their right to be heard; he was one of the few American writers of distinction to express concern over the conviction of Sacco and Vanzetti. He also had a strong feeling for underdogs of all kinds even if he was never sentimental about them. Unlike the younger cultural rebels of the 1920s, he was fascinated with American politics and a most acute judge of American politicians. To him politics was a spectator sport; he was always the observer, never personally involved. The end of World War I found him in a truculent mood, angered by the "anti-Hun" hysteria of the war years and the bigotry, prudery, and know-nothingism that surfaced after 1919. So he stepped into the cultural forays of the decade with gusto and extreme assurance. He did not need to create an audience; it was there, avid for leadership, eager and responsive. He had seeded this rebellion, of which he was the prime catalyst, during the war years when he edited *The Smart Set*.

Mencken was not primarily a literary critic, much less a systematic political or social thinker. He was first and foremost a gifted journalist and editor. In fact, he had not written much about literary matters until his monthly articles on books began to appear in *The Smart Set* in 1908. From then on he did a good deal of reviewing for magazines and newspapers, but these writings, he once wrote me, "were not important . . . My real work always went into *The Smart Set*." *The Smart Set* was another of those curious, offbeat, bohemian journals that began to appear around the turn of the century, such as *The Lark* (1895–97) in San Francisco; *The Chap-Book*, launched in Cambridge in 1894 and later published in Chicago; *M'lle New York*, which lasted only fifteen issues (1895–96, 1898–99); and *Reedy's Mirror* (1909), published in St. Louis. *The Chap-Book*, first of the self-consciously avant-garde magazines of this type, had been directly inspired by *The Yellow Book*. There was an interesting note of rebellion in these magazines, but, as Larzer Ziff has pointed out, the young American writers of the period apparently were reluctant to divorce themselves "from the mainstream of their commercial culture even while feeling oppressed by it."[7] The onset of the Spanish–American War and the jingoism it aroused may also have had something to do with putting a hex on these first feeble stirrings of cultural revolt. In any case, *The Smart Set* provided the bridge between this earlier incipient literary and cultural revolt and the rebellion of the 1920s.

Willard Huntington Wright, who had been literary editor of the Los Angeles *Times,* served as editor of *The Smart Set* from 1912 to 1914. He had recruited Mencken and George Jean Nathan as contributors and was responsible for their selection to succeed him as editors. In the years they edited the magazine (1914–23) it was, as it had been under Wright, a lively and stimulating publication. Ostentatiously risqué in tone, disreputable in appearance, aggressively irreverent, it was consistently hospitable to the best in new writing. It published the first works of many important writers from Scott Fitzgerald to Robinson Jeffers. Even during the war years the magazine struck a consistent note of cultural defiance and thumbed its nose at many of the idols and totems of American society. But its maximum influence was exerted from 1918 to 1923; in these five years it moved from a marginal to a central position in the cultural quarrels of the period. But by 1923, the year Mencken and Nathan withdrew, its influence had crested. Largely confined to newsstand sales, *The Smart Set*'s circulation had hovered at or around fifty thousand from 1914 to 1920 but had dropped to twenty thousand by 1923. In a sense the magazine was the victim of its own success: by 1923 the cultural rebellion of the 1920s was well launched.

Mencken's writings did not begin to attract national attention until 1914, when he became co-editor of *The Smart Set.* I once queried him about a change that seemed to have come over his writing about that time, and he replied:

> The change that you notice circa 1913 probably came in 1914, when Nathan and I took over the complete editorial management of the magazine. I naturally felt more free when there was no editor over me, although those I served seldom bothered me. . . . My reviews got little notice until about 1919. They were denounced by certain academic critics, but there was little discussion of them. They got a great deal more after the Armistice. In fact, *they came in on the tide of the post-war reaction.* [My emphasis.] I had been writing about social and political matters in the Baltimore *Evening Sun* since 1910. The war naturally made such things seem important, so they also got into my literary criticism. I was never, in fact, a purely literary critic. I have always detested them. Literature is nothing when it bears no relation to life.

With the war at an end, the range and sharpness of Mencken's social criticism increased. In a 1921 policy statement issued in the name of the editors, he had written:

> Both of us are opposed to all such ideas as come from the mob, and are polluted by its stupidity: Puritanism, Prohibition, Comstockery, evangelical Christianity, tin-pot patriotism, the whole sham of democracy. Both of us, though against socialism and in favor of capitalism, believe that capitalism in the United States is ignorant, disreputable, and degraded, and that its heroes are bounders.

At the time, this was a refreshing and pertinent note to strike; disrespect has its uses, and many aspects of American life invited scornful satire and sharp criticism. But the owners of *The Smart Set* showed little enthusiasm for the new tone it had assumed. When, in September, 1923, they demanded the removal of a satirical piece about President Harding's funeral train, Mencken and Nathan resigned to launch a new magazine. In announcing their withdrawal, Mencken wrote that the editors' "desire and interest now lead them beyond *belles lettres*." And in the first issue of *The American Mercury* (January, 1924) he told its readers that the editors were determined "to shake up the animals, in politics, in economics, sciences, etc., as well as the fine arts." So well did he succeed that Nathan, who did not share his broader interests, resigned as co-editor at the end of 1924.

In the first years of Mencken's editorship, particularly from 1924 to 1927, the new magazine exerted a far-ranging and rapidly expanding influence, well beyond that which *The Smart Set* had attained. "As a literary arsonist," writes Peter Buitenhuis, Mencken "burned many rubbishy intellectual constructions and outmoded temples." He was, in Murray Kempton's phrase, "a gloriously destructive force," whose assaults on the "booboisie" helped set the stage for the New Deal he hated. But even before he withdrew as editor in 1933 (the repeal of Prohibition in that year was a fitting tribute to his influence), *The American Mercury* had lost much of its interest and relevance.

In retrospect it should be emphasized, as Douglas C. Stenerson has done, that Mencken played a key role in precipitating and perpetuating the great quarrel within American culture which developed between his boyhood in the 1880s and his heyday in the 1920s. Edmund Wilson made much the same point in an article in *The New Republic* of December 15, 1926, in which he commented on Mencken's Democratic Man.

This character [Wilson wrote] is an ideal one: it is an abstraction like Swift's Yahoo and it has almost the same stature and distinctness. It has, in fact, impressed itself upon the imagination of the general public in America as perhaps no other literary creation with the exception of Scott Fitzgerald's flapper. Sinclair Lewis's Babbitt and other inhabitants of his Main Street are merely particular incarnations of the great American boob, evidently inspired by Mencken . . . Mencken has planted the conception of the American boob, not only in the minds of those writers whom he has influenced, but also in the minds of all persons, all the otherwise undistinguished citizens, who are to be seen in every state of the Union carrying *The American Mercury* under their arms. And he has inculcated, along with this image, the moral ideal which it implies. We may not always like the somewhat heavy-footed superman (who is the positive inference to be drawn from the negative caricature) as we sometimes encounter his embodiment in some of Mencken's admirers; but we must admit that to have made the Americans recognize themselves in this super-boor and turn from the revelation in horror is no inconsiderable achievement.

But there was another highly significant aspect to Mencken's influence—namely, his insistence that the cultural rebels of the 1920s should concentrate on the American scene. Again and again he reminded contributors that the name of the new magazine was *The American Mercury* and that it was "very strictly confined to the American scene." There was always a sharp tension between his preferences—those aspects of American life and culture he liked and hugely enjoyed—and his "prejudices," i.e., his distaste for mindless conformity, bigotry, and hypocrisy. Actually he was endlessly fascinated, to the point of obsession, with these United States. Despite his cosmopolitan interests and air of being a man of the world, he was as American as apple pie. No one had a greater enthusiasm for Americana or did more to stimulate a new interest in the American language and American folkways. Few aspects of American life failed to engage his attention. He had little firsthand knowledge of the Middle West or the West or the West Coast, but he was actively interested in these regions. For all his harsh strictures about democracy, he was a notably democratic person. He was not overawed by names, titles or reputations. He published articles by convicts, lumberjacks, tramps, cowhands, stevedores, and sailors, as well as scholars, famous authors, and the reverend clergy. Manuscripts—often their first published writings—were accepted from unknown Italian Americans, Yugoslavs, Armenians, and other ethnics. He was hospitable to blacks. He published many women authors. He liked nothing better than to publish a new writer who had something of interest to say about some aspect of American life not previously chronicled. As an editor he would allow an author's offbeat phrase to stand if it had the ring of native authenticity to it. He was immensely interested in American writers of quality whose work had been overlooked by academic critics. For example, he encouraged me to write about the careers and books of Harold Frederic (*The Damnation of Theron Ware*) and Vincent O'Sullivan, whose fine novel *The Good Girl* had been suppressed on publication in 1914 by the Watch and Ward Society in Boston. He also encouraged me to write about such diverse subjects as religious cults, the folklore of earthquakes, farm labor tensions in California, and the life and times of Ambrose Bierce. He also published the first writings of many of my California friends: John Fante, Louis Adamic, Clarkson Crane, William Saroyan, and others. His emphasis on the American scene was timely and valuable; many cultural rebels on returning from expatriate years in Europe were turned off by the stupidities of the 1920s and needed to be reminded that the native scene offered inviting subjects for critical attention.

By the end of the decade the "great quarrel" in American culture began to assume new forms and Mencken's influence swiftly declined. But he did "shake up the animals," and his emphasis on the American scene gave the cultural rebellion of the 1920s a dimension it would otherwise have lacked. In a review in 1926, Walter Lippmann referred to Mencken as "the most powerful person and influence on this whole generation of educated people." This is perhaps an exaggeration, but I can attest that he was a prime influence in my "education."

4. FROM MENCKEN TO BIERCE

One day in 1923, a year after I had arrived in Los Angeles, I came across the imposing *Collected Works of Ambrose Bierce* in the open stacks of the Los Angeles Public Library. I knew that Mencken admired Bierce, but I had never read him. It did not take me long, however, to devour the twelve volumes, starting with *The Devil's Dictionary*. The line of succession from Bierce to Mencken was clear, in thought, style (the same direct and forceful prose), and outlook. Like Mencken, Bierce was, in the phrase of John G. Neihardt, "a congenital outsider," part of that "maverick and outlaw" strain that has kept a tradition of dissent alive from generation to generation. What intrigued me about Bierce, apart from his irony and wit, was an undercurrent of passion and deep feeling I did not find in Mencken. Mencken was an amiable critic of the American scene; there was little animus in his tirades; he was often amused by the Bryans and the Comstocks. But Bierce was "bitter." He did not share Mencken's relish for buffoons. He had no feel for Americana. There was little in the post–Civil War decades that aroused his enthusiasm. At an earlier date and under more difficult circumstances, he had zeroed in on many of the same targets that drew Mencken's fire, but with greater directness and candor. What, I wondered, had made him so bitter?

There were, of course, numerous hints and leads in the *Collected Works,* but most of what had then been written about Bierce was not very helpful. It consisted in the main of a welter of misinformation, some fine critical appreciations of his short stories, and a maze of feature news stories ("Who Was Ambrose Bierce?" "Whatever Happened to Ambrose Bierce?") that shed little light on the questions they raised. So I began to toy with the idea of writing a biography. But the practical difficulties were intimidating. I had no credentials for the task, I was a sophomore in college, holding a job which I could not afford to abandon. But somehow I managed to steal enough time from work and studies to begin the task of finding out what I could about the mysterious Ambrose Bierce. A year or so later I wrote a piece on Bierce for *The Argonaut* (March 14, 1925), a San Francisco weekly he once had edited. I sent a clipping to Mencken, and he promptly asked me to write a longer article for *The American Mercury;* when it appeared Albert Boni offered me a contract to write a biography. Mencken was helpful in other ways as well; he had known Bierce slightly, admired his writing, and was greatly intrigued by aspects of Bierce's personality and background which he did not understand. Publication of the *Mercury* article opened a number of doors and drew some interesting mail.

So I set out on the trail of Ambrose Bierce, interviewing those who had known him, visiting old haunts and places where he had lived—St. Helena, Calistoga, Los Gatos—endlessly hunting for documents, letters, and clippings. Unlike Twain and Harte, Bierce had not moved east until fairly late in life; many Californians had known him. The list I interviewed was a long one and included some fascinating Californians: Fremont Older, James Tufts, Mary Austin, George Sterling, Gertrude Atherton, Colonel Charles Erskine, Scott Wood (at his famous hilltop estate at Los Gatos overlooking the Santa Clara Valley), and many others, friends and enemies, admirers and detractors. The experience yielded a wealth of previously uncollected information about Bierce and many valuable insights about California; it also enabled me to examine Bierce's journalism in the context of the times, which is the way, for example, his famous column "Prattle" in the San Francisco *Examiner* should be read.

One of the individuals who encouraged my efforts was George Sterling, the San Francisco poet, who had been Bierce's protégé. From a first meeting in 1925 until his death slightly more than a year later, I saw a good deal of him, at the Bohemian Club in San Francisco, where he lived, and in Los Angeles, where he came from time to time to visit his sisters. An enormously generous and kindly person, Sterling proved to be an invaluable source.[8] In September, 1926, Sterling wrote me that he was preparing a lively reception for Mencken, who was scheduled to visit San Francisco a few weeks later. He had laid in a fine stock of liquor but had been on the wagon for "53 days now, though of course it seems longer," since he was afraid to start drinking, because of his health, before Mencken arrived. As he put it: "I have sworn to stay sober but was I sober when I swore?"

On October 29, Mencken stopped off in Los Angeles for a few days en route to San Francisco and I met him for the first time, at one of the Huerta cottages at the Ambassador Hotel. When he arrived in San Francisco, Sterling was not at the station to greet him; he had slipped off the wagon the day before and was quite ill. Later in the day Mencken called at the Bohemian Club, chatted briefly with him, and reported that his friend seemed to be in great pain. When he returned the next morning, he was told Sterling was sleeping. The following day, November 17, 1926, Sterling was found dead in his room; he had apparently taken poison during the night. He was only fifty-seven years of age but was tired and lonely and had been ill for a long time. Mencken attended the funeral services in Cypress Lawn Memorial Park and wrote a fine short tribute to his friend in which he referred to Sterling as "one of the last of the free artists."

It was through leads that Sterling provided that I was finally able to locate Bierce's daughter, whose whereabouts had eluded me. Ironically, she was living in Los Angeles, having moved there about the same time I did. In the introduction to the 1967 edition of my Bierce biography I have told of my friendship with Helen Bierce. Of all the characters I met on the trail of Ambrose Bierce she was one of the oddest, also one of the most likable. She had her father's good looks and bearing but was bouncy and exuberant, a devout Christian Scientist, highly susceptible to "new thought" credos of all kinds. She was also extremely improvident, accident prone, and difficult to help; in fact, she caused me no end of anxiety and concern from the time we first met until her death on December 16, 1940. But we remained the best of friends. A sentence or two from one of numerous emergency messages suggest what she was like better than anything I might say: "Carey, dear—Just got a 'job' from Jensen in County Welfare and here I am! Thank the Gods! Now will you leave a couple of dollars at your office so that I can eat until I get *rich*? O, am I a busy child! *I am!* This is written between *breaths*. Love from Little Helen." But between breaths, as it were, she was most helpful.

Somehow the Bierce biography got written and was published late in 1929, a few weeks after the stock market crash. The timing was perhaps symbolic, for my interests were about to take a new turn. The experience of writing it was so improbable, in view of the practical difficulties, that it left me with an eerie feeling that I had been tapped for the task by the ghost of Ambrose Bierce. It all seemed a bit too pat—the good luck, the fortunate timing, the way the discoveries about Bierce kept falling into place. The feeling prompted me to quote on the title page something the character Spandrell has to say in Aldous Huxley's *Point Counter Point:* "I doubt if anything is really irrelevant. Everything that happens is intrinsically like the man it happens to. . . . In some indescribable way the event's modified, qualitatively modified, so as to suit the character of each person involved in it. It's a great mystery and a paradox."

After the book was published, I began to receive important information and material of which I was unaware when I wrote it. This material, and some of the more recent research on Bierce, helps explain how he came to occupy the important place he does in the "maverick and outlaw" tradition of native American dissent.

5. BIERCE'S "GILDED AGE"

I had known, of course, about Bierce's famous uncle, General Lucius Verus Bierce (given that title when he headed an unsuccessful filibustering expedition against Canada in 1838), though his remarkable journal of a visit to the antebellum South, *Travels in the Southland (1822–1823),* was not published until 1966. Lucius Verus had attended Ohio University at Athens before moving to Akron, where he became one of the leading antislavery advocates in the Midwest. He was something of a scholar, possessed a fine library, and was prominent in Ohio politics, having served as prosecuting attorney and later as mayor of Akron. Impatient of dogmas and arbitrary definitions of "the nature of God and his revelation," he was as much opposed to religious bigotry as he was to slavery. From the outset he gave active support to his old Akron friend and neighbor, John Brown. When Brown stopped at Akron on his way to Kansas in August, 1855, he was given arms, ammunition, and some "artillery short swords" on each of which was emblazoned an American eagle. The swords were the contribution of General Bierce and were used in "the terrible work at Pottawatomie."[9] After Brown's execution, General Bierce delivered the funeral oration at an impressive public meeting held in Akron in which he referred to Brown as "the first martyr in 'the irrepressible conflict' of liberty with slavery." In this oration he publicly admitted having provided aid for Brown's Kansas foray. "Thank God! I furnished him arms—as did others in Akron—and right good use he made of them." Of the Fugitive Slave Law he said: "Whether the order comes from a Judge or a Commissioner or a President, if it is to transport a citizen of this to a slave state, without the protection of our laws, *I say resist it,* and let the South and her servile minions of the North know that she sleeps on a magazine that a spark from the North can at any moment explode."[10]

George Knepper's study of General Bierce confirms my conclusion that Ambrose "modeled himself upon his purposeful, active and opinionated Uncle Lucius, possibly even to the extent of copying and improving upon his style." He could hardly have avoided being influenced by his uncle's views on slavery. Throughout the Western Reserve, to which the Bierces had moved from Litchfield, Connecticut, abolitionist sentiment reached the highest pitch of indignation and excitement. Bierce's father was an early subscriber to *The Northern Indianan,* an antislavery paper founded in Warsaw, Indiana, in 1856, on which Ambrose worked as a printer's devil when he was still in his teens.

Among American writers none had a Civil War record of active service in any way comparable to Ambrose Bierce's. He had enlisted on April 19, 1861, when he was nineteen—the second person in the county to enlist after the firing on Fort Sumter—and had been assigned to Company C, Ninth Indiana Infantry. Known as "the Bloody Ninth," it participated in front-line combat at Shiloh and suffered the heaviest casualties of all Union regiments in that action, the first major battle of the war. He was twice severely wounded, the second time at Kennesaw Mountain, where his head, he once told a friend, had been "broken like a walnut." The rolls of his regiment contain not one mark against his record, and he was cited some sixteen times for gallantry in action and efficient service.

Such a record, set against the antislavery idealism which was part
of his family inheritance, goes far toward explaining his subsequent bitterness about the war and the kind of society that emerged
in its wake. He once wrote that it had been his good fortune to
command a company (he emerged with the rank of major) "of just
plain, ordinary American volunteer soldiers, who loved their country and fought for it with never a thought of grabbing it for themselves; that is a trick which the survivors were taught later by
gentlemen desiring their votes." The truth is that Bierce was not
the mocking misanthropist of legend but, as Lawrence I. Berkove
has demonstrated,[11] "a humanitarian deeply stirred by the tragedy
of life." Like Justice Holmes, his heart had been "touched with
fire"; it had been given to him, as it was to Holmes, to learn at the
outset that "life is a profound and passionate thing."

An important episode, at the midpoint of Bierce's career, confirmed his jaundiced view of the Gilded Age. Shortly after he had
returned to San Francisco after three years in London as a journalist, the Black Hills of the Dakotas were opened to unrestricted
development (February 28, 1877). Bierce, who had served on the
staff of General William B. Hazen during the war, had accompanied him in the same capacity on a tour of Western military posts
in 1866. That he knew something about the gold-mining district in
the Black Hills is shown by the fact that, in 1877, Bancroft, the San
Francisco publisher, had issued a map of the district which he had
prepared. In this way he became involved in the Black Hills Mining
Company, which had been incorporated December 8, 1879, by a
group of Gilded Age financiers including S. B. Eaton, who had also
served on General Hazen's staff during the war and who later
became president of the company known today as General Electric.
For four months in 1880, Bierce tried desperately to carry out his
assignment, which was to supervise construction of a dam and a
huge wooden flume, tunneling through hills and winding around
and across gulches, some eighteen miles to the rich diggings at
Rockersville. But he soon discovered he had been called to rescue
the affairs of a company that had been looted by its incorporators.
The Black Hills Mining Company failed, but the flume was actually
completed and operated for some fifteen years. Maurice Frink,
who studied the episode in detail, concluded that all Bierce received for his gallant efforts—he got not one cent in salary—was
bitter experience "in a dose sufficient to sour a man on the human
race."[12] Worth noting is the fact that Bierce never mentioned the
Black Hills episode directly, although there is a reference to it in
"A Sole Survivor," a sketch he wrote some fifteen years later. That
he was badly used in a characteristic swindle of the times there can

be no doubt. Soon after he returned to San Francisco he became editor of *The Wasp,* in which some of his most savage journalism appeared. He had become Bitter Bierce.

But it would be a mistake to attribute the change that came over his journalism after 1880 solely to personal disappointments. Over the years, as Berkove points out, he had been driven to the conclusion that "life was a war, and conflict of some kind a truer and more natural state than peace." He was obsessed with war and wartime experiences, and his typical theme after 1880 became "war in a larger sense," of man against nature, of man against man. His view came to be that man was "sentenced to life" and that overt warfare was simply "a visible and honest representation of the true state of things." Hence to live was to be a soldier. Bierce's tales of soldiers transcend the particular historical event and rise to the more subtle theme of "man in a hostile universe" in which "soldiers" make common cause with "civilians" who are also doomed to fight and lose. "The idealist who had been brutally awakened to war and surprised by the role Chance played in it," writes Berkove, "was equally struck by the brutality of 'normal' life and by the formidable part Chance played in it, too."

Some interesting parallels can be noted in the careers of Bierce and Justice Oliver Wendell Holmes. Both had been born in 1842. Both had participated in some of the heaviest fighting of the war. Both had been wounded. Both had been intensely idealistic on enlistment but had emerged from the war in a somewhat different state of mind. Neither ever forgot or fully recovered from the effects of the war. In neither case was their early idealism eclipsed; it simply assumed a deeper form. Both were men of rare courage who took a clear-eyed stoical view of human experience. Both were deeply troubled by the corruption of the Gilded Age. Yet, as Edmund Wilson noted, both were too much old-fashioned Americans, shaped by earlier experiences and social inheritance, to embrace the clamor for "social justice" with much enthusiasm. Holmes, the more favored, was able to make a better adjustment to post–Civil War America than Bierce. He had a name, family connections, a sound education, a measure of inherited wealth. Bierce had none of these. "Bierce's mind," Van Wyck Brooks once wrote in *The Freeman,*

> had nothing upon which to feed but the few books, old and well tried, that had nourished his youth. . . . While his interests were parochial, his outlook was broadly human. No man was ever freer of personal bitterness. It is impossible to read his letters without feeling that he was a starved man; but certainly

it can be said that, if his generation gave him very little, he succeeded in retaining in his own life the poise of an Olympian.

Bierce, like Mencken, had his limitations as a social critic. He had little sympathy with the vague socialist ideals that began to be voiced in the 1880s, but he thoroughly detested the tycoons of the period. In 1896 Congress was ready to pass the Funding Bill, an outrageous giveaway designed to add to the plunder of the Big Four—Huntington, Crocker, Stanford, and Hopkins—who had built the Central Pacific (later the Southern Pacific) largely at public expense. At William Randolph Hearst's request, Bierce went to Washington, where for a year or more he directed a savage, unrelenting, brilliant attack on the bill which finally resulted in its defeat. It was this victory that set the stage for the long struggle to break the Southern Pacific's dominance in California politics which culminated in Hiram Johnson's election as governor in 1910. This was nearly a decade before Lincoln Steffens and the other muckrakers began to attract national attention. Years later, Charles Edward Russell, one of the leading muckrakers, had high praise for Bierce's articles and cited them as one of the earliest manifestations of muckraking journalism. And there were other precursors, not many but a few, for example Charles and Brooks Adams, E. L. Godkin, Oswald Garrison Villard, and John Jay Chapman. The *Political Nursery*, which Chapman edited and published in New York between March, 1897, and January, 1901, was shrewd and perceptive about the sources of corruption in a society in which business was dominant. Chapman was another early enthusiasm; I collected his writings, corresponded with him, and wrote several articles about his work. Steffens was right in saying that the muckraking impulse was the "reflex of an old moral culture." But it was the spokesmen for this earlier moral criticism who kept alive the tradition of dissent and managed to trouble the conscience of thoughtful Americans before the muckrakers appeared on the scene.

So where was I, politically speaking, at the end of the 1920s? In joining the Mencken contingent I had rebelled against aspects of the dominant culture, and my reading of Bierce had provided an antidote to the brassy optimism not merely of the decade but of the conventional reading of the American experience. I felt alienated from the Main Street consensus but remained committed to the view that rebellion was a form of protest without specific ends. What does it mean to be a rebel? Alan Sillitoe's hero in *Saturday*

Night and Sunday Morning has the answer: "Once a rebel, always a rebel. You can't help being one. You can't deny that. And it's best to be a rebel, so as to show 'em it don't pay to try to do you down."

In the summer of 1928, Louis Adamic and I drove to San Francisco. On the way we detoured to Carmel, and late that afternoon I took him around to meet Robinson and Una Jeffers. On this as on previous occasions Una did most of the talking. Before we left she took us through the slightly ritualized ceremony of inspecting the Irish reed organ in the Hawk Tower, the grove of newly planted trees, and had us gape at the mottoes and legends in Old English that were painted on the beams and panels of Tor House. As usual, Jeffers said very little, but what he did say made a deep impression on both of us. He made us feel that World War I—with which he seemed obsessed—marked the beginning of the end of the kind of civilization we had known. He had brooded about the war in ways we had not. Beyond the brief parenthesis of the 1920s, he saw a darker decade looming up in which various forms of Caesarism were likely to emerge. In his eyes, America was a "perishing" Republic. As we drove up through the pines and the cypresses and struck the main highway at Salinas, we talked excitedly about what he had said and what his silences implied. For both of us the visit marked a realization that the "world" of the 1920s was drawing to a close and would probably be followed by a time of turbulence and upheaval.[13]

CHAPTER **IV**

THE SURGING THIRTIES

I was two years into the practice of the law when the stock market crash ushered in what John Steinbeck called "the terrible, troubled, triumphant, surging thirties." To Malcolm Cowley, the first five years of the 1930s were a time of intellectual ferment when one could see the bubbles rising as in a jug of cider, but after 1935 the bubbles stopped rising. In California the sequence was different: most of the excitement was crowded into the years from 1934 to 1939. In 1929, just as the decade of the twenties was drawing to a close, Steinbeck published *Cup of Gold,* an apprentice work on a romantic theme; a few years later, "frantic with material," he had written *In Dubious Battle* (1936) and was hard at work on *The Grapes of Wrath.* When my biography of Bierce was published in 1929, I had only a marginal interest in political and social issues. If anyone had told me then that I would be writing a book on farm labor in 1935, I would have been truly astonished.

In those first years of the 1930s, I was a very busy young lawyer. After passing the bar examination in 1927, I had found a place immediately in what was by local standards an "old" and prestigious law firm. The two senior partners were Princeton graduates who had joined the firm founded by their fathers, who had also been Princeton graduates. In the 1920s a second-generation firm was regarded as "venerable" in Los Angeles. Daniel Hammack, Jr., before going on to Princeton, had attended Occidental College, "the Princeton of the West," where he had been a classmate and close friend of Robinson Jeffers; the two of them used to go on long hiking trips through the Sierra Madre Mountains. It was in fact through Dan that I first got to know Robinson and Una Jeffers. Both senior partners were quite conservative; one was a Democrat, the other a Republican, but neither had an active interest in politics. Their clients included the Jameson Oil Company, one of the first to tap the rich Huntington Beach fields, Occidental College, cement plants, independent oil operators, loan-and-investment companies, industrial corporations, some wealthy "pioneer" first families, and quite a number of upper-middle-class residents of San Marino, South Pasadena, and Pasadena (in the Los Angeles region these were "old money" preserves). Needless to say, there were no trade unions on the list.

I liked and respected my associates, and our personal relations remained consistently warm and friendly despite growing differences on many issues. When I joined the firm it occupied space in an ancient office building; the high-ceiling rooms were laid out in a crazy-quilt pattern, the library was vast but largely obsolete, the atmosphere sedate, musty, and slightly Dickensian. Neither partner liked to make court appearances, one being too shy, the other too lazy, so with the brash self-confidence of the young lawyer I set to work to catch up with an incredible backlog of untried cases. Within a few years I had become a junior partner, the firm had moved into a modern office building, and its clientele had expanded, so I had little time for politics and only a slight interest in social issues. Three years out of law school I had married Dorothy Hedrick, the daughter of Dr. and Mrs. E. R. Hedrick. A distinguished mathematician, Dr. Hedrick was tapped a bit later as vice-president of the University of California and placed in charge, as provost, of the UCLA campus at Westwood. Wilson Carey Mc-Williams, nowadays professor of political science at Livingston College at Rutgers University, the author of *The Idea of Fraternity in America* (1973), a more prescient work than any written by his father, was the only child of this marriage. So in the early 1930s I seemed programmed as a reasonably successful young lawyer with a conventional practice, a promising future, and sobering responsibilities. (Some years after an amicable separation in the middle 1930s Dorothy obtained a divorce. In 1941 I married Iris Dorn-feld, of Roseville, California, and we have a son, Jerry Ross Mc-Williams. A novelist, Iris is the author of *Jeeny Ray* and *Boy Gravely*.)

But I did not need to leave my office to appreciate the extent of the 1929 debacle. I had, in fact, a prime view of the ravages of the Depression and its human consequences. I seemed to be endlessly involved with foreclosures and evictions (either bringing them or attempting to stave them off), bankruptcies, receiverships, savings-and-loan failures, collapsed business ventures, investigating real-estate swindles, tracing lost equities, salvaging something for widows from shrunken estates—the whole range of legal tangles that resulted when the bottom fell out of the Coolidge-Hoover "boom." What I saw distressed but did not surprise me; on the contrary, it confirmed my Colorado experiences of 1919–21 and strengthened my distrust of "the system." But I soon came to feel trapped in a professional role that had little meaning; at best we were technicians attempting to alleviate hardships and repair some of the damage, but I found little satisfaction in what we did. I became impatient and irritated and, above all, bored with the kind of law we practiced. And, as Saul Bellow once noted, boredom has probably had more to do with precipitating modern political revolutions than social injustice.

At about this same time, the social scene suddenly began to come alive. From 1932 on I became increasingly interested in what was happening at the grass roots of California politics: the social-protest movements, the dramatic farm labor strikes, the rebirth of the labor movement. The sense of social excitement was contagious; at long last that curious numbness and political paralysis of the first years of the Depression was rapidly giving way to a sense of rebellion. California—particularly Southern California—was the place to be in the years from 1934 to 1939; in no other part of the country did so much happen so fast. If their initial response to the Depression had been one of confusion and uncertainty, Californians more than made up for it in the last years of the decade.

It was this combination of personal dissatisfactions and mounting social excitements that brought about a radical shift in my interests. Almost before I knew what was happening, I found myself facing in new directions. Most of my writing in the first years of the Depression continued to be on literary themes and subjects. I kept turning up interesting letters and materials about Ambrose Bierce. I was for a time intensely interested in regionalism and regional culture, much in the manner of the Southern Agrarians but with a Western emphasis. In 1931 the University of Washington Press, as part of its chapbook series, published a long essay of mine on *The New Regionalism in American Literature,* and I did pieces on various aspects of the subject for *The Saturday Review of Literature, The Bookman, North American Review, The Nation, Southwest Review,* and other publications. I carried on an extensive literary correspondence with such Western writers as Mary Austin, collected rare books, developed a lively interest in American folklore and Californiana, wrote articles about little-known American writers for the university quarterlies, and contributed tony pieces on literary themes to magazines with such fancy names as *The Double Dealer, Hesperian, Contempo,* and *Apéritif.* But these literary interests swiftly receded as the Depression deepened. After 1932 I was writing almost exclusively about social issues, politics, and labor. In brief, once I began to respond to "the beat of the times," I soon found myself, like Steinbeck, "frantic with material."

1. THE POLITICS OF SOCIAL PROTEST

Southern California was the spawning ground for social-protest movements that quickly attracted national attention in the 1930s. Four were of major interest: the Utopian Society, Upton Sinclair's EPIC (End Poverty in California), the Townsend Plan, and Ham-'n-Eggs, another pension scheme. From the outset the national press took a lively interest in these defiant forms of political action, which it rightly sensed were distinctly California innovations. Nothing quite like them developed elsewhere; they could have originated only where and when they did, in Southern California in the 1930s. New, different, colorful, these four movements immediately aroused my interest, and I began to write about them for such publications as *The New Republic, The Nation,* and the Baltimore *Sun.* The experience taught me something about the politics of social protest by contrast, say, with radical politics or conventional party politics, and it marked phase one of my political education.

The first of the social-protest movements to surface was the Utopian Society. The society was an offshoot of a brief flurry of interest in technocracy which had been stimulated by a series of articles in the Los Angeles *Daily News* (December, 1932), then edited by Manchester Boddy, who had a real flair for the journalism of ideas. So great was local interest that crowds gathered each morning at the door of the pressroom to scramble for copies. The Utopian Society's vision of abundance, which was in essence an imaginative projection of technocracy's blueprint, had immense popular appeal in that season of scarcity. But part of its phenomenal success was due to the "secret" or "fraternal" mode of organization in which initiates kept repeating a vow of secrecy as they moved from one cycle to the next. For a modest fee, new recruits were initiated, in small groups, into the mysteries of the new economics of abundance at a series of secret dramatizations or "cycles" as in a fraternal lodge. I found it quite easy to sit in on these supposedly secret initiation rites, which dramatized mankind's quest for abundance in a series of revelations as in a Biblical play or parable. The formula piqued curiosity and offered a measure of protection against police "red squads" on the lookout as always for subversives, and the neophytes immensely enjoyed the ceremonies.

In the hothouse political atmosphere of the time, the Utopian Society grew like a gourd in the night. By midsummer 1934 the secrecy factor had become laughable: the Society then claimed an initiated membership of 500,000 and was holding as many as 250 meetings a night. The first big public rally, staged in the Hollywood Bowl on June 23, 1934, drew a capacity crowd of 25,000. But the promoters could never agree on the ultimate revelation—that is, how to usher in the society of abundance, having demonstrated its feasibility in six cycles. So the Utopians soon faded from the scene, but not until the stage had been set for a political movement that had a plan to end poverty if not to usher in an era of abundance.

In September, 1933, Upton Sinclair decided to seek the Democratic nomination for governor on a platform pledged to "End Poverty in California." The timing was propitious. By then the ravages of the Depression, as one observer noted, had "coalesced all the dissident elements of the state into one great surging political movement." Roosevelt had carried the state by a margin of 476,000 votes in 1932, but officials of the Democratic Party in California had little sympathy with the New Deal. Almost any reasonably presentable, fairly credible New Deal candidate could have won the governorship in 1934, but those who filed were discredited hacks, and so Sinclair's defiant movement filled the vacuum. EPIC had some good, indeed gifted, organizers, but Sinclair was not one of them. He was, however, a superb propagandist and educator. For more than a year he campaigned tirelessly from one end of the state to the other, insisting that poverty was anachronistic and that EPIC had the answer. What he proposed in essence was creation of a land authority and a production authority, financed by an increase in income taxes; these authorities would then put the unemployed to work on a variety of useful projects.

By January, 1934, some three hundred EPIC clubs had been organized; by the fall of that year there were two thousand. Financed by pennies, nickels and dimes, EPIC was without a doubt the finest example of a truly grass-roots campaign in the state's political history: a movement formed outside the Democratic Party with the objective of taking it over. Although viciously red-baited, Sinclair captured the Democratic nomination by a handsome margin, the opposition being divided, stupid, and ineffectual. When the returns were tallied in November, a record number of ballots had been marked: 2,330,132, or 32,000 more than had been cast in the presidential election of 1932. Of the total, Sinclair received

879,519, or 37.3 percent; Raymond Haight, running as an independent to draw votes from Sinclair, 320,519, or 12.9 percent; and Governor Frank Merriam, the Republican incumbent, 1,138,620, or 48.8 percent. When Sinclair had run for governor as a Socialist in 1930 he had polled 50,480 votes. In the 1934 election, the Communist Party gubernatorial candidate got 5,826 votes, the Socialist a mere 2,947.

I had come to know Sinclair quite well by the early 1930s. From time to time I would drive such distinguished visitors as Edmund Wilson out to see him at his place in Monrovia. I was an early admirer of Wilson's writing and had written what I later learned from him was the first article to be devoted to his work.[1] When Wilson had come to Southern California seeking material for *The American Jitters*, I served as his guide and chauffeur. The tour included a visit to Angelus Temple, where the Reverend Aimee Semple McPherson always provided excellent entertainment, and a trip to San Diego to inspect the Hotel Del Coronado, which I knew he would appreciate. While there we studied the city's suicide rate, then the highest in the nation; the research yielded one of the most interesting chapters in the book. It was on returning from this junket that I drove Wilson out to meet Upton. The three of us spent the afternoon talking about politics, the Depression, and socialism. Neither then nor before he took us to dinner, at a posh hotel with a splendid view of Pasadena's Arroyo Seco, did Upton, the teetotaler, offer us a drink. Wilson, I remember, wanted to know how Sinclair, a confirmed Socialist, had found capitalism endurable for so many years without benefit of alcohol. But all he got by way of an answer was a benign smile.

Of many vignettes of the EPIC campaign, one is sharply etched in my memory. At the time of the San Francisco general strike of July 19, 1934—a watershed event in the state's political history—I had a long interview with Sinclair at his home. A forest fire was burning in the nearby Sierra Madres—a not uncommon occurrence in the dry summer months—and the blinds had been shuttered and the drapes drawn to keep out the glare and the heat. During the interview, which took place in a suffocatingly hot living room, I tried repeatedly to get Upton to say what measures he would have taken had he been governor. (Governor Merriam had sent in troops with drawn bayonets, although San Francisco authorities had not requested intervention.) But he insisted on giving me a politician's answer: If he had been governor the strike would never have been called. I found his position evasive and said so, which resulted in one of several spats I had with him although we remained good friends. It was my impression that Upton was somewhat skittish about the strike because he did not like or trust Harry Bridges, the leader of the striking longshoremen. But he did, of course, express sympathy and support for the strikers.

Shortly after Sinclair won the Democratic primary, he paid President Roosevelt a visit at Hyde Park in the company of my friend Robert Brownell, his press secretary. Roosevelt, of course, was most cordial, and he flattered Upton by telling of the deep impression *The Jungle* had made on him when he first read it. Sinclair returned to California on cloud nine, convinced Roosevelt would endorse his candidacy, but of course he never did. In the last weeks of the campaign a somewhat similar California "summit" conference was arranged between Sinclair and Manchester Boddy which took place at Boddy's handsome estate at La Canada. Upton's "second" was Robert Brownell, while I sat in as Boddy's. The Los Angeles *Daily News* had given Sinclair a fair amount of coverage but had not endorsed his candidacy. Boddy had discussed every phase of the campaign in his widely read and quite influential column, without indicating whether in the end he would support Sinclair. The entire afternoon was taken up with political talk, but nothing much came of it. Boddy remained affable, hospitable, and wholly noncommittal. As at Hyde Park, Sinclair left convinced that an endorsement would be forthcoming. But during the final seven days of the campaign, Boddy left on a sudden vacation and filled his column each day with excerpts from Plutarch's *Lives!*

The EPIC campaign revamped the map of California politics by giving the state, for the first time, a New Deal Democratic Party. Previously there had been a strong old-guard Republican Party, a Progressive Republican faction (a heritage from Hiram Johnson and the Bull Moose campaign), and a notably ineffectual Democratic Party. After 1934 the Democratic Party came of age. EPIC-endorsed candidates won in twenty-four State Assembly and 3 State Senate races. Culbert L. Olson, elected to the State Senate from Los Angeles County, went on to win the governorship in 1938—the first Democrat to hold the office in forty years. Between January and June, 1934, the Democratic Party gained more than 350,000 new members, most of them EPIC supporters. Of the unknown politicians swept into office by EPIC votes, many became prominent figures in the Democratic Party. Sheridan Downey, Sinclair's running mate, was later elected to the U.S. Senate, and a number of EPIC-backed representatives still serve in the House. I covered every phase of the EPIC campaign, which was of intense interest to the national press. I was not surprised when Sinclair lost—I had reported he would—but I had great respect for his achievement.[2]

A day or two before the November election, I had a final interview with Upton. The Sinclairs—Upton and his wife, Craig—were staying at the time in the home of a rich Beverly Hills friend. Once again the drapes were drawn and the blinds shuttered in midafternoon. This time the reason was Craig's morbid fear that Upton might be assassinated. As we sat there in the rich friend's elegantly appointed living room discussing the campaign to end poverty in California, I suddenly sensed that Upton not only realized he would be defeated but seemed somehow to have lost interest in the campaign. In that vivid imagination of his, he had already acted out the part of "I, Governor of California," the title of one of his leaflets, so why bother to enact it in real life?

The pension plan movements which originated in Southern California in the 1930s were less interesting than the Utopian Society and EPIC but exerted a significant influence on state and national politics. Francis E. Townsend, a displaced Midwesterner, had moved to "the capital of the aged," Long Beach, California, in 1919. A graduate of Omaha Medical College, he practiced medicine briefly, engaged in various real-estate promotions and other get-rich-quick ventures, and nearly went bankrupt in the Depression. On September 30, 1933, a letter of his appeared in a Long Beach newspaper in which he set forth the elements of a scheme to retire everyone at age sixty on pensions of $150 a month (later raised to $200). On January 24, 1934, the plan was incorporated as Old-Age Revolving Pensions, Ltd., and by November some twelve hundred Townsend Clubs had been formed. Originating in Southern California, the movement quickly became national in scope, since Congress would have to adopt the plan. To the conservative Townsend, Sinclair was a "socialist" and hence beyond the pale, while to Upton, Townsend was a well-meaning quack. So the two movements went their separate ways. The rapid rise of the Townsend movement nationally was a major factor in prompting Roosevelt to sponsor social-security legislation. Ironically, adoption of the Social Security Act in August, 1935, sounded the death knell of the Townsend movement. Furious that Roosevelt had cleverly co-opted its appeal, Townsend teamed up with Father Charles Coughlin and Gerald L. K. Smith to support William Lemke for President in 1936.

Ham-'n-Eggs, the gaudiest of the Southern California pension schemes, was the brain child of Robert Noble, a talented radio demagogue who had been active in the EPIC campaign. Noble's program on Station KMTR in Los Angeles had overnight acquired a large audience and strong public support because of his sharp attacks on the corrupt administration of Mayor Frank Shaw. To give his program added zing and broader appeal, he began to spout about a plan that would pay every oldster twenty-five dollars every Monday. But he had made the mistake of contracting for radio time through an agency operated by two shrewd and cynical promoters, Willis and Lawrence Allen. On discovering this fact, Captain Earl Kynette, who was in charge of the "dirty tricks" squad of the Los Angeles police, hit on a scheme to get Noble out of Mayor Shaw's hair and at the same time muscle in on what appeared to be a lucrative promotion. So he made a loan which enabled the Allens to take over Noble's radio contract in their name. The next night when Noble arrived for his regular appearance he found Willis Allen seated behind the microphones. And when he got noisy, he was quickly and rudely escorted from the studio by the beefy aides of Captain Kynette. A little later, Kynette, emboldened by this coup, went a bit too far and planted a bomb in the car of one of Mayor Shaw's critics; for this particular dirty trick he served time in San Quentin.

In taking over Noble's radio program, the Allen brothers renamed his pension scheme Thirty-Every-Thursday, although it was popularly known as Ham-'n-Eggs, and began to promote it vigorously (their previous promotion had been Grey Gone, a hair tonic). Impractical as the plan was, it caught on rapidly and soon claimed 360,000 supporters. It was narrowly rejected by the voters when presented as an initiative measure in 1938 but proved to be a factor in the election of Culbert L. Olson as governor.

Not long after Noble had been brushed aside, a sixty-four-year-old unemployed widower notified the editorial offices of a San Diego newspaper that he intended to commit suicide because he could not get a pension. The threat was greeted with guffaws, but Archie Price then proceeded to take his own life and was buried in a pauper's grave. Sherman Bainbridge, one of the best of the Ham-'n-Eggs spellbinders, promptly organized a motorcade which wound its way down the 120-mile coastal highway from Los Angeles to San Diego, where Price's body was exhumed and reburied, with class and style. Thousands joined the motorcade and thousands more attended the funeral services, at which Sheridan Downey delivered a memorable oration. No other demonstration in Southern California in the Depression years was quite as impressive as this funereal motorcade, which moved slowly through the string of beach communities stretching from Los Angeles to San Clemente, then a new subdivision, and on to San Diego. Southern California has not produced many martyrs in the cause of social

•

justice, but Archie Price must rank as one, even though he has long since been forgotten.

Southern California's hothouse, rootless social setting was responsible for the rapid growth of these four movements, which had no exact counterparts nationally. They came out of nowhere, flourished briefly, and then subsided. The EPIC movement functioned within the Democratic Party; the others had no specific party connections. Sinclair was a Socialist who thought and spoke as a Socialist; but none of the four movements had ties with existing left parties. The leaders of the Socialist Party, including Norman Thomas, bitterly opposed Sinclair's campaign. These were not ideological movements; in each instance support for a specific plan was used to register a protest against the rigors of the Depression. Neither farm nor labor groups were significantly involved, although EPIC and Ham-'n-Eggs had some labor backing. No special efforts were made to recruit blacks, Mexican Americans or other minorities. Young people were not attracted in large numbers, and most intellectuals remained aloof or critical. The appeal was primarily to middle-aged and elderly whites of lower-middle-class and middle-class backgrounds who had been hurt by the Depression. The Utopian Society and the pension movements were autocratically controlled; EPIC was not. Movements like these, which urged adoption of particular plans, were easy to organize in the 1930s— the appeal was simple and direct—but seldom survived an initial defeat at the polls. Politicians learned to play one off against the others. Townsendites, for example, supported Republican Governor Frank Merriam, while Ham-'n-Eggs initially supported Olson but later caused him no end of trouble. But credit the Southern California social-protest movements with this: they voiced deep concerns, shook up state and national politics, and set the political wheels spinning.

It was these movements which first aroused my active interest in politics. Personally I had mixed feelings about them. I admired the superb grass-roots organization the EPIC leaders had put together. I also admired Sinclair's remarkable talents as a publicist and shared his criticism of the "free-enterprise system." But I never thought the EPIC plan would be adopted or that it would work if it had been enacted; on this score I agreed with much of the Socialist and Communist criticism of the plan. I spent hours debating EPIC with myself and others and always came out at the same point: I was sympathetic with the protest, with the politics of the movement, but skeptical of the plan. I found it easy, however, to vote for Sinclair. The other movements I distrusted because of the ease with which they could be and were in fact manipulated. But social-protest movements were merely one phase of California's dramatic response to the Depression. From them I moved on to reporting still more significant aspects of the surging thirties.

2. *FACTORIES IN THE FIELD*

Factories in the Field is subtitled "The Story of Migratory Farm Labor in California." The subtitle defined my intention: to piece together the dramatic and fascinating story of migratory farm labor. What prompted me, a busy young lawyer, to undertake such a task? The answer is quite simple. A series of dramatic large-scale farm labor strikes captured my interest. The headlines were so insistent, the social drama so intense, that I felt compelled to find out what was going on.

The troubles started in the spring of 1930 in Imperial Valley, California's great truck garden, with a series of spontaneous strikes by Mexican and Filipino field workers. Hundreds of arrests were made, and eight of the strike leaders were convicted under the Criminal Syndicalism Act (its first use against farm labor) and sentenced to San Quentin Prison. Then in 1931 and 1932 a rash of strikes broke out in the San Joaquin Valley, some of which were suppressed with violence and brutality. The next year workers at the Tagus Ranch near Fresno walked out in August. A large corporate enterprise, Tagus was noted for its tough antiunion tactics. When the strike succeeded, to nearly everyone's surprise, all hell broke loose. Strikes were reported throughout the state: at Oxnard, Tulare, Fresno, San Jose, Merced, Chico, Lodi, San Diego, Gridley, and Sacramento. Most of these strikes were spontaneous. Only a handful of left-wing organizers were involved, and their role was not significant; workers would not have struck on this scale in the absence of deep grievances of long standing. The climax came on October 4, 1933, when eighteen thousand cotton pickers went on strike at a string of cotton "farm factories" that stretched down the San Joaquin Valley for a distance of 114 miles. The next year another rash of strikes occurred. Coinciding with the San Francisco general strike and Upton Sinclair's EPIC campaign, the 1934 strikes stimulated the formation of a militant antilabor organization, the Associated Farmers, which promptly launched a statewide campaign to prevent the organization of farm workers. A series of mass arrests was staged, culminating in still another Criminal Syndicalism Act prosecution, this time in Sacramento, in which eight organizers were convicted after one of the longest trials in the state's history (the convictions were later reversed on appeal). These 1933–34 strikes were the most extensive in the farm labor history of California and the United States; in scale, number, and value of crops affected, they were quite without precedent. The 1933 strikes alone involved more than fifty thousand workers.

It took little imagination to sense the importance of this extraordinary social upheaval. So as time permitted I began to make forays into various strike areas to see and report on what was happening. In the summer of 1935, I made a tour of areas from Bakersfield to Salinas in the company of my friend Herbert Klein, checking up on the results of the 1933–34 strikes, interviewing workers, labor contractors, growers, and officials, taking a look at living and working conditions, and talking to organizers. Armed guards ordered us off the Tagus Ranch. Near Salinas we inspected a large camp or stockade which had been built, we were told, to protect strikebreakers but seemed much better designed to serve as a concentration camp for striking farm workers in case of mass arrests. I returned to Los Angeles from this trip determined to tell the story of migratory farm labor in California and promptly set to work.

The following year there were still more strikes, including a major strike in the citrus industry in Southern California which lasted for some weeks and was finally suppressed in a crude and brutal fashion. What impressed me most about the strike was not so much the violence, which was commonplace, but the way residents of the beautifully laid out "citrus belt towns," with their ivy-covered Protestant churches, permitted local police to issue shoot-to-kill orders and deputize college football stars to round up Mexican-American strikers and hold them in improvised stockades. But, as I found out, the owners of the groves had little to do with labor relations; that vulgar and often unpleasant activity was handled by the large cooperative fruit exchanges which represented the collective power of the industry. In fact, this was the general pattern of farm labor relations in California. On a regional or crop-by-crop basis, growers would meet in advance of each labor operation and fix a "minimum" rate which invariably proved to be the maximum they would pay, all without benefit of any kind of collective bargaining.

Migratory farm labor was an old if largely unreported California story by the mid-1930s, when it suddenly and dramatically became invested with a new national interest. So-called "Okies" and "Arkies" had been trekking to California since the early 1920s, when cotton first began to be grown in the San Joaquin Valley. As the acreage increased, so did the influx. Then drought sent thousands of refugees moving westward; in 1935 alone some 87,302 Dust Bowl migrants entered the state. Actually the influx was never quite as menacing as it was made out to be. In all, perhaps 350,000 to 400,000 entered California between 1935 and 1938. What alarmed the growers—and local residents—was the fact that most of these migrants stayed on after the crops were harvested, living in labor camps, improvised "shacktowns" and "Little Oklahomas" on the outskirts of established towns. Most of them lacked the means or any incentive to return to the Great Plains areas from which they had fled. With little federal aid available, local communities became concerned about budgets for schools, hospitals, health services, and, of course, relief payments.

The large growers were particularly disturbed by the fact that Dust Bowl migrants could not be hustled out of the state once the crops were harvested. They were citizens: whites of Anglo-Saxon Protestant backgrounds, former yeomen farmers who had come west seeking a new life for themselves and their families as a majority of Californians had done before them. Although stereotyped as an undesirable minority—lazy, shiftless, ignorant, improvident, with too many children and notoriously loose sexual standards—they stayed on, and others kept coming. So ludicrous expedients were invoked to stem the tide. In May, 1933, a law was passed making it a criminal offense for anyone knowingly to transport an indigent person into the state. In a famous case, the Reverend Fred Edwards was convicted under this statute of having brought his brother to the promised land (the United States Supreme Court eventually held the act unconstitutional). Also, a special border patrol was established in 1935–36 in an unsuccessful but widely publicized attempt to turn back indigent migrants at the Arizona border. Largely ignored in all this headlined excitement was the fact that farm production was increasing while labor costs remained at a low level.

Intrigued by the new turn events had taken and obsessed by a sense of urgency—the times had begun to take on apocalyptic overtones—I somehow managed to finish *Factories in the Field*, working nights, weekends, and holidays. Published in July, 1939, shortly after *The Grapes of Wrath*, it promptly became a best seller. The timing was, of course, excellent. But an unanticipated development catapulted the book into the thick of the controversy then raging in California about farm labor and Dust Bowl migrants. In January, the newly elected Governor Olson had named me to head the Division of Immigration and Housing. A unique agency, set up in 1913 by Governor Hiram Johnson at the time of the Wheatland hop pickers' riot, it had authority to inquire into the welfare of alien immigrants, inspect farm labor camps, and concern itself with some forms of rural housing. Simon J. Lubin, John Collier, and Carleton Parker had worked with the agency in its early years—it was really Lubin's idea—and some remarkable results had been achieved. But under successive conservative Republican administrations it had become moribund. Neither Governor Olson nor his aides had a nominee in mind until someone reminded the Governor that I had written a book about farm labor. I was not an applicant, nor had I known that my name would be proposed. But I had worked in the Governor's campaign and I found his argument unanswerable: if I wanted to do something about farm labor, here was my chance. For all practical purposes, the appointment marked the end of my career as a lawyer.

In that first exciting year, 1939, the division began to come alive. A branch office was opened in Fresno, in addition to those in San Francisco, Sacramento, and Los Angeles. New labor camp inspectors were added to the staff. The number of camp inspections tripled—there were then some 4,500 labor camps in the state, with a peak-season camp population of 160,000 or more—and growers were compelled to spend more than a million dollars in improvements. Most of these camps, often with as many as sixty or more cabins, were located off the beaten paths, invisible to nearby townspeople and to motorists on the main highways. So we organized caravans of social workers, churchmen, teachers, and housewives and took them on guided tours so that they could see for themselves, often for the first time, what the camps were like. Repeated radio appeals were made by way of securing tips on where labor camps were hidden; often they would be set up in abandoned barns or old warehouses. I addressed groups from one end of the state to the other on the need to improve living and working conditions for migratory farm labor. Special reports were issued on labor camps and shacktown settlements. With the Governor's approval, I convened, in Fresno on May 26–27, a large meeting of local, state, and federal officials concerned with various aspects of migratory farm labor, attracting statewide attention. Naturally this burst of activity did not endear me to the large growers and the Associated Farmers. But it was two specific actions that made me, as they put it, "Agricultural Pest No. 1, worse than pear blight or boll weevil."

In May, 1939, I got Governor Olson to let me hold a public hearing in Madera for the purpose of recommending a fair wage rate for chopping cotton (i.e., weeding and thinning). The state could not enforce such a rate, but it could refuse to cut able-bodied adults from relief rolls if they declined to work for less. *These were the first hearings of the kind ever held in California.* When I recommended twenty-seven and a half cents an hour—the going rate was twenty cents—the growers screamed like banshees. And that fall when it came time to pick cotton, I talked the Governor into letting me set up a commission which included growers, academic experts, labor spokesmen, and public citizens to recommend a fair rate of payment. Held in Fresno's City Auditorium September 28, 29, and 30, the hearings drew an estimated attendance of 3,500 and received wide press coverage. That year a man and wife picking cotton for sixty-six days, the average season's length, at the going rate of eighty cents a hundred pounds, would make $140.57. At $1.25, the rate recommended by the minority of which I was one, they would have made $229.41. The majority came up with a lesser rate, but the growers promptly rejected it, and a major strike ensued.

Thus, when *Factories in the Field* appeared on the heels of *The Grapes of Wrath,* the growers were convinced a conspiracy had been hatched to defame large-scale corporate agriculture. A kind of mass hysteria developed, with a concerted public-relations campaign being directed against both authors and their books at luncheons, public meetings, on the radio, and in the press. Answering books appeared with such titles as *Grapes of Gladness* and *Plums of Plenty.*[3] But the more violently the books were denounced, the better they sold. Almost overnight the migrant issue became a national news story. "After mid-1939," writes Walter J. Stein, "Americans could no longer hear the word 'migrant' without thinking of the Joads."[4] The release of John Ford's fine screen version of the Steinbeck novel in January, 1940, gave the issue still greater national exposure. But the conspiracy charge was a fantasy. The fact is I never met John Steinbeck. Both of us were active in the Simon J. Lubin Society, we exchanged a few letters, and I served as chairman of the Steinbeck Committee to Aid Agricultural Workers until succeeded by Helen Gahagan Douglas. (The committee once staged a memorable Christmas party attended by five thousand children of migrant farm workers in a huge circus tent at Shafter, California.) But our paths never crossed.

In the fall of 1938, some of us began a campaign to induce the La Follette Committee to investigate violations of civil liberties in California farm labor disputes, but Senator La Follette remained lukewarm to the idea until *The Grapes of Wrath* and *Factories in the Field* "provided the necessary thrust."[5] Once the committee arrived, I spent a great deal of time with the staff, briefing them, lining up witnesses, and cooperating in other ways. When public

hearings opened in San Francisco on December 6, 1939, Governor
Olson was the first witness. I remember meeting with him early
that morning at the Fairmont Hotel, while he was having breakfast
in his nightshirt, to go over the statement I had prepared for him.
Later, on December 21, I testified and presented a sixty-page report on farm labor conditions. Unfortunately, the committee's final
report and recommendations were not issued until October 19,
1942, and by then we were at war. But the widely publicized hearings and twenty-seven volumes of published transcripts—over four
hundred witnesses were questioned—had enormous impact. In
effect the hearings put the Associated Farmers out of business.

As a result of all the excitement in 1939, a stream of reporters
visited California, and the radio networks were alive with debates,
discussions, and interviews. *Factories in the Field* remained on the
best-seller lists for months and I was invited to discuss the issues at
many public meetings. I debated Phil Bancroft, son of the famous
California historian, vice-president of the Associated Farmers, and
Republican senatorial nominee in 1938 and 1944, on a *Town Meeting of the Air* program from New York, before the Commonwealth
Club in San Francisco, and at the Friday Morning Club in Los
Angeles. Arthur Eggleston, then labor editor of the San Francisco
Chronicle, summed up the effects of the tumult and the shouting
by saying that it had finally become respectable in California to
discuss, openly and publicly, any aspect of the farm labor problem.
The logjam of taboo, ignorance and misinformation had finally
been broken, and "a mighty river of words flooded out over the
land" and, he added, "is still flowing."

Before Governor Olson left office, I had so succeeded in arous-
ing the ire of the growers that I became the target of the only bill
of attainder ever passed by the California legislature. In February,
1941, Assemblyman Earl Desmond of Sacramento introduced a
bill (AB 2162) which proposed to abolish the Division of Immigration and Housing. The sponsors made no secret of the fact that
their purpose was to drive me from office. The bill was opposed by
an impressive array of unions, church groups, civic and professional organizations, and a significant section of the press. But the
war in Europe had crowded the Okies off the front pages, and
Olson's enemies had moved in to strike at him by striking at me.
The measure passed the Assembly by a vote of forty-eight to seventeen and the Senate by twenty-three to nine, but was pocket-
vetoed by the Governor because, so he said, it was primarily aimed
at me and he had received no complaints that I was inefficient or
incompetent.[6]

Looking back on those years, I find it difficult to believe that so much excitement, action, controversy, and conflict could have been squeezed into such a brief span. But even before the outbreak of war in Europe, I sensed we had come to a big bend in the stream; that nothing would ever be quite the same again. As the preparedness program got under way, the despised Dust Bowl migrants moved into the rapidly expanding shipyards and defense industries, with immense benefit to the state and the nation. And not only that: a new migration of far greater significance had been set in motion.

> For every Okie who made the trek from 1935 to 1940 [writes Walter Stein], two Okies came during the wartime boom. For every migrant California gained from 1930 to 1940, she gained three the following decade. Many of the migrants of the war years were as penniless as were the Okies who had displaced the Mexicans in California's fields during the depression years. The new Okies did not frighten Californians, however, for they rapidly found work. In any case, the state had found a new bogey in the Japanese.

It was, as Stein notes, a great pity that "the events of 1940 marked a tragic lost opportunity in America's confrontation with rural poverty." The stage had been set, the issues defined, and an enormous national audience was eagerly attentive; then the war curtain descended. But it was not all wasted effort; those exciting years at the end of the 1930s had "brought the harvest gypsy to national attention for the first time in the nation's history."[7]

It was the misfortune of the Olson administration to come to power too late; by 1939 the New Deal was dead. But if his legislative achievements were disappointing, Olson should be credited with several notable acts of political decency. His first official act had been to present a pardon to Tom Mooney in an impressive ceremony in the State Assembly Chamber on January 7, 1939, which I witnessed. (Mooney and Warren Billings, labor organizers, had been convicted of the bombing of a Preparedness Day parade in San Francisco in 1916. Their case became an international *cause célèbre* during the twenty years they spent in prison for a crime which it is today almost universally conceded they did not commit.) The Governor also supported and approved my efforts to secure the release of Henry Cowell, the distinguished musician-composer, from San Quentin Prison. Cowell's parents had sought my aid shortly after I joined the administration. It took months of patient negotiation—the Hearst press had a vested interest in his conviction—and the aid of John Gee Clark, director of the Department of Penology, and State Senator Robert W. Kenny, both friends of mine, to bring about Cowell's release on parole. He had foolishly pleaded guilty to a morals charge which should never have been filed. Incredible as it sounds today, he had served three and a half years of a fifteen-year sentence before we were able to secure his release. Nothing in my term of service gave me greater pleasure or more lasting satisfaction. In a letter dated July 7, 1940, Cowell wrote to say that his release was "due in much part to your most appreciated efforts on my behalf"; years later I received his personal thanks in New York.

3. "ORGANIZE!"

At the midpoint of the 1930s "Organize!" suddenly became a one-word battle cry as labor sought to regain overnight the ground it had lost after World War I. The catalyst was Section 7-A of the National Industrial Recovery Act of 1933, which for the first time in American history gave legal recognition to the right of workers "to organize and bargain collectively through representatives of their own choosing," a right firmly implemented by the National Labor Relations Act of 1935.

The electrifying effect of the legislation was felt immediately; in plant after plant, industry after industry, workers wanted to know how to exercise the new rights they had been granted. This was notably true in Los Angeles, which for years had been the capital of the "open shop." It was, in fact, a nonunion city, and, not surprisingly, labor lawyers were in short supply. After 1933 organizers and elected officers came knocking on the doors of young lawyers who were rumored to have an interest in labor. My credentials were not impressive. I had written about the new labor legislation and was known to have an interest in the history of labor in Southern California; but prior to representing some Mexican-American workers in a 1934 citrus strike, at the request of the American Civil Liberties Union, I do not remember having been involved in a labor case, nor had I represented any unions. But such were the social urgencies of the time and the place that I got caught up almost overnight in the organizing campaigns of the 1930s.

Shortly after the National Labor Relations Board opened a regional office in Los Angeles, I was asked to serve as trial examiner in one of the first major proceedings in Southern California. The case involved charges of union discrimination brought by the Mine,

Mill and Smelter Workers Union against the American Potash and
Chemical Company of Trona, California.

Located near Searles Lake at the lower end of the Pannamint
Range on the edge of Death Valley, Trona was the classic company
town. Every lot and building was owned by the company. The
setting was dramatic and intimidating: town and plant were pin-
points in an encompassing desert of sand and barren mountain
ranges; the isolation was awesome. The hearings were scheduled
to be held in a portion of the space rented by the U.S. Postal
Service, but the company promptly threatened to cancel the lease.
So permission was obtained to use the American Legion Hall in the
desert town of Randsberg some thirty miles distant. The hearings
opened there in May, 1935, but had to be adjourned to Los Angeles after a week because the Legion, responding to company pressure, revoked permission to use the hall. Just who owned and
controlled this company which exhibited such sovereign contempt
for an agency of the federal government? It took the NLRB's counsel several days to trace the chain of ownership back to an international mining cartel with offices in Brussels and a Belgian count as
chairman of the board. Later I learned that among the company's
other holdings was the Compagnie des Potasses du Congo, in
Holle, Congo. After the hearings concluded in Los Angeles, I filed
a report sustaining some of the charges of union discrimination,
but when the Supreme Court handed down its decision in the
Carter Coal Company case, the NLRB decided to dismiss the action
for lack of jurisdiction. Later I served as trial examiner for the
Board in a number of other proceedings and then began to represent some of the new unions that came along at that time. For
me Trona was an eye-opening experience, one I never forgot. The
arrogance of the company, the extent and ramifications of its interests and connections, the desert setting, and the courage exhibited
by union members and organizers made a lasting impression.

Still another milestone in my labor "education" had to do with
the first organizing campaigns of the Los Angeles Newspaper
Guild, which were greeted with less than total enthusiasm by local
newspaper managements. I was more or less drafted by the Guild
as its first counsel, largely because many of its members were
friends and drinking companions and thus felt no need to discuss
retainers or fees. On May 14, 1938, the Hollywood *Citizen-News*
discharged Roger Johnson, a well-known and widely respected reporter who headed the local Guild unit which was attempting to
organize the paper, and a strike was called. Since the locale was
Hollywood, the strike promptly assumed show-biz aspects. Prominent stars paraded on the picket lines and signed autographs. Tea

was served. Mannequins twirling parasols pirouetted in fancy gowns. For several weeks the picket lines were the best show in town. But management was not amused, and the strike soon took on ugly overtones as Johnson and two Guild organizers were arrested and some thirty-three contempt citations were issued.

Judge Harlan G. Palmer, the publisher of the *Citizen-News*, was a leading figure in the local "reform" movement: a man of integrity, piety, and "liberal" views, on most issues. Roger Johnson might have been Palmer's son: he was the same kind of person, held essentially the same political views, but believed strongly in collective bargaining. A campaign had been launched that summer to recall Mayor Frank Shaw. The recall candidate was Judge Fletcher Bowron, who won the election and served three terms for a total of fifteen years, during which he administered city affairs in an honest but not notably enlightened manner. He too was much the same kind of person as Palmer: a "reformer," something of a "liberal." It was, indeed, an odd situation. The four of us were friends, all of us were active in the recall campaign (I served as chairman of a Labor-for-Bowron Committee), and yet there we were, caught up in a bitter strike which one might have thought we could easily have resolved.

The strike was finally settled, but it raised some significant questions in my mind about the limitations of "reform" politics. After the strike I could better understand why organized labor in general preferred corrupt mayors who were prolabor to honest mayors who were not. Most of the city's unions supported Mayor Frank Shaw; only a minority backed Bowron. So the strike drew no support from either Shaw or Bowron and little, if any, from organized labor; the Guild was, in fact, lucky to win it. That "reformers" had closer ties with the economic Establishment than with labor represented, I came to feel, a weakness on the part of both organized labor and the reform movement. Either labor did not want reform ("honest") government or the reform movement preferred honest government to decent working conditions.[8]

Still another episode in my brief but hectic involvement with the labor movement is one I shall not soon forget. Piece-rate workers who shelled walnuts in one of the large cooperative grower exchanges in Los Angeles asked me to explain their rights under the new labor legislation. The meeting was held on a warm and humid evening in a large hall in East Los Angeles. In a letter to Louis Adamic (October 3, 1937) I jotted down some impressions for his interest and amusement. I was the only male in the hall, in which fifteen hundred women of all ages, shapes, sizes, and nationalities had gathered. Questions and answers had to be translated into several different languages, the audience being a bizarre mix of Armenians, Russian Americans, Mexican Americans, and other ethnics. The front-row seats had been reserved for some older women from the Russian Molokan colony, mostly peasant types with colorful scarfs and shawls who spoke not a word of English. As I wrote Adamic: "You should have been there if only to have gotten the *feel* of the meeting, its tension and excitement. And you would have been fascinated to watch some of the women get to their feet and attempt to explain how they felt about their work, their jobs."

The ladies heard me out politely, but the NLRA was not their primary interest; that was obvious. They wanted to express their feelings, to talk about their problems. It seems there were never enough hammers available for all the women who reported each day to crack walnuts—a primitive operation in those days, paid at piece rates. Many workers had to shell walnuts by hand. Dozens held up swollen, bruised, and blackened fists to prove it. Some complained because the floors were not swept regularly and said they often slipped on shells. A pretty young blonde suddenly jumped up laughing, raced down the center aisle, bent over, and lifted her skirt high to show me a large black-and-blue mark which was right where you would expect it to be. The audience howled with laughter. Women and girls stood on benches, crowded the aisles and doorways, and applauded every time they heard the word "organize." It was the one English word all of them understood. The spirit that animated that meeting was the spirit of the New Deal, which had reached full tide with the rebirth of the labor movement.

Curiosity, not ideological commitment, was responsible for my involvement with labor unions. I was interested in Marxism in the 1930s—as who wasn't?—but I never succeeded in mastering the sacred texts. Nor had many of the persons I met in the labor movement. I knew and admired Harry Bridges and was active in the Bridges Defense Committee. What I most admired about Harry was his shrewd practical approach to trade-union problems. He may have been deeply imbued with Marxist dogmas, but he never spent much time mouthing them in my presence. It was his tactical skill and astute leadership that brought about the remarkable victory of the longshoremen in the 1934 strike. The largest maritime walkout up to that time, it precipitated the most widespread general strike in American labor history, one that transformed the labor and political scene in California. Between 1934 and 1939 union membership in the state increased by eight hundred percent, "much of the growth coming with the active support, advice, and leadership of Harry Bridges."[9] For nearly twenty years the Democratic Party had run a poor second to the Republican Party in San Francisco; even in 1934 the Democratic vote for Sinclair had accounted for only 38.9 percent of the total. But four years later, nourished by the growth of the labor movement, the Democratic vote had jumped to 53.4 percent and was a major factor in the election of Culbert L. Olson as governor.

The years in which I was actively involved in labor's organizing campaigns (1935–39) were exciting and illuminating and provided a wonderful anodyne for the pain of boredom. But they were not remunerative and involved some troublesome personal experiences and adjustments. Needless to say, the two senior members of the firm of Black, Hammack and McWilliams did not share my new social interests; indeed, they took a rather bleak view of labor unions, as did most of our clients. To their credit, my associates never once suggested that I should cease to represent unions, then a notoriously time-consuming and unprofitable form of practice that frightened off better-paying clients. But I did not need to be told of their displeasure; it was a source of painful concern. I liked and respected and felt deeply obligated to both of them. Also I had heavy commitments to clients most of whom also took an unfriendly view of labor. And I had, by then, sizable personal responsibilities. The dilemma was real, but the truth is I had grown irredeemably bored with the kind of law my associates wanted to practice; in the context of the times it did not seem exciting or "socially significant," nor was it relevant to my personal interests. By contrast, the new "world" of labor seemed vastly more interesting and important. How I might have resolved this dilemma if I had not been named to head the Division of Immigration and Housing in 1939, the year *Factories in the Field* was published, I do not know; but I did not have to make the decision. It was made for me by events over which I had no direct control but to which I readily responded.

No experience did more to shape my political point of view than this brief engagement with labor. It pushed me beyond the liberalism of the period in the direction of a native American radicalism with which I could readily identify. That the experience took place in Southern California was of special importance, for the region still lacked a broad industrial base, and labor had not fully recovered from the setback it had suffered after the dynamiting of the Los Angeles *Times* in 1910.* Representing unions in Los An-

*The dynamiting of the Los Angeles *Times* is the subject of Louis Adamic's *Dynamite* and fills a large chapter in the social history of the city. A long fight against the open shop had culminated in a strike of metalworkers which the *Times* bitterly opposed. J. B. and J. J.

geles in the 1930s was like being in on the birth of the labor movement: it enabled one to see how, and why, labor organized. Not until the CIO held its first statewide convention in Los Angeles on August 20, 1938, could one say that the city's open-shop phase had finally come to an end.

Exhilarating as my brief involvement with the upsurge of labor organizing in the 1930s proved to be, it was not without some dark and troublesome aspects. I could understand why labor officials were often wary of "dollar-honest" reform politicians who better served the dominant economic interests than the working people they were supposed to represent. But alliances with corrupt politicians were, I came to feel, invariably short-sighted and self-defeating. More troublesome were the connections between union officials with Mafia connections and corporate executives who dealt with them knowing of their ties with criminal elements. An encounter I had with the gangster Willie Bioff, which had unintended and far-reaching consequences, added an important chapter to my labor "education."

4. THE LIFE AND TIMES OF WILLIE BIOFF

Not without ironic overtones, my dramatic brush with labor racketeering in Hollywood taught me something about the undercurrents of crime, violence, and corruption that permeated sections of organized labor even in the period of its remarkable resurgence. Phases of the story did not come to light until some time after the events occurred. Only then did I learn that Louis B. Mayer of MGM had been threatened by a Chicago gangster who mistakenly thought Mayer had fingered him, whereas I was the party responsible. Still later I learned how I had more or less inadvertently set in motion a chain of criminal prosecutions and investigations that revealed how the motion picture industry had been shaken down in a multimillion-dollar caper described by George Murray as the single most dramatic shakedown of the Capone syndicate.[11]

Shortly after the National Labor Relations Act was adopted, a group of rank-and-file studio workers consulted me about a new and dramatic turn that events had taken in the always volatile Hollywood trade-union scene. The motion picture industry has

McNamara, of the ironworkers' union, were arrested and charged with the dynamiting, in which twenty employees lost their lives. Clarence Darrow, with an assist from Lincoln Steffens, finally made a deal by which the McNamaras pleaded guilty but escaped the death penalty. Then Darrow was tried for attempted jury tampering and narrowly escaped conviction. The dynamiting episode and its aftermath set labor back several decades and snuffed out a strong socialist movement.[10]

always presented a hodgepodge pattern of craft unionism. But one union, the International Alliance of Theatrical and Stage Employees, had the potential of becoming a vertical, or industrial, union. That it had jurisdiction over projectionists in motion picture theaters simply underscored the potential threat it represented to producers and single-craft unions. In the aftermath of a disastrous strike in 1933, Local 37 of the IATSE—the big Hollywood catchall local—lost most of its nine thousand members to other unions. As a result, the IATSE was dropped from the basic agreement and by 1936 had only 158 dues-paying members. Then suddenly, on April 21, 1936, notices were posted in all studios announcing that it had been reassigned jurisdiction over the jobs lost in 1933. This meant that some ten thousand studio employees would have to take out cards in the IATSE, which had been granted a closed shop. No election had been held, none was scheduled. But that was not all: soon a two percent assessment was levied on the entire membership. Over a period of six years, this assessment yielded some $6,500,000, which was divided "up the middle" by George Browne and Willie Bioff, two Chicago gangsters who with the aid of Frank Nitti ("the Enforcer") and other syndicate elements had seized control of the IATSE. Not a penny of this sum cleared through the books of the union.

Confident that the closed-shop agreement and the assessment could be set aside, I initiated the necessary legal proceedings, but I soon realized that other tactics would have to be pursued, since the litigation might drag on for years. Having obtained information from the Chicago Crime Commission that Browne and Bioff had gangster ties, I took the material to the Speaker of the State Assembly, a law school classmate then associated with the firm of McAdoo and Neblett (Senator William Gibbs McAdoo and Colonel William Neblett), and suggested that a legislative committee should investigate. The Speaker said no; my materials were too meager. But a few days later he changed his mind. Apparently he had decided that such an inquiry might be good politics or good business or both. The hearings opened on November 8, 1937, in the auditorium of the State Building in Los Angeles to a capacity audience, with intensive press coverage. My clients testified that when they had tried to protest the closed-shop agreement and the assessment they had been beaten up, suspended from their jobs, and expelled from the union. Then Bioff was called to the stand and was asked one or two vague questions about his background in Chicago. But before the next day's session opened, the hearings were indefinitely postponed. I learned why the following year when I was the lead-off witness at an open, or public, grand-jury hearing in Sacramento on August 8, 1938, called to hear evidence which Herbert Philbrick, a special investigator, had assembled bearing on legislative corruption.[12]

According to Philbrick, the firm of McAdoo and Neblett had received a five-thousand-dollar retainer from the IATSE while also acting as counsel for the Assembly Labor Committee at the request of the Speaker. The IATSE had regular counsel in Los Angeles, and McAdoo and Neblett had never previously represented it. Philbrick had also come across evidence that Joseph Schenck of 20th Century–Fox had given Bioff $100,000. A series of subsequent federal investigations and prosecutions, aided by some hard-hitting columns by Westbrook Pegler, brought the full facts to national attention. In the meantime, I had bowed out as counsel for the rank-and-filers, having been named to head the Division of Immigration and Housing.

Browne and Bioff had been petty racketeers in Chicago until Browne became head of the important projectionist local of the IATSE. Bioff, incidentally, was never at any time a member of the union. Motion picture theater owners have little defense against projectionists who want to cause trouble. Films can be shown upside down "by mistake"; lights can be turned off and on at the wrong time; stench bombs can be rolled down darkened aisles. So Browne and Bioff had little difficulty in shaking down the major theater chains. Intoxicated by their easy success, they began to talk and spend too much in nightclubs and thereby came to the attention of Frank Nitti, who had succeeded Capone as head of the syndicate. A deal was then worked out whereby the mob would help Browne win election as national president of the IATSE at the 1934 convention with the aid of gangster-controlled projectionist locals in New York and New Jersey. It has been reported there were more gunmen than delegates at this convention. Nitti made it clear that the shakedown of the theaters would continue, but as part of a larger plan to levy tribute on the motion picture industry. Payoffs from the theater owners and the industry would be split: half to Browne and Bioff, half to the syndicate. Later the syndicate's share was upped to two-thirds, and John Roselli—the CIA's hit man in the plots to assassinate Castro; his body was found in an oil drum off Miami in the summer of 1976—was assigned to Hollywood to see that Browne and Bioff honored the agreement.

A first step in the larger design was the gangster-style execution on February 4, 1935, of Tommy Maloy, who "owned" a motion picture operators' local in Chicago. The next step was to have Browne call out the Chicago projectionists briefly, just by way of demonstrating what might happen on a national scale. So when the producers met with the heads of the Hollywood unions in New York to negotiate the basic agreement of 1936, Browne and Bioff were there with a set of stiff demands: the IATSE must be readmitted to the agreement; it must be given a closed shop; it must be granted jurisdiction over workers and jobs it had lost in 1933; there would be no local autonomy, none. In addition, in private sessions, they demanded money, a lot of it. The producers howled but soon capitulated. Indeed, the meetings adjourned on a note of joviality and mutual satisfaction. In the words of Judge John W. Kern, the producers not only "knowingly and willingly" paid off Browne and Bioff but "had in a sense lent encouragement" to their activities. Court records indicate that a minimum of $1,827,000 was collected during the time the agreement was in effect, but the actual amount was much larger, and it did not include the $6,500,000 collected under the two percent assessment.

The denouement was interesting. First Bioff was extradited to Cook County, Illinois, on April 5, 1940, to serve a jail sentence for pimping which he had successfully evaded for nearly twenty years. Six months later he and Browne were indicted on charges of having extorted large sums from the producers, and they were later convicted. Accepting bribes would have been a more appropriate charge. Payoffs were being made at the time of the legislative-committee hearings in Los Angeles and while the grand jury in Sacramento was investigating the evidence Philbrick had assembled. Both hearings provided the producers with splendid opportunities to complain of "extortion," but no complaints were voiced. On the contrary, the producers did everything in their power to protect Browne and Bioff. When he was first summoned to appear before the legislative committee in Los Angeles, Bioff was furious. Convinced that Louis B. Mayer had instigated the hearings, he lost little time in letting his displeasure be known both to Mayer and to the New York headquarters of the producers' association. As a result, Nicholas Schenck, president of Loew's, Inc., was hastily dispatched to Los Angeles, where he conferred with his brother, Joseph Schenck, Mayer, Leo Spitz and other top industry figures at a meeting held at Joe Schenck's home on November 11, 1937.

Witnesses present at the November 11 meeting later testified that Mayer was "panic-stricken," "terribly nervous," "really pale." He told the others how Bioff had accused him of initiating the legislative hearings through Colonel Neblett and said he feared for his life. Later Browne and Bioff showed up. Bioff "abused Mayer," pointed his finger at him, and said, "Look, Mayer, there is not room for the two of us in this world and I am going to be here." Mayer, "absolutely white, and trembling at the time"—the quotes are from the court record—assured Bioff he had not instigated the hearings, which was true. To prove it, he phoned Colonel Neblett and, with Bioff listening in, got Neblett to say he would, if necessary, explain to Bioff that there was nothing to the charge. Mayer then turned to Bioff and said, "Well, are you satisfied?" to which the response was, "Never mind what Neblett said, I still don't believe you." But once it was clear that the legislative hearings would not be resumed, his belligerence abated; even so, the executives who were present were at some pains to keep him in an amiable mood. Joe Schenck gave him a photo autographed "To my friend Willie" and signed "Affectionately." On January 17, 1938, he presented to Bioff and his wife tickets for a cruise on the *Normandy* to Rio de Janeiro, and he later made it possible for them to continue on to Europe. When the Bioffs sailed, the producers threw a party for them, and Mr. and Mrs. Harry Warner sent orchids to Mrs. Bioff.

Convicted of extortion, Browne and Bioff served brief jail terms and then agreed to testify for the government in a prosecution against Nitti and other members of the syndicate. Nitti committed suicide the day after the indictments were returned, on March 18, 1943. But the other defendants were tried and all but one convicted. They were later paroled in what was patently a deal backed by top figures in the Truman Administration. As to Browne and Bioff, they were soon paroled and managed to do quite well for themselves. Browne bought a posh country place in Illinois, and Bioff, who changed his name to William Nelson, retired to a handsome home near Phoenix. There for some years he enjoyed quite a pleasant existence. He sported a seven-carat diamond ring, usually carried large sums in cash, and hobnobbed with Senator Barry Goldwater, to one of whose campaigns he contributed five thousand dollars.

But when Bioff surfaced as the person in charge of entertainment at Gus Greenbaum's new Riviera Hotel in Las Vegas, in March, 1955, the mob was not at all pleased. On the morning of November 4, 1955, in full view of his wife, who was standing at the kitchen window of their home, Bioff stepped on the starter of his car and a tremendous explosion wrecked the car, destroyed most of the garage, tossed portions of his body a distance of twenty-five feet, and scattered debris over a wide area. The seven-carat diamond he admired so much was never found. Mrs. Bioff told police that her husband was "sort of retired and dabbled in real estate." Asked if she thought he might have committed suicide she said, "Oh, God, no. He got a lot out of life. He was so good and kind. He was too nice a person for anybody to get mad at. He didn't have an enemy in the world." Thus did Willie Bioff depart this life, not with a whimper but with a bang.

Bioff had taken one route to Hollywood. The Schencks had taken another. But when their paths crossed they soon reached a meeting of minds, for they came from much the same backgrounds and shared essentially the same values. Willie, born in Russia, was a full-fledged hood on the streets of Chicago before he was out of knee pants. He started out as a pimp with a string of teenage prostitutes and then began to shake down kosher restaurants. Later he provided the muscle for the joint Browne-Bioff shakedown of motion picture theaters in Chicago. Nicholas and Joseph Schenck were born in Rybinsk, a Volga River village. At the turn of the century they sold newspapers on the Lower East Side, and later they operated nickelodeons and amusement concessions in Paradise Park. In 1919 their friend Marcus Loew, a theater owner who had financed some of their early ventures, acquired a studio in Hollywood, and Joe Schenck soon joined him there, to become, in time, president of United Artists. By 1927 the two Schencks were said to be worth $20 million and had a combined income of $1 million a year. When Bioff intruded in their operations they thought they knew how to deal with him, and he was equally sure that he had their number. Both were right. Bioff once said movie executives were "nothing but two-bit whores with clean shirts and a shine." Of course, the executives who paid off Browne and Bioff and the mob had to cover up the payments, deceive their stockholders, and trick the government (Joe Schenck was convicted of income tax evasion and served time briefly), but "the bottom line" was right. While these executives may have feared Bioff, knowing of his connections, they demonstrated remarkable confidence in him. Nicholas Schenck, for example, used him as a courier to deliver large sums in cash to his brother, Joe. The Schencks, Mayer, and the other industry executives had great influence in Washington. They could have secured the cooperation of the FBI and the Justice Department at any time by simply snapping their fingers. Harry Warner, a witness at the Los Angeles legislative-committee hearings in 1937, was asked these questions in a later, 1943, proceeding:

Q. Now, in this legislative investigation under oath you had every opportunity, did you not, not only to tell the committee but the world the character of the man Bioff?

A. I would not take that chance, sir.

Q. So Bioff was above the legislature of California, was he?

A. I would say as far as my life was concerned, yes, sir.

Yet this was the same Harry Warner who sent the Bioffs orchids and bon-voyage messages.

The Bioff episode left me with a feeling that the army of sleuths, informers, and House Un-American Activities Committee investigators who descended on Hollywood in the 1940s to ferret out "reds" and radicals and expose "Communist" plots might better have devoted their talents to investigating corrupt labor practices in the motion picture industry. The perspective of a quarter century confirms this impression.

5. THE ANTIFASCIST PHASE

In the 1930s the forces of Armageddon and social reform raced toward a climax that came at the end of the decade. The shock waves from abroad seemed to strike at regular intervals of two years or less: Japan's invasion of Manchuria, Hitler's seizure of power, Mussolini's invasion of Ethiopia, the march into the Rhineland, the Spanish Civil War, the occupation of Austria, and, finally, Munich. Up to a point the effect was to quicken the pace of social reform; coalitions broadened, concerns deepened, perspectives shifted. But as the war clouds darkened, a lengthening shadow was cast across the New Deal. With the fall of Madrid in the spring of 1939 and publication of *The Grapes of Wrath* a few weeks later, the decade, in Harold Clurman's phrase, "boomed its farewell salute."

The Nazi seizure of power in 1933 was, of course, the major seismic happening overseas, but Ethiopia and Spain registered high on the scale in terms of domestic interest and response. A classic case of aggression, the invasion of Ethiopia provided the acid test: a small, virtually unarmed nation, brutally assaulted by a major power, had resisted with exceptional courage and determination. Not only did France and England fail to act: they encouraged the aggression. At the League of Nations, only the United States, Russia and China opposed the Italian conquest. A green light was immediately flashed to Hitler; predictably more aggression was in the offing. But despite the indignation it aroused, the invasion of Ethiopia did not become a major issue: there was no Ethiopian political constituency in this country to beat the drums. It did, however, evoke protests, even in Los Angeles. A mass meeting was organized by the American League Against War and Fascism to enable those troubled by the aggression to voice their feelings. None of the speakers—I was one—knew anything about Ethiopia, but the meaning of Mussolini's flagrant and undisguised aggression for the future was clear enough. For me that meeting marked the beginning of the antifascist phase of the politics of the 1930s.

The Spanish Civil War was even more momentous; it provided the key or set of keys to almost everything that followed. In Spain, as Senator Borah put it, fascism produced its masterpiece. Support for the Loyalist regime quickly became an international cause, the point of resistance to the outbreak of a second world war. Pro-Loyalist sentiment steadily increased, but not enough to reverse the policy of nonintervention. The first public meeting in support of the Loyalists in this country was held at the Hollywood Women's Club on September 11, 1936; the speakers were the author Lewis Browne, Manchester Boddy, Lionel Stander and myself. It had been organized not by leftists but by the editor of a small Jewish weekly who happened to be a well-known "anti-Communist." As the war continued, a parade of visitors came to California, mostly to Hollywood, to rally support for the Loyalists: André Malraux, Hemingway, Joris Ivens, José Bergamin, Ralph Bates, Ramon Sender, and others. Large sums were raised for ambulances and medical aid; in fact, there was probably more activity of this sort in California than in any other state. A glance at the long list of sponsors of the Western Writers Congress held in San Francisco, November 13, 14 and 15, 1936, is enough to demonstrate how deeply writers of the most widely varied political views had been affected by the antifascist ferment. The list embraced the entire political spectrum. But even before the fall of Madrid (March 29, 1939), the fervor had begun to abate. I chaired the last pro-Loyalist mass meeting in Los Angeles, at the Trinity Auditorium, at which Theodore Dreiser was the main speaker. I can still see him stalking back and forth across the platform; growling about what he had said to Roosevelt on the need to lift the embargo and what Roosevelt had replied; silent for embarrassing intervals; muttering to himself; but strangely eloquent and impressive. Between that first meeting in Hollywood in September, 1936, and this last, December 22, 1938, much of the initial ardor and enthusiasm had subsided.

With the Soviet-Nazi Pact of August, 1939, the antifascist coalitions fell apart. The period from then until the Nazi invasion of the Soviet Union in June, 1941, can be described only as a nightmarish season. Name-calling and denunciations became the order of the day; old friends ceased speaking; new political alignments emerged. The savage "anti-Communist" witch-hunting of the late 1940s had its origins in this period. I did not see the issues in the same way as the Communists, who were denounced as appeasers, or the liberals, many of whom turned violently anti-Communist. I felt that the Communists should have foreseen the likelihood of such a pact and the distinct possibility it would soon be breached. From the early years of the decade it had been obvious that the Soviets were militarily vulnerable. It was equally clear that Hitler was determined to dominate the area from the Rhine to the Urals. Nor could there be the slightest doubt that British policy sought to encourage him to move in this direction. Again and again France and England yielded to Hitler's escalating demands—in part because they feared Germany might go Communist if his regime were to collapse. Mussolini's invasion of Ethiopia had been encouraged for much the same reason. Any significant show of force, it is now conceded, would have compelled the Nazis to withdraw from the Rhineland. Austria held guarantees from Britain, France, Italy and *Germany,* but Hitler marched in unchallenged. When Russia became alarmed and signed the Franco-Soviet Pact, Britain was anything but pleased. Nonintervention on the part of France and England doomed the Loyalists. But it was Munich that sealed the fate of Europe. Czechoslovakia had a defensible border: twenty-one regular and fourteen or more second-line divisions, with strong industrial and defense resources. To abandon the Czechs and *then* make a commitment to Poland was suicidal. Poland would not permit Russian troops to enter the country; it could not be effectively aided by France or England; and its military strength was negligible. Under the circumstances, therefore, it did not seem surprising to me that the Russians should have signed a pact with the Nazis, however shameful it might be in moral terms. The effect was to turn the Nazis against the West which had been trying for years to turn them against Russia. The Anglo-German Naval Pact had given Hitler virtually everything he wanted, yet it had not been denounced with anything like the vehemence directed against the Nazi-Soviet Pact.[13]

Following the outbreak of war in September and notably after Hitler smashed the Maginot Line, the feuding and infighting in what had been the antifascist coalition became truly savage. My problem was and always has been that I am a pacifist by conviction but have never been able to make the commitment total. After Munich my confidence in the French and British *governments* was minimal; I thought them quite capable of making a deal with Hitler. So I did not favor direct American intervention. In June, 1941, as I was driving down the coast highway from San Francisco to Los Angeles, I stopped at Pismo Beach, the halfway point, and there, at a restaurant famous for its clams, met Haakon Chevalier and J. Robert Oppenheimer, who were driving north. Both were deeply pessimistic about the Nazi invasion of the Soviet Union launched the day before. As they saw it, Russia would soon be defeated. I did not agree, I was, in fact, certain that Hitler had signed his death warrant. For me this was the turning point in the war. Later I was convinced the Japanese would never have struck at Pearl Harbor in December had it not been for Hitler's invasion of the Soviet Union in June. After these momentous developments, the infighting ceased for the duration of the war, but it left a heritage of bitterness and ill-will which was to erupt after 1945.

In its September 1, 1941, issue, *The New Republic* conducted a symposium on whether the United States should declare war immediately. To the editor's query I replied:

> It is my belief that the United States should not at this time make a declaration of war against the Axis powers. I believe that Carl Sandburg is right when he points out that in the present "war of nerves" the President's tactics are well calculated to drive the Nazis crazy. The uncertainty of our policy is more exasperating to them than a forthright declaration of war. After the dramatic meeting with Churchill, the President returns and the headline reads: "U.S. No Nearer War, President Declares" (August 17, 1941). This sort of thing is maddening to the Nazis: a bold diplomatic move, aggressive in tone, followed by a baffling non-committal interview. As usual the President is leading the country along and, at the same time, sparring with the domestic political opposition. This seems to me to be the best strategy at the moment. May I add, however, with respect to Japan, that I strongly favor a hard-boiled aggressive policy—an absolute embargo, enforced if necessary by blockade.

6. THE ORDEAL OF HUMPHREY COBB

The murderous tensions and crosscurrents of this nightmare season (1939–41) came to a sharp and dramatic focus in the life of Humphrey Cobb, who had come to live in Southern California shortly after *Paths of Glory* was published in June, 1935. Based on an actual incident in World War I (reported in the New York *Times* of July 2, 1934), the novel became a best seller, was adapted to the stage by Sidney Howard but closed after four or five performances and was later—in 1957—produced as a motion picture by Stanley Kubrick; it was, in fact, his first film. Most of those who have read the novel will probably agree with Warren Eyster's conclusion (in an afterword to the 1971 paperback edition) that Cobb hated war "to a degree that makes Remarque's *All Quiet on the Western Front* seem merely sentimental, and current anti-Vietnam talk a mere kindergarten protest." What he hated was the ruthless system of militarism.

I knew Humphrey from the time he came to work in Hollywood—he was employed at different times by MGM, Warner Brothers, Goldwyn and Paramount—until his death in 1944. We were, in fact, close personal friends. A small man, five feet five inches or thereabouts, weighing perhaps 150 pounds or less, with closely cropped hair, his speech clipped and tart, Humphrey was amusingly irascible and never suffered fools gladly. Nor was he ever known to walk away from an argument. Born in Siena, Italy, on December 5, 1899—his father an artist, his mother a doctor— he had been sent to private schools in England until age fourteen, when the family returned to this country. He then attended Newman School in Lakewood, New Jersey, and was admitted to Princeton. But he never enrolled; in 1916 he falsified his age in order to enlist in the Royal Montreal Regiment of the First Canadian Division and saw active service in France.

When I first knew him he was recovering from a heart attack and worked mostly at home, first in Brentwood, then in Flintridge. He hated the atmosphere of the studios and, in fact, had little interest in films. As the international situation began to heat up in the middle 1930s, he became so obsessed with what was happening that he could think or talk of little else. The situation was ironic and tragic. Hating war as profoundly as he did, he was so outraged by the failure of world opinion to check fascist aggression that he could hardly wait for the next war to start. His wife, concerned about his health, asked me to visit him as often as possible, since he seemed to be less agitated when he talked politics with me than with some of his other friends. So I made a point of spending as much time with him as I could, particularly when the various crises crested. Now and then I brought visitors along to help relieve the tension: Robert Dell, Otis Ferguson, Louis Adamic, and others. During the Munich crisis, Louis and I sat up most of the night with him, listening to short-wave radio broadcasts. The next day he wrote a magnificent letter to Neville Chamberlain, renouncing the dual British citizenship he had acquired by service in the Canadian Army and returning a handful of decorations.

After the Nazi-Soviet Pact, he was beside himself with anger and indignation and quarreled with many of his "left" friends in Hollywood. Later he determined to help in the war effort, at whatever risk to his health, and signed on with the Writers War Board of the Office of War Information. But he soon became disenchanted with the thrust of our wartime propaganda. In a letter of December 23,

1942, he rather plaintively inquired, "Do you think this war will win us anything better than before?" He died of a heart attack at Port Washington, New York, on April 25, 1944—before we had dropped the bomb at Hiroshima, before the Cold War had gotten under way, and long before we tried to win the hearts and minds of the Vietnamese.

On two occasions he revisited the scenes of engagements in France in which his regiment had taken part: once shortly after the armistice when the devastation had not been repaired and the trenches still gaped at the sky; and again some years later when the fields were covered with beautifully waving wheat and the trenches had disappeared. He understood, he once wrote me, why Ambrose Bierce had revisited in old age the scenes of Civil War engagements in which he had taken part: "It is a pilgrimage to ground that is in a sense holy no matter how much we may hope that no more acres will be baptized."

None of Humphrey's other writings ever quite measured up to *Paths of Glory*. He once started a novel based on the Tom Mooney case which was to have been titled "Without Remedy"; we had many long talks about it. But after he had written five or six chapters, he decided, with characteristic abruptness, to shelve the project. He was bitterly disappointed in the Tom Mooney who emerged from San Quentin, although he liked the man he had interviewed there. So his reputation rests on *Paths of Glory,* which, as Warren Eyster wrote in 1971, is

> more typical for the American today than it was at the time of its publication. No current explanation of the moral problems of United States troops in South Vietnam, and no current investigations of reported atrocities at My Lai, Song My, and Son Thang offer such graphic evidence of the real causes of inhuman behavior and moral perversion as *Paths of Glory.* . . . To Cobb, mud was mud, and rain was rain, and dying was dying. . . . *No* writer has ever opposed the power structure that exists within modern armies more relentlessly than Cobb. No writer has shown the gap between officers and enlisted men, between front-line troops and the high command, to be so tragic and absurd.

CHAPTER V

THE WAR YEARS

1. THE RACIAL REVOLUTION

By contrast with labor's remarkable insurgence, racial minorities registered only slight gains in the 1930s. Some of the new CIO unions were relatively free of bias, but in general the labor movement was reluctant to organize workers regardless of race or to tackle the problem of discrimination. Nor was the New Deal, in its early phases, much concerned; the growth of black political power came later. The outstanding *cause célèbre* of the decade was the Scottsboro case, which Elias M. Schwarzbart, associate counsel for the defense, has described as "a lightning flash that signaled the reawakening of the civil rights movement after the long sleep of Reconstruction." But the modern civil-rights movement dates not from that flash; it stems, rather, from the racial revolution that began with our entrance into World War II.

Today we have forgotten what prevailing racial attitudes were like as late as 1940. Miscegenation was an impermissible concept; intermarriage was taboo; "touching" was frowned upon; social intercourse was severely restricted. Franklin Frazier, the distinguished Negro sociologist, had to ride a freight elevator to attend a meeting of a learned society in Washington, D.C. Roland Hayes and his wife were beaten and jailed by police in Rome, Georgia, for no reason. Marian Anderson had a celebrated row with the Daughters of the American Revolution. Blacks could not play professional baseball. The 1940 convention of the AFL turned down, with no more than a murmur of protest, A. Philip Randolph's proposal to create a committee to investigate discrimination. The simple fact is that prior to our entry into World War II race had not become a national issue.

In retrospect it is easy to identify what it was that precipitated the change. "A war," Dr. Robert C. Weaver once pointed out, "is a social revolution. For society it means dislocation of temporary equilibriums incident to fundamental problems. In such a period, the basic, unresolved problems come to the fore and force our attention to them."[1] That World War II was a total war, global in scope, with distinct racial overtones, necessarily brought racial issues to the surface. As Roy Wilkins observed: "Hitler jammed our white people into their logically untenable position. Forced to oppose him for the sake of the life of the nation, they were jockeyed into declaring against his racial theories—publicly."[2]

Yet with emergency war preparations under way, Vultee Aircraft announced on August 2, 1940, that "only members of the Caucasian race will be employed in our plant." Not one black was to be found among its 6,500 employees. On May 20, 1941, Boeing Aircraft in Seattle had precisely three blacks on the payroll. In 1940 none of Lockheed's 42,000 employees were blacks, and about this time the president of North American Aviation said, "No matter what their qualifications, they will only be used as janitors." Despite the existence of a national emergency, it took tremendous pressures to open these and other defense plants to racial minorities. Blacks had to march on Washington (June 25, 1941) to secure the first executive order (No. 8802) against discrimination in employment, and as late as October 28, 1942, the New York newspaper *PM* could quote a top official of the Boilermakers Union as saying, "Do you know when a white man sweats, salt comes on his skin to take the smell away but when a nigger sweats, he's got no salt."

But wartime needs were not to be denied. *PM*'s editor, Ralph Ingersoll, put the issue succinctly on May 3, 1942: "This country is not strong enough to go on persecuting—discriminating against—10 per cent of its population and win the war, too." By April, 1944, nearly 5,300,000 blacks were employed in civilian jobs, up a million from the 1940 census; more than 500,000 had joined trade unions in the same period, and the number in skilled jobs had doubled. Blacks were quick to push for further change. Membership in the National Association for the Advancement of Colored People jumped from 100,000 in 1941 to 500,000 in 1944. Roy Wilkins reported from South Carolina that blacks were organizing all over the state to secure their rights: "They are not frightened. They are being joined, sometimes openly and sometimes quietly, by whites who believe in justice." Significant Supreme Court decisions accelerated pressures for change: in 1944 the Court struck down the all-white primaries; in 1938 it had sounded the death knell of segregation in higher education. Concurrently defense manpower needs brought about a broader and more typical distribution of the black population. In the war years 250,000 blacks moved to the West Coast states, an estimated 150,000 left the South annually to take up residence in such Northern cities as Chicago, Philadelphia, Detroit and New York (the migration continued at this level throughout the decade), and some 300,000 moved from rural to urban areas in the South. For the first time, racial issues began to assume truly national significance.[3]

From the early 1930s on I had been interested in the racial and ethnic minorities that figured prominently in the history of migratory farm labor in California. But it was not until I was named to head the Division of Immigration and Housing that I became interested in "the racial problem" as such. The experience gave me a chance to observe how racial minorities lived in rural and urban areas and to become familiar with some of their problems. It also convinced me that California provided an ideal setting in which to study majority–minority relations. In a relatively brief span of time the state's population had grown so rapidly, communities had formed so swiftly, that the "history" of social relations was visible, so to speak, to the naked eye; time had not blurred the record. One could, for example, easily trace the pattern of discrimination against any particular minority. Also, with the arrival of blacks in large numbers after 1940, California had become the one state in which virtually all racial minorities, including Indians, were represented.

The more I thought about the fascinating California racial mosaic, the more dissatisfied I became with the prevailing theories of prejudice and discrimination. Sociologists then devoted elaborate studies to measuring the "social distance" between the majority and various minorities in different relationships but had little to say about what had created the distance in the first place. The conventional wisdom, reflected in many court decisions, held that racial prejudice was deeply embedded in the mores and that hence little could be done about it. The mores would simply have to change, and that would take time. But the California experience convinced me legislation had been a key factor in shaping the mores. There was little doubt, for example, that discriminatory legislation had stimulated bias against the Chinese and the Japanese. So over a period of time I came to believe that since the law had been a factor in shaping the mores, it could be used to change them, as by the enactment of civil-rights legislation.[4] But it was not so much this growing theoretical interest as a series of wartime emergencies that got me involved in "the racial revolution." The first of these had to do with the removal, as a wartime measure, of 126,000 Japanese, citizens and aliens alike, men, women and children, from the three West Coast states and their internment in "relocation" centers.

2. "RELOCATING" THE JAPANESE

Few episodes in the racial revolution of the war years were more significant than the removal of the resident Japanese, two-thirds of whom were citizens, from the West Coast states. A tragic mistake, shameful and unnecessary, the program had the paradoxical effect of forcing a reexamination of the traditional bias against Orientals, which was more pronounced in California than elsewhere. From the outset, I was drawn into the controversy that raged around the issue; in fact, I became an active participant. It was not a matter of choice: I was co-opted.

My book *Prejudice* was the first to appear on the ouster of the Japanese; it was published in 1944, before the internment program had terminated or the war had ended. Since then the number of studies has steadily increased; indeed, there seems to be more interest in the subject now than there was at the time. But despite the advantage of hindsight and a wealth of new documentation, confusions and misconceptions persist primarily because so much of the action took place off stage.

By midsummer, 1941, alien resident Japanese (the Issei) were being squeezed by various federal regulations aimed at aliens in general. A kind of economic paralysis had begun to spread throughout the Little Tokyo communities. The Japanese were not integrated in the economy to the same extent as in Hawaii; they occupied special niches, such as fishing, truck farming, the floral industry. As a result of four decades of intermittent harassment, the older generation had adopted a defensive attitude. The Little Tokyo communities were well organized to look after their own but maintained a low profile. The Nisei, or American-born, were eager to win general acceptance but lacked political sophistication and experience; most of them were quite young. Even so, Pearl Harbor might not have activated the historical fault separating resident Japanese from the rest of the population had it not been for certain special factors.

Given the excitement that prevailed immediately after December, 1941, there were surprisingly few incidents. Mass evacuation did not stem from widespread popular demand or antagonism; by and large the Japanese were well regarded. Nor was "military necessity" a prime consideration. In the fall of 1941 the State Department had sent a representative, Curtis B. Munson, to survey the situation in the three West Coast states, and he had reported (November 7, 1941) that the resident Japanese did not present a security problem. In Hawaii, martial law was proclaimed immediately and, in fact, was not terminated until October 24, 1944. But the Japanese simply could not be removed from the islands; they were too numerous (150,000) and too essential to the economy and the war effort.[5]

On the mainland, industrial and business leaders were anxious to avoid the imposition of martial law, which would have involved endless red tape, costly delays, and vexatious restrictions. Prompt removal of the Japanese, it was argued, would obviate the necessity of imposing martial law. Also, various interest groups saw a chance to move in on Japanese-controlled segments of the economy if the resident Japanese were removed. More important were the political pressures exerted by the three West Coast congressional delegations under the leadership of Senator Hiram Johnson, long active in the "anti-Oriental" movement in California and a power in the Senate. On February 13, 1942, Johnson presented a letter to the President in the name of the three delegations, demanding "immediate evacuation of all persons of Japanese lineage" without the imposition of martial law. I am convinced that Roosevelt, overwhelmed with critical military problems at the time, felt he had to yield to the demand, otherwise the implacable Johnson would keep knocking at the door of the Oval Office and "the Japanese problem" might blow up into a politically divisive and diversionary issue. This does not, of course, excuse what was done but suggests why the President acted as he did.

Most of the recent studies fail to emphasize the speed with which the program unfolded; there was simply not time to marshal the potential opposition. The Department of Justice began arresting "dangerous enemy aliens" on December 7 and 8, and subsequent orders required the removal of "enemy aliens" from particular areas, near airports, harbors, and power lines. On February 14, 1942, General J. L. De Witt recommended mass evacuation, and on February 19 President Roosevelt signed Executive Order 9066, which authorized the War Department to set up military areas and exclude any and all persons from them if necessary. This authority was passed along to De Witt, who on March 2 issued orders defining certain military zones. The next step was to prohibit all persons of Japanese descent from leaving these areas. Then by a series of orders, the first of which was issued on March 24, the Japanese, citizens and aliens alike, began to be moved, first into assembly centers and later to "relocation" centers—i.e., concentration camps, American style. The exclusionary orders were issued without formal hearings or any semblance of due process; racial lineage was the sole criterion.

Immediately after Pearl Harbor, Nisei friends and spokesmen for Japanese organizations converged on my office at the State Building, seeking advice and assistance. An endless series of meetings ensued, some public, some private, with many midnight sessions, all as part of an effort to avert the trauma and tragedy of mass evacuation. The immediate objective was to gain time so that Washington might be induced to listen to those who really knew something about the resident Japanese. Naval Intelligence officers who had studied the West Coast Japanese communities for years did not feel mass evacuation was necessary, nor were they alone in this view. I did not know then but later learned that J. Edgar Hoover strenuously opposed mass evacuation. As part of this effort to avert a hasty and irrevocable decision, I hit upon the idea of inducing the House Committee on Inter-State Migration (the Tolan Committee) to hold hearings in California. The committee could justify the inquiry because of its concern with migration, and a public airing of the facts and issues might quiet the growing demand for removal of the Japanese. Dr. Robert Lamb, the director, and several members of his staff had served with the La Follette Committee and were good friends of mine. After much wire-pulling, intrigue, and importuning, the Tolan Committee finally decided to hold hearings, but it arrived in California too late to influence the decision. When Bob Lamb called at my office in Los Angeles on February 19, I had just received word that summary action could be expected momentarily. The next day as I was conferring with Lamb and his staff, we were told President Roosevelt had signed Executive Order 9066, which, of course, had the effect of making the subsequent hearings anticlimactic.

The authors of four books on the internment program credit me with having induced the Tolan Committee to hold hearings in California, but I am not sure I want the credit. As events worked out, the hearings did not have the effect we had hoped. In the confusion and excitement of those hectic weeks it proved difficult to get opposition spokesmen to appear. The shock of Pearl Harbor was a fresh memory, the headlines were alarming, the demand for mass evacuation kept growing. As early as December 9, Westbrook Pegler published the first of a series of columns demanding immediate removal of the resident Japanese which set the tone for much of the subsequent news coverage and commentary. On February 12 and 14, two extremely influential columns by Walter Lippmann, based on talks with Earl Warren, then attorney general of California, tipped the scales of national opinion in favor of mass evacuation. Early in February, also, the House Committee on Un-American Activities—the Dies Committee—issued a lengthy report which repeated every false charge ever leveled against the resident Japanese. And on February 24 the papers carried sensational reports of the shelling, by a Japanese submarine, of the Barnsdale oil fields north of Santa Barbara. From the start, the Tolan hearings were dominated by politically potent elements demanding mass evacuation. These elements were vociferous, well organized, and numerous, and their presentations were strongly backed by the press. Most state and local officials, including Governor Olson and Mayor Fletcher Bowron of Los Angeles, testified in favor of removing the Japanese. Ill-informed and biased, Earl Warren's testimony received wide media coverage and was quite influential. So, too, was the testimony of Tom Clark, chief spokesman for the Roosevelt Administration on the issue. Years later both Warren, then Chief Justice, and Clark, then an Associate Justice of the Supreme Court, expressed regret for the position they had taken at the hearings.

The next round in the controversy took place behind the scenes and centered on the question of how and by what means mass evacuation should be carried out. Those who opposed the program felt that the Army should be eased out of the picture as quickly as possible. They also agreed that the idea of a special War Relocation Authority offered the best practical alternative. Milton Eisenhower, the first director of the authority, was known to be a humane and decent man, and so, too, was Dillon Myer, who soon succeeded him. Our main concern then was to safeguard the future of the evacuees by insisting on the earliest termination of the internment program, before the end of the war if possible. This general strategy succeeded. The Army's role was soon brought to a close, and the WRA did as good a job, in an impossible situation, as could be expected. But what really saved the program from irredeemable disaster was the good sense, orderliness, and intelligence of the evacuees.

For nearly three years I was actively involved, in one way or another, with the evacuation program. I visited the various assembly centers, including the one at the Santa Anita Race Track, which held eighteen thousand evacuees. There I had the disturbing experience of chatting with Nisei friends housed in stable stalls. Later I visited most of the relocation centers, where WRA officials made it possible for me to move about freely, interviewing anyone I wished. On these visits I met evacuees who became and have remained close friends, including Mine Okubo, the distinguished artist, whose sketches and drawings appear in *Citizen 13660* (published in 1966). When I first met Mine, she was sloshing about in the mud and snow at the Topaz Center. On a visit to the Granada Center in Colorado, I was asked to speak to the students. Looking out over that sea of young faces, so quiet and attentive, I was suddenly shaken and nonplused. What could I say except to express the hope that a better day was coming and that Washington would eventually regret the action that had been taken. From its inception I tried to keep a spotlight focused on the internment program in the form, first, of a long report (1942) for the Institute of Pacific Relations, a later report (1944) for Public Affairs Pamphlets, and articles which appeared in *Harper's, PM, The New Republic, Common Ground,* and *The Nation.* And once again a book of mine was well timed. Wallace Stegner wrote me that *Prejudice,* published in October, 1944, had appeared "at a critical time, if there is any such thing in California as a moment more critical than any other"—a shrewd and perceptive qualification.

The sharpest phase of the conflict came as the war drew to a close. If the evacuees were permitted to return to their former homes before the end of the war, there was reason to believe that appeals to good citizenship, wartime sentiments, and the like would help persuade local communities to accept them with a minimum of friction. But the opposition was formidable. Earl Warren, by then governor, took the position that not a single "Jap" should be permitted to return until the war had ended. The American Legion, demagogic politicians, the inquisitorial committees (state and federal), and a large section of the press joined in a campaign against lifting the ban. The ensuing debate, which was bitter and clamorous, brought the issue to national attention and also provided an occasion to discuss neglected aspects of "the racial question."

I debated the issue on three *Town Meeting of the Air* programs, from Santa Barbara (July 15, 1943), New York (February 17, 1944), and Sacramento (August 3, 1944), and spoke about it at numberless meetings in California. Also, I campaigned in Colorado on behalf of a local fair-play committee that was able to defeat a statewide initiative aimed at excluding the Japanese. In the course of this protracted controversy "the Japanese problem" received the thorough airing it should have had years before. Those of us who served as spokesmen for the evacuees—they were not in a position to speak in their own behalf—lost the first round (on whether they should be evacuated) but won the second, which permitted them to return before the end of the war. The ban was partially lifted on December 17, 1944, just before the Supreme Court handed down its decisions in the Korematsu and Endo cases, and the next day the WRA announced that all centers would be closed within six months to a year. I was able to report in *PM* on August 27, 1945, that, while some fifty-six "incidents" had occurred in California, by and large the return of the evacuees had taken place with less friction than had been expected. The superb record of the all-Japanese 442nd Regimental Combat Unit in the Italian campaign was one of a number of factors that helped create a public opinion favorable to acceptance. Of major importance was the firm leadership of State Attorney General Robert Kenny, who was able to keep California law-enforcement officials in line with an assist from Governor Earl Warren, who, to his credit, backed Kenny's stand once the ban was lifted.

The internment program had a profound impact on race relations. For one thing, it lifted "the racial problem" out of the traditional black–white (slavery) and Indian–white (reservations) context and placed it in a larger setting. Since the war had definite racial overtones, Axis propagandists were quick to seize on the removal of the Japanese to demonstrate that this country was biased against Oriental races. There was enough truth to the charge to make it acutely embarrassing in a wartime setting and to prompt enactment of measures designed to disprove it. In California, "anti-Oriental" agitation began to be played down and a number of legal restrictions against the Japanese were removed or declared unconstitutional, including the prohibitions against land ownership and practicing certain professions. As part of the same strategy, Congress was induced to repeal the odious Chinese Exclusion Act which dated from the 1880s. So paradoxically the internment program, for all its harshness and unfairness, helped the Japanese to escape from a ghettolike status and ushered in a new phase of race relations on the West Coast and in Hawaii. Today the Japanese have been characterized as "the most successful racial minority in U.S. history."[6] At the moment, Hawaii has two U.S. senators who are Japanese Americans; California has one. Japanese Americans serve as legislators, city councilmen, mayors and judges; on May 5, 1976, Robert Takasugi, who spent three years as a youngster in one of the relocation centers, was confirmed as a U.S. District Court judge in Los Angeles.

But if the stigma of evacuation has been removed, the experience has not been forgotten. The most serious violation of civil liberties of the last half century, the mass removal of the West Coast Japanese has proven to be a source of continuing national embarrassment. Interest in the subject has grown, not abated; fresh studies appear nearly every year. It now occupies a major chapter in the history of civil liberties and race relations, as well it should, if only because of the dangerous precedent it established. On May 21, 1959, U.S. Attorney General William P. Rogers announced completion of the process by which citizenship was restored to 4,978 evacuees who had renounced it because of the treatment accorded them at the Tule Lake Center; the action was taken, he said, by way of "making up for a mistake our nation made." Still later, on February 19, 1976, President Ford, in the presence of Senators Daniel K. Inouye and Hiram L. Fong and Representatives Patsy T. Mink and Spark M. Matsunaga, formally rescinded Executive Order 9066. "This kind of error," he said, "shall never be repeated," for the order had marked "a sad day in American history."

On January 6, 1943, Earl Warren announced, with considerable fanfare, that his first official act as governor would be my removal from the office I had held in the Olson administration. He was obviously eager to make the announcement, and I must confess that I felt flattered by it. We had been on opposite sides of many highly controversial issues: the Mooney-Billings, Ship Murder, and Harry Bridges cases; the Japanese-American issue; the right of farm workers to form unions; and the right of indigent Dust Bowl refugees to enter California and register as voters. While I came to respect Warren greatly after he was named Chief Justice, I did not admire his record as attorney general of California and saw little in his performance as governor to cheer. There are, incidentally, curious omissions in Warren's memoirs. He does not, for example, mention his close identification with the Native Sons of the Golden West, which was to anti-Oriental agitation in California what the KKK was to Southern racism, albeit in a somewhat more decorous manner. Nor does he discuss the La Follette Committee hearings or his efforts to frustrate its inquiries or the role he played in blocking Olson's appointment of Max Radin to the California Supreme Court.[7] Actually Warren's record on the Supreme Court is all the more impressive when contrasted with his California performance on racial and civil-liberties issues. But for the record: Warren did not remove me from office. All of Olson's term appointments automatically expired on December 31, 1942. With four hectic years in state office behind me, I was by then deeply immersed in the racial revolution that, starting with World War II, had begun to accelerate by 1943. The Japanese-American controversy formed an early and significant chapter of this revolution, but there was more, much more, to come. (As an ironic footnote to my feuding with Warren in California before he became Chief Justice, I might note that at its annual meeting on December 10, 1978, in San Francisco, the ACLU Foundation of Northern California presented me with its Earl Warren Civil Liberties Award.)

While this new racial phase in my "education" was unfolding, I wrote another book about migratory farm labor. *Ill Fares the Land* (1942) deals with national aspects of the farm labor problem and examines the large-farm/small-farm controversy about which I later prepared a special report for Public Affairs Pamphlets: *Small Farm and Big Farm* (New York, 1945). In writing *Ill Fares the Land,* published in Britain with an introduction by the Earl of Portsmouth, I visited most of the areas with well-established patterns of migratory farm labor: the Northwest (apples, hops); Arizona and Texas (cotton and vegetables); Colorado and the Plains States (sugar beets); "onion migrants" in Ohio and Indiana; "berry migrants" in Arkansas and the Ozarks; the East Coast migration from Florida to New Jersey, upstate New York, and Connecticut; and the "big swing" of Mexican migrants from Texas to Michigan. The experience greatly stimulated my interest in the Spanish-speaking. It enabled me to unearth invaluable sources of information and to establish contact with many Mexican Americans, particularly in the border states. Also, I was privileged to visit New Mexico in the spring of 1942 for a conference at the University of New Mexico and was taken on an unforgettable tour of remote Hispanic mountain villages and settlements in northern New Mexico. My hosts were officials of the Bureau of Indian Affairs and the Soil Conservation Service who proved to be a continuing source of prime information about the Spanish-speaking and their problems. The experience added an entirely new dimension to my growing interest in Mexican Americans, border relations, and the Spanish-speaking influence in the Southwest.

3. THE SLEEPY LAGOON CASE

One of our largest minorities, the Spanish-speaking were slow to make their debut on the national scene. Little was known about them, although they had long been a familiar aspect of the social landscape in the Southwest (as Puerto Ricans had been on the East Coast and Cubans in Florida). As late as 1940 they were to Dr. George Sanchez still "an orphan group, the least known, the least vocal minority in the nation."[8] Still later, in 1966, a Mexican-American spokesman was quoted in *Newsweek* as saying, "We're the best-

kept secret in America." With the eight-month-long grape pickers'
strike that began in Delano, California, on September 8, 1965,
under the brilliant leadership of Cesar Chavez, the Spanish-speaking ceased to be "an orphan group" or a "well-kept secret." But the
first signs of a new political and cultural maturity on the part of
this large minority—a submerged subclass in the Southwest since
the Mexican War—really date from the early years of World War
II. For me the Sleepy Lagoon case marks the inception of the
Chicano movement.

On the afternoon of August 1, 1942, Henry Leyvas, a young
Mexican American, had taken his girl for a swim in a gravel-pit
pool in East Los Angeles. In the early evening hours the two of
them had been roughed up by members of a neighborhood youth
gang which had been feuding with the one to which Leyvas belonged. Later that night he returned with some friends, only to
find the pool deserted. But a party was in progress at the nearby
Delgadillo residence, and they proceeded to crash it. The next day
the body of young José Díaz was found in the immediate vicinity.
An autopsy disclosed he had been engaged in a fight of some kind
and had probably been drunk at the time. He had left the party
with two friends, who were never called as witnesses.

With wartime tensions mounting, the press promptly pounced
on the case, dubbed the gravel pit "Sleepy Lagoon" after a current
motion picture of that name, and began to demand tough police
action against Mexican-American youth gangs. Twenty-four Mexican Americans—Leyvas, nineteen, was the oldest—were arrested,
indicted, and charged with the murder of José Díaz. After a thir-
teen-week trial before an all-white Anglo jury, the defendants were
convicted (January 13, 1943) in what was, up to that time, the
largest mass-murder trial ever conducted in Los Angeles. The trial
took place in an atmosphere of intense prejudice, before a biased
judge, and with a stubborn and courageous but inadequate defense.

When the indictments were returned, a loosely organized defense committee had been set up by individuals some of whom had
close ties with the Communist Party. Red-baited by the press and
State Senator Jack Tenney's Committee on Un-American Activities, it had been severely handicapped. After the guilty verdicts
were returned, several members of the defense committee asked
me to serve as chairman (I had not previously been identified with
the case) to help raise funds needed to prepare an appeal, which
promised to be costly; the transcript, for example, totaled more
than six thousand pages. I agreed on three conditions: that the
committee would be reorganized and broadened; that new counsel

and office personnel would be selected; and that, once the committee was disbanded, a formal audit of the books, showing all receipts and disbursements, would be deposited at the library of the University of California at Los Angeles, where it could be inspected by anyone with a legitimate interest in the facts. The committee was broadened to include some well-known civic, business, and labor leaders and such Hollywood figures as Orson Welles, Joseph Cotten, and Anthony Quinn. New counsel were selected to prepare and argue the appeal, and the brilliant Alice Greenfield took over as secretary. In all, the committee raised approximately $50,000— a sizable sum for that time. On October 4, 1944, the District Court of Appeals, in a unanimous decision (*People v. Zamora et al.*) reversed the convictions and sharply reprimanded the trial judge. Later all charges were dismissed.[9]

In the wake of the Sleepy Lagoon arrests, the Los Angeles police rounded up over six hundred young Mexican Americans on the evenings of August 10 and 11, 1942, often treating them with less than tender loving care. The reporting of these arrests was anything but restrained. As background the press made sensational use of a report which Captain E. Duran Ayres of the sheriff's office had submitted to the grand jury in which he theorized that Mexican Americans had inherited a lust for violence, knives, and bloodletting from Aztec ancestors. It should be emphasized that Mexico was then our ally, having declared war against Germany, Italy and Japan on May 22, 1942. The Axis radio quoted passages from the Ayres report and devoted much attention to the dragnet raids, the mass arrests and the trial of the Sleepy Lagoon defendants.

One of the members of the grand jury that year was Harry Braverman, a well-known businessman prominent in the Jewish community and a friend of mine. Outraged by the Ayres report and the general behavior of the police, he persuaded his fellow grand jurors to air the issues on October 18 at a public hearing, at which I testified.[10] I pointed out that unless proper corrective measures were taken, and promptly, the community could anticipate further unrest and possible violence. Much the same point was made by other witnesses, including spokesmen for the Office of the Coordinator of Inter-American Affairs (Nelson Rockefeller), who stressed the harmful effect that sensational press coverage of incidents involving young Mexican Americans was having on Latin-American relations. Always anxious to oblige, the press began to write about "zoot-suit hoodlums" and "pachuco gangs" instead of "Mexicans" and "Mexican gangs." It was easy to foresee there would be more trouble soon, and it came the following summer with the zoot-suit riots.

When charges against the Sleepy Lagoon defendants were finally dismissed, after they had served nearly two years in San Quentin Prison because they could not raise bail, thousands of wildly jubilant Mexican Americans gathered at the Hall of Justice to greet the defendants as they emerged from detention quarters. As the Los Angeles *Times* reported: "Hysterical screams and shrieks, laughter and cries of jubilation welled from the crowd. The atmosphere was electric with excitement as the liberated men were besieged by well-wishers who enthusiastically pumped their hands and slapped their backs. Tears flowed unashamedly." For the first time in the memory of the living, Mexicans had won a major round in the courts.

In the past, Mexican Americans had been isolated—set apart—from the rest of the community; in the Sleepy Lagoon case their allies were Anglo doctors, lawyers, film actors, writers, and business executives as well as blacks and Hispanics. For the resident Spanish-speaking it represented an historic breakthrough, the first significant forward step in what has proved to be a steady advance. The work of the defense committee won the praise of ex-President Cárdenas and high Mexican officials. The magazine *Hoy*, in Mexico City, devoted a three-page spread to its work (September 10, 1944), and wartime information agencies in Washington made excellent use of the court victory in their campaign to counter Axis propaganda. But even more pleasing were the hundreds of letters received from Mexican-American and other GI's, often enclosing small contributions and thanking the committee for its efforts.

The work of the Sleepy Lagoon Defense Committee had an important sequel. I had known Fred Ross since the 1930s, when he was with the labor camp program of the Farm Security Administration in California. After the war he joined the staff of the Industrial Areas Foundation of Saul Alinsky (another old friend) in Chicago and was soon assigned to Los Angeles to see what might be done to stimulate self-organization among Mexican Americans. Largely because of his interest in the Sleepy Lagoon case, Harry Braverman, at my request, raised a fund of some $9,000, which enabled Alinsky to lend Ross to the Community Service Organization. A brilliant organizer, Fred directed the CSO's voter registration drive among thousands of East Los Angeles Mexican Americans that resulted in the election of Edward Roybal to the City Council in 1949—the first time a Mexican American was elected to that body (since then he has continuously represented the district in Congress).

In 1952 Ross chanced to meet Cesar Chavez in a San Jose barrio known as Sal si Puedes—"Get Out If You Can"—and persuaded him to sign on with the CSO. From 1952 to 1962 Chavez worked with the Community Service Organization and then organized the National Farm Workers Union at a meeting in Fresno on September 19, 1962, out of which came today's Farm Workers Union which has made labor history in California.

4. THE 1943 RIOTS

Brothers Under the Skin, my book about racial minorities, was published on April 23, 1943. Almost before the first reviews appeared, the mounting racial tensions of the war years suddenly exploded right under my nose—in Los Angeles. The week-long "zoot-suit" riots which began on June 3 were the first of a series of similar riots that came in rapid succession in other defense centers across the country: San Diego June 9, Philadelphia June 10, Chicago June 15, Evansville June 27, followed by major riots in Detroit, Beaumont, and Harlem. The Sojourner Truth Housing Project riot in Detroit on February 28, 1942, had been a portent of things to come, but it was the rash of riots in 1943 that marked the climax. The Detroit riots of June 20–21 were perhaps the worst: twenty-five blacks and nine whites were killed and property damage was extensive. The Harlem riots of August 1–2 resulted in five deaths, over 500 arrests, 565 injuries, and property damage estimated at $5 million. Coming at the midpoint of the war, at the end of the North African campaign, the 1943 riots had tremendous impact. Overnight the need for affirmative action was acknowledged, and, for the first time, a truly national opinion against racial discrimination began to form.

By midsummer 1943, the major defense centers were booming and manpower needs had become critical. Job prospects for racial minorities brightened; sizable numbers began to move into semiskilled and skilled positions from which they had been previously excluded. These gains, as Dr. Robert C. Weaver pointed out, "represented more industrial and occupational diversification for Negroes than had occurred in the seventy-five preceding years."[11] But every gain for blacks and other minorities sharpened the hostility of the traditionally biased groups and contributed to mounting tensions.

Southern California was, of course, a major zone of military activity and booming defense production. Thousands of soldiers and sailors moved in and out of Los Angeles. Manpower needs were critical, in part because of the removal of the Japanese Americans. Once again Mexicans began to cross the border in large numbers, but, as always, they were relegated to the least skilled, lowest-paying jobs, for which they competed with the native-born Spanish-speaking. At the same time a disproportionate number of Mexican Americans were being drafted because they lacked jobs which carried draft-deferral status. For all groups, housing was in short supply, rationing a nuisance, and transportation a problem; in brief, wartime tensions had reached the boiling point. In such a situation, scapegoats were in order, and, inevitably and predictably, Mexican-American youngsters were prime targets. In an article in *The New Republic* of January 18, 1943, I described the setting and warned, as I had in my grand-jury testimony of the previous October, that future violence was unavoidable if corrective measures were not taken.

The Los Angeles zoot-suit riots began with some fighting between sailors on shore leave and young Mexican Americans in a largely Spanish-speaking neighborhood close to the downtown sections. The next night sailors organized fleets of taxicabs and roamed the streets looking for teenage Mexicans wearing zoot-suits "with reat pleat and stuff cuff." Egged on by sensational news stories and encouraged by police indifference, the mobs grew larger; on successive nights zoot-suiters were dragged out of downtown motion picture theaters, roughed up, beaten, and chased through the streets, their fancy suits, which seemed to have an infuriating effect, ripped and torn from their bodies. The Sleepy Lagoon case of the previous year and the excitement it had caused had, of course, helped set the stage for the riots, which lasted for a week.[12]

On the second night of the rioting there was an emergency meeting of several hundred citizens, which I chaired, to see what might be done to "cool" the situation. The imperatives of the hour were obvious: to check if possible the unbelievably wild rumors then sweeping through the community, to correct the false, hysterical, and provocative reports that kept appearing in the press, and, hopefully, to call attention to a few of the underlying sources of tension. Out of this meeting came the Council for Civic Unity, which, for some years, played an active role in fostering better race relations. At the close of the meeting, I phoned State Attorney General Robert Kenny in Sacramento and urged him to induce Governor Earl Warren to name an official committee of inquiry. The Governor agreed and accepted four of five names I had submitted to Kenny. The fifth was his own selection: Leo Carrillo, the actor, one of those "early Californians" who don sombreros and serapes for the annual Fifth of May celebration and then forget about their Mexican-American heritage for the rest of the year. Happily, Carrillo was a minority of one on the committee.

The next morning I met Kenny, who had flown in from Sacramento, for breakfast at the unholy hour of six in the cavernous empty dining room of the elegant California Club. In this slightly absurd setting, we went over plans for the proposed hearing and discussed a draft report I had prepared for him to submit to the Governor's committee later in the morning. With some slight modifications it was adopted and released the next day. Warren, of course, did not know that the idea for the committee was mine or that I had prepared the draft report. But it really didn't matter. The committee's prompt action in issuing the report had the desired effect: a measure of calm was restored, the press took a more temperate line, and some of the recommendations were heeded by local authorities. Later I prepared, at Kenny's request, a manual for police officers to follow in handling racial disturbances; it was issued by the State Attorney General's office in a somewhat watered-down version, "Interim Report of Peace Officers Committee on Civil Disturbances," Sacramento, December 15, 1943.

No book of mine coincided more precisely with maximum national interest in the subject than *Brothers Under the Skin,* which promptly became and for months remained on the best-seller lists. The timing was not based on calculation, nor was it purely accidental. The book was well timed because it grew out of the action it described; it was a part of the "racial revolution" it reported. Reflecting a phase of my postgraduate "education" in social realities, it could have been written only by an active participant in the racial ferment of the war years. Only those who were part of that ferment can properly appreciate the excitement and high hopes it generated. No public figure of the period understood what was happening better than Wendell Willkie. In a series of syndicated articles in 1944, on the eve of the national political conventions, he identified race as one of the critical issues of the war and postwar periods. "When we talk of freedom of opportunity for all nations," he wrote, "the mocking paradoxes in our own society become so clear that they can no longer be ignored. . . . Our world is breaking to pieces. And with the break-up arises the opportunity to fashion a newer and a better life." Unfortunately not everyone was listening.

But the opportunity did exist, and significant gains were registered. The fact is—and it deserves emphasis—that the civil-rights movement of a later period is to be understood only in terms of what happened from 1941 to 1945. In those years racial issues began to be seen in a new light. For half a century, American social scientists had discussed "prejudice" as theologians might discuss original sin. They "deplored" but had little to propose. From 1900 to 1940, as E. Franklin Frazier pointed out, social-science theory simply rationalized, in different ways, the existing racial status quo. It was not until Franz Boas and some of his colleagues began to dissect Nazi racial theories in the late 1930s that the accumulated mythology began to be challenged. Books such as *Brothers Under the Skin* (1943) and Gunnar Myrdal's *An American Dilemma* (1944) should be compared with pre-1940 writings on racial minorities and racial discrimination. The comparison will show a radical change in outlook and perception. Both books stressed that racial discrimination was a national problem with international ramifications; both emphasized that overt forms of discrimination could be minimized if not entirely eliminated by legislation. Both insisted that the war had created an opportunity to carry programs of this type into effect. In his preface, Myrdal wrote: "not since Reconstruction has there been more reason to anticipate fundamental changes in American race relations, changes that will involve a development toward American ideals." In *Brothers Under the Skin* I emphasized that "the racial problem" had many facets, not merely black–white relationships, and urged adoption of civil-rights legislation of the kind enacted twenty years later.

If it did nothing else, the wartime ferment and discussion ended the paralysis of will that had prevailed since Reconstruction. Some five hundred civic unity councils came into being shortly after the June, 1943, riots, and a wide variety of action programs were adopted. The California Federation for Civic Unity, the Southern Regional Council, and the American Council on Race Relations were formed in 1944. Much of this and similar activity can be discounted as "crisis patriotism" destined to end with the war. Nevertheless, it was significant, if only because it set the stage for important subsequent developments. Out of it emerged a new national public opinion against racial discrimination. The volume of discussion and activity was without precedent. A flood of books, articles, wartime pamphlets, and radio programs kept a spotlight on the issue. The number of forums, programs, conferences, seminars, and institutes held in these years on "the racial problem" would invite disbelief today. I crisscrossed the country not once but twice a year during the war, speaking on racial issues to the most diverse groups and organizations from university audiences to dinner meetings of Knife-and-Fork Clubs. Sartre is right: catastrophe initiates social change; it was the war that set the racial revolution in motion.[13]

CHAPTER VI

THE COMING OF THE COLD WAR

In retrospect I can see that January 25, 1945, marked the beginning of the end of my California experience. That was the day *The Nation* named me its West Coast contributing editor. In themselves my duties were not burdensome. For a minuscule stipend, I was supposed to contribute one or more unsigned editorials each week and articles at the rate of one a month or thereabouts. But the moment my name appeared on the masthead, I became a target-of-opportunity for every left-of-center group and politician in the vast area west of the Rockies. And a great deal was happening just then. What made the difference in my life was the convergence of a steadily escalating involvement with *The Nation*, well beyond anything I had originally intended, and an unexpected change in the political atmosphere. In the "futile interlude" from 1945 to 1949, the high hopes of the war years swiftly gave way to the fears and tensions of the Cold War, not immediately, not overnight, but all too soon. To Arthur Miller, 1949 was the last year of the postwar period, but as I see it there never was a postwar period: the Cold War began before World War II had ended.

1. FIRST SIGNS AND PORTENTS

In the summer after Roosevelt's death, President Truman and his new Secretary of State, James Byrnes, eagerly awaited word at

Potsdam of the first test of the atomic bomb at Alamogordo. Once word came that the test had been successful, Churchill noted that the President acted like a changed man; now he could tell those Russians where to get off. The coded signal was flashed immediately to use the bomb against selected targets in Japan. I still remember the shock and dismay with which I stared at the headlines announcing the bombing of Hiroshima on August 6, and of Nagasaki on August 9. Even though little was known then about how and when and why the decision had been taken, I felt intuitively that a terrible mistake had been made. But these initial misgivings were momentarily submerged in the noise and excitement which came with word that Japan had surrendered on August 14. Not until John Hersey's famous report appeared in *The New Yorker* the following year did people dare to think of Hiroshima; previously it had been, in Mary McCarthy's phrase, "a kind of hole in history."

The end-of-war euphoria, however, did not last long. Most wars are followed by a period of reaction, and World War II was no exception. But it took the Roosevelt liberals some time to realize that the bombings marked the inception of a new—a "cold"—war and that there was to be no "postwar" period. Nor were they quick to perceive how easily the rhetoric and ideology of "antifascism," which had won wide acceptance during the war, could be made to serve the uses of "anti-Communism" and "containment" by simply changing a few phrases and substituting new "enemies" for old.

No one knows, of course, what might have happened if Hiroshima and Nagasaki had not been bombed. But nowadays it is clearer than it was then that the bombings were not motivated by military necessity. With its naval and air power virtually destroyed, Japan was, in Eisenhower's phrase, "utterly defeated." Tokyo had sent peace overtures to Moscow, and Washington knew that the Russians would soon enter the war. Later the U.S. Strategic Bombing Survey reported that even if the bombs had not been dropped and Russia had stayed out of the war, Japan would probably have surrendered and in all likelihood before November 1. Actually the decision to use the bomb does not seem to have been carefully reviewed; it was simply assumed it would be used if the tests proved successful. And no acceptable rationale for dropping the second bomb has ever been offered. Contrary to what most Americans thought at the time, it is today generally conceded that bringing the Russians to terms was part of the decision to use the bomb. Truman, we now know, was convinced its use would make the Soviets more "manageable" in Europe and restrict their role in Asia; it would give us "a hammer on those boys." But it had almost exactly the opposite effect. The secrecy with which the bomb was developed and the oblique way in which Truman referred to the "new explosive" in his much-too-casual conversation with Stalin at Potsdam immediately confirmed Soviet misgivings based on their prewar fears. Combined with other actions, such as the abrupt cancellation of Lend-Lease four days after Germany surrendered—an action Stalin described as "unfortunate and even brutal"—the bombings were clearly a major factor in poisoning Soviet-American relations at a critical juncture of the war. Stalin and his colleagues got the "signal" Truman and Byrnes had flashed; for them the Cold War began at Potsdam.[1]

But relief that the fighting had finally ended was so great that even Truman's critics were inclined to give him the benefit of the doubt, at least initially. It was easy to sympathize with the position in which he found himself after Roosevelt's death. At a critical point in world history, terrifying responsibilities which he was ill-prepared to assume had descended on him overnight. A product of the Pendergast machine in Kansas City, he had had no experience in foreign affairs; indeed, he had not visited Europe since World War I. Of limited educational background, he brought a storybook conception of history and world politics to the Oval Office. As Vice President he had not been briefed on the major issues; for example, he had not been told of the atomic-research project. Shocked and alarmed by Roosevelt's death, most Americans sympathized with Truman, wished him well, and wanted him to succeed. Even later, when I became convinced he had set American policy on a tragically mistaken course, it never occurred to me to think of him as an "evil" person. He seemed to me to be just what in fact he was: a decent human being, personally honest (despite the Pendergast connection), well-meaning, and not without courage. But Truman was neither tactful nor sensitive. In 1958 the City Council of Hiroshima, in a politely worded resolution, urged him to reconsider a statement in which he had said that he felt no compunction about the decision to drop the bombs on Hiroshima and Nagasaki. In a bristling rejoinder, he in effect told the Council to mind its own business; he had no qualms whatever about the decision.

Despite the bombings, remarkably little "anti-Truman" sentiment surfaced in 1945; only in 1946 did dissatisfaction with his leadership become widespread.

Nor was much notice taken of the fact that the center of gravity had begun to shift to the right before the war had ended. Of this there were many signs. In January, 1945, Representative John E. Rankin, catching the liberals unprepared, had secured adoption of a resolution setting up the House Committee on Un-American

Activities as a permanent committee. More "no" votes were cast than on earlier tests; even the press seemed surprised that Rankin's coup had succeeded. But red-baiting had merely been suspended during the war; now it would be resumed and in a more dangerous form. In Hollywood, the Motion Picture Alliance for the Preservation of American Ideals, a right-wing organization that worked closely with the inquisitorial committees, was set up in 1944 for the declared purpose of purging the industry of "reds" and "radicals" but really to weaken the unions and guilds which had gained strength during the war. In the spring of 1945, the strike—actually a lockout—of the Conference of Studio Unions erupted, and it continued, in one form or another, for a decade. More than any single event of the time, this bitter internecine dispute convinced me the specious wartime unity had ended. Out of it came the purges and blacklists, which were aimed at undercutting the progressive unions and guilds, a process that culminated in the case of the Hollywood Ten. Nor was Hollywood an isolated case; similar tensions began to surface nationally as the war drew to a close. But despite these signs, the illusion of "unity" prevailed well into 1946.[2]

2. THE DOMESTIC COLD WAR

The years 1945–46 were busy ones for me. I was increasingly preoccupied with *The Nation* and its problems; I went on nationwide lecture trips twice a year (speaking mostly on racial minorities and their problems); and at the start of 1945 was hard at work on the first of two books about California. *Southern California Country: An Island on the Land,* published in the spring of 1946, was a labor of love. I had been obsessively interested in the region since I had gone there to live, and I had reported on many aspects of the California scene for national publications over a period of two decades. In addition, for six years (1933–39) I had contributed a regular two-page feature to the magazine *Westways* about anything and everything related to California—writers, folklore, climate, history, cults, politics—that interested me. Also, four years as an official of the state government had given me a chance to visit every part of California not just once but often. The fine reception *Southern California Country* received encouraged me to start work on *California: The Great Exception,* which came along later, in 1949. Incidentally, the fact that all my books represent efforts to relieve my ignorance on subjects of compulsive interest often prompted me to wonder if I had selected the subjects or whether it was the other way round. In one way or another the books came out of my

California experience and were very much a part of the times and the place. *Southern California Country,* for example, *had* to be written at that time. It could not have been written earlier, and there would have been little point in trying to write that kind of book about the region at a later date, for too much happened too soon. It had to be written then or never.

But while I was very busy with my writing and *Nation* affairs, I could not have avoided becoming directly involved in California's hectic "postwar" politics even if I had wanted to remain aloof. Four years in the state government had whetted my interest, and the *Nation* connection constantly drew me to the center of the action. In effect politics came knocking at my door.

During the war the possibilities of progressive political action had necessarily been circumscribed. But with the end of the war in sight and demobilization soon to follow, hopes soared for a just and lasting peace and a resumption of the interrupted New Deal. To strengthen the Roosevelt coalition for the tests ahead, Sidney Hillman and his colleagues had set up the National Citizens Political Action Committee, and in no state was the response quicker or more enthusiastic than in California. On January 25, 1945, Hillman addressed a large dinner meeting in Los Angeles, and the next day I presided at a luncheon for him at the Alexandria Hotel. The response at both meetings, measured in terms of attendance and funds raised and pledged, was quite extraordinary.

That spring Roosevelt's death dealt these hopes for a resurgence of progressive politics a cruel and jarring blow. Coming as it did at the high point of the war, when victory was in sight, it left a leadership void that was never filled. Acting in concert, Roosevelt and Willkie might have been able to win and implement the kind of peace that both desired. The loss of the two of them at so nearly the same time momentarily created a mood of profound uncertainty and apprehension. But the rush of events foreshortened any disposition to dwell on the magnitude of the loss. In fact, the immediate effect of FDR's death, it soon became apparent, was to invest the movement to win the peace with a new urgency and importance. Strenuous efforts were made to strengthen the Roosevelt coalition and build support for new initiatives such as the one Hillman had launched.

Despite some disquieting signs, the Roosevelt coalition seemed to be holding together during most of 1945 under the uncertain banner of Harry Truman. But progressives and liberals and their allies in the labor movement and on the left had become more dependent on Roosevelt's political magic than they realized. Also, they had acquired an exaggerated notion, during the years he was in the White House, of their own strength. Nor were they quick to sense that the Cold War had already been set in motion. And in later years I came to feel that Hillman's death on July 11, 1946, had dimmed the prospects for a resumption of New Deal politics. A brilliant organizer and tactician and a total pragmatist, he might have succeeded in keeping the movement he had initiated on a more realistic course.

For liberals, in any case, 1946 began as a year of bright promise and keen anticipations. This was the year—the election—everyone had been waiting for and thinking about. A decade had elapsed since there had been an election not dominated by war or the threat of war. No one could be sure to what extent political attitudes had been affected by the enormous social and economic changes the war had brought. With an eye to the "postwar" period, parties and politicians had been jockeying for position, but there had been no real tests; now the contours of the new political landscape would be revealed. Bemused by visions of a prosperous America in a world at peace and still charged with wartime enthusiasms, liberals and progressives were eager and confident, thoroughly convinced that majority sentiment supported their positions. Roosevelt was dead, but the name was still magic and they carried the Roosevelt banners. On April 19 Henry Wallace came out to address a huge gala dinner meeting at the Beverly Wilshire Hotel. I was one of several other speakers and vividly remember the excitement and enthusiasm the meeting reflected.

That year a strong slate of liberal Democratic nominees had been selected in California: Will Rogers, Jr., home from the war (he had given up his seat in the House to enlist) for senator; Robert W. Kenny, Jr., for governor; Edmund G. ("Pat") Brown for attorney general; and State Senator John Shelley of San Francisco for lieutenant governor. The four were well-known, popular, attractive nominees, with excellent liberal credentials; all were Roosevelt New Deal Democrats. Kenny, Rogers and Brown were personal friends in whose campaigns I played an active role, writing speeches for them, advising about campaign materials, and doing whatever I could to further their candidacies. Kenny was an intimate friend; we had hobnobbed for years, shared an intense interest in Southern California (my book on the region is dedicated to him), and had engaged in many joint political and intellectual ventures. But Kenny and Brown had good organizations and needed less help than Rogers, in whose campaign I was particularly active. Rogers was an excellent political performer and waged a most refreshing, stylish, and unconventional campaign. But much as I liked him personally, he gave me some bad moments; one never knew what he might do next, and his political judgments were often erratic. Of the four, however, he ran the best and the strongest campaign. Twirling a rope and ad-libbing at rodeos and county fairs, he was a dream candidate. But the slate had been chosen, and campaigned, on the false premise that we were about to enter the glorious "postwar" period, when in fact a sharp reaction had already set in and the Cold War had begun.

That fall, at my insistence, *The Nation* held a two-day conference (September 21 and 22) at the Ambassador Hotel in Los Angeles on "The Challenge of the Post War World to the Liberal Movement," for which I edited a forty-eight-page supplement on the prospects for liberal politics in the Western states. Oscar Chapman, Under-Secretary of the Interior, Will Rogers, Jr., Chet Huntley, Freda Kirchwey and other well-known liberals spoke, including Ronald Reagan, who then fancied himself a liberal; his conversion to "conservatism" came some years later. The sessions drew standing-room-only attendance and netted *The Nation* more than $25,000— a handsome sum in those days. But despite the enthusiasm, one could sense sharp underlying tensions between Truman and anti-Truman elements; sentiment had, in fact, been shifting steadily to the right since the first of the year. In November, the entire Democratic slate went down to defeat in California. As a portent of things to come, a newcomer, Richard Nixon, defeated the much-admired and respected Representative H. Jerry Voorhis (an alumnus of the EPIC movement), in the first of the red-baiting smear campaigns which he and his aide Murray Chotiner waged at intervals for nearly thirty years. Nationally, the Republicans scored a landslide victory, capturing control of the Senate (51 to 45) and House (246 to 188) and bringing the curtain down on the New Deal. Among the new senators were Jenner, McCarthy, Knowland, Malone, and Bricker. The class of '46 had arrived, the domestic Cold War had begun.

In retrospect it is easy to see what had happened. Voters were annoyed with controls, shortages, and labor difficulties, but, above all, they were surprised and disappointed by the turn events had taken after the death of Roosevelt (although the reaction had set in even earlier). Our enemies had been defeated, but had we really won the war? By 1946 the bombings in Japan had begun to arouse deep undercurrents of fear and apprehension. Few consequences of Truman's decision were more significant than the paradoxical way in which the bombings stimulated a sense of foreboding at a time when this country's preponderant military and industrial power, on a worldwide basis, was overwhelming and self-evident.

But there were other reasons. For Truman, 1946 was a succession of disasters; his weaknesses and inadequacies were on full display. He fumbled nearly every major issue that year. In a temper tantrum, he threatened to draft striking railroad workers and then vetoed an antistrike measure. But the vote which sustained the veto was so close it encouraged Senator Robert A. Taft to draft the Taft-Hartley Act, which was enacted over Truman's veto the following year. While professing loyalty to Roosevelt's policies, Truman conveyed the impression he neither fully understood nor approved them. He mishandled price controls; seemed not to know what, if anything, to do about mounting racial violence in the South; and puzzled even his supporters with his erratic stands and snap judgments. His mind, as Henry Wallace noted, seemed to move in different directions simultaneously. A major exodus of top- and middle-level officials got under way. Officials who had given the New Deal its vitality, as the New York *Post* observed, were "brushed out" of Washington. Both symbols of the New Deal, Harold L. Ickes resigned in February, Wallace in September. Cronyism permeated the White House in the persons of John W. Snyder, Jimmy Byrnes, Edwin Pauley, James K. Vardman, Jr., Harry Vaughan, and pudgy George Allen. Of Truman's early appointments to top posts, Howard K. Smith observed that the locus of government seemed to have shifted "from Washington to some place equidistant between Wall Street and West Point." On the few occasions when he made the right decision, it was usually for the wrong reason or by accident or by way of correcting an initial mistake. Angry, frustrated, and hungry for power, the Republicans seized the opportunity his inept leadership presented and began to attack and red-bait the Democrats with gusto. By year's end, Truman's rating in the polls had dropped to thirty-two percent; up to that point his performance had been, as Max Lerner noted, "one of the sorriest in the history of the Presidency."

But it was not alone this abject record on domestic issues that spread disaffection among New Deal liberals and progressives: during 1946 the Cold War surfaced as a political issue. On February 22, George F. Kennan's famous "long telegram" was greeted with immense enthusiasm by James V. Forrestal and like-minded elements in the Defense and State Departments and used as a kind of Cold War manifesto. Later Kennan conceded that the message was not unlike "one of those primers put out by alarmed congressional committees or by the Daughters of the American Revolution . . . to arouse the citizenry to the dangers of the Communist conspiracy." But for years to come the containment concept set the pattern for American thinking about the Soviet Union. Friction was indeed increasing with the Soviets in Korea, Germany, Iran and other areas, but, as Robert J. Donovan notes, it was the interaction of events in both countries that brought about the sharp turn in Soviet-American relations in the winter and spring of 1946, a turn which led to an increasingly divided world "totally at variance with the dreams and expectations of World War II."[3] Then on March 4, at the President's encouragement and with his full approval, Churchill delivered his famous speech in Fulton, Missouri, which was tantamount to an informal declaration of cold war. At about the same time, Wallace had urged Truman to try a new approach to the Soviets along economic and trade lines by way of demonstrating our willingness to continue the wartime cooperation, but the recommendation was ignored. From March 4 on, the new hard-line Iron Curtain policy was never seriously questioned.

After the election, Truman's wretched performance on domestic issues, the new turn foreign policy had taken, and the resumption of red-baiting led to much talk in California about the need to set up a new organization of liberals and progressives that would keep the Democratic Party committed to New Deal objectives. There was also much talk about an alternative nominee in 1948; even the California "regular" Democrats were not enthusiastic about Truman. One faction insisted that the proposed new organization must specifically exclude Communists and other left-wing elements. Such a bar, it was thought, would protect liberal candidates against red-baiting charges. The issue was discussed at great length in a series of meetings initiated by Dr. Harry Girvetz of the University of California at Santa Barbara, in which I participated. I could not go along with the suggestion that a specific ban or bar against particular groups would insure protection against red-baiting; on the contrary, I was convinced it would have the opposite effect and only lead to endless splits and dissension. In New York, where a similar debate was under way, Stanley M. Isaacs, a consistent and widely respected liberal Republican, took the same position: "I grant the difficulty of dealing with well-organized Communists who want to dominate. But I am not afraid of Communist infiltration and certainly will not abandon a just cause because I object to some of those who join in its support."

It was clear to me then that this was the issue on which attempts to reconstitute the Roosevelt New Deal coalition would flounder. As the weeks went by, the debate over the interlocking questions of foreign policy and "anti-Communist" immunization programs largely determined, as Norman D. Markowitz has pointed out, "the future of social liberalism in the postwar period."[4] Progressive Citizens of America came into being in December, 1946; Americans for Democratic Action, in the spring of 1947. In a diary entry of

January 19, 1947, I noted that the split this division reflected would only make it easier for both Republican and Democratic politicians to red-bait those with whom they disagreed. Regretfully I had to part company with Harry Girvetz and other California friends who joined ADA. I joined PCA.

In the wake of the 1946 elections, Truman's advisers began putting together the elements of a new game plan. The strategy was to combine an increasingly tough "anti-Communist" stand in foreign affairs, the better to outflank the Republicans, with greater rhetorical emphasis on domestic issues such as civil rights which had strong appeal to New Deal Democrats and blacks. In December, a Commission on Civil Rights was named as a response to increased racial violence in the South and as a gesture to black voters. And to offset Republican red-baiting and by way of taking "the ball away from Parnell Thomas" (J. Parnell Thomas, a Republican from New Jersey, was chairman of the House Un-American Activities Committee; later he was convicted of criminal charges and served time in Danbury Prison until he was pardoned by Truman), a Temporary Commission on Employee Loyalty was set up shortly after the election.

The Truman Doctrine, announced with great fanfare on March 12, 1947, ushered in the new strategy. In February the British ambassador in Washington had notified the State Department that his government would no longer be able to continue financial assistance to Greece and Turkey after the end of the British fiscal year on March 31, 1947. The note also reiterated the Anglo-American position that the Soviet Union ought to be prevented from acquiring a dominant position in these countries. In his speech to a joint session of Congress at noon on March 12, broadcast nationally by radio, Truman not merely took the position that aid must be supplied to Greece but in effect said that this country must support "free peoples" who were resisting "attempted subjugation by armed minorities or by outside pressures." The overblown rhetoric and ideological emphasis made it sound like a formal declaration of the Cold War that Churchill had proposed the previous year. The scope of the doctrine was worldwide; we would support "free peoples" everywhere. The ideological emphasis necessarily fed "anti-Communist" sentiment in this country and immediately stimulated the red-baiting mania. By placing the emphasis on conflicting ideologies rather than on any specific military or security threats posed by the Soviets, the Truman Doctrine encased American policy in a rigid mold that, as Robert J. Donovan notes, inhibited a turn in the Cold War for a generation.[5] Promptly hailed by Henry Luce as fulfillment of his "American Century" manifesto of

1941, it was greeted with equal enthusiasm by most of the press.[6] That it was proclaimed so close to the Moscow Conference (April 24) seemed both tactless and provocative, the more so since Russian intervention was not a prime source of the trouble in Greece, where a royalist and reactionary regime was in power. The day after the doctrine was announced, Wallace said it "marked a turning point in American history"; the President had, in effect, said that henceforth we would police Russia's every border. In retrospect it is hard to fault Wallace's conclusion. As Godfrey Hodgson has pointed out, the Truman Doctrine contained "the seeds of a habit of intervention: clandestine in Iran, Guatemala, Cuba, the Philippines, Chile and the CIA alone knows where else; overt in Korea, the Lebanon, the Dominican Republic, Laos, Cambodia and Vietnam . . . by the end of the 1940s . . . the United States had set out on the road that led to Vietnam."[7]

Nine days after the Truman Doctrine was proclaimed, the President signed Executive Order 9358 setting up the "loyalty program." In effect the program was the counterpart of the new doctrine. The interaction between the two created an atmosphere in which it became hazardous to criticize Cold War policies and programs or to question the assumptions on which they were based. Later the loyalty criteria were changed so that it became even easier to oust government employees suspected of some form of heresy. It was these changes, as Richard M. Fried has written, that made it possible for "the dragon's teeth of charges sown by McCarthy in 1950" to sprout at a later date.[8] A day or so before signing the executive order, Truman had written former Governor George Earle to say that all the talk about reds in government was nonsense. Obviously he thought the program would protect his administration against red-baiting charges, but it had, of course, exactly the opposite effect. In later years Dean Acheson frankly acknowledged that its handling of the loyalty issue had been one of the worst blunders of the Truman Administration.

Then in June came the Marshall Plan, which, as we now realize, was really not so much a plan for the economic reconstruction of Europe as it was a strategy to insure German recovery and rearmament on terms that Britain and France would accept.[9] The plan was sold as a means of saving Europe from Communism and as a tonic for the domestic economy. To congressional leaders Truman made it clear that most of the funds would actually be spent in this country. And indeed more than $13 billion was spent here, a billion for coal alone. The Marshall Plan confronted the liberals with a real dilemma. It was fairly close, in some ways, to their favorite plans and projects, and it was not wholly objectionable. But when related to the Truman Doctrine, it had disturbing overtones. Politically it split the liberal movement: one faction, supported by organized labor, jumped aboard the bandwagon, while the other had difficulty in trying to formulate a sensible criticism of the plan.

But there were other plans and projects afoot of which the public was only dimly aware. On January 22, 1946, again by executive order, Truman had set up the Central Intelligence Group—the forerunner of the Central Intelligence Agency, which came along in 1947 with a vague grant of power to perform "other functions and duties." By the end of the year, the CIA had begun to carry out covert missions and "dirty tricks" of which, thirty years later, we still do not have a complete list. The fact is, of course, that the Truman Administration had a great deal to do with shaping the Imperial Presidency, notably by the use it made of emergency powers. Without formal congressional approval or UN sanction, Truman's decision to intervene in Korea established an extremely dangerous precedent. Some eighty-five prior instances were cited to justify his action, but as Senator Arthur V. Watkins pointed out in a scholarly speech in the Senate (January 22, 1951), none of them had any relevance to the facts in Korea. Presidents Eisenhower, Kennedy, Johnson and Nixon all made use of the Korean precedent in support of their overseas interventions. The Korean intervention postponed the Sino-Soviet split and foreclosed the possibility of an American-Chinese rapprochement for two decades. Timely recognition of the new regime in China might have avoided the war in Indochina. Truman and Acheson could see the North Vietnamese only as puppets of China, just as they were convinced Russia was behind the actions of the North Koreans. In their eyes even Mao Tse-tung was a puppet of the Kremlin. Both misconceived the significance of the Asian revolutions and by stressing ideological differences aligned American policy with reactionary regimes on a worldwide front. Perhaps an accommodation with the U.S.S.R. could not have been reached, but by 1947 American policy had been set on a course that precluded the possibility. By then, we had in effect renounced diplomacy.[10]

3. THE WALLACE MOVEMENT

In the early months of 1947 the Wallace movement made remarkable headway in California. The crowds were large and enthusiastic. When permission to use Hollywood Bowl for a major rally was revoked, the meeting was shifted to Gilmore Stadium, where, on the night of May 19, the *paid* attendance totaled more than 28,000 and a pass-the-hat collection netted $33,000. Addressed by Henry Wallace, Katharine Hepburn, Dr. Linus Pauling and others, it was the largest political rally ever held in the community. On July 19 a Democrats-for-Wallace meeting was held in Fresno with similar success. Wallace was then drawing thirteen percent of the Democratic vote in the polls, and Truman's advisers were alarmed, not that Wallace might win but that Republican Thomas E. Dewey might. Reacting to the Wallace threat, Truman began to speak of his "Fair Deal" in a manner reminiscent of the New Deal. His veto of the Taft-Hartley Act assured support of all but a handful of unions. Release of the report of the Commission on Civil Rights in October ("To Secure These Rights") was well timed in relation to the 1948 election and virtually insured the support of black voters. By the end of the year the early enthusiasm for the Wallace movement had begun to subside. Fearing there would not be enough time to launch a third party after the 1948 conventions, the leadership of PCA induced Wallace to announce his independent candidacy in December, thereby sealing the isolation of the movement. An idealist with fine insights—most of his foreign-policy statements stand up remarkably well—Wallace was not a good politician. He did not seem to realize, for example, the extent to which the liberal-labor-minorities wing of the Roosevelt coalition was committed to the Democratic Party.

Freda Kirchwey and *The Nation* looked with favor on the Wallace movement at the outset but did not go along with the idea of a third party. J. Raymond Walsh, active in PCA from the beginning, pointed out in *The Nation* that the launching of a third party would set back progressive politics for many years. In the end *The Nation* made no endorsement. In general I shared this point of view. When it became clear that Wallace was committed to the third-party strategy, I resigned from PCA but voted for Wallace nonetheless. My reasons for opposing the third party were the same as those voiced by Freda and Ray Walsh, but with a difference. In California the Wallace movement had been presented from the outset as a movement *within* the Democratic Party. Despite the fact that Truman was an incumbent, there was an outside chance a Wallace delegation might have been chosen in California. But the moment it became clear that Wallace intended to run as the nominee of a new party his support sharply declined. I wanted a serious effort made to carry the fight to the Democratic convention regardless of the outcome. Within the Democratic Party, the Wallace movement could have survived; it could not as an independent party. In 1968 critics of the war in Vietnam wisely decided to carry the issue to the Democratic convention. True, they lost, but Johnson was forced to bow out as a candidate. The circumstances were, of course, different, but it should not be forgotten that in 1948 there was much sentiment against Truman in the Democratic Party; a long list of liberals who later denounced Wallace were initially opposed to Truman. ADA leaders, for example, openly intrigued with other "dump Truman" elements, and these intrigues might have succeeded if the liberals had not been split. In California, many Democrats felt let down if not misled when Wallace decided to run as an independent; they had joined a Democrats-for-Wallace movement, not a third party.

Clark Clifford's famous memo of November 19, 1947, provided Truman with an excellent blueprint for the 1948 campaign. He should attack Congress incessantly and bombard it with New Deal–type programs, which would of course be voted down. He should strengthen his position as a Cold Warrior. He should make a strong pitch for the black vote, which, as usual, was being neglected by the Republicans. He should largely ignore the Wallace movement: ADA would assume the burden of discrediting it. Truman's 1948 State of the Union Message, reflecting this advice, was a distinct improvement over what he had been saying. After some weird flip-flops, he finally took a strong position on the partition of Palestine. The Dixiecrat revolt enhanced his appeal to black voters in the pivotal states, and, overall, he probably benefited from Wallace's candidacy, which drew most of the fire from the red-baiters. Truman's strategists had seen to that: the timing of the indictment of twelve Communist Party leaders on July 21, just two days before the Progressive Party convention, was no coincidence. Then, too, the death of Jan Masaryk in March and the Czech crisis had a devastating impact on the Wallace movement. Throughout the year, the spreading anti-Communist paranoia—witness the enormous interest shown in the tall tales that Whittaker Chambers began to tell about Alger Hiss—made it hard for Wallace to get a hearing. I returned to California from a lecture trip in the late spring of 1948 convinced that a witch-hunt far more serious than any we had known was shaping up; I had, in fact, signed a contract to write a book about it.

Somewhat to my surprise, Truman carried California by a narrow margin that fall. I had thought, and so reported (in the Manchester *Guardian*), that Earl Warren's presence on the Republican ticket as Dewey's running mate, coupled with widespread dissension in Democratic Party ranks, would enable the Republicans to win. And it was a close election in terms of the popular vote: with a low turnout, Truman received 49.5 percent, Dewey 45.1 percent. A small shift of votes in Ohio, Illinois and California would have elected Dewey. Robert J. Donovan has drawn the correct conclusion: the Roosevelt coalition held together just long enough to elect Truman; twenty-three of the twenty-eight states he carried had voted for Roosevelt every time FDR ran.

For Wallace's backers the returns were disastrous. They had predicted he might receive as many as four million votes; the actual count was 1,156,000, somewhat less than Dixiecrat Strom Thurmond received. That Wallace drew only 2.37 percent of the popular vote flashed a green light to the Cold Warriors: the only articulate challenge to their policies had been crushed. Before much time had passed, even ADA was being red-baited despite its "anti-Communist" stance. In a word, the stage had been set for the debut of Joe McCarthy. But in spite of their failure, Norman D. Markowitz is right in saying that the Progressives had faced

> the real questions confronting postwar America. They had sought the political alignment that all social liberals believed in and that was necessary to save and fulfill what was worthwhile in the New Deal heritage. They had realized that a democracy is only as strong as its treatment of dissenters and that religious and class unity obtained in the name of a mindless anti-Communism would ultimately tear the country apart or erode it from within. They had struck at those who held the real power in the country—the corporations and the military. They had called for a foreign policy that recognized what the Soviet Union had suffered in the war and what Russia and America must do to live together in the years ahead. Truman and his supporters had linked the domestic policies of the Economic Bill of Rights with the foreign policy of containment, leaving in the aftermath of the elections the Achesons to indulge in their geo-political fantasies and the McCarthys to usurp the banner of the common man.[11]

I would only add that the Wallace movement made political history in the United States with its nonsegregated political rallies in the South and the way in which it forced Truman's hand on civil rights.

4. "THE CAPITOL OF ANTI-SEMITISM"

Once a writer becomes identified with a controversial social issue—in my case racial minorities—it is difficult to retreat to the sidelines. After publication of *Brothers Under the Skin* and *Prejudice,* I was appalled by the amount of time I was spending on lecture junkets, attending conferences, and conferring with government and agency officials about social-action programs. Then, too, a book is never finished; there are always sequels. In traveling about the country on lecture trips, it was often suggested that I should interest myself in anti-Semitism, but I was wary of the ramifications and complexities, nor was the subject directly related to my California experience. But over a period of time I became fascinated by manifestations of anti-Semitism uncovered in the course of these trips. I was, for example, greatly intrigued by the strange pattern of anti-Semitism in the Twin Cities.

Moving in and out of St. Paul and Minneapolis in the war years, I had acquired some exceptionally fine sources and contacts, particularly in the Jewish community. What surprised me was the discovery of a pattern of anti-Semitism not precisely duplicated elsewhere in the Midwest. For example, Jews had never been accepted into membership in the local Kiwanis, Rotary, Lions, Toastmasters, or other service-club organizations. One or two had once belonged to the Minneapolis Athletic Club, but at a later date Jews were barred. Nor were they eligible for membership in the local automobile club! Except for an alderman from a predominantly Jewish district, there were no Jews in elective offices. More significantly, Jews were not visible in milling, lumbering, transportation, private utilities, banking, insurance, or, for that matter, in department-store merchandising. St. Paul was less uptight, perhaps because the Catholic influence was stronger there. Minneapolis was a newer city, more industrial, largely Lutheran, and the Jewish community had a heavier representation of fairly recent immigrants, many of Russian and Polish backgrounds.

I was also intrigued by the fact that the non-Jewish majority in both cities seemed actually surprised and to a degree embarrassed when I called attention to the prevailing pattern of anti-Semitism in an article in *Common Ground* ("Minneapolis: The Curious Twin," Autumn, 1946). Reprinted in the local press, the article drew widespread comment at civic meetings and in editorials, sermons, and radio programs. The new mayor of Minneapolis, Hubert H. Humphrey, invited me to confer with him and the members of the Council on Human Relations which he had just established—the first such agency to be set up by city ordinance. In fact, his friend Max M. Kampelman years later wrote in the New York *Times*[12] that Humphrey had been deeply troubled by the article, which appeared at about the time he became mayor, and that it prompted him to order a community self-survey in which every part of the city could see itself in the mirror, so to speak. But the article had still wider ramifications. Dean E. W. Ziebarth of the University of Minnesota later wrote to say that it had prompted CBS to launch a radio series, *Neither Free Nor Equal,* which won nearly every national award in the field of race relations. In a remarkably short period of time after the article appeared, nearly every exclusionary discrimination in the Twin Cities was lifted. Years later, in a special issue devoted to the present status of Jews in St. Paul and Minneapolis, the magazine *MPLS* (November, 1976) took note of the article's impact and reported that "anti-Semitism is no longer a problem in Minneapolis."

Incidents such as the Twin City inquiry gradually led me to believe that just as California was an ideal place to study race relations, so the United States offered the best setting for a study of *modern* anti-Semitism. The medieval heritage, which formed the background of "classical" anti-Semitism in Europe, never had much meaning here, although vestiges of it could be detected in colonial America. With the exception of a few discriminatory measures enacted in a dozen or more states, most of which were later repealed, Jews had never labored under *official* disabilities—i.e., legally sanctioned discriminations. Moreover, I was curious about how anti-Semitism fitted into the pattern of my thinking about prejudice and discrimination.

So once *Southern California Country* was out of the way, I began work on *A Mask for Privilege: Anti-Semitism in America,* and I kept at it for the next two years, intermittently making notes and accumulating materials for *California: The Great Exception.* For me, writing a book, any kind of book, in California in those years was like trying to study in a shipyard. California politics had acquired a feverish intensity, and Southern California, in particular, was a caldron of Cold War pressures and tensions. Many of the key issues of the period came to a sharper focus in Hollywood than elsewhere; witness the case of the Hollywood Ten. Just how I managed to complete the book I don't quite know; the phone rang constantly and there seemed to be a new emergency every day, another meeting every night. And I had lectures, journalistic assignments, and *Nation* commitments to worry about. Not surprisingly, *A Mask for Privilege,* which was published in the spring of 1948, indirectly reflects the severe tensions of this period.

I had decided to trace the pattern of anti-Semitism from the point in the middle 1870s when it first began to attract national attention. This was, of course, a critical period in group relationships, what with the "Compromise of 1876," which brought Reconstruction to a halt, the beginnings of a reservation policy for Indians, and enactment of anti-Chinese legislation on the West Coast which set the pattern for much of the subsequent Jim Crow legislation in the South. Invidious distinctions of a new kind began to be emphasized, particularly in the upper reaches of society. A famous incident of the period, the denial of accommodations to Joseph Seligman and his family at the Grand Union Hotel at Saratoga Springs in 1877, highlighted the rising anti-Semitism of the Gilded Age. The Seligmans were a New York family of wealth and social prominence, but this alone would not have accounted for the interest the incident aroused. Blatant discrimination of this kind was then sufficiently novel to come as a shock to many Americans. But the pattern quickly spread—at certain levels, in certain relationships. After 1877, in fact, social discrimination became quite common as nouveau-riche elements sought to protect their recently acquired status in the emerging industrial society of the postbellum period. Social discrimination against Jews was part of a broader pattern of discrimination invoked to keep immigrants, blacks, and other minorities in their place.

The more I thought about the post–Civil War pattern of discrimination against Jews and other minorities, the more I came to believe there are two basic racial-ethnic stereotypes. One arises when there appears on the scene a minority usually marked by some badge of difference—race, ethnic background, language, or religion—and handicapped by late arrival, lack of educational skills, and occupational training. The older Jewish encyclopedias, in fact, once defined prejudice as "the dislike of the unlike." But unlike groups do not necessarily dislike each other; initially, differences often stimulate curiosity and mutual attraction. The antagonism comes later when the dominant economic element (not always a numerical majority) senses an advantage in keeping the newcomers in subordinate roles. Members of such minorities then begin to be stereotyped as lazy, shiftless, irresponsible, improvident; they are said to have too many children, to be dirty, to be sexually promiscuous, etc. The function of the stereotype is to maintain an unequal relationship between groups competing for place, power, and position. Even similarity of racial, ethnic, and religious background will not always protect a minority against discrimination under special circumstances. For example, Okies and Arkies were stereotyped as an undesirable minority when they first began to arrive in California in large numbers during the Depression.

But there is another kind of minority: the mercantile or trading minority. Here the stereotype assumes a different form. These minorities—Jews, the overseas Chinese, Indian merchants in East Africa, Moslem traders in Central Asia, and, at one time, Quakers and Huguenots—are characterized on initial contact as aggressive, too industrious, too hard-working, too competitive, excessively clannish and much too clever. Being better trained, better organized, and more agile, this kind of minority is difficult to subordinate but can be kept at a distance for a time. So a pattern of social discrimination is invoked, the purpose of which is to prevent encroachment on the privileged preserves of the dominant economic elites. But as members of these minorities gradually become part of the economic and social Establishment, the half-forgotten barriers begin to be lifted in an often apologetic manner. This, in general, was the theme of *A Mask for Privilege,* which was a Book Find Club selection and won a Page One Award from the New York Newspaper Guild.[13]

Even before *A Mask for Privilege* was published, Louis Adamic had asked me to write the volume about Mexican Americans for the "Peoples of America" series he had begun to edit for J. P. Lippincott Company in 1943. The series was an outgrowth of his editorship of *Common Ground,* which he had helped launch in August, 1940. I had written for the magazine and had helped Louis line up authors for some of the volumes in the series, specifically, as I recall, D'Arcy McNickle for the book on Indians, and J. Saunders Redding for the one on blacks. Knowing of my long-standing interest, Louis asked me to do the volume about the Spanish-speaking, and I agreed. When *North from Mexico: The Spanish-Speaking People of the United States* appeared in January, 1949, it attracted little attention; the Spanish-speaking were still "a well-kept secret." But in 1961, Monthly Review Press brought out a new edition which sold fairly well and resulted in a Spanish-language edition which appeared in Mexico City in 1968. That same year Greenwood Press decided to bring out an edition with a new introduction, and the book promptly became a best seller—nearly twenty years after it was first published! Later a documentary film based on the book was produced under the title *North from Mexico: Exploration and Heritage.* In this instance my record of accidental good timing on books was off by several decades, but the new edition happened to coincide with the rise of the Chicano movement, which it is credited with having helped set in motion.

During the 1940s, then, I had written four books about minorities: *Brothers Under the Skin, Prejudice, A Mask for Privilege,* and *North from Mexico,* in that order. In a sense, all of these books were an outgrowth of the new interest in racial and ethnic minorities which World War II had stimulated. But by 1949 the Cold War was well under way and the wartime ferment had subsided, not to reemerge until the Montgomery bus boycott of 1955. For a time it had seemed that the racial revolution might accelerate after the war, as Willkie and others had hoped; but that was not to be—not just then.[14]

5. *THE HOLLYWOOD TEN*

From the outset I was actively interested in the case of the Hollywood Ten, which raised perhaps the most important civil-liberties issue of the period. Could a congressional committee make a mockery of the First Amendment by hailing witnesses before it and grilling them in public hearings on their political beliefs, particularly when their answers might have adverse consequences? To raise this issue the defendants had to rely solely on the First Amendment. If they had pleaded the Fifth Amendment, they would not have gone to jail, but they would almost certainly have been discharged and blacklisted—for no offense other than having invoked the protection of a right guaranteed by the Constitution. To raise the First Amendment issue, they had to refuse to answer key questions on the ground that the committee had no right to question them about their political beliefs. In other words, they had to contend that the First Amendment protects the right *not* to speak—the right to remain silent—as well as the right to speak. This was the position the Ten took, and it might have been upheld by the Supreme Court but for the deaths, pending the appeal, of Justices Wiley B. Rutledge and Frank Murphy, who were replaced by Truman appointees.

The defendants—Dalton Trumbo, Herbert Biberman, Edward Dmytryk, Adrian Scott, Alvah Bessie, Lester Cole, Ring Lardner, Jr., John Howard Lawson, Albert Maltz, and Samuel Ornitz—were articulate and intelligent men; they were well represented (by Robert W. Kenny, Bartley Crum, and Charles J. Katz); and they had resources to publicize their position. But they had great difficulty in getting the press and the public, in the atmosphere that then prevailed, to understand the nature of their contention. Many liberals were sharply critical. To them it seemed inconsistent to rely on an amendment which guaranteed freedom of speech in refusing to answer questions about one's political beliefs. Noisy, disorderly, and conducted in a glare of publicity, the hearings did not provide an ideal forum for presentation of a major constitutional issue. And it must be confessed that for all their intelligence and verve and courage, the defendants somewhat confused the issue by trying to talk while, at the same time, refusing to answer the key questions. If they had simply said that the First Amendment protected them against a public inquisition into their political beliefs, which they had a right to discuss or not to discuss as they saw fit (the one right being the counterpart of the other), it might have made for a better understanding of their position.

In an effort to clarify the issue at stake, Alexander Meiklejohn and I submitted an amicus curiae brief to the Supreme Court in which we argued that the First Amendment implied a right of silence; that citizens might hesitate to participate actively in politics if they could be hailed before inquisitorial committees and questioned about their beliefs under circumstances where the answers might have damaging consequences. As Meiklejohn later pointed out in *The Nation* (December 12, 1953): "A legislative committee which asks the question, 'Are you a Republican?' or 'Are you a Communist?,' accompanying that question with the threat of harm or disrepute if the answer is this rather than that, stands in contempt of the sovereign people to whom it owes submission. . . . The intent of the Constitution is that, politically, we shall be governed by no one but ourselves." Years later the Supreme Court in *Wooley v. Maynard* (April 20, 1977) affirmed this contention by ruling that the First Amendment protects the right to refrain from speaking about one's political beliefs as well as the right to speak, both being complementary components of the broad concept of individual freedom of mind. Today this point of view is not exceptional; then it was. In fact, it was regarded as heretical. It is hard to believe today but true that William L. Shirer was blacklisted for a time because his name had appeared in *Red Channels*—a publication which purported to identify Communists in the radio and television industries—as one of many distinguished Americans who had sponsored the brief that Meiklejohn and I had prepared.

Before the Hollywood Ten hearings opened in Washington, industry spokesmen had solemnly affirmed they would never, but never, establish a blacklist. But on November 26, 1947, Eric Johnston, speaking on their behalf, said that the producers would "discharge or suspend without compensation those in our employ, and we will not re-employ, any of the ten until such time as he is acquitted or has purged himself of contempt, and declares under oath that he is not a Communist." Dore Schary, then with MGM, was one film executive who had taken a good position at the first HUAC hearings. He would, he said, have employed Hans Eisler if offered convincing assurances he was not a foreign agent. But it was Schary who made the announcement at a meeting of the Screen Writers Guild in Hollywood that the Ten would be fired and blacklisted and that no writer who was believed to be a Communist would be hired in the future. Somewhat later he told Lillian Ross of *The New Yorker* (February 21, 1948) that he had been faced with the alternative of supporting the stand taken by his company or quitting his job. Then, in 1952 (July 27), Hedda Hopper, the Hollywood gossip columnist, wanted to know if he would buy a story from a Communist if the script was brilliant and contained no Communist propaganda. His answer was no. I promptly asked him to write a piece for *The Nation* in which he would explain his reasons. He agreed but then reneged on his promise. Ironically, Schary was later eased out of Hollywood; even his brand of liberalism had become a bar to employment. He was quoted by *The Reporter* (April 18, 1957) as saying, apropos of his departure from Hollywood, that he had made too many speeches.

Today the Hollywood Ten—the few that survive—are national folk heroes. Plays, television scripts, films, and books have told their story; even onetime detractors honor them. All this is as it should be. But I cannot help remembering the blighted careers, ruptured friendships, and personal and family hardships that the blacklist—ultimately expanded to include all phases of the entertainment industry—imposed. Some of those named managed to survive fairly well, but they were the exceptions. Lionel Stander, who told off HUAC with rare spirit and courage, paid heavily for his stand, as did others. Ring Lardner, Jr., was blacklisted for fifteen years—actually seventeen years between screen credits. With varying degrees of consistency, the blacklist was enforced for approximately fifteen years; it was not lifted in Hollywood until 1960. Unless one had reason, as I had, to be familiar with the hardships experienced by those blacklisted and graylisted, it is difficult to appreciate what a fifteen-year suspension can mean in the career of a screenwriter, an actor, or a director. Under the intense social pressure to conform, to capitulate, many were uncertain whether they should stick it out or change careers, not knowing how long the ban would last or when, if ever, it might be lifted.

I also knew many "friendly" witnesses—i.e., those named as reds and radicals who had decided, out of fear or expediency or for whatever reason, to testify. For some of these I had real sympathy; for others I had none. For example, I knew and liked Robert Rossen, the director, who was on the next list of those to be summoned after the Hollywood Ten. I spent hours listening to him as he agonized over the decision he had to make, and I was not surprised when he finally decided to testify. Unless he could make films, life had little meaning for him, and, as it turned out, he did not have long to live. Back in May, 1946, the two of us had served as co-chairmen of a committee which raised more than $20,000 to aid some CIO strikers who were having a rough time of it. So I had reason to know something about his basic social views and sympathies. On the other hand, I was puzzled when Edward Dmytryk, in an article written for *The Saturday Evening Post* (May 10, 1951) after he decided to cooperate with his inquisitors, said

that Thomas Mann and I had been "used" by the defendants. I
had no feeling of having been used; it was a privilege to support
the Ten in the position they had taken. And I wondered if it had
occurred to Dmytryk that he was being used by the committee
when he decided to testify.

*   *   *

   To Eric Goldman, 1949 was "a year of shocks," to Arthur Miller
"the year it fell apart." The Wallace movement had been routed;
the wartime unity had ceased to be; the liberal-progressive forces
were divided; the left had been silenced; the New Deal was dead.
And the shocks came thick and fast: the "loss" of China; the purge
of the left unions, begun in May, concluded in November; the first
trial of Alger Hiss, which opened in May; the eighty-one-day trial
of Harry Bridges, which started in November; the Smith Act convictions, coming after a long and tumultuous trial. A report that a
few grams of uranium were missing from an Atomic Energy Commission laboratory triggered something like a national panic. Senator Pat McCarran spoke of "treason in the State Department,"
and the Peekskill, New York, riots made a shambles of freedom of
speech and assembly. The most dramatic confrontation of the period, the Peekskill riots—one on August 27, the other on September 4, 1949—arose out of efforts of local residents to disrupt a
Paul Robeson concert held on private grounds as a benefit for the
Harlem Chapter of the Civil Rights Congress. Mobs blocked roads
and entrances to the grounds—five miles from the town of Peekskill—with shouts and catcalls directed against "reds," Jews, and
Negroes. Many women and children were among those injured.
Local police did little to prevent the violence. The second meeting
was held to vindicate the right of assembly. It was staged after a
fashion, with state troopers standing by, but was also accompanied
by much miscellaneous violence. No event of the period did more
to discourage freedom of assembly by dissident groups.[15]
   In September, Truman announced "with elaborate calm" that
the Russians had the bomb; the monopoly he had thought we
might enjoy for a decade or longer had suddenly ended. On February 1, 1950, he overruled the unanimous recommendation of a
panel of distinguished scientists and ordered the H-bomb program
to proceed. Long since forgotten was Henry L. Stimson's initial
advice that we should offer to share atomic "secrets" with the Russians as a quid pro quo for international controls.
   In 1949 the pursuit of heretics began in earnest. Given ideological sanction by the loyalty program, it spread from profession to
profession, throughout every level of government, from defense

industries to the private sector. That year saw the ouster of University of Washington professors—a shameful action set in motion by the hearings of the Canwell Committee, one of numerous committees established by state legislatures, in this case the state of Washington, to investigate un-American activities.[16] Then the embittered "loyalty oath" controversy got under way at Berkeley and dragged on, in one form or another, until October 31, 1952, when it finally began to be phased out—but not before it had caused severe hardship to many individuals and substantial damage to the university. Having covered both cases from the beginning, I was inescapably drawn into the ongoing controversy they set in motion. I spoke against the Washington ousters at a large mass meeting in Seattle's Civic Auditorium, discussed the two controversies at many meetings, and took part in public debates on the issues they raised. Later I devoted chapters to both controversies in *Witch Hunt: The Revival of Heresy.*[17]

For me, 1949 was a savage and depressing year. The political lines were sharply drawn; the tensions severe. Old friends ceased speaking, as they had, briefly, in 1939. Feuds multiplied and vendettas flourished; name-calling became endemic, and a kind of mindless pall spread across the land. There was a surreal quality about that year that made me want to laugh and curse at the same time. To cite merely one experience: the day I received an award from the Council Against Intolerance in America for work on behalf of racial minorities, the American Legion forced the Teachers Institute of Riverside, California, to cancel a meeting at which I had been invited to speak on, of all subjects, racial minorities. To add to the confusion, I had just recorded a series of radio talks on the same subject for broadcast overseas to the armed services. It was an odd feeling to be blasted as subversive by the Legion for voicing views which the Army and the State Department officially approved. But a group of Riverside residents, aided by the press, took a hand in the matter; the meeting was rescheduled and I did speak, despite continued protests from the Legion.

Thomas Mann had a few somewhat similar experiences, but he took a more serious view of this kind of harassment than I did. He thought fascism was coming in America. When Abe Polonsky, the Hollywood writer-director, reminded him that reaction was not quite the same thing as fascism, he replied, "Well, I had the European experience. I am leaving. As much as I love this place, I have to leave it. This is not the country that I became a citizen of." To me the country had not changed, but it was momentarily exhibiting a face that I did not like and that I found depressing. Why, I kept asking myself, had we become so fearful? Why did we insist on beaming a mirror image back to the Soviet Union? How had it happened, as Arthur Miller later asked, that "the only solvent nation in the world" had become "unhinged by fear," that "the inner coherence of the American world view" should have become so quickly "invested with phantoms"?

It was in search of answers to such questions that I wrote *Witch Hunt: The Revival of Heresy.* Once again my timing was or seemed to be impeccable. I had written a book about McCarthyism which was completed so soon after McCarthy's famous Wheeling, West Virginia, speech of February 9, 1950, in which he made his national debut as an "anti-Communist" demagogue, that I could refer to it only in the introduction. Corrected proofs were returned to the publisher on June 16, 1950, a few days before the outbreak of the Korean War, just as the last of the Hollywood Ten were departing for prison, and as the tenth anniversary of the adoption of the United Nations Charter was nearing. By then McCarthyism was rapidly becoming a national scourge. The book had chapters about the Hollywood Ten, the assaults on academic freedom, the inquisitions, the panic triggered by the thirty-two missing grams of uranium, the Berkeley crisis, the University of Washington ousters, the loyalty obsession, and other aspects of McCarthyism. By the time copies arrived in California in early November, the witch-hunt was well under way, but apparently few people wanted to read about it just then. Perhaps they were too preoccupied with the subject, or they may have been merely inattentive; more probably they thought I had become "invested with phantoms." Whatever the reason, the sales were not impressive; the book sells better today, in a reprint edition, than it did then.

With its publication, the long California chapter in my "education" came to a close. Shortly after the first copies arrived, Freda Kirchwey asked me to come east to help with *The Nation,* which had become a target of the witch-hunt. (Incidentally, of the ten books I wrote prior to leaving California, all but two are still in print.)

BOOK  II

CHAPTER VII

THE KIRCHWEY YEARS

Although I had contributed to *The Nation* for a decade or longer, it was only after being named West Coast correspondent in January, 1945, that Freda Kirchwey and I became close friends. One of her instructors at Barnard said of Freda that she was the prettiest, most intelligent, and most radical girl in her class. The Freda I came to know so well was this same girl grown older: attractive, intelligent, and still a radical. She was also fun-loving, lighthearted, vivacious, "a natural born Bohemian," in the words of Joseph Wood Krutch. A delightful companion at all times, in all settings, she was also an incomparably fine working colleague and a loyal and devoted friend. I have never known a less self-righteous person. The courage, unflappability and grace she invariably exhibited under stress were wholly admirable. She and I had our differences, but I cannot remember that we ever had a serious quarrel.

Freda had joined the staff of *The Nation* in the fall of 1918, shortly before the armistice and not long after she had graduated from Barnard. There were few tasks at the magazine she had not performed. She liked to edit copy and was very good at it. One of her first assignments was to serve as *The Nation*'s "New Woman— Modern Morals" editor. In the early 1920s she assembled an important series of anonymous autobiographies, most of them by famous women, which were published under the title "These Modern Women." A major contribution to the history of American feminism, the articles are only now being issued in book form.

Later she edited another widely read series on "Our Changing Morality" which became a book of that title. (Feminism, incidentally, was an early and continuing concern of *The Nation,* due in part to the interest and influence of Mrs. Henry Villard, William Lloyd Garrison's daughter, who was a pioneer in the movement.) As editor–publisher (1937–55), Freda was primarily interested in foreign affairs; one of her first assignments at the magazine had been to edit a section on international relations. Admired and respected in United Nations circles, she played a key role in *The Nation*'s campaign to exclude Franco's Spain from the UN and to secure the partition of Palestine. Her predecessor, Oswald Garrison Villard, knew the hinterland fairly well—he was enthusiastic about the Grand Tetons, Jackson Hole, and Yellowstone National Park—but never quite outgrew his preoccupation with the Boston–New York–Washington axis. Freda's life and interests were also deeply rooted in New York; she did not know or care too much about the country west of the Hudson. On most domestic issues, she took a left-of-center position, and for years she was a personage of consequence in the liberal movement. Liberal and reform politics were, in fact, very much a part of the Kirchwey family tradition. Freda's father, George Kirchwey, for years dean of the Columbia University Law School, had been a leader in penal reform (one of the first presidents of the League to Abolish Capital Punishment), had helped draft the Progressive Party platform in 1912, and had run for state office on its ticket.

From 1945 on—and particularly after the successful *Nation* conference in Los Angeles in 1946—I was increasingly drawn into discussions of *The Nation*'s editorial and financial problems both with Freda and with Lillie Shultz, the gifted organizer and publicist who directed the activities of The Nation Associates. With the exception of a few years, roughly from 1938 to 1942, when for once it found itself in the mainstream of national opinion, *The Nation* had never been self-supporting. But the annual deficit had usually been met without too much strain and effort until the late 1940s, when sharp changes in the political atmosphere suddenly made it difficult to raise funds through public functions. After 1949 the "freeze" became acute. Many left-liberals and radicals felt that *The Nation* should have supported the independent candidacy of Henry Wallace, while not a few liberal Democrats resented its criticism of Truman's Cold War policies. Traditional sources of support became cautious and apprehensive. The magazine had weathered crises in the past, but this one was different: it was sharper, more pervasive and persistent, with new dimensions. Many of the attacks, for example, emanated from sources once regarded as neutral if not friendly and supportive. With the inception of the Cold War and the rise of McCarthyism, some "liberal" intellectuals, frequently those with a Communist past, became so committed to the new "anti-Communist" ideology that they vehemently denounced as un-American and pro-Soviet any criticism of American policy not coupled with stronger criticism of Russian policy and practice. As Alonzo L. Hamby notes, *The Nation* became their prime target.[1] What these elements could not abide was the magazine's criticism of Cold War policies of the kind that finally resulted in the Vietnam disaster and its consistent denunciation of the witch-hunt which was in part a consequence, in part a cause, of these policies.

Late in 1950 Freda summoned me to New York for an emergency conference. She was having great difficulty in raising funds and was particularly concerned about attacks then being directed at *The Nation* by "anti-Communist" Cold War intellectuals which seemed to be mounting in volume and intensity. As a personal favor, she asked if I would come east for a time and lend a hand with some of the problems the magazine then faced. I was reluctant to say yes; among other reasons, I had just started a new book (which, incidentally, has yet to be written). But I was thoroughly convinced the domestic witch-hunt would get much worse, and soon, and that it should be sharply challenged. In fact, I had been urging *The Nation* to take the offensive by bringing out a special civil-liberties issue.

Once Freda agreed I might edit such an issue, I said I would come east for a month or so to help in any way I could. I had no thought then, nor I am sure did she, that I would be staying on, for more than a quarter of a century. Much less did either of us have in mind that I might one day succeed her as editor. But hardly had I set foot in the office before Harold Field resigned as managing editor, for reasons wholly unrelated to my being there, and Freda asked me to take over his tasks while continuing to help in her round-the-clock fund-raising activities. I never fancied myself a fund raiser, but I did succeed in enlisting the support of a few individuals of means whose continued support proved to be of critical importance in keeping *The Nation* alive in those lean years and later. Functioning as an editor was an equally novel role for which I was not prepared, undertaken in a new setting with which I was not familiar. Yet before I quite realized what had happened, I found myself saddled with major editorial and financial responsibilities. I kept thinking that the crisis at the magazine, which reflected mounting tensions in the Cold War, would soon pass, but it got steadily worse. There was no time to think of anything else.

I did what had to be done, hour by hour and day by day. By the end of that first year in New York, I found myself tightly "locked" into *The Nation*'s structure, and the key had been tossed out the window—for the duration.

1. "HOW FREE IS FREE?"

In that odious spring of 1951, the McCarthy rampage was in full swing. Everything McCarthy did or said was top news; the newspapers were never able to develop a formula to counter his formula, which was to keep one jump ahead of them with his endless charges and accusations. In one form or another, McCarthyism was the dominant domestic issue for the next four years; it became, in fact, a national obsession. It posed not one but many interrelated issues. There were the hearings of the various inquisitorial committees, the purges, the loyalty screenings and investigations, the Smith Act prosecutions, the key cases involving individual victims, the harassment of artists and gallery owners, of publishers, editors, librarians, actors, network personnel, directors, the contempt citation cases, the book burnings and bannings, local vigilante "incidents," a long list of important civil-liberties cases, repressive legislative proposals, and, above all, the politics of McCarthyism and its relation to the Cold War.

My California experience, on which *Witch Hunt* was largely based, was of some help in coping with these assorted issues, but it was not entirely relevant. California had a tradition of free-wheeling radicalism that dated back to the 1870s. There were shadings of difference between West Coast and East Coast Communists and in their relations to liberals and other radicals. Witch-hunting was a kind of outdoor political spectator sport in California: noisy, crude, relatively unsophisticated. The infighting on the left and in intellectual circles was much more vicious in New York, although it was bad enough, at times, in Hollywood. The first phase of the witch-hunt (1945–50) left some social wreckage in California, including many blighted careers; even so, the resistance was stronger there than in the East and the consequences less serious.

By and large, the West Coast red-baiters were an even crummier lot than those in the East. Jack Tenney, chairman of the California Committee on Un-American Activities, onetime president of the powerful Los Angeles Musicians Union, state assemblyman and later state senator, was best known, when I first knew him, as the composer of the popular song "Mexicali Rose." He was then as red as a Mexicali or any other kind of red rose. In the first session of the state legislature after Olson's election in 1938, Tenney and Sam Yorty, later mayor of Los Angeles, were miles to the left of the Governor—that is, for the first few months. Then both swung sharply to the right. Tenney joined the Republican Party and later shocked the veteran, patriotic, and civic groups that had long applauded his "anti-Communist" tirades and investigations by turning anti-Semitic and joining forces with Gerald L. K. Smith, a product of the Huey Long movement in Louisiana and one of the most obstreperous demagogues of the period. I was neither shocked nor surprised. It was hard for me to take Tenney seriously for any purpose: I had known him too long and too well. McCarthy was hardly more impressive as a person, but he had one talent Tenney lacked: he knew how to manipulate the media.

The second phase of the witch-hunt, with which I had to contend in New York, was far more dangerous than the first; it was also more difficult to report. Much of the action was fairly easy to follow. The hearings, for example, presented no problem. The press, most of which backed McCarthy, gave massive coverage to whatever he did or said, and television carried the turgid committee sessions to a vast national audience. Then, too, victims of the witch-hunt came trooping to *The Nation*'s offices in single file and platoons, to tell their stories, to seek advice, to gain publicity and editorial support, bringing bales of documents, clippings, and personal statements. But some aspects of the witch-hunt were not easily reported; much of the action went on behind the scenes, notably in the New York media world. Often the victims were not sure just what had happened or who was responsible. Some did not want to be identified by name or were reluctant to verify facts. Sources declined to be quoted; inquiries were brushed off; blacklists multiplied, but their existence was denied. Those on the "inside" did not always know the full story.

But even in the least accessible, murkiest areas, *The Nation* had exceptionally good sources. For some time before I came east, a group of writers, editors, and journalists known as "The Observers" had been meeting informally to discuss strategies for countering McCarthyism in the media world. To *The Nation* they offered to provide occasional reports on censorship and blacklisting incidents which would simply be signed "The Observers." Freda liked the idea, and I was invited to serve as liaison. The Observers had no formal organization; there were no bylaws, dues, or officers. They were merely individuals, perhaps two dozen in all, well known to each other, of kindred sympathies, all engaged in the media in one way or another, who met from time to time to compare notes and monitor the witch-hunt. Jack Goodman and Joseph

Barnes, both of Simon and Schuster, were among the moving spir-its; other observers included Millard Lampell, Merle Miller, Edgar Snow, June Wallace, Matthew Josephson, Ira Wolfert, Gerard Piel, Arthur Miller, Jack Belden, Ernestine Evans, William Shirer, Judy Freed, and some whose names I have forgotten. Meetings were generally held in Jack Goodman's Village apartment and went on and on, far into the night. In fact, the Observers usually had such fun rapping that it was difficult to get much copy out of them, but the exchange of information was valuable, as were the leads, and *The Nation* was able to publish a few first-rate reports the group provided, including one that described how Max Lowenthal's fine book on the FBI had been suppressed on publication. Then one day Jack Goodman, who had not the most remote ties with any left groups, was summoned to Washington and minutely questioned about the meetings in his apartment. Committee members and staff were able to refer in elaborate detail to actual discussions that had taken place. Obviously there was an informer in our midst— even in that select, innocent, and friendly circle. Someday I would like to learn the identity of the stool pigeon responsible for ending those lively sessions, for, sadly, there were no more meetings of the Observers after Jack had been questioned by the inquisitorial com-mittee.

During the first four years I was in New York, McCarthyism was a major—a constant—editorial preoccupation. Despite its limited resources and meager staff, *The Nation* managed to keep a spotlight on the main issues. More than a year after I came east, the special book-length civil-liberties issue finally appeared: "How Free is Free?," with contributions by Matthew Josephson, Vern Country-man, Arthur Miller, Zechariah Chafee, Jr., and others, and a hand-some cover drawing which Ben Shahn insisted on giving us as his contribution (*The Nation*, June 25, 1952). If anything the delay had improved the timing; the issue appeared when McCarthy was at the peak of his power and a presidential election was in the offing. Fortunately a large press run enabled us to fill thousands of special orders throughout the balance of that year and the next. What most readers liked about the issue was its tone, which was neither apologetic nor defensive but indignant and defiant. But Richard Rovere was not pleased; in a piece in *The New Leader* he said it would provoke cheers in the Kremlin, and *Time* thought well enough of his silly comments to reprint them (July 21, 1952).

Encouraged by the response to "How Free is Free?," we decided to bring out a second special issue on a civil-liberties theme: "Does Silence Mean Guilt?" (June 6, 1953). The authors were two brilliant legal scholars, Norman Redlich, later staff director of the Warren

Commission, now dean of the New York University Law School, and Laurent Frantz, a Midwest law school librarian. The manuscript had an interesting history. Each author submitted a version, and each edited and criticized the other's manuscript. Then a final version was put together and the three of us went over it carefully. I was most anxious to get a clear, forceful, readily understandable statement of the history, purpose, and meaning of the Fifth Amendment. The response was phenomenal; we sold single copies and filled bulk orders for a year or more. Today we have forgotten the low esteem in which the Fifth was held in those years; to invoke its protection was tantamount to a confession of guilt. In the post-Watergate era, scores of corporate executives, labor leaders, politicians, officeholders, police, and Mafia figures invoke the amendment's protection without inviting catcalls from the press or the public, but it was not always so. Later that year we brought out still another special issue on civil liberties: "Freedom and the American Tradition" (December 12, 1953), with contributions by Alexander Meiklejohn, Howard Mumford Jones, Irving Dillard, Allan Seager, Kermit Eby, Harold Wolfram, and others, and we followed up with another, on the informer system and how it worked, which Frank Donner prepared (April 10, 1954). Whether any of these special issues were cheered in the Kremlin I would not know, but they make good reading in retrospect and were of great help to *The Nation* at a critical point in its history.

2. THE GREENBERG INCIDENT

Shortly before I arrived in New York in the spring of 1951, the celebrated Clement Greenberg incident confronted Freda with a major problem. Greenberg, who had been *The Nation*'s art critic, submitted for publication a letter in which he leveled some libelous accusations against J. Álvarez Del Vayo, the magazine's foreign editor. A world-famous figure in antifascist and socialist circles, Del Vayo had served as Spain's ambassador to Mexico and as Foreign Minister of the Spanish Loyalist government from 1936 to 1939. As such he had eloquently pleaded the Loyalists' case at the League of Nations and later, in New York, had played a key role in *The Nation*'s successful effort to delay the admission of Franco's Spain to the United Nations. When Freda refused to publish the Greenberg letter it appeared in *The New Leader* (May 19, 1951), and, after consultations with her advisers, she decided to file suit for libel. I had no part in the making of this decision, which had been discussed at great length before I arrived in New York, but I did say to Freda that, in my judgment, the suit should not have been filed. Later when she asked me to take over as editor in 1955, I made it a condition of acceptance that the action would be dismissed, and this was done, with neither party making any admissions or retractions and each paying its own costs.

To his credit, Del Vayo did not want Freda to take court action. Pugnacious as always, he was inclined to "punch Greenberg in the nose" and let it go at that. But Freda saw it differently. As a stateless refugee, Del Vayo was in a position of considerable peril; he could have been deported instanter. Greenberg had implied that Del Vayo was some kind of agent of the Soviet Union. To anyone who knew Del Vayo this was a humorous suggestion. He was never in his life anyone's "agent." A brave man, he never hesitated to voice his views, which were, in fact, a matter of international notoriety. He was certainly not noted for his discretion about anything, including his personal safety. The Soviets would have had to be out of their minds even to think of him as an agent. A latter-day Don Quixote, he was gallant, intrepid, generous, proud, and loyal to a fault, but he was not an "agent," nor was he a Communist. He was an internationally known and widely admired left socialist. As a journalist, he was quite right in thinking Greenberg's charges should have been ignored or published with a sharp rebuttal. Libel actions are not for newspapers and magazines. But Freda, who greatly admired Del Vayo, felt personally responsible for his safety and the security of his family. Also, she was convinced that failure to challenge the accusation in the courts would be damaging to the magazine at a time when it was under severe attack, and would stimulate further slanders. Filing the action, however, did not stop the attacks: it encouraged them; worse, it imposed a major financial burden on *The Nation* which it could ill afford.

But if Freda erred, as I think she did, in making a legal issue of the Greenberg letter, her concern for the Del Vayos was not a fantasy. On returning from Europe in February, 1952, Del Vayo and his wife were seized and detained incommunicado at Ellis Island for three or four days. I thought then and think now that *The Nation*'s "liberal" critics who disagreed with its stand on the Cold War instigated this action. Frantic wires, cables, phone calls, and personal intercessions finally secured the conditional release of the Del Vayos, but their "parole" was not lifted for some months. Writing in retrospect, tapping a wealth of latter-day research, Alonzo Hamby, an impartial scholar, concluded that "Greenberg's polemic was debatable at best, scurrilous at worst; in an atmosphere of McCarthyism, it was at the outer limits of legitimate liberal debate."[2]

A few years later, when it seemed that the court action might be set for trial, Sol Stein of the American Committee for Cultural Freedom tried to plant a story with the New York *World-Telegram and Sun* that Del Vayo was "a Soviet espionage agent." Asked for proof, he said he had none. Nor would he permit his name to be quoted in any way, so the tip was ignored. But Bernard Nossiter, the reporter who took Stein's call, gave me a memo of the conversation dated November 13, 1954, which is referred to in *The Agony of the American Left*, by Christopher Lasch (p. 89).

3. THE CULTURAL COLD WAR

Oddly enough, *The Nation* was never singled out for attack by McCarthy, although it was responsible for a disproportionate share of the critical attention devoted to McCarthyism. But its consistent refusal to rubber-stamp American Cold War policies, some of which it thought were stupid and self-defeating, and its stubborn defense of civil liberties invited constant sniping from "anti-Communist" intellectuals. For the most part, these self-appointed censors were ex-Communists, many of whom were to blossom out later as "neo-conservatives" actively devoted to defending the capitalist status quo in intellectual circles. Spokesmen for this claque singled out *The Nation* and Kingsley Martin's *New Statesman* for abuse largely because both publications insisted on assessing Cold War issues from an independent critical point of view. An opening blast in their carefully orchestrated attack was an article by Granville Hicks in *Commentary* for April, 1951. From a later perspective, Alonzo Hamby found that there was "something sinister" about this article; from first to last it implied that *The Nation* had become mesmerized by Soviet propaganda and was following a pro-Soviet line. But so convincing was Freda's long and eloquent rejoinder (*Commentary*, May, 1951) that at least one of her severest critics, Peter Viereck, praised it as "able" and, parting company with his colleagues of the "anti-Communist" persuasion, was even gracious enough to concede that *The Nation* and *New Statesman* were undoubtedly "loyal to America and England"![3]

The Greenberg incident was not the cause of these attacks, which had begun before the letter was written and continued long after the litigation had been dismissed. But because it was a party to the Greenberg controversy, *The New Leader* naturally became a favorite "launching pad" for attacks against *The Nation*. For instance, its issue of August 28, 1951, carried a long article by Daniel James in which he attacked what he called *The Nation*'s pro-Soviet bias. Similar articles by N. Muhlen had appeared in the issues of May 21 and 28 of that same year; in fact, this kind of sniping—waspish, malicious, and tiresome—continued for years. Nor was it confined to *The New Leader*. Worth noting is the fact that not a few of our critics had once been members of the Communist Party (as Granville Hicks had been) or had once had close ties with other left parties. As a group they seemed to be furious that *The Nation* should continue to defend the civil liberties of those who had not joined in the exodus. In ideological feuds, hell hath no fury like that which apostates exhibit not so much toward former co-religionists as against those who defend their rights and refuse to join in the crusade against them. In other words, it was not *The Nation*'s position on issues that annoyed these critics so much as it was its refusal to join in the witch-hunt.

As an indication of the attitude that many "anti-Communist" intellectuals adopted toward civil liberties in this period, one might cite Irving Kristol's much discussed article in *Commentary* for March, 1952. In this piece, Kristol pontificated that those liberals who had expressed doubts about the culpability of Hiss, Owen Lattimore, the well-known scholar and expert on Far Eastern affairs, William Remington, a minor figure in the federal bureaucracy, and Harry Dexter White, a distinguished economist and top official in the Treasury Department, all prime targets of the "anti-Communist" inquisition, should be compelled to expiate their political sins by conceding the guilt of these men. Of this article Hamby writes: "Purporting to present an anti-McCarthy strategy, Kristol actually agreed with the fundamental assumptions and tactics of McCarthyism."[4] And in much the same arrogant tone, Leslie Fiedler, who later was to have some extremely unpleasant experiences with high-handed police methods which may have taught him something about civil liberties, labeled as "innocents" those who defended Hiss and insisted that the guilt of Julius and Ethel Rosenberg had not been clearly established (*Encounter*, October, 1953). The American Committee for Cultural Freedom took much the same position in announcing that the Rosenbergs must "openly acknowledge" their guilt before intellectuals should even consider signing appeals for clemency.

If there was one publication that Kristol, Rovere, James, Hook, Viereck, Hicks, and the others detested and were determined to discredit and silence if possible, it was *The Nation;* they simply could not abide its independent stance on Cold War issues or its willingness to defend the rights of those who dissented on these issues. While the charges that these and other Cold War intellectuals directed against *The Nation* were demonstrably not true, they made it very difficult to stage fund-raising functions. For instance, in May, 1952, *The Nation* sponsored a meeting at the Waldorf on "Arab-Israel Peace: Key to Stability in the Middle East," hardly a controversial issue and one which, at that time, was not directly related to the Cold War. But *The New Leader* promptly joined forces with *Counterattack,* the right-wing newsletter, in denouncing the meeting and succeeded in enlisting the aid of Frederick Woltman of the New York *World-Telegram and Sun* in their campaign. From a long list of what were conceded to be "respectable sponsors," *The New Leader* singled out a few names—Algernon Black, Thomas Mann, Langston Hughes, Gardner Murphy, Dirk Struik (of the Massachusetts Institute of Technology), Bishop Arthur W. Moulton, and Mordecai Johnson (president of Howard University)—and drew the inference that inclusion of these well-known and respected individuals, whom it labeled "dubious 'liberals' " and "assorted Stalinoids and muddleheads," gave the meeting a dangerous "red" taint. In a shrill editorial of April 28, 1952, *The New Leader* demanded to know how *The Nation* had been able to induce so many honest democrats to lend their names to such "a questionable cause." Arab-Israel peace, a questionable cause? Backed by the *World-Telegram and Sun,* this slanderous campaign reached such proportions that, for a time, Freda considered canceling or postponing the meeting. But it was held as scheduled. The attendance was excellent, but the media coverage was minimal and the financial response disappointing. In fact, this was one of the last public fund-raising functions *The Nation* attempted during the McCarthy years. A savage public attack by McCarthy would have been much less damaging; in fact, it might have had exactly the opposite effect. In 1918, when *The Nation* was spun off from the *Evening Post* and Oswald Garrison Villard became editor, it had a circulation of only 11,000. By November, 1919, thanks largely to violent attacks by the rabble-rousers and demagogues of that period, circulation had risen to 53,000, an all-time high, but, predictably, it declined once the attacks abated.[5]

Unlike the red-baiting that came after World War I, "anti-Communism" rapidly became the dominant ideology of the 1950s. It buttressed Cold War policies, offered protection and absolution to those who had once been Communists, and appeared to be "the wave of the future," as indeed it was, for quite some time. A rigid comprehensive ideology, it lent credence to McCarthy's charges and sharply divided the intellectual opposition. The ideology was largely the handiwork of ex-Communists, who, with the fanaticism of apostates, waged a holy war against those who refused to accept it. Not a few of these ex-Communist intellectuals had been brought to national attention by the inquisitorial committees. Whittaker Chambers was one, but there were others. Nothing these voluble "witnesses" said, in the context of the times, sounded improbable or farfetched. Discrepancies in their lurid narratives went unnoticed; multiple acknowledged perjuries were ignored. And in the nature of the situation no effective rebuttal was possible. The left parties were silenced or discredited, and the testimony of those who had never been Communists was dismissed as worthless. To reject any aspect of this rigid ideology was to run the risk of being branded "pro-Soviet." In the general nuttiness of the times, one's patriotism was judged not in terms of a demonstrated commitment to constitutional freedoms but by the shrillness with which one denounced repression in the Soviet Union.

But to couple every statement about the denial of civil liberties in this country with denunciations of similar or more flagrant denials in the U.S.S.R. was to divert attention from the immediate— the nearest—danger which was McCarthyism. As Conor Cruise O'Brien has pointed out, there is something dubious and tactically self-defeating in "the convenient localization of slavery 'over there' and liberty 'over here' "; it is always easy to beat up on the remote external evil but much more difficult—even dangerous at times— to oppose the evil close at hand, particularly when it happens to be supported by powerful forces in the society, including such agencies as the FBI and the CIA. That McCarthyism went unchecked as long as it did is to be explained in no small measure by the "shame" of those intellectuals who insisted on regarding it as merely an insignificant aberration or who actually condoned it and joined in the attacks.[6]

Two organizations in particular played a key role in spreading the chic well-financed "anti-Communist" ideology among American intellectuals and in waging a kind of cultural cold war against those who, in a notably hostile environment, refused to accept it. One was the Congress for Cultural Freedom, formed at a meeting in West Berlin in June, 1950, which had been initiated by a former CIA agent. Among the active American participants were Sidney Hook, Arthur Schlesinger, Jr., and Elliot Cohen, editor of *Commentary*. Its affiliate, the American Committee for Cultural Freedom, was formed in 1951. Sidney Hook was the first chairman; Irving Kristol served as executive secretary. Other members included Schlesinger, Diana Trilling, Richard Rovere, and Peter Viereck. Both committees were heavily larded with ex-Communist intellectuals and liberals who had turned hawkish. The line these committees pushed was of major assistance to Cold War policy chieftains in Washington, who had good reason to be concerned by the apprehension McCarthyism had aroused among many European intellectuals.

Using acceptable liberal rhetoric, both committees "lashed out" boldly at the denial of intellectual and cultural freedom in the Soviet Union and the other Communist regimes but were strangely silent about the denial of these same freedoms in many of the regimes which received lavish military and economic aid from Washington. Both committees took quite a benign view of McCarthyism; in fact, they tried, and quite successfully, to avoid mention of it. Not once did either committee ever challenge or criticize any significant aspect of American policy. Both were conceived, as we now know, as part of a CIA strategy to mute criticism of Cold War policies among intellectuals here and abroad. Small wonder, then, that the American Committee for Cultural Freedom often acted as though it had been given an official mandate to censor this country's intellectuals and keep them in line. A few kind words were said now and then about social democrats in Europe and elsewhere, but care was taken not to question Washington's leadership of the "free world." With the exception of one or two vague and belated references, the committee maintained a stony silence on McCarthyism.

From the outset, I was convinced that both "cultural freedom" committees were receiving government subsidies either directly or indirectly; their pronouncements smacked of propaganda and not very clever propaganda at that. So I began to gather as much material about them as I could. Eventually I turned this material over to Christopher Lasch, having gotten him interested in the subject, and he made excellent use of it in his long essay "The Cultural Cold War" which *The Nation* published as a special issue (September 11, 1967). (It was later reprinted in Lasch's *The Agony of the American Left,* 1969, and in *Towards a New Past,* a volume which Barton Bernstein edited in 1968.) Shortly after the issue appeared, evidence came to light that the CIA had for sixteen years provided secret funding to the Congress for Cultural Freedom for a variety of projects, including a covert subsidy to *Encounter* magazine, edited by Melvin Lasky, one of the founders of the Congress. From 1953, when *Encounter* first began publication, until 1964, it had been the recipient of CIA funds, which had also been channeled, indirectly, to the American Committee for Cultural Freedom. Yet as late as 1958 Richard Rovere, who was associated with both committees, insisted the parent Congress for Cultural Freedom was "a worthy organization, anti-Communist and gen-

erally libertarian in outlook and associated with no government.
. . . The rule in the West is that intellectuals and politicians stay out
of each other's way."[7]

When *The Nation*'s special issue on the cultural cold war appeared, Melvin Lasky and his colleagues threatened legal action,
demanded retractions, wrote angry letters, and even had the ef-
frontery to make disingenuous denials of facts they were later compelled to acknowledge. In England the same strenuous pressure
tactics were used in an effort to force Conor Cruise O'Brien to
retract charges similar to those Lasch had made in *The Nation*, but
with no greater success. All, of course, in the name of "cultural
freedom." At one point in the controversy, a covey of distinguished
American intellectuals, most of whom had enjoyed all-expenses-
paid junkets of the Congress for Cultural Freedom, sprang to its
defense in a series of public statements, but these expressions of
robust confidence ceased abruptly once the fact of the CIA subsidy
was confirmed. The most the press was ever able to get out of
Lasky was a cryptic statement to the effect that he had been "insuf-
ficiently frank" about the funds *Encounter* had received from the
CIA via the Congress for Cultural Freedom. But his associate,
Stephen Spender, who had not known of the subsidy, had the
candor to acknowledge that he and other intellectuals had been
used for "concealed government propaganda." Through subsidies
of the kind paid to the Congress for Cultural Freedom, the CIA
succeeded in aligning a significant and influential section of American intellectuals, spearheaded primarily by those who had come
"up from Communism," in a cultural "front" which consistently
supported Washington's Cold War policies and tactics in the sense
that they were never criticized or questioned. A comment by Andrew Kopkind, quoted by Lasch, on the way the strategy worked,
is pertinent: "The illusion of dissent was maintained; the CIA supported socialist cold warriors, fascist cold warriors, black and white
cold warriors . . . but it was a sham pluralism and it was utterly
corrupting."[8] And in the end it backfired on the CIA and its "witting" and "unwitting" agents and retainers.

Actually, as the record shows, it was not *The Nation* but its critics
who had reneged on the obligation to defend civil liberties, with
particular reference to the right to dissent on major political issues.
A glance at Irving Kristol's *Commentary* article of March, 1952,
amply confirms this statement. Nor was *The Nation* the dupe, wit-
tingly or unwittingly, of Soviet propaganda; it tried to assess Cold
War issues on the merits. But, with few exceptions, its most vociferous critics in intellectual circles were individuals closely identified
with the American Committee for Cultural Freedom, which was

the beneficiary of the CIA funds via the Congress for Cultural Freedom. Kristol, Rovere, Schlesinger, Hook, and Viereck were all identified with the committee; Viereck, who thought *The Nation* was quite naïve, was a member of its executive.

It is hard to believe that such gifted intellectuals were unaware that both "cultural freedom" committees were little more than fronts for the CIA. Some of the organizers and officials may not have known of the secret subsidy but were charged with notice of facts that should have prompted some inquiries. H. R. Trevor-Roper, one of the British delegates, noted that "a political tone" had been definitely set and clearly maintained at the meeting out of which the Congress for Cultural Freedom had emerged; this might not, he thought, have been objectionable if it had been frankly avowed, but it was not. So the defense of "innocence" is a bit hard to accept, although it is available to some, at least, of those active in the American Committee who were eager to believe what the CIA wanted them to believe. To Peter Viereck, for example, Marx's prophecies had proved to be "almost 100 per cent wrong"; hence American intellectuals should have faith in capitalism, whose profit system had been "sufficiently modified by ethics" so that it no longer violated, if it ever had, "the demands of humanity."[9] He was convinced, in fact, that his colleagues in the crusade for "cultural freedom" should join with him in opting for "a new conservatism," which, in effect, is what happened. Today "neo-conservatives" are the chief apologists for American capitalism in intellectual circles. This, of course, is their privilege; too often, however, they have acted as though they had a franchise from the Establishment to function as an ideological constabulary to keep dissenting intellectuals in line.

On the other hand, some "anti-Communist" intellectuals were in fact "witting" collaborators with the CIA in some of its fancy capers. The New York *Times* articles on the CIA and the media on December 25, 26, and 27, 1977, tell part, but only part, of the story. One learns, for example, that Arnold Beichman, long active in the "anti-Communist" contingent, accepted material from the CIA which was used to prepare an article about a Russian defector that appeared in *The Christian Science Monitor*. Beichman never met the alleged defector. In an interview, he told the *Times* that he had "pieced the story together from officials in the American Embassy" in Rangoon. "For all I know," he conceded, "he [the alleged defector] might never have been in the embassy. It might have been a fraud." The *Times* series also documents how Daniel James, former managing editor of *The New Leader*, author of that savage 1951 article about *The Nation*, had taken material from the CIA about an

East German woman who had joined Che Guevara's guerrilla group in Bolivia and made her out to be "the biggest, smartest Communist there ever was," as well as being an operative of the East German Ministry of State Security and the Soviet KGB. When interviewed, James offered no proof that the woman was in fact connected with the KGB but admitted that he had received and used materials from the CIA without identifying the source.

But far more serious, in a way, than these and similar incidents were the disclosures in the *Times* series about how the press had permitted itself to be managed and manipulated by Washington Cold Warriors, on many issues, for nearly three decades. A long list of publishers and editors, network executives and personnel, magazines, news agencies, journalists, and book publishers were named as "witting" and "unwitting" collaborators with the CIA. But these disclosures were "news" only in the sense that the *Times* had been able to secure semiofficial confirmation of facts and relationships that had been bruited about for a long time. Denied access to key documents and reports, the press often took handouts from official agencies and used them in a way that implied that the facts had been verified. Again and again the media accepted policy pronouncements as gospel truth; in the process the adversary role of the press was largely abandoned. The effect, of course, was to strengthen the extreme Cold War position on many issues both with the public and in the Congress. Any number of books have documented the way in which the press was manipulated by government agencies prior, say, to the Watergate scandals and the withdrawal of U.S. troops from Vietnam. One of the best is the report issued in 1969 by the American Friends Service Committee, "The Anatomy of Anti-Communism," which both provides an excellent analysis of the sources of McCarthy's popular support and explains, in detail, how "anti-Communism" became a political strategy that opposed not only Communism but neutralism and democratic revolution as well. "The doctrine of anti-Communism," as the authors of the report point out, "conceives of Communism as a major enemy, not because it is totalitarian or dictatorial, but because it challenges the status quo."

4. NOTES ON McCARTHYISM

There were of course many reasons why the contagion of McCarthyism spread so quickly. By 1950 we had been waging Cold War for five years, since the bombing of Hiroshima and Nagasaki, but we did not seem to be winning; quite the contrary. We had "lost" China, the Soviets had the bomb, and the prospects for peace were dim and growing dimmer. Then suddenly we were fighting in Korea, and a world war seemed likely. In such a setting the response to McCarthy's charges was massive and instantaneous. In effect the witch-hunt heated up because the Cold War had turned hot; the one development was the counterpart of the other. Once a cease-fire was negotiated in Korea, the hysteria began to abate and McCarthy was soon in trouble. But by then the damage was done: McCarthyism had been institutionalized. With the expanded funding of defense programs that came with the Korean War, as Daniel Yergin notes, "the architecture of the national security state was complete." [10] From then on, national security became an end in itself more or less divorced from "foreign policy" as conventionally conceived. But the expansion of American military power did not lead to a greater sense of security; it simply stimulated new fears which resulted in still heavier defense spending. McCarthyism did not create this state of affairs, but it was a major factor in consolidating the power of the Cold War "anti-Communist" consensus which made it possible.

McCarthy did not invent McCarthyism. He was a "populist" demagogue, not an ideologue. He was not really concerned with U.S.-Soviet relations or foreign policy, nor was he interested in ideologies. But he skillfully exploited the "anti-Communist" ideology which had been fashioned by policy-makers in the State Department quite some years before he made his appearance on the national scene. This ideology was less concerned with any specific threat posed by Soviet military power than with checking or containing the spread of Communist influence. McCarthy greatly reinforced this position by rallying domestic political support for the "anti-Communist" crusade. In fact, he succeeded in welding a massive bipartisan consensus which made it possible to wage Cold War with little criticism or restraint. At the same time, official policies and pronouncements strengthened his appeal by lending credence to his charges. In retrospect it is difficult to see how McCarthyism differed in any fundamental way from the policies, programs and tactics of the Truman Administration. "The practices of McCarthyism," writes Richard M. Freeland, "were Truman's practices in cruder hands, just as the language of McCarthyism was Truman's language in less well-meaning voices." [11]

The fact is that McCarthy was a Johnny-come-lately to "anti-Communist" politics. By the time he came along most of the paraphernalia of the witch-hunt had been in use for years. [12] As a demagogue his stock in trade consisted of two threadbare themes which he tirelessly and cynically exploited. The first, "reds in government," was a hoary hoax long before he brandished his first list of

205-odd names in his Wheeling, West Virginia, speech of February 9, 1950. His other theme, the Communist Party as a threat to national security, was equally bogus. By 1950 the party had been virtually outlawed; it was completely on the defensive; it had fewer members than in 1932. Severely isolated as it was, its marginal position in a few unions and "front" organizations had been gravely weakened if not destroyed. Members of the Communist Party ran the risk of being discharged and blacklisted and of possible criminal prosecution. The party's close ideological ties and sympathies with the Soviet Union were an insurmountable political handicap in a Cold War setting. Similarly its slavish adherence to a "line" made nonsense of the charge that it was a devious criminal conspiracy. The line was never difficult to detect; it was advertised in the party's publications and propaganda.[13] Interest in both these tawdry themes had actually begun to abate when McCarthy made his dramatic debut on the national scene, and he was never seriously concerned with either. He was interested in power. Not only did he demonstrate skill in exploiting the Cold War atmosphere and in the use he made of time-tested witch-hunting techniques, but he also had a canny intuitive understanding of the national psychosis on Communism.

In a year's-end issue of *The Nation* (December 30, 1950), Jean-Paul Sartre noted that American "anti-Communism" was more dangerous than the European variety precisely because this country had so few Communists:

> Frenchmen who hate Communists or feverishly condemn Soviet policy meet Communists every day and everywhere. Thus, however violent their antipathy, they have to recognize that their opponents are men and not devils; they know that it is possible to talk to a Communist. It is difficult and irritating and does not always give results but it is possible. In short, for French anti-Communists, Communists are a civilian adversary. For Americans they are always a military enemy. And because the enemy is unseen and unknown, he is the devil and must be fought to the death. Moreover, he appears to be everywhere, just because he cannot be pinned down in a definite place; suspicion grows, infects everybody. Is this man a Communist? or he? or he? With us, if a man belongs to the party, we think him perhaps a fanatic; with you he is of necessity a traitor, because by definition he is ranged on the enemy side. And since communism is evil, all that is evil is communist. In that way we try to explain that the United States, which has virtually no Communists and where there is not the slightest danger of

red revolution, is obsessed by the fear of communism. It is
because it fears treason more than revolution.

Still another acute French observer made much the same point.
"Communists are so scarce," Claude Bourdet wrote in *The Nation*
of December 12, 1953, "that practically nobody in the United States
has ever met one; thus any amount of fear and horror can be
aroused against them."

Numerically insignificant, Communists made an ideal target:
they could be baited with political impunity. And since we had
always regarded socialism or Communism as alien philosophies, it
was easy to regard reds and radicals as possessed of no rights that
the majority was obliged to respect. In the 1950s even the American Civil Liberties Union had qualms about defending the rights
of individuals who were or once had been Communists or who
were accused of once having belonged to an organization "on the
list." Indeed, for some six or seven years, officials of the ACLU
sought the aid of the FBI in screening its own boards and committees and even fed information to the FBI about the political beliefs
of some of its members. To fill this dangerous gap in the defense
of civil liberties, some of us—I. F. Stone, Corliss Lamont, Paul
Lehmann, H. H. Wilson, Clark Foreman, and others—took the
initiative in setting up the Emergency Civil Liberties Committee.
Even before the committee was formed, Stringfellow Barr,
Thomas I. Emerson of the Yale Law School, and I signed an open
letter which called attention to the critical need to provide adequate
legal defense for the political pariahs of the Cold War. Arthur
Schlesinger, Jr., the distinguished historian, was so incensed by this
appeal that he denounced the three of us in his column in the New
York *Post* (September 2, 1951) as "dough-faced typhoid Marys of
the left" and became quite angry when I observed in *New Statesman*
(December 8, 1951) that this was the language of McCarthyism
even if spoken with a Harvard accent. Yet it should have been
obvious—even in a Cold War setting—that to deny any group of
citizens rights guaranteed by the Constitution solely because of
their political beliefs and associations would dangerously weaken
the whole structure of constitutional freedoms. Happily the ACLU
eventually shifted back to its original position, but in the 1950s it
shied away from some critically important civil-liberties issues.
Slight wonder, then, that press and public, parties and politicians,
succumbed so quickly to McCarthyism.[14]

But if at home we feared treason more than revolution, throughout the world we feared revolutions more than any specific military
threat posed by the Soviet Union. Abroad we divided peoples into

two categories: "good guys," those on our side, and "bad guys," those who weren't. We could distinguish good Nazis from bad, but all Communists were alike, all were evil. The fate of mankind was at stake in the Cold War "exactly as in the war against Nazism," so Dean Acheson had said on March 10, 1950. But were the situations "exactly" the same? As allies the Russians were entitled to much of the credit for the defeat of the Nazis; their losses (twenty million dead) had been much heavier than ours. But that didn't matter. Every revolution, including the nationalist anticolonial variety, was seen as a threat to American capitalism and an extension of Soviet influence. So we opted for a counterrevolutionary strategy inconsistent with our professed political values and ideals. The Soviets could hardly have foisted on us a strategy better suited to serve their purposes. By simply giving lip service to revolutionary ideas, they reaped substantial political dividends (which, in many cases, they later squandered). Their costs were minimal by comparison with ours, and their risks were not as great. They could always abandon a revolutionary regime when it suited their interests. As Nixon pointed out in one of the David Frost television interviews, we did not always approve the repression some of our allies practiced, but they could be counted on to oppose revolutionary change, which is what mattered most to us.[15]

In exploiting the national psychosis on Communism, McCarthy helped fashion the "anti-Communist" counterrevolutionary ideology. The methods he advocated against reds and radicals were adopted as defensible aspects of our Cold War policies. A report prepared by a blue-ribbon panel (the Hoover Committee) for the CIA in 1954—the year McCarthy was condemned—warned that American concepts of fair play must be reconsidered; we must learn to subvert, destroy, and sabotage; to fight fire with fire. By 1960 we were quite prepared and willing to invoke the most despicable methods, including murder, assassination, sabotage, and arson against the "bad guys," these being the methods we charged them with using against us and our allies. As Richard Bissell of the CIA explained in a CBS interview of June 10, 1977, such methods were sanctioned by "the prevailing ethic" which McCarthyism had helped establish. It was this "ethic" that permitted us to wage a secret war against Fidel Castro after the Bay of Pigs and, later, to train Cuban exiles to carry out hundreds of raids and numberless acts of terrorism against his regime from "safe houses" and bases in Florida, in clear violation of the neutrality laws. This same ethic also sanctioned American intervention in Vietnam and the methods used there. And later it provided tacit sanction for the abandonment of both Cuban and Vietnamese collaborators. By "ditching" them in the way we did, we made it clear that they were never more than pawns in the Cold War, to be used when it served our interests and then abandoned when those interests had shifted.

More than anything else, it was the bipartisan fear not so much of Communism as the way the national psychosis on Communism could be exploited, that made it possible for McCarthy to spread fear and panic through the land. Politicians lived in mortal fear of the charge of being "soft on Communism." In 1948 Truman had made clever use of "anti-Communism" to ward off attacks from the right. But in 1952 the Republicans did not make the mistake of running a "cool" campaign as they had done four years before. On the contrary, they promptly preempted the "anti-Communist" position by doubling and redoubling the bid. Instead of curbing McCarthy, Taft and Eisenhower and the Republican leadership generally let him tear into the Democrats. Even in the wake of McCarthy's blitz, with Eisenhower in the White House, liberal Democrats could conceive of no better response to McCarthyism than to become more "anti-Communist" than the Republicans. In 1954 I covered the United Auto Workers convention in Chicago and heard Senator Paul Douglas, in a passionate defense of Cold War policies, charge that the "anti-Communist" provisions of the McCarran Act were not nearly tough enough. That same year—the year McCarthy was condemned—the Senate agreed to a conference report on a set of vicious amendments to the McCarran Act by a vote of 79 to 0. "Liberalism," the Chicago *Daily News* commented, "in the noble and historic sense, did not have one vote in the Senate last week. The self-styled Democratic liberals could think of no answer to their detractors except to outdo them in their sponsorship of repression."[16] By then both major parties had become one on issues relating to the Cold War and the witch-hunt; both had become pawns of the national-security state.

In my log of events, 1952 marked the high point of McCarthyism. In the early months of that year, *The Nation*—largely on my initiative—tried to trigger a boom for William O. Douglas, but the effort quickly collapsed when it became clear that Truman's choice was Adlai Stevenson. Douglas would probably have fared no better against Eisenhower than Stevenson, but he might have waged a better campaign. Once Stevenson was nominated, *The Nation* endorsed him, but with no great enthusiasm. Throughout the campaign, Eisenhower was content to let McCarthy and Nixon badger the Democrats with being "soft on Communism" but in a way that implied his approval. Stevenson endorsed the Smith Act prosecutions, thought it was proper to discharge teachers tainted with heresy, and said we should continue to wage war in Korea "for as long as we have to."

In December, following the election, I had an hour's interview with Stevenson in the Governor's Mansion in Springfield and came away thinking that perhaps *The Nation* should have made no endorsement. He told me, for example, that Eisenhower's promise to go to Korea was merely a gimmick to attract votes from women. On civil rights, there was little need for legislation: anti-lynching and anti–poll-tax measures and a fact-finding FEPC-type commission would be sufficient. Nor did he reflect much concern about the witch-hunt. The night before, I had spoken at a dinner meeting in Chicago along with Harry Bridges. The Governor seemed curious about Bridges, whom it was obvious he had never met. I found it hard to believe that the nominee of the Democratic Party in the year 1952 could harbor so many misconceptions about a labor leader of Bridges' prominence or show so little interest in the long uphill struggle that West Coast longshoremen had been forced to wage to achieve an honest union controlled by the rank and file. But there was so much to admire about Stevenson as a person that one kept minimizing his limitations as a politician. So when 1956 rolled around, *The Nation* again endorsed his candidacy, largely because the state of Eisenhower's health made us mindful of the fact that Nixon was a heartbeat from the Presidency. But Stevenson's campaign that year was an embarrassment: bland, inept, and, on civil rights, shameful.

At about the time of my interview with Stevenson, President Truman, flanked by Chief Justice Vinson, took part in a Bill of Rights ceremony in Washington (December 15, 1952) that had ironic overtones. The original Bill of Rights was enclosed in a brass-bound glass receptacle from which the air had been exhausted and helium substituted. With great fanfare, the document was then lowered, like a corpse, into a twenty-foot vault, the better to protect it against the ravages of time and possible national catastrophe. The symbolism was appropriate. On a substantial list of critical issues, Truman and Vinson had done their best to entomb the Bill of Rights. Loaded with Truman appointees—Vinson, Burton, Minton, and Clark—the Vinson Court was a disaster for civil liberties; not one of the four merited appointment. If an exception be noted for Justice Whittaker, Eisenhower's appointments—Warren, Harlan, Brennan, and Stewart—were superior on all counts and notably so on issues involving the Bill of Rights. In fact, Warren's appointment as Chief Justice in October, 1953, marked a turning point in the witch-hunt and for civil rights; in effect if not in fact, the Bill of Rights was exhumed. And this too was ironic.

For if Eisenhower had known the kind of Chief Justice that Warren would turn out to be, he would not have kept his promise to name him to the first vacancy on the Court. But not even Joe McCarthy could have found much in Warren's record as district attorney, attorney general, and governor in California to criticize, so how was Eisenhower to know that, unwittingly, he had made one of his best appointments?

5. THIS NEWFANGLED TREASON

Today we have a new-fangled treason; we call it subversion. We don't imprison for it; we just make a man unemployable, an outcast.
              —CHIEF JUSTICE WALTER L. POPE,
                  Ninth Circuit Court of Appeals

McCarthyism had far more serious consequences than earlier witch-hunts. The harassment of political dissenters was carried out thoroughly, systematically, remorselessly. By 1955 a comprehensive system of "antisubversive" legislation had been enacted at every level of government. Similar mechanisms were also adopted in the private sector, first by defense industries and government contractors, then by other industries, including communications and entertainment, by licensed businesses and professions, by the trade unions, and by many civic organizations. It was bad enough when congressional committees badgered individuals about their politics, but when large corporations, such as General Electric and the Columbia Broadcasting Corporation, began to demand non-Communist affidavits and disclaimers as conditions of employment, the controls were extended to embrace virtually the entire work force and thus became more or less self-enforcing. Political prosecutions invite protests; legislative hearings sometimes result in disturbances; but blacklists operate quietly and efficiently. "The pulse of freedom," Justice Douglas told the Authors' League in December, 1952, "was never feebler. . . . The suppression comes not from fear of being jailed, but from the fear of being dismissed from employment, banned from radio work, disqualified from teaching. . . . These sanctions are effective and powerful. They often carry as much sting as a fine or a jail sentence."

In no area were "antisubversive" controls more important than in the labor movement. On May 19, 1950, the Supreme Court upheld Section 9(H) of the Taft-Hartley Act, which required officers of trade unions to file affidavits at six-month intervals that they were not Communists and did not support any organization believing in or teaching the overthrow of the government by force or illegal or unconstitutional means. What these vague and sweeping affirmations meant, in practical effect, was that officers of trade unions had better not stray off the political reservation. Thereafter organized labor was firmly attached to the corporate Establishment as a junior partner in the Cold War. No single decision had a more significant impact on the politics of the period. In it the Court ruled, for the first time, that the Communist Party was *sui generis,* a special case, outside the protection of the constitutional guarantees. In his earliest major dissent in a political case, Justice Hugo Black warned that "restrictions on prescribed groups are seldom static even though the rate of extension may not move in geometric progression from discrimination to arm band to ghetto and worse." As he saw it, the majority's decision would invite endless trouble, and it did.

More important than the actual controls imposed were the attitudes and the atmosphere they fostered. For example, a measure requiring tenants in federal housing projects to sign sworn statements that neither the tenant nor any member of his family belonged to any organization "on the list," even if not strictly enforced, could hardly fail to breed a sense of political caution and restraint. In the same way, knowledge that a huge sixth column in government and industry constantly fed—and was encouraged to feed—information about co-workers to the FBI and the committees inhibited open discussion of political issues. So, too, did the circulation of "lists" of subversives by a variety of organizations. Red Channels, Aware, Inc., the American Vigilante Intelligence Federation, Circuit Riders, Inc., and other organizations of this sort did a thriving business selling "lists." Circuit Riders, for example, distributed a six-hundred-page report on the activities of 6,000 teachers and educators who had "assisted the Communist cause," as well as a list of 9,000 clergymen suspected of political heresy. "We doubt," *The New Yorker* observed in its issue of October 4, 1952, "that there was ever a time in this country when so many people were trying to discredit so many other people. . . . Discreditation has become a national sickness for which no cure has so far been found, and there is a strong likelihood that we will wake some morning to learn that in the whole land there is not one decent man."

Jessica Mitford correctly points out that it was the local heresy hunts that did "the deadliest damage in destroying livelihoods and muzzling dissent at the grass-roots level." HUAC admitted that it had compiled dossiers on one million Americans. Not only were these dossiers available to government agencies, federal, state, and local, but other use was made of them as well. From 1949 to 1959, for example, the committee furnished data on 60,000 individuals and 12,000 organizations to inquiring employers. In addition HUAC published a "Cumulative Index" and supplement listing some 45,000 individuals and thousands of organizations mentioned in its hearings. The fact that this material was known to exist and could be consulted probably had an even greater effect in inhibiting free political expression and activity than any actual use that was made of it.[17]

Informers were a terrible scourge. If they testified before a legislative committee they could not be sued for slander, and with one exception—Harvey Matusow—I can think of no informer who was ever prosecuted for perjury. The testimony of Louis Budenz, a star informer, was refuted under oath by twenty or more well-known individuals, but the government continued to use him as a witness. Attorney General Herbert Brownell and J. Edgar Hoover vouched for Elizabeth Bentley long after she had been proven to be a clumsy and confused liar.[18] False rumors and mistaken identifications did serious damage to reputations and careers. "Clearance" rackets flourished on both coasts. In Hollywood, victims of the blacklist beat a path to the offices of certain lawyers and psychoanalysts who, for substantial fees, could arrange rites of political purification for the craven and the penitent. Lillian Ross reported in *The New Yorker* (February 21, 1948) that the kind of political self-consciousness encountered at Hollywood parties was on the whole rather cheerful. "I never cut anybody before this," one actress remarked. "Now I don't go anywhere without cutting at least half a dozen former friends." John Huston told Ross he had been forced to drop the line "Gold, Mister, is worth what it is because of the human labor that goes into the finding and getting of it" from a script: it was thought to be subversive. Networks refused to present *The Male Animal* because one of the characters in the film reads a letter of Bartolomeo Vanzetti.[19] In Bloomington, Indiana, patriotic groups tried to force the removal of a book about Robin Hood from the local library because it sounded "socialistic." In Ohio, the Motor Vehicle Department refused to renew the license of a local resident who had once been a Communist; a *Nation* editorial brought about a reversal of this decision. In Miami, an ordinance was enacted requiring Communist Party members to register with the authorities if they stayed in the city for more than forty hours (why precisely forty hours?).

Many aspects of the witch-hunt have never been properly documented. Unknown is the number of Americans who were required to sign non-Communist affidavits or disclaimers or were investigated with or without their knowledge because of their political beliefs and activities. In 1955 Ben Bagdikian estimated that one out of every ten American adults had been investigated for loyalty, ideas, and associations. Some twenty million were given security clearances, 3.5 million in defense industries alone. Even if the clearances were more or less perfunctory, the non-Communist affidavits remained on file, and the oath-takers did not need to be reminded of this fact. And we do not know the number of individuals who lived for years in fear of being hailed before one or another of the federal and state inquisitorial committees but were in fact never called. Nor do we know the number who either resigned employment rather than face investigation and possible public interrogation or were eased out of their jobs or actually forced to resign.

Nor do we know the number of cases similar to that of Eugene W. Landy, an honor graduate at the U.S. Merchant Marine Academy who was dismissed because his mother had once been a Communist. Unknown also is the number who took up residence abroad to avoid political harassment, as Charles Chaplin did in 1952, or the grand total of political deportations. Nor do we know the number of involuntary exiles. As an undergraduate at Harvard and later at the Yale Medical School, Dr. Joseph H. Cort was a member of the Communist Party. While on a fellowship in England he was informed that his passport had been revoked, and he was ordered to return. When he refused he was drafted, and later he was indicted when he failed to report for preinduction examination because he feared he might be prosecuted as a subversive. Ousted from Britain, he went to Prague, where, at the Czech Academy of Science, he engaged in important medical research of great current interest to American scientists. Leonard Boudin finally got the draft indictment dismissed, and now, after more than two decades of exile, Dr. Cort is continuing his research at Mt. Sinai Hospital in New York.[20] Any number of similar cases might be cited. Nor has anyone estimated the number of suicides attributed to the witch-hunt or the number of individuals who, for varying periods of time, were "graylisted" or blacklisted.

Formal government "clearance" procedures were farcical. Dr. Edward U. Condon finally felt compelled to resign as director of research at the Corning Glass Company after four clearances failed to stop the harassment to which he had been subjected. John Paton Davies, Jr., was tried nine times on loyalty charges and then cashiered after twenty-three years of honorable service with the State Department. John S. Service was cleared six or seven times by the State Department Loyalty Review Board and then fired on his eighth attempt to win vindication. John Carter Vincent, another

State Department officer, was cleared three times and then eased out.

A major consequence of McCarthyism was the imposition of a nationwide integrated system of indirect controls that, without formal censorship or blanket suppression, restricted free debate on critical issues relating to the Cold War. Dissent was never wholly suppressed even on these issues, and the number of persons arrested, cited for contempt, or jailed was minimal by police-state standards; but after 1950 certain thoughts became "unthinkable," certain positions untenable, certain issues nondebatable. At the time, some of my friends and associates thought we were on the threshold of fascism, but I never did. European-style fascism could not have been imposed, nor was it needed. The controls invoked were quite adequate to minimize opposition to the Cold War consensus. Claude Bourdet once pointed out in *The Nation* (December 12, 1953) that this country had opted for what he called "demo fascism," in which normal democratic procedures were tolerated so long as "the accepted truth," that is, the dogmas and assumptions on which Cold War policies rested, was not questioned. Everyone was quite "free" to remain silent or to speak on other matters or to affirm the official Cold War line, but to question it was to invite trouble. It was remarkable how quickly, in the atmosphere that McCarthyism had created, people got the point and went along with "the accepted truth."

Indeed, the most shameful aspect of the "plague" was not so much the overt intimidation—hearings, purges, blacklists—as the expediency which made the system work as well as it did as long as it did. As Dalton Trumbo wrote,

> The terrible thing that happened to us during the oathing 1950s is that we have been so strongly engaged in swearing what we aren't that we have altogether forgotten what we actually are. The fevers of the Cold War have not only left us without a sense of identity but have also robbed us of our original sense of moral purpose. Thus, decent men and women, persons with intelligence and good will and high aspirations, having submitted to the expediency of the negative oath, have been compelled to accept expediency as a way of life.[21]

Equally shameful was the way the federal government harassed individual critics of Cold War policies. In May, 1952, Dr. Linus Pauling was denied a passport to attend a scientific symposium in London because of his outspokenness on issues related to the Cold

War. Two years later he was invited by Nehru to dedicate a new scientific laboratory in India and was also invited to lecture at the University of Athens and at the Weizmann Institute. He was told there would be some delay when he applied for a passport. Eventually he was forced to cancel the invitations after spending a month's time and nearly two thousand dollars in an unsuccessful effort to obtain a passport. Later that same year—1954—when he was awarded the Nobel Prize in Chemistry, he was able to obtain a passport after some initial hassling, but the Voice of America was forbidden to mention his name. And as late as June 21, 1960, he was hauled before the Senate Judiciary Committee and badgered about his views and public statements. Harry Kalven, Jr., of the University of Chicago Law School, found the hearings "wasteful, hypocritical, and offensive" and pointed to "the thin line that separates the ludicrous from the sinister." The hearings were indeed ludicrous, but they were also sinister, for, as Kalven noted, they represented "an expression of the *official* climate of opinion, of the *official* sense [my emphasis] of the fair use of government power in the United States in the year 1960"²²—six years after the condemnation of McCarthy. Yet because of Dr. Pauling's antiwar activities, Presidents Kennedy, Johnson, and Nixon ignored recommendations from the scientific community that he be given the National Medal of Science. For this honor he had to wait until September 19, 1975, when President Ford presented it to him as part of the new "mood of conciliation" which had by then invaded the White House.

The press was always quick to criticize Soviet methods of dealing with dissenters but often failed to protest when similar methods were invoked here. In its issue of March 15, 1958, *The Nation* carried an article by Ernest J. Simmons on the writings of Boris Pasternak which was accompanied by an editorial in which we urged that he should be nominated for the Nobel Prize in Literature. Later, when Pasternak was nominated, *Literaturnaya Gazeta* (October 25, 1958) took note of the article and the editorial and said that it was not "until the American *Nation* suggested that Mr. Pasternak be awarded the Nobel Prize that Western critics took him seriously."²³ And there was some truth to this report. But once the Soviet authorities forced Pasternak to reject the award, the American press joined in denouncing the action. Yet only a few newspapers took exception to the treatment accorded Dr. Pauling.

By transforming "the issue of Communist subversion into a shibboleth of domestic political alignment," as Godfrey Hodgson has pointed out, McCarthyism froze American policy into a pattern of "moronic rigidity."²⁴ "Anti-Communist" policies and programs were rubber-stamped, not debated; alternative policies were not considered. Not until the Vietnam crisis broke in 1965 did the liberal Democrats voice much opposition to the war.

One of the worst consequences of McCarthyism, in fact, was the distortion it worked in the party system. Without an independent "left" or any significant opposition within or between the two major parties on Cold War issues, the center of gravity shifted steadily to the right. A few liberal Democrats did speak out against aspects of McCarthyism, but, as Hodgson notes, "the lesson the Democrats drew was that never again could they afford to expose their foreign policy to the charge that it was soft on communism." Actually it was the impact of McCarthyism on politicians, principally the liberal Democrats, rather than on the electorate as reflected in congressional elections, that produced the distortion in the party system. Bipartisan adherence to "anti-Communist" dogmas buttressed the Imperial Presidency and kept us bogged down in Vietnam for a quarter of a century (not to mention other disastrously misconceived policies and programs). And there were other consequences as well. Not to debate foreign policy is to stack the cards, to narrow the options, and to dictate choices on domestic issues. What commentators now refer to as "the end of liberalism" dates from the triumph of the Cold War consensus. McCarthyism also had a baneful influence on aspects of American intellectual life. In a word, as Hodgson emphasizes, the overall effect of McCarthyism is to be measured not "only in individual careers destroyed but (more significantly for the nation as a whole) in assumptions unchallenged, in questions unasked, in problems ignored for a decade."[25]

"A successful seditionist," David Marquand once wrote in the Manchester *Guardian*, "must believe in his seditions; McCarthy believed in nothing—not even in his own lies." He was not a gifted rabble-rouser as were Huey Long and Father Coughlin. His talent, such as it was, consisted in the skill and daring with which he manipulated the media. He had no sense of strategy or tactics. A Catholic, he gave great offense to Jews and Protestants. A junior in the Senate, he maligned the senior leadership of both parties. He had no sense of organization. He never really tried to transform his large national following into a coherent movement. A fortune came his way in the form of cash gifts and contributions, but instead of using it to build a movement, he spent most of it on soybean futures and large bets on slow horses at Belmont and Pimlico. And his final folly, of course, was his attack on the Republican Secretary of State and the Army brass. Even so, he had an extraordinary influence on American politics and was largely responsible for consolidating the Cold War consensus.

Eisenhower had hardly been installed in the White House before the Republicans began to have trouble with McCarthy. He could not be programmed; he would not accept discipline. In turn Herbert Brownell, John Foster Dulles, Nixon, William Rogers, and Eisenhower sought to reason with him, but he would not listen. So when he began to attack the Army and take potshots at Eisenhower and Chief Justice Earl Warren, the leadership decided to dump him, the better to preserve McCarthyism. McCarthy was personally vulnerable and could be safely discarded, but only the man, not the ism, was condemned.

The vote on the Senate resolution condemning McCarthy was cunningly delayed until after the November election, but was finally approved on December 2, 1954. The resolution was one of the rare instances, as I. F. Stone noted, when the conservatives of the Senate acted as one had a right to expect them to act on an issue of this kind. Senator Ralph Flanders, a New England conservative, showed rare courage in pressing the charges. The members of the select committee were old-fashioned conservatives from some of the less populous states: Arthur V. Watkins and Wallace F. Bennett of Utah, John C. Stennis of Mississippi, Frank Carlson of Kansas, Francis Case of South Dakota, Sam Ervin of North Carolina. Lyndon Johnson was, of course, responsible for their selection, and his stage management of the proceedings was brilliant. He kept a tight rein on the Democrats during the debate, thus pitting Republicans against Republicans; but when the roll call came, not one Democrat voted against the resolution. Thus almost before he knew what had happened, McCarthy was condemned, isolated, and put down. What surprised everyone was the swiftness with which his apparent power had collapsed; once the bipartisan Cold War coalition which he had helped forge turned against him, he was through. Almost overnight he was defanged. He lost the power to dominate the headlines almost as suddenly as he had acquired it. No one any longer cared what he said or did. There was even something rather pathetic about his last days; he never seemed to realize what had hit him. Eisenhower snubbed him; he was the one member of Congress not invited to a White House function in 1955. And two years later—May 2, 1957—he was dead. But his name had become an eponym in *Webster's International Dictionary*, where McCarthyism is defined as the "use of indiscriminate, often unfounded, accusations, sensationalism, inquisitorial investigative methods, etc., ostensibly in the suppression of Communism." Here the operative word is "ostensibly."

By the summer of 1955 the liberal press—elated by the vote on the resolution of condemnation—was proclaiming "the twilight of McCarthyism." *The Nation* did not share this optimistic view.[26] In the short term the damage was irreparable, and it is not possible even yet to assess the long-term consequences. With the death of Stalin, the cease-fire in Korea, and Warren's appointment as Chief Justice, some of the hysteria abated, but McCarthyism remained a major force in American politics. The apparatus of the witch-hunt was not dismantled; loyalty screening and testing continued; no files or dossiers were destroyed. The liberal Democrats, or most of them, still toed the line. On April 12, 1954, the investigation of charges against J. Robert Oppenheimer got under way just as the Army–McCarthy hearings were about to open. As "the father of the bomb," Oppenheimer might have been expected to enjoy a degree of immunity from slanders of the type leveled against him, but the committee voted four to one against his reinstatement and the press was nearly unanimous in its approval. The fact is that McCarthyism long survived McCarthy's condemnation and his death. We seem to have forgotten that the radical-right movement which led to Barry Goldwater's nomination in 1964 dates from the condemnation of McCarthy and that the decision to escalate the war in Vietnam was taken nearly a decade after his death.

6. COLD WAR CASUALTIES

Any number of excellent books by a new generation of historians, political scientists, and journalists have been published of recent years about the witch-hunt that began in 1945. But most of them fail to convey—how could they?—the emotional feel of the times or how particular events affected a person's outlook and "politics." It is one thing to comment objectively on a suicide or personal tragedy as an incident in a larger pattern of events; perhaps that is the way it should be seen in retrospect. But it is a different matter if the tragedy was observed at close range and thus became part of one's own experience. Four friends of mine, F. O. Matthiessen, Louis Adamic, Albert Dekker, and Edgar Snow, were, in a very real sense, Cold War casualties; three were suicides. Knowing how their lives were affected by the political passions of the period formed an important part of my "education." What I remember most vividly about McCarthyism are these personal tragedies, not the shouting and the headlines; these have faded but not my feelings about what happened to these friends. The experience made me realize that the witch-hunt involved more than a bitter political hassle with ideological overtones; that it was actually a kind of domestic civic war with extended, if often unpublicized, casualties. In fact, I was forced to conclude that a national—an American—tragedy was implicit in what happened to these four friends.

Death of a Scholar

A suicide is not a simple death, bringing peace with it. It haunts; it asks a question.
　　　　　　　　　　　　—MAY SARTON, *Faithful Are the Wounds* (1955)

I first met F. O. Matthiessen in the early 1940s on a lecture junket to Cambridge. Later I would see him on trips to Boston; and when he came to the West Coast, as he did nearly every year, he always spent some time with us. My wife and I came to think of him not as an intimate friend—I doubt that he had many intimate friends—but as a guest we were always delighted to have in our home. We had many mutual friends; we viewed politics from somewhat the same perspective; and we shared an enthusiasm for many of the same California scenes and landscapes. Few books of the period made a deeper impression on me than *American Renaissance* (1941), which confirmed and strengthened my attachment to the indigenous American democratic-radical tradition. I also greatly admired his study of Theodore Dreiser, particularly the long chapter "The Business Novel."

Of my memories of Matty none is more vivid than the last time he was our guest in Los Angeles, which, as I recall, was in the late summer or early fall of 1949. Politically it was a bad year for those on the left (the worst, in the view of Arthur Miller). Of it the narrator in May Sarton's novel based on Matty's life comments, "We're all as nervous as cats . . . it's become a crime to subscribe to *The Nation*." I sensed immediately that something was wrong; this was not the Matty we had come to know so well. That afternoon and evening proved to be a painful experience. He seemed terrified by thoughts he was unable or unwilling to voice. He wasn't really listening to anything we said, yet he seemed reluctant to leave. Long after midnight I drove him out to Santa Monica, where he was staying, but found it virtually impossible to get a word out of him. In the past we would have been rapping about politics and the state of the world the entire time, but not this night. When we got to his beach hotel, he sat quite still in the car for several minutes. Finally I said, "Matty, tell me, what's the trouble? What's bothering you? Are you ill?" He gave me a very thin smile, shook his head, and got out of the car.

Neither my wife nor I was greatly surprised when we read that he had leaped to his death from a twelfth-floor room in the Hotel Manger in Boston on April 1, 1950. I have never been in the presence of a person in a more tormented frame of mind than he was on the occasion of that last visit. A note left in his hotel room said that he did not know how much the state of the world had to do with his state of mind but added: "As a Christian and a Socialist believing in international peace, I find myself terribly oppressed by the present tensions." No doubt his depression was complicated by personal factors, but the vituperation, slander, and abuse directed at him, particularly by certain faculty colleagues at Harvard, on his return from a year in Prague had cut him to the quick and contributed to his sense of isolation. This much he told me. However grievous his personal "wounds" may have been, they were not the only cause of his wretched state of mind. Apart from the Cold War and the witch-hunt, I would agree with Leo Marx that Matty's final depression was deepened "by painful recognition that the world of righteous respectability, the tough official downtown America which Dreiser recreated, was every day more firmly in power and would demand an even more absolute conformity."[27]

After Spain and Munich, Matty found it difficult to believe that Britain and France could ever be counted on to resist Nazi aggression, but his attitude changed when the Nazis moved eastward. Although a pacifist by inclination—he never ceased to believe that war was the greatest catastrophe that could overtake a society—he sought to enlist in the Marine Corps after Pearl Harbor but was rejected. Active in Progressive Citizens of America and the National Citizens Political Action Committee, he seconded the nomination of Henry Wallace at the Progressive Party convention in 1948. He was, I feel, a classic example of the intellectual of "unshielded sensibility" caught in the vicious ideological and political crosscurrents of a turbulent time. For natures as sensitive and complex as his, a succession of defeats, as his friend Ernest J. Simmons pointed out, "can obliterate all the roads back and leave one a lonely island in a sea of despair."[28] To Barrows Dunham, the Cold War had claimed its first "martyr among scholars" with Matthiessen's death. "One cannot feel more helpless," he wrote, "than in a place and a time when slander settles everything."[29]

Edward, the name May Sarton gave the central character in her novel, was a person driven by keen intellect and sensitive conscience to become a political activist, a role for which he was not fitted because of his uncompromising beliefs and strong moral convictions. At one point Edward exclaims, "I feel locked in, locked up, stifled." But there seemed to be no means of escape without appearing to repudiate positions he had taken in which he still believed and principles he had affirmed to which he was still committed. So his isolation became total. As the narrator comments, "There have to be absolute people," guardians of conscience, but theirs is seldom a happy lot. Intellectuals cannot avoid involvement in politics in a time of crisis, but their primary concern should be with values, not with the business of politics. "The effect in politics of the pure intellectual," as Conor Cruise O'Brien has written of Simon Weil, "is normally exerted through the impure intellectuals, the only kind that that domain will tolerate. Save in exceptional circumstances, the pure intellectual can only, in consequence, be a small influence indirect, filtered, and perhaps distorted." [30]

Matty may not have been the first martyr among American scholars, but that he was a casualty of Cold War tensions I am quite sure. He had become convinced that the native American democratic-radical tradition with which he identified had been eclipsed by the kind of society that emerged during and after World War II. While I shared many of his political beliefs, I had some reservations about this one, perhaps because I was not a "pure" intellectual in the sense that he was and also because I had had a longer and more active involvement in politics. But knowing him infused my brand of radicalism with valuable historical and cultural insights. "It is appalling," he once said, "how much can get left out of an American education." A great deal had been left out of mine, which is why knowing him was for me a memorable experience.

Death of an Immigrant

Leaving *The Nation*'s office for lunch on September 4, 1951, I stared in utter dismay at a headline in the New York *Post*: "Louis Adamic Found Shot in Blazing Home." The story went on to say that Adamic had been found dead that morning in his farm home near Milford, New Jersey, "under mysterious circumstances." His body had been discovered in an upstairs bedroom with a bullet hole above his right ear and a .22-caliber rifle across his knees. After some frenetic telephoning, I located his wife, Stella, and arranged to meet her in Milford. By the time I arrived the place was swarming with police and reporters, but I did manage to have a long talk with her. The next day I was interviewed at length on WCBS about Adamic, whom I had known for many years.

It was George Sterling who had suggested to Louis that he should look me up, since we both lived in Los Angeles. Louis was employed at the time in the pilot station office located on the breakwater at the entrance to San Pedro Harbor. Born in Slovenia in 1898, Louis had passed through Ellis Island in 1913, taken up residence in New York with relatives, and gotten a job on a Slovenian-language newspaper. In December, 1916, he enlisted in the Army and served in Panama, Hawaii, Louisiana, and California. When he left the service in January, 1923, he settled in San Pedro, which had a small Yugoslav fishing colony. From our first meeting on September 11, 1926, until Louis moved to New York in 1929, we spent much time together, exploring Los Angeles and Southern California and going on numberless junkets up and down the state. Both ardent Mencken fans, we wrote for *The American Mercury*, read and discussed many of the same books and periodicals, and shared a great number of interests. For one thing, we had come to live in Southern California at about the same time and never tired of comparing notes about it. While our backgrounds could hardly have been more dissimilar, we became close friends. We were both Americana enthusiasts and yet, in different ways, felt alienated from the mainstream of American life in the 1920s. Rebels but not yet radicals, we were wary of being caught up in what Louis called "the turbulent, superficial, temporary, non-essential America" which we endlessly discussed but could never quite accept on its own terms. Being foreign-born, Louis could take a somewhat more objective view than I, but I shared his estrangement from many aspects of the current scene, much as they fascinated me.

High-strung and extremely sensitive, Louis had a magnificent sense of humor, of the robust peasant variety; I have never known anyone who laughed more or whose laughter was more infectious. He was intensely interested in people; to him every American, without exception, was a story. His enthusiasms were boundless, his interests far-ranging, his social perceptions acute. What drew us together more than anything else was my interest in his view of America and the American experience, which both influenced and, to some extent, reflected my own. His novel *Grandsons* (1933), in which he developed his intriguing concept of a "shadow America," is dedicated to me and with good reason, for we had spent many hours discussing the main theme. In fact, I wrote a long essay, *Louis Adamic and Shadow America* (published in 1935 in a limited edition by one of Southern California's fine printers), in which the theme and its implications are analyzed.

After Louis left California, we continued to see each other at frequent intervals, in New York, at the Mountain View Farm near Milford which he acquired in 1937, and on his trips to the West Coast. When I first knew him, Louis carefully avoided direct political involvements. As he put it, he did not want "to plunge too far into the economic and social issues of American life. One is too apt to be caught up in their ramifications, overwhelmed and crushed, without beneficial results to anyone"—a prophetic insight in view of what later happened. But by 1931 he was writing in the New York *Sun* that "what was amusing in 1923 is no longer funny. . . . There probably won't be any more pleasantly cynical laughter for some time. We are living in a serious, tragic period." Even earlier he had written me (September 10, 1930): "The more I see of America the less I think it is a land of laughs." As the decade unfolded, his political involvements steadily increased. With its emergence he became a partisan of Tito's regime in Yugoslavia. In 1948 he served as vice-chairman of Progressive Citizens of America, and in the 1949, 1950, and 1951 reports of the California Un-American Activities Committee he was tagged as "pro-Communist," meaning that he had become active in left-liberal politics. At the time of his death a clipping was found in his wallet with the headline "Adamic Red Spy: Woman Charges." The woman was Elizabeth Bentley. She, of course, knew nothing about Louis, and the charge was pure slander but hateful and damaging.

By 1950 a combination of political and personal pressures with which he was not prepared to cope began to converge on Louis. Winston Churchill had filed a libel action against him and his publishers which proved costly and embarrassing but was essentially a tempest in a teapot. Also, tensions began to develop in his marriage. While in Yugoslavia gathering material for his last book he learned that Stella was seriously ill, and on returning in June, 1949, he hurried to join her in California, where she was recuperating. A reconciliation of a sort was worked out, but the marriage was never quite the same. One of the last times we saw them was in January, 1951, shortly before I left to come to New York. Both were extremely tense and ill at ease. This was not the Louis we had known. Obviously exhausted, he had divided the day and the night into three work shifts, one of which extended from midnight to dawn. He had seen few of his old friends and did not want to see them. He did not laugh once, which was truly alarming. He was greatly disturbed about the witch-hunt and bitterly disappointed that there was so little opposition to it. He was also profoundly concerned about the intensification of the Cold War and "the big fix," the corruption that seemed to be spreading through all levels of American life.[31]

I was of course deeply shocked to learn of Louis's death, but I was not entirely surprised. As with Matthiessen, personal and political tensions had fused in a way that proved to be unendurable. In none of the talks I had with Stella—she survived Louis by a decade—did she suggest that his death was not self-inflicted; quite the contrary. But some close friends were not convinced. Jess Gitt, publisher of the *York Gazette and Daily* was one; Representative John Blatnik was another. Louis had received a number of threatening letters and messages from Croatian nationalists because of his pro-Tito views. But there was only one contemporary report of his death that gave me pause: a story by Henry Beckett in the New York *Post* of September 20, 1951, which called attention to some odd details and unexplained discrepancies in the first news reports. In 1976, through the courtesy of Simon Bourgin, I saw for the first time a detailed report by *Time*'s stringer in northern New Jersey, dated September 9, 1951—never published—which raised a number of significant unanswered questions. But my feeling is still the same as Stella's: that he had surrendered so much of himself, over a period of time, to the passion of politics, that he found it impossible to go forward with his work; life had closed in on him much as it had on Matthiessen.

Louis Adamic was an important influence in my thinking about racial and ethnic minorities and the problem of "identities" in American society, which is what he was getting at in his concept of "shadow America." Someday, when Henry A. Christian finally completes his biography of Louis, a new generation will be able to appreciate his remarkable contributions to the American immigration saga, its meaning and consequences. In his books and articles and lectures and through his editorship of *Common Ground* (from 1940 to 1949), he did more to call attention to ethnic values and dramatize what he called "the secondary consequences" of immigration than any other American of his time. Whatever conclusions are ultimately reached about his death, whether it was suicide or murder, there can be little doubt that he found himself imprisoned in Cold War pressures in a way that made it difficult for him to see a clear path to the future. Stella and Timothy Seldes, his editor at Doubleday, completed the final draft of his last book, *The Eagle and the Roots,* which was published in 1952. It ends on a note of uncertainty. Was a new birth of freedom possible?

> Hardly. That was utopianism cried the self-styled Marxists and the hysterical "private enterprise" voices in unison. But, *if* it didn't occur— *If* it occurred, it would have to begin to occur everywhere: within the roaring Industrial Revolution in America, in scarcely developed Yugoslavia, in Russia too—but how? How? [Emphasis in the original.]

The agony of the last months of his life is implicit in that question.

Death of an Actor

I came to know Albert Dekker shortly after he arrived in Hollywood from New York in 1937 or 1938. The Dekkers—"Van," as
Albert was always known to us, Esther, and their children—became
close family friends. A six-foot-two, 220-pound bear of a man,
Dekker was a marvelous companion, an always genial host. I have
never known anyone quite so "full of life." He was a most popular
figure in Hollywood circles, left, right, and center; it was difficult
not to like him. Before coming to Hollywood he had appeared in
a dozen or more Broadway plays after making his debut in 1927.
In all, he appeared in some thirty Hollywood films, and after his
return to the stage he starred in *Death of a Salesman* (after Lee Cobb
bowed out of the leading role), *The Andersonville Trial, A Man for
All Seasons,* and other plays and television productions here and in
London.

In 1944 the Hollywood Democratic Committee induced Dekker
to run for the State Assembly from the Fifty-seventh District and
he was elected by a margin of 6,500 votes, in the same election in
which Helen Gahagan Douglas won a seat in Congress; her
congressional district embraced his assembly district. He was the
first Hollywood actor to be elected to state office and, with Mrs.
Douglas, one of the first to enter politics, perhaps charting the way
for George Murphy and Ronald Reagan. Van liked politics, had a
talent for it, and made an excellent record in the state legislature.
But he had never intended to make politics a career, and each six-
month session during the two years he served in Sacramento cost
him more than fifty thousand dollars in lost Hollywood earnings.

Even before his first term expired, his views—and his prominence as a Hollywood actor—had made him a target for demagogues and red-baiters. Also, he had taken part in a number of
nationwide radio programs including one on "Communism in Hollywood" which, coupled with his liberal voting record, had drawn
fire from "anti-Communist" columnists and kindred types. Dekker
was never a member of the Communist Party any more than Matthiessen or Adamic had been members, and his "popular front"
identifications were neither numerous nor significant. He was active in the Democrats-for-Wallace movement but resigned from
Progressive Citizens of America when I did, once Wallace decided
to run on a third-party ticket. In the atmosphere that prevailed
after 1948, he soon found that he was not getting the number and
kinds of roles he had formerly been pressed to accept. In 1949 the
California Un-American Activities Committee named him in its

annual report, and his serious troubles began. A piece I wrote for *The Nation,* "The Hollywood Gray List" (November 19, 1949), dealt with cases such as his, of Hollywood figures who were never black-listed or called before the committees but lived and functioned in the shadow of the blacklist. Indeed, I had Van in mind when I wrote the piece; I had spent hours listening to him describe the baffling, elusive, unreal situation which he and others on the "gray list" then faced.

In an effort to escape from being a kind of "dangling man" in Hollywood—not blacklisted and yet not regularly employed—Dekker decided to return to New York in 1950. But by then the same blight had spread to the theater. There were "incidents" on road trips, in Peoria, in Syracuse, in Dallas. In effect the Hollywood experience was repeated; he found himself in the position of being a part-time actor, confined to a kind of theatrical limbo. Pride did not keep him from talking to those who were supposed to have the "connections" and the power to deal with such situations. He spoke to Jay Lovestone, Roy Brewer, and other "anti-Communists" who had close contacts with the inquisitorial committees. But since he would not compromise his principles, there was little they could do for him. So for a period of perhaps fifteen years he kept battling a form of "graylisting" that had a crippling effect on his career. Between the occasional roles that came his way, he appeared in nightclubs, gave solo performances and readings, and kept knocking on doors. This can be—at least it was for him—an utterly demoralizing experience. Zero Mostel, once blacklisted, could spend more time painting and, eventually, was given some fine roles on the stage which he probably would not have accepted had he remained in Hollywood; he survived fairly well, as did some of the other blacklistees. In some respects graylisting was a worse form of punishment for equally imaginary offenses, since the victims never knew whether they were in or out of Hollywood, or on or off the stage.

Like Matthiessen and Adamic, Dekker had personal problems which stemmed in large part from his political difficulties. But, like them, he was truly a casualty of the Cold War and the witch-hunt. On May 6, 1968, he was found dead in Hollywood, a suicide. I had watched this political-personal tragedy unfold; in fact, I felt very much a part of it. The caption on the New York *Times* obituary summed it up: "On and Off the Shelf." For fifteen years or longer his career had been just that: on again, off again, never terminated, never given a chance to go forward—a baffling, unnerving, surreal experience for him and for his family. Even after he returned to the stage and scored some major successes, the partial ban was never lifted. On one occasion he sought the advice and help of Arnold Forster of the Anti-Defamation League. Forster recalls that "he thrashed around the office, a bull of a man, growing more furious all the time. Finally, he just said, 'Fuck 'em! I *won't* compromise. I won't give in, I'll wait them out. I'll lecture. I'll go on one-man tours, but I won't *crawl* to those bastards. Never!' "[32] And he never did. To observe a personal-political tragedy of this kind at close range, as it unfolds over a period of years, is to acquire the perspective of the victim, to feel as he felt; latter-day investigators, no matter how sympathetic, can never fully share this feeling.

The "Exile" of Edgar Snow

Blacklisting in the 1950s took different forms. Some journalists, for example, found themselves blacklisted in the sense that publications which had long used their work suddenly decided not to— "for the time being" or "until pressures ease up a bit." In some cases they were blacklisted for reasons that had nothing whatever to do with political activities or affiliations. Consider, as a case in point, the "exile" of Edgar Snow.

Red Star Over China (1932) was the first and best contemporary account of the Chinese Revolution to be published in this country. No American journalist had better sources of information inside China or knew more about the revolution or enjoyed more cordial relations with the Chinese Communist leaders. But Ed was not a "left" journalist or ideologue. He wrote for mass-circulation magazines. He had been an associate editor of *The Saturday Evening Post.* He had reported brilliantly from China, the Soviet Union, India, and Southeast Asia. A large reading public had confidence in his work; he had enjoyed the respect and friendship of Roosevelt and top officials in Washington. Yet for nearly twenty years he was kept on the sidelines during a critically important period in this country's relations with China when his reports would have been invaluable. During these years—roughly from the late 1940s to the middle 1960s—the market for his work shrank in this country to a handful of publications, of which *The Nation* was one. Ironically, it was the triumph of the Chinese Revolution, which he had predicted, that made him unpublishable in the mass media.

Ed and I had become friends in California, and I saw a great deal of him in New York in the years from 1951 to 1959, before he moved to Switzerland, and on each of his subsequent return visits. *The Nation* made good use of his talents; we published him as often as possible. But the editorial budget made it impossible for me to send him to China, Russia, or India, which was a major disappoint-

ment for both of us. But of all the fine journalists the blacklist
turned our way, Ed was the prize catch. (One of his pieces, "Nationalism–Colonialism: The New Challenge," won a top prize in
the second National Mayers' Peace Competition.) That such a
gifted journalist, with such unique insights and experience, should
have felt compelled, as he did, to join a year-long world "study
abroad" safari of high-school students in 1959–60 is a sad commentary on the know-nothingism which then beset the American
press, the academic world, and official circles in Washington. Of all
persons, James Reston referred to Ed in a front-page piece in the
New York *Times* as being part of a "mixed bag of Communists and
liberals," a grotesque statement for which he later apologized, but
the damage had been done. Equally grotesque was the blacklisting
of Lois Snow, a fine actress, whose career was blighted by an idiotic
and utterly erroneous reference which had crept into the files of a
blacklisting agency.

I never ceased to marvel at the philosophical way in which Ed
put up with the unpleasant consequences the tacit blacklist had
imposed. After he moved to Switzerland, his writings were more
widely published, but by then his life was nearly over. Fortunately
he was finally able to revisit China, in 1960, 1965, and 1970. Yet
when he returned from China in 1960, Dean Rusk was too busy to
see him or had only a few minutes to spare. It was a hint dropped
by Chou En-lai on Ed's last trip that "the door was open" which
resulted in Kissinger's initial visit to Peking. Nothing could be sad-
der or more ironic than the fact that Ed should have passed away
on February 14, 1972, just as Nixon was preparing to leave for
China. At least someone in the President's entourage had the tact
to prompt Nixon to send a letter of condolence to Lois. Ed was
scheduled to have preceded the President's party to Peking as correspondent for *Life,* which after twenty years of thumb-sucking
had decided it was again safe to make use of his remarkable talents
and unique credentials. As John Service wrote Lois:

> Ed would certainly have savored the historical significance (and
> irony, after all that had happened in the past twenty-three
> years) of an American President shaking hands with Mao Tse-
> tung and Chou En-lai. But what could be done with a "corre-
> spondent" who was much more than that, who was really a
> ghost at the banquet? How could he be expected to be one of
> the horde of confused and frustrated news and television men,
> watching from afar and gleaning little? He could hardly be a
> member of the President's party (though that might be fitting).
> And his presence could only have posed awkward problems

for the innate courtesy of his old (and very important) Chinese
friends.[33]

Nor was Edgar Snow the only American journalist to be caught
in "the twenty years of treason" hoax which, as he once pointed
out, resulted in twenty years of folly. Anna Louise Strong was
another. Gallant, courageous, generous, Anna Louise was an en-
thusiast turned journalist; she was a kind of grandmotherly anar-
chist with missionary impulses. All the same, she deserved fairer
treatment from both this country and the Soviet Union than she
received. In the late 1930s I drove her from San Francisco to
Sacramento one night—we were good friends—and spent most of
the time trying to convince her that the newly elected Governor
Culbert L. Olson was neither Franklin D. Roosevelt nor yet Mao
Tse-tung!

Agnes Smedley, another friend, was a very different type. I first
met her in Los Angeles in the early 1940s. She had just returned
from China and was ill, frustrated (no assignments, no outlets),
exhausted, dead broke, but defiant and determined to carry on.
She and Edgar Snow had succeeded in "writing their way" to China
in 1928 and had remained good friends. Her books *Chinese Destinies, China's Red Army Marches,* and *China Fights Back,* all published
in the 1930s, provided important insights into the Chinese Revolution. But on February 10, 1949—that meanest of years—the
Pentagon made public a 32,000-page report in which she was
named as a "Comintern agent." She promptly denied the accusation and demanded an apology; eight days later the Army admitted
that it had no proof to back the charge. But the widely publicized
smear did not make it any easier for her to find a market for her
writings. She died in England at age fifty-six, on May 8, 1950, the
same year she went there to live as an "exile" from America. A
remarkable woman. By exceptional courage and iron determination, she had managed to liberate herself from a life of brutal
poverty and cruel cultural deprivation. *Daughter of Earth* (1929),
her autobiography, is an American testament of rare moral courage and social insight.

To a degree, Edgar Snow, Anna Louise Strong, Agnes Smedley,
and Owen Lattimore became victims of "the deadly aberration of
McCarthyism" because they had become China symbols and, as
such, infuriated the demagogues who had succeeded in commit-
ting this country to a disastrously mistaken China policy. The true
object of propaganda, as Leonard Schapiro once pointed out, is
neither to convince nor to persuade but to produce a uniform
pattern of utterances in which the first trace of unorthodox

thought immediately reveals itself as a jarring dissonance. The propaganda of the Chinese Nationalists and the China Lobby in this country succeeded brilliantly in achieving this objective. Until it finally lifted, the fog of propaganda was impenetrable. I once calculated that in the 1950s alone *The Nation* had published seventy or more articles and editorials pointing out fallacies, misconceptions, and false assumptions in this country's China policy. One of the first and best of these articles was by Edgar Snow—"What We Could Do About Asia" (January 28, 1950)—but the list also included pieces by Howard K. Smith, Harold R. Isaacs, Owen Lattimore, Joan Robinson, Aneurin Bevan, V. K. V. R. Rao, Mark Gayn, Nathaniel Peffer, O. E. Clubb, many articles by Snow, and excellent reports from the Australians W. Macmahon Ball (who served as Australia's ambassador in Tokyo) and C. P. Fitzgerald, both of whom I recruited as contributing editors. But until the pall of Cold War propaganda began to be dissipated by events, opinion leaders (so-called) and decision-makers marched in lockstep. At times it seemed the State Department was afraid of the truth; in 1960, for example, it tried to suppress publication of Ross Y. Koen's *The China Lobby in American Politics.* Townsend W. Hoopes has revealed how, after the Tet offensive of February, 1968, the secret doubters and silent dissenters began to emerge from official bureaucratic closets in Washington; then and only then did they learn who the other doubters and dissenters were and when each of them had "fallen off the boat."

In retrospect it is easy—even tempting—to minimize the consequences of McCarthyism. At its worst, the "terror" was livable; most of the victims survived; not too many went to jail; not all those "fingered" lost their jobs. Some actually did better on "the outside" than on "the inside." But it was a brutal business just the same. I never felt I had been a victim, but what happened to my friends happened to me vicariously and it is this I remember. The experience left me with a bitter aftertaste which I have not lost. McCarthyism was a phase of my "education" I would readily have forgone.

7. *"WATCH THE CLOSING DOORS."*

Although no member of the staff was ever called before the inquisitorial committees, *The Nation* was savagely sideswiped in one of the zaniest episodes of the McCarthy years.

In its issue of April 10, 1954, *The Nation* published Frank Donner's long manuscript "The Informer," one of the first exposés of the informer system and how it worked. Widely distributed by many organizations, it attracted a great deal of attention. Shortly after it appeared, Harvey Matusow, then living in New York under the name Harvey Marshall, got in touch with Donner, who was intrigued by the stories he had to tell of his life in the political underground and sent him to see me. He came bringing a manuscript captioned "Blackmail Was My Business," which I rejected because I did not see how the facts could be readily verified. Then one day, October 27, 1954, to be exact, he phoned from New Mexico to say he had decided to make amends for the false testimony he had given as a government informer. Wondrously, he had joined the Church of Jesus Christ of Latter-Day Saints, repented his falsehoods, and rewritten the manuscript, which was destined, he was sure, to create as great a sensation as Whittaker Chambers' *Witness*.

When Matusow's publishers called a press conference on February 3, 1955, to announce early publication of *False Witness,* Attorney General Herbert Brownell reacted immediately. His primary concern, of course, was that Matusow's admission to having given false testimony might endanger a number of major political prosecutions in which the Department of Justice's prestige and credibility were at stake. Moreover, if Matusow recanted and got away with it, other informers might be tempted to repudiate their testimony. This in turn would endanger other pending prosecutions and vastly annoy the inquisitorial committees, who were dependent on informers as key witnesses. So on February 8 Brownell announced that a federal grand jury in the Southern District of New York would investigate an alleged plot or "conspiracy" to undermine the informer system. The grand jury then promptly subpoenaed the publishers—even the printers—in a frantic effort to lay hands on the manuscript and thereby prevent or delay publication of the book. But the publishers made the issue moot by releasing the book, which indeed created the sensation Brownell had feared. Matusow was the first important informer to recant testimony he had given. To discourage, if possible, further recantations, Brownell then decided to continue the grand-jury probe.

In the meantime, quite unknown to *The Nation,* an important development had taken place behind the scenes. A young man, Paul Hughes, had presented himself to a group of Washington and New York liberals as a disaffected member of McCarthy's entourage. For a price, he was willing, he said, to tell them what he already knew and might be able to learn about McCarthy's antics and the work of the Senate subcommittee McCarthy headed. The group included Joseph L. Rauh, Jr., the prominent Washington, D.C., lawyer, James Wechsler, editor of the New York *Post,* who had had a most unpleasant encounter with McCarthy in 1952— both Rauh and Wechsler were active in Americans for Democratic Action—and the editors of the Washington *Post.* For payment of slightly less than eleven thousand dollars, Hughes agreed to pro- vide—and did provide—a steady flow of tantalizing memos and reports. But on the eve of publishing their exposé, the sponsors became convinced that most of the information was of dubious authenticity. By inference Hughes or someone had tipped off McCarthy, who had in turn informed Brownell; hence the latter's charge that a "conspiracy" existed to undermine the informer sys- tem. *The Nation* had no connection whatsoever with this subplot; in fact, we knew nothing about it.[34]

It so happened that at this same time charges were pending before the Federal Communications Commission that Edward Lamb, the Toledo industrialist and financier, had falsely denied membership in the Communist Party in applying for renewal of radio and television licenses for stations he owned. Ted was an old friend of mine from the 1930s. Since I knew that some of these charges stemmed from the Ohio Un-American Activities Commit- tee, I put him in touch with Matusow, who had once worked for the committee. This circumstance, plus the fact that *The Nation* had kept a spotlight on the Lamb case (articles on it appeared in the February 5 and March 3, 1955, issues), apparently prompted the Justice Department to conclude that it was part of the "conspiracy" of Rauh, Wechsler, and the editors of the Washington *Post* to use informers to undermine the informer system. The Republican Ad- ministration was also anxious to do what it could to prevent a renewal of licenses for Lamb's radio and television stations. Inci- dentally, these hearings, which were themselves a form of political prosecution—Lamb was obviously being harassed because of his liberal views—dragged on for three years; not until June 14, 1957, was he finally cleared of all charges, at a cost of something like $900,000. In the course of the hearings two informer witnesses recanted their testimony.[35] But a weirdly unrelated chain of cir- cumstances contributed to the Department's paranoia and provides a sorry footnote to the general nuttiness of the times.

When Matusow first called at the office, I had sent him to see R. Lawrence Siegel, *The Nation*'s attorney. Siegel was active in the American Civil Liberties Union—he served as counsel for one of its committees—and had clients some of whom might be interested in Matusow's recantations. On one of several visits to Siegel's office,

Matusow was directed to a nearby restaurant, where Larry was
having dinner with a famous client, the actress Gloria Swanson.
Brash as always, Matusow promptly joined the party and began to
entertain Siegel and his guest with lively stories about his life as an
informer. At that time, Siegel was representing Swanson on a
purely private matter, of no political importance whatsoever, which
was wholly unrelated to *The Nation*. The pattern of subsequent
events suggests that government investigators were aware of the
meeting—they undoubtedly had a tail on Matusow—and wanted
to learn more about it.

Not long after the restaurant session, I was subpoenaed (March
8, 1955) to appear before the grand jury, as were Freda Kirchwey,
Martin Solow, *The Nation*'s business manager, and Siegel. None of
us knew anything about the alleged plot to discredit the informer
system, nor were we aware, in any way, of the Paul Hughes caper.
All I could tell the grand jurors was, yes, *The Nation* had published
Frank Donner's piece "The Informer," and, yes, I had put Matusow in touch with Lamb, but, no, we had never published anything
Matusow had written. Later I learned that in submitting a memorandum to the grand jury of his meetings with Matusow, Siegel
had made no mention of the session at which Swanson was present.
Apparently he felt that it might be embarrassing to his client, and,
after all, it had no relevance to the inquiry. But the upshot was that
Larry and his assistant found themselves in serious legal difficulties. Marty Solow also got caught in a somewhat similar contre-
temps. Initially he had been unable to locate a few letters or copies
of letters which he had exchanged with officials of the Mine, Mill
and Smelter Workers Union, who had been interested in our special issue "The Informer" because of testimony Matusow had given
against Clinton Jencks, one of their organizers (the conviction of
Jencks was subsequently reversed on appeal). The misplaced correspondence was soon found and the case against Solow was then
dismissed, but the damage was not easily repaired.[36]

The grand-jury hearings continued for some time but were finally phased out once the Justice Department became convinced
its conspiracy theory was a fantasy. But for several months Freda,
Lillie Shultz, and I were preoccupied days, nights, and weekends
with this weird tangle of events. The courage and loyalty Freda
displayed throughout this ordeal were beyond praise. None of the
stormy experiences we shared in those years was quite as agonizing
as this one. For weeks afterward, I never heard the singsong sub-
way refrain "Watch the closing doors" without thinking of this
Kafka-like episode. Somehow we managed to keep the doors from
closing on *The Nation*, but it took some doing.

When Harvey Matusow finally emerged from prison after serving a three-year sentence for perjury, the Madison *Capitol-Times* referred to him as "a hero of the McCarthy era" (September 9, 1960), which, in a sense, was certainly true. It took real courage to recant testimony he had given, for he had every reason to know it would lead to his indictment for perjury and a stiff prison sentence. Ironically, he was prosecuted because he had decided to admit having given false testimony against others; in effect, therefore, he was prosecuted because he finally told the truth! Dozens of other government informers who committed perjury but did not recant managed to lead charmed lives. W. H. Taylor presented to the Civil Service Commission's Loyalty Review Board a brilliant 107-page detailed refutation, item by item, of testimony Elizabeth Bentley had given against him, but no action was ever taken against her. Obviously the Department of Justice was itself a party to a conspiracy to smear the good names and reputations of hundreds of citizens by sponsoring informer witnesses whose testimony it had every reason to believe was false.

In retrospect, I find it nothing short of miraculous that we were able to keep bringing out *The Nation* week after week in those years of perpetual crisis from 1951 to 1955. To add to its difficulties, the consequences of earlier decisions continued to plague the magazine. Filing the court action against *The New Leader* over the Greenberg letter was one such decision; another was Freda's decision to initiate legal proceedings in an effort to restore *The Nation* to the library racks of the New York City schools. With publication of Paul Blanshard's famous series of articles on the Catholic Church in 1948, which were primarily concerned with the politics of the hierarchy, the superintendents of the Board of Education abruptly banned *The Nation* without notice or a prior hearing or so much as a formal announcement. A number of civic groups, including Protestant and Jewish organizations, urged Freda to challenge the legality of this arbitrary censorship in the courts and promised support, but later most of them reneged on their promises. The litigation proved to be interminable, the costs prohibitive. No doubt the ban had to be protested, but I was never convinced that court action was the proper remedy. As in the Greenberg incident, it imposed a heavy financial burden and narrowed the base of support at a time when *The Nation* was coming under severe attack for its stand on the Cold War and its opposition to the witch-hunt. When I became editor, I insisted that both actions be dismissed, and this was done. And eventually the ban was lifted—on February

9, 1963, fifteen years after it had been imposed! Both of these legal ventures cost *The Nation* dearly.[37]

In those troublesome years from 1951 to 1955 it often seemed to me that I was spending as much time helping Freda fend off attacks on *The Nation* and in fund raising as I was with editorial matters; she, of course, was almost entirely preoccupied with these issues. When I could I dashed off on numberless quick solo junkets to the West Coast, the Midwest, and up and down the East Coast in quest of donations and support. The experience was taxing but had its rewards. I seldom came back empty-handed, and in the process I managed to acquire valuable insights into the nature of the magazine's readership; in fact, I came to be on a first-name basis with many of the readers with whom I met to discuss its problems and to seek their help. To this day I cherish a special feeling for their loyalty and devotion. In New York many nights and weekends were devoted to similar activities in the company of Freda and Lillie Shultz. On Monday mornings the first order of business was usually a hurried conference on how to meet that week's payroll and printing bill. Not that *The Nation* lacked friends, loyal readers, and generous sponsors; that it survived is proof to the contrary. But the Cold War had created a climate of opinion in which wealthy donors were reluctant to be identified as sponsors. And the continued sniping of "anti-Communist" and "neo-conservative" intellectuals did not make matters any easier.

But *The Nation*'s problems were not unique. To a much lesser extent, *The New Republic* was subjected to similar attacks, but it had the good fortune to be edited by men—Michael Straight and Gilbert Harrison—who had access to substantial family fortunes; also, its stand on Cold War issues deflected much criticism of the kind directed against *The Nation. PM,* launched in June, 1940, had more than $5 million poured into it by Marshall Field but was finally forced to suspend publication in 1948. *PM* was then succeeded by *The Star,* under the aegis of Joseph Barnes and Bartley Crum, but it expired in 1949. *The Compass,* under Ted Thackrey, managed to survive, but barely, from 1950 to November, 1952, when it too suspended publication. The *National Guardian,* edited by Cedric Belfrage and James Aronson, came along in 1948 and did fairly well for a time, but its opposition to the Korean War caused circulation to drop from 55,000 to nearly half that figure in one year. (*The Nation* was also critical of the Korean War but did not suffer a similar decline in circulation; in fact, circulation remained fairly steady throughout the McCarthy years, but fund raising proved to be a tortuous process.) In 1953 the editors were subpoenaed to appear before the McCarthy subcommittee, and as a result Belfrage, a British citizen, was arrested and held for deportation. After spending four months in prison as part of an unsuccessful two-year effort to reverse the deportation order, he finally left the United States in August, 1955. Jim Aronson stayed on as editor until April, 1967, when he resigned.

Max Ascoli, married to the daughter of Julius Rosenwald of Sears, Roebuck, managed to keep *The Reporter* alive from April, 1949, to June, 1968, but then gave up. A resolute anti-Communist and dedicated Cold Warrior, Ascoli supported the Vietnam War and later endorsed the candidacy of Richard Nixon. It was his belief that a vacuum existed between what he considered "the didactic liberal weeklies" and "the superficial newsweeklies," a vacuum which *The Reporter* might fill. The stand the magazine took on the Cold War should alone have won it immunity from red-baiting despite its generally good positions on civil liberties and other controversial issues. But no quarter was given, no exception allowed; it too was savagely red-baited. In fact, there were some years when only *National Guardian*, I. F. Stone's newsletter which dated from January, 1953, and *The Nation* survived as critics of the Cold War and the witch-hunt—i.e., in the category of "intellectual" publications of general interest. With a fraction of the funds that went into the support of *PM, The New Republic, The Star, The Compass,* and *The Reporter* (although it took a different stand on the Cold War),[38] *The Nation* was lucky to stay alive.

In fact, the finances became so precarious in 1954 that I had to arrange for *The Nation* to be published at the plant of Aubrey Williams' *Southern Farmer* in Alabama. Costs were lower there, and, fortunately, the shop had a union label. But the real advantage was the credit we enjoyed with Aubrey. We installed a Teletype system over which copy, corrections, editorials, etc., were transmitted from New York to the plant in Alabama, where Al Maund, the novelist and short-story writer, had been installed as copy editor. Somehow we managed to make this highly improbable arrangement work, after a fashion, for nearly a year.

The Nation was, of course, Freda's life, but by the summer of 1955 she realized that an impasse had been reached. For more than a year she had tried without success to develop new sources of support or to find an acceptable successor as publisher. Would I, she wanted to know, be willing to see if I could ferret out a new publisher and then take over as editor so that she might be relieved of both burdens? I agreed; how could I say no? But I had about given up on the assignment, after weeks of effort, when one day, as luck would have it, I learned that George Kirstein, whom I had met on just one prior occasion, was at loose ends, having recently resigned as executive vice-president of the Health Insurance Plan of Greater New York, a post he had held for some years. Harvard Class of '32, brother of Lincoln Kirstein and Mina Curtis (the distinguished biographer and critic), George had served as executive secretary of the War Labor Board for two years before going off to the South Pacific as a naval gunnery officer. So I sought him out, and after a series of meetings *The Nation* had a new publisher for what proved to be a ten-year term. Freda knew George scarcely better than I did, but we both knew he was an excellent executive with many valuable contacts and a keen interest in public affairs. More important, we had good reason to know that he understood, appreciated, and honored the tradition *The Nation* represented. In the issue of September 17, Freda announced she had turned the magazine over to the two of us and made it clear the succession had been arranged at her request.

One day that summer, shortly before final details of the transfer had been worked out, I happened to be having lunch with Bartley Crum, who had played a key role in Wendell Willkie's brief political career. In the course of a rambling discussion of our experiences on both coasts in the domestic Cold War, in which we fancied ourselves veterans, Bart suddenly exclaimed, "And to think that we have survived ten years of this!" I had to confess that "the nightmare decade"—the title of Fred J. Cook's fine book on the period—did seem like an eternity. But the mere fact that we had been able to survive that long offered some assurance, I suggested, for the future even though the Willkie-Roosevelt vision of "one world" at peace, which had appealed so strongly to both of us, seemed less realizable then than it had in the middle 1940s.

CHAPTER **VIII**

THE KIRSTEIN YEARS

By the fall of 1955 I had completed a hectic editorial apprentice-ship at *The Nation*. I can't honestly say I was prepared to assume the editorship, but at least I was forewarned: I knew what I was getting into. During four years of extraordinary political turbu-lence, mounting Cold War tensions, and aggravated business and financial problems, I had become familiar with basic editorial rou-tines and had developed some ideas about how to give the maga-zine a new emphasis and direction. Fortunately, 1955 happened to be a logical time to transfer ownership and control. A decade of Cold War was ending. New social landscapes were emerging; a new generation was maturing; fresh perspectives and responses were needed. But, as I was to discover, the nature of the "new times" made it difficult to steer a steady editorial course. The 1955–65 decade was full of contradictions and paradoxes; few things were quite as they appeared to be. McCarthy had been condemned, but McCarthyism persisted; indeed, in a sense, it had triumphed. The cease-fire held in Korea, but another war was heating up in Viet-nam. Economically it was supposed to be the best of times, but it wasn't. Accelerating social, cultural, and technological changes made it difficult to sort out and properly evaluate the new issues; by comparison those of the first half of the 1950s were crystal-clear.

The circumstances, however, were now different. After Freda left, I had a freer hand with editorials and articles and was able to make changes in personnel and procedures. Del Vayo ceased to function as foreign editor, although he continued to send occasional articles from Europe, where the best use could be made of his insights, experience, and wide contacts. Del Vayo did not know or understand the Washington scene; he was not an expert on American politics, his English was barely understandable, his articles were written in Spanish and had to be translated, and increasingly foreign policy was being made in Washington, not at the United Nations. The shift was entirely amicable. I personally raised a sum for him which was equivalent to the amount he would have received in severance pay had he been a member of the Newspaper Guild. Shortly before Freda's departure, I had induced her to take on Harold Clurman as drama critic. Margaret Marshall, who served as back-of-the-book editor for fifteen of the twenty-four years she spent at *The Nation,* had resigned in January, 1953. New York media gossips promptly attributed her resignation to political differences with Freda. Such differences did exist, but the tradition of autonomy for the back-of-the-book section was so deeply entrenched at *The Nation* that Freda never, at any time, sought to interfere with Margaret's editorial responsibilities. Moreover, they had been close personal friends for a quarter of a century. Whatever her reasons for resigning, Margaret was not "eased out"; she left of her own volition. For a time we operated without benefit of a back-of-the-book editor, but, once named editor, I lost little time in bringing in Robert Hatch, one of the finest editors in New York magazine journalism, to succeed Marshall and also serve as film critic. When Victor Bernstein, another splendid working colleague, retired, Hatch succeeded him as managing editor. We then had a succession of book editors: Warren Miller, the novelist, who died not long after he joined the staff, Elizabeth Sutherland, Grandin Conover, Beverly Gross, Helen Iglesias, and Emile Capouya; but Bob Hatch continued to supervise the regular back-of-the-book columns.

Carl Dreher was coaxed into coming to the office once a week to help with editorials. A friend from California, Carl had an excellent background in science and technology (he was the author of such books as *Automation* and *The Coming Showdown*) and for years proved to be an invaluable editorial resource. Maurice Mandell, another California friend, was induced to come east from his retirement in Carmel to give us—quite literally—a year of his time to help with promotion and circulation. Bruce Catton was named Washington correspondent but after a time moved on and was succeeded by Edgar Kemler. After Kemler's untimely death, I tapped Robert Sherrill for the Washington assignment. As part of a new emphasis on labor coverage, B. J. Widick, Harvey O'Connor, and William Gomberg were recruited as correspondents. Although he could not be named "foreign editor" because of his commitments to the Field newspapers, Frederick Kuh provided United Nations and Washington coverage on foreign affairs along with Alexander Werth, Claude Bourdet (founder and editor of *France observateur*), Basil Davidson, Mark Gayn, Geoffrey Barraclough, Carleton Beals, Edgar Snow, O. E. Clubb, and other correspondents. I also put together a new group of contributing editors and lined up regional correspondents out across the country. And Mina Curtis, Kirstein's sister, was induced to lend a hand with the book section. Kirstein's special interest in labor matched my own; he was of major help in this and other areas where he had a special interest, such as health services, and in planning the editorial section. More attention was focused on domestic issues; the range of subject matter was broadened; and a much greater interest was shown in what was happening west of the Hudson. As often as possible, I tried to get out of the office on lecture trips, which in the give-and-take of question periods offered an opportunity to listen to a wide diversity of points of view and compare Eastern Seaboard preoccupations with those of other regions.

During the Kirstein Years—1955–65—my "education," particularly the editorial phase of it, took a new turn as *The Nation* sought to revive the muckraking tradition and began to zero in on such issues as the new affluence, the civil-rights movement, the peace movement, changing aspects of the social and cultural scene, Cold War alarums and interventions, the military-industrial complex, the Bay of Pigs fiasco, and, of course, the first phases of the war in Vietnam. By the end of this second decade of the Cold War, in 1965, the magazine had rounded out the first century of publication, was very much alive and kicking, and in a mood to celebrate its centennial, being happily out of debt for the first time since 1945. But by then another "world" had emerged, and it was time, once again, for a change in ownership and control.

1. THE GREAT AMERICAN BARBECUE

It was one thing to plan issues in the first half of the 1950s when people were worried about the Cold War, Korea, and McCarthyism; articles almost assigned themselves. It was far more difficult to draw a bead on significant aspects of the "affluent society" that surfaced in the second half of the decade. By 1955 the American people had begun to "cash in" on Cold War policies and programs. A strategy of "autoimperialism"—the phrase is Edgar

Snow's—had been devised by which we were induced to tax ourselves ostensibly to aid and defend other peoples but with most of the money being spent in this country in ways that profited some a great deal more than it did others. By then, too, we had become prisoners not so much of our fears as of our assumptions. Cold War expenditures were uncritically approved by a nearly unanimous—a virtually automatic—bipartisan consensus. Defense spending steadily increased, and foreign economic aid (much of it for military assistance) flowed back in the form of lucrative contracts. Payments for raw materials purchased abroad created an expanding market for American products, and overseas investments began to soar (a 1977 estimate puts the total at $133 billion). For the first time in our history, powerful, articulate, well-organized groups acquired a vested interest in a constantly expanding military budget. By 1955 defense spending had become a prime factor in sustaining high levels of employment and economic activity.

An abundance of alternative job-creating programs existed in such fields as housing, education, health, and transportation, but funding them presented serious political problems compared with the ease with which defense appropriations were consistently voted. Defense spending did not compete with the private sector. Also it provided, notably in the period of the Korean War, lucrative opportunities for small-business subcontractors. Pratt & Whitney, for example, gave out 5,278 subcontracts to firms in twenty-eight states; fifty producers of airplanes, engines, and components negotiated a total of sixty thousand subcontracts. The geographical spread of these subcontracts was impressive; it covered nearly every congressional district. Major interest groups routinely approved defense spending in the absence of alternative programs. After the merger of 1955, organized labor became a willing and active junior partner in the military-industrial complex. Defense-industry lobbies, with the aid of these auxiliary forces and the active support of powerful friends in the Defense and State Departments and in Congress, had little difficulty in securing prompt enactment of defense appropriations.[1] Heavy and continuous arms spending entailed higher taxes, but a disproportionate share of the burden was gradually and cleverly shifted to the lower- and middle-income groups in ways that did not at first arouse much opposition. Payroll taxes offered an efficient and relatively painless form of collection; over a period of time, employees became psychologically conditioned to regard "take-home pay" as their actual wage or salary.

With so much money being pumped into the economy, mass

consumption was greatly stimulated. Easy credit and intensive advertising—television proved to be a marvelous selling aid—made
consumer goods available on a scale that helped create the illusion
of affluence. Superficially, consumption was "equalized" in the
sense that there was a wider distribution of cars, gadgets, clothes,
food, and housing, but the relative distribution of wealth and income remained as unequal as in the last century. The flight to the
suburbs stepped up the demand for homes, appliances, highways,
and with it came the supermarket boom. Service and white-collar
job categories expanded. "Gross national product" became a term
of mystical import. What was produced did not matter, nor were
the social costs calculated. The discovery of environmental, occupational and product hazards came later. To be sure, obstinate
pockets of poverty remained, but the public was assured that the
shift of a percentage point or two in gross national income would
eliminate them. Leisure was growing; disposable income was increasing. Endless stories of technological marvels achieved or on
the drawing boards made criticism of what T. Balogh called "the
voodoo prosperity" of the period seem like ill-natured kibitzing.[2]
The threat of nuclear war was always present, but it failed to discourage what some commentators called "the Great American Barbecue" and others "the New American Celebration." The morbid
fear of a postwar depression had finally been exorcised; it was time
to celebrate—and consume.

Throughout the early phases of this celebration—when we were
consuming more and demanding still more to consume—a firm
consensus developed around the theme that American capitalism
had ushered in an age of perpetual and expanding prosperity. The
celebrants were not prepared to concede that "prosperity" on this
scale had never previously been sustained in a capitalist society
over an extended period of time without the stimulus of war or
preparations for war. Military spending is not, of course, the best
type of spending to raise employment levels. Sustained at high
levels over long periods, it can have harmful effects on the economy. An enormous waste is implicit in military spending; materials
are misallocated, manpower and other resources misdirected. Arthur Burns once pointed out that if the defense sector has stimulated economic developments in some direction, it has retarded
growth in others. But considerations of this sort were ignored, as
were the rapid growth of population, the spiraling arms race, the
destruction of limited raw materials, and the wanton waste of energy resources. Ignored also was the fact that Cold War "affluence"
was not based on any significant redistribution of income; but the
proliferation of consumer goods, however achieved, was tangible,

and the costs were deferrable. That military spending and related programs might have harmful long-term effects on the economy did not matter; in the absence of alternative programs, expanding military and foreign-aid appropriations were voted with little opposition or criticism.

After 1955, *The Nation* kept hammering away, with increasing insistence, on the theme that heavy arms spending was distorting the economy, diverting resources from critical domestic needs, and contributing to Cold War tensions. Major pieces by Seymour Melman, Paul Baran, Matthew Josephson, Stanley Meisler, Al Toffler, Walter Millis, Fred J. Cook, and other contributors kept a spotlight on the problem. The election returns consistently demonstrated that arms cuts, to be politically feasible, had to be closely tied to the simultaneous adoption of alternative programs. With this in mind we devoted two special issues in 1959 to the imperative need to create other sources of jobs and income, but to little avail. At the same time we published a barrage of pieces—by Sidney Lens, Kermit Eby, Harvey Swados, Henry Berger, Bernard Nossiter, Harvey O'Connor, Richard Sasuly, B. J. Widick (named labor editor on my recommendation), and others—devoted to exposing organized labor's role in marshaling support for Cold War policies. But in the absence of significant political pressure from the left for alternative programs aimed at maintaining high levels of production and employment, heavy arms spending continued to receive massive bipartisan support.

The headlines might be frightening—they often were—but the ongoing American Celebration, the great consumer binge, served to quiet apprehension and stifle doubt and criticism. The mass media provided jubilant orchestration and endless distractions. The new residents of suburbia were easily convinced that the poor had somehow vanished, since they had not joined in the flight from the cities. After 1955, it was actually necessary to *prove,* in the face of media assurances to the contrary, that poverty persisted, that urban slums were real, and that large sections of rural America might best be described as disaster areas. Not until the middle 1960s did poverty begin to be rediscovered in a significant way, thanks to the findings of Michael Harrington, Herman P. Miller, Robert Lampman, V. Lewis Bassie, Richard Cloward, and Frances Piven, all *Nation* contributors, and others. Long after these studies appeared, however, the self-congratulatory, all's-well tone continued to echo in the mass media.

The Protestant ethic, which had been such an important factor in the rise of capitalism, was an early casualty of the Cold War boom. Oddly enough, business journals and spokesmen seemed quite pleased with the demise of the work or thrift ethic. Kenneth Burke was one of a number of *Nation* contributors who called attention to changing attitudes toward the Protestant ethic, notably in a piece captioned "Recipe for Prosperity: 'Borrow, Buy, Waste, Want.' "[3] The quoted words were from *Business Week,* which had recently stated: "Just past the midmark of the 20th century it looks as though all of our business forces are bent on getting everyone to borrow, spend, buy, waste, want," and had then added: "Today a penny saved is just too bad." About that same time the *Wall Street Journal* quoted a Midwest banker as saying, "The noise you hear around here at night is not the katydids; it's just the noise all those debts make, amortizing." By way of encouraging the new trend, *Fortune* formulated a new concept known as "budgetism," which it defined as "a person's desire to regularize his income by having it removed from his own control and disciplined by external forces." And *Newsweek* cheerfully noted: "Never before have so many owed so much to so many . . . Time has swept away the Puritan conception of immorality in debt and godliness in thrift."

But it was not merely that people were spending more and saving less: more of them were on the take. John Kenneth Galbraith once pointed out that the "bezzle" zooms in "good times" when a lot of money is in circulation. Again and again, *The Nation,* like a nineteenth-century scold, kept pointing to the scandals and corruption that became alarmingly widespread after the midpoint of the 1950s: quiz-show frauds, police scandals, packaging frauds, the price conspiracy cases, employee thefts (considerably in excess of the amounts stolen by professional thieves), bank robberies (some staged by suburban housewives behind in their payments on installment purchases), scandals in the highway program ("the biggest highway robbery in history," with graft estimated at $100,000 a mile), the systematic pilfering by employees and customers that cut deeply into profits of supermarkets (adding a reported fifteen percent to the national food bill), shoplifting on a massive scale, white-collar crimes, heists, bribes, rip-offs, and tax evasion schemes of all kinds.

But the extraordinary proliferation of scandals of this sort failed to dampen enthusiasm for the special kind of "prosperity" that had produced them. C. Wright Mills was one of the first social critics to point out that much of the defiant behavior of the 1950s was "primarily a matter of a corrupt society" or what he called "structural immorality." There was surely nothing novel about individual greediness and social misconduct; what was new was the way an affluent society seemed to encourage sleazy practices of all kinds. In a neglected little volume, published in 1963, called *The Pseudo*

Ethic and subtitled "A Speculation about American Politics and Morals," Margaret Halsey demonstrated how politics and morals had come to a definite parting of the ways. As she saw it, the new American pseudo-ethic, which had replaced the Puritan ethic, was a combination of cowardice, anti-Communism, and consumerism. In an interview some years later she explained its emergence in this way: "In World War II we built a tremendous industrial plant, the output of which was being burned up or exploded in the war. After the war this plant was left over, and the only way to absorb its output was to change the people—from a producing to a consuming economy."[4]

Affluence also bred its own special discontents. During the years of the Great American Barbecue, any number of thoughtful observers—Archibald MacLeish, E. B. White, John Steinbeck, Walter Lippmann and others—expressed concern that we seemed to have no great or exciting goals. If we had a dominant purpose it appeared to be to negate the Russian purpose. Saul Bellow was quoted as saying, "The American today is an enthusiastic consumer of goods. . . . The picture of the U.S. therefore seems to be—sometimes—that of a pig in heaven . . . The revolution of abundance may have brought with it certain possibly unfavorable consequences; it may have left us without a sense of values . . . There are very few value systems based on abundance." Reece McGee, a *Nation* contributor, sharpened the same point: "Goods are not in themselves satisfying (and certainly not when produced in today's profusion). They are, in fact, incapable of producing satisfaction. So when we judge ourselves according to their possession we give hostages to a fortune that could destroy us. We worship the goods which, since they are symbols of ourselves, mean we worship ourselves, and no one . . . can be satisfied with gods *that* small."[5] And another perceptive *Nation* piece, "The Happiness Rat Race," by George Y. Elliott, cast a revealing light on the discontents of an affluent society.[6]

After 1955 I spent a great deal of effort in quest of irreverence and satire by way of jarring the complacency of what our poetry editor, John Ciardi, had called the "Icondic" years. David Cort was one of several happy discoveries. A gifted journalist, veteran of the *Time-Life* school, Dave had been foreign editor of *Life* when Whittaker Chambers covered the same field for *Time*. As the political winds shifted, Luce became more interested in Chambers' fantasies than in Cort's quirky brand of liberalism, and Cort was eventually eased out. Dave had been a classmate of Chambers at Columbia and never ceased to view him with loathing and contempt: "master of the big lie," "not entirely mad," "a genius imposter," "a true monster who simultaneously fooled the American Right, Center, and Left," "a congenital liar of such magnificence as to deserve enduring fame."[7]

Fortunately I came knocking at Dave's door shortly after his departure from *Life* and was able to enroll him as a frequent contributor. His articles provided a good antidote to the foibles of an affluent society. Dave was one of those contributors who delight editors because they too have been editors and know and understand their problems. He would take almost any suggested assignment and usually manage to make something of it. At our prompting, he wrote about flying saucers, crossword-puzzle addicts, gossip columnists, changing sexual mores, supermarkets, Madison Avenue capers, Robert Moses ("The King of Babylon"), organic soils, bank robbers, book clubs, the zoo, quiz shows, the highway construction mania, and kindred topics. His *Nation* contributions fill most of three volumes: *Is There an American in the House?* (1960), *Social Astonishments* (1963), and *The Glossy Rats* (1967). Social astonishments and glossy rats were not traditional *Nation* fare, but the pieces Dave did for us offered a welcome offset to the pomposities of the period. Irreverent, endlessly curious, ferociously independent, he struck just the right note. As often as not he was in disagreement with *The Nation*'s editorial positions—and he never hesitated to tell us how wrong he thought we were—but, in a curious way, there were some fundamental agreements: on attitudes, on the need for dissent, on the importance of ideas.

Good use was also made of the irreverent talents of Nelson Algren, Kenneth Rexroth, Roy Bongartz, Terry Southern, Kenneth Burke, Wade Thompson, and others. I discovered Wade at Brown University, where, as a brash young instructor, he had brought new life to a campus then notably in need of a little excitement. In my experience, humorists are a rarer breed than satirists, and Wade is an authentic American humorist in the tradition of Mark Twain. His first piece for *The Nation*, "My Crusade against Football," was reprinted in many major newspapers and a large section of the college press. Other Wade Thompson "crusades" were directed against fraternities, the launching of a Polaris submarine, HUAC, J. Edgar Hoover, Norman Vincent Peale, the DAR, and Radio City Music Hall, where Wade, then a graduate student at Columbia, had been employed as a singer with the Rockettes. As a part-time union organizer, he dreamed up the gaudy idea of pulling the Rockettes out on strike during the Christmas season. But New Yorkers were to be denied the thrill of seeing the Rockettes, in all their flimsy finery, on a picket line in wintertime. While negotiations were still pending, a huge stage elevator, conveying the entire troupe of Rockettes, descended out of control and sheared the little toe off Wade's left foot. Rushed to the hospital, he had a fine time being petted and pampered by adoring Rockettes, but the strike was never called. At Brown, Wade's crusades finally undermined his position and he was compelled to move on. Many of his *Nation* pieces were collected in a volume (1962) with the engaging title *Egghead's Guide to America*—affluent America, that is.

But try as we might, satire and irreverence could not seem to penetrate the fog of complacency that prevailed in the late 1950s. In such a setting, social pressures and a sense of expediency kept dissent carefully muffled. External policing of the kind the McCarthy hearings imposed was no longer needed; self-censorship was even more effective. "Continuous and subtle pressures," the novelist Allan Seager wrote in *The Nation*, "are applied to make you feel wretched if you don't have what everybody else has around you . . . The very process of manufacture demands conformity, so much so that McCarthy seems to be a symptom rather than a cause."[8] Ironically, conformity came to rival Communism as a major concern in intellectual and academic circles. Novels were written about men in gray flannel suits, and "the new conformity," as it was called, was examined in any number of books, including *The Exurbanites*, by A. C. Spectorsky (1955), *The Power Elite*, by C. Wright Mills (1956), and *The Organization Man*, by William H. Whyte, Jr. (1956).

One day in 1957 the young novelist Alan Harrington—I had previously recruited him as a contributor—brought me a manuscript which described in amusing and vivid detail the elegant office environment a mammoth corporation had fashioned for the comfort, convenience, and peace of mind of a small army of publicists, including Alan, who served in its public-relations department. The office was a "palace," with wall-to-wall carpeting, air conditioning, noiseless typewriters, a splendid view, beautiful furnishings and works of art, handsome rest lounges, a clublike dining room, fancy lighting, and piped-in music. It took some brutal arm-twisting on my part to get him to agree to let us publish the piece under his name; he was sure it would mean the end of his stay in the palace. As a matter of fact it did, but not for the reasons he anticipated. Much to his surprise, his supervisors rather liked the piece and thought it amusing. More to the point, he received two simultaneous unsolicited offers: a sizable foundation grant for further research and a generous contract for publication of a book based on the article. So he was able to resign his post and devote full time to his writing. What he had to say about *Life in the Crystal Palace* (1959) goes to prove that the structure of large organizations and the cozy and often luxurious environments they create can foster conformity even though no direct pressures are applied. In the 1950s the number of "crystal palaces," in the form of urban high-rise towers and stylish modern structures in sequestered suburban wooded areas, began to mass-produce a new breed of conformists.

At about the same time, also, student apathy became a major topic. In retrospect it is hard to believe that educators who, only a few years later, were being driven frantic by angry students, should have been deeply worried by the dense quiet prevailing on most campuses. Student apathy suddenly became a fashionable conference subject, discussed in books, articles, seminars, forums, and academic gatherings. In a puckish mood, the editor of the University of Chicago *Maroon* suggested formation of an Apathy Party with the sloth as its symbol; he might join such a party himself, he said, if he were not so apathetic. To find out what was happening on the campuses, I projected a series of annual Commencement Day special issues. The first appeared in the spring of 1957 (March 9) and was captioned "The Careful Young Men: Tomorrow's Leaders Analyzed by Today's Teachers." In it a number of perceptive faculty observers, including Carlos Baker, Stanley Kunitz, Leo Marx, Allan Seager, Karl Shapiro, and George R. Stewart, from a wide range of institutions, reported that most students were silent, satisfied, and not much interested in new or challenging economic or political ideas.[9] But a subsequent issue in the same series, "Tensions Beneath Apathy: The Myth of the Bland Generation" (May 16, 1959), with articles by William Sloane Coffin, Jr. (Yale), Dr. Louis Reik (Princeton), and others, clearly foreshadowed a significant shift in attitude. By the time Commencement Day rolled around in 1961, even the appearance of apathy had vanished. That issue (May 21), accurately titled "Rebels With a Hundred Causes," heralded the arrival of what Jessica Mitford Truehaft, one of the contributors, called "the indignant generation." There seemed to be little reason for further concern with student apathy, but a final report on the class of '67 noted that the indignant generation had become "the acid generation": bitter, explosive, disaffected. One of the contributors, Wallace Stegner, observed that many students had become bored with the goals and incentives of an affluent society and were beginning to reject most conventional values.

Thus, in less than a decade, the cycle had moved from apathy to indignation to disgust, which is a measure of the rapid pace of social and cultural change in those years.

2. CIVIL RIGHTS: IN PERSPECTIVE

Prospects for progressive political action were bleak indeed in 1955, but in at least one area it seemed to me significant gains might be scored. The 1947 report of the President's Commission on Civil Rights had placed that issue on the national agenda for the first time since Reconstruction. However, congressional sabotage of the commission's proposals in 1948, 1949, and 1950 appeared to have shelved the issue for the duration of the Cold War. But the "racial revolution" of the war years had aroused expectations among blacks, particularly among Southern blacks, that were not to be denied. The problem had always centered there—in the South. Until Southern blacks were prepared to lead the way, with the aid of white liberals, there was little chance of forging a strong national movement in support of civil rights. But reaction to such "incidents" as the brutal Christmas Day bombing in Mims, Florida, in 1951, which resulted in the death of Harry Moore, a courageous black activist, offered dramatic proof that a new day had dawned. More than anything else, it was the proliferation of such incidents throughout the South that convinced me there could be no return to the prewar racial status quo.

But there was another reason why I felt that the issue of civil rights could be restored to the national agenda: it was one major domestic issue that Cold War politics could not submerge. Red-baiters had tried to account for increasing racial unrest in the South as the product of "Communist" agitation but had never fully succeeded. Left-wing organizations, including the Communist Party, had so consistently botched their efforts to organize Southern blacks that it was patently absurd to hold them responsible for protests and actions in which the black churches of the South had played a far more significant role. Besides, most Americans knew better; at least the more thoughtful realized that the "racial problem" was deeply rooted in the national experience. As racial tensions continued to mount, and in the South more than elsewhere, a troubled national conscience, stirred by the fervor of the war years, began to respond. I was persuaded, therefore, that a strong nationwide movement in support of civil rights could be organized despite the Cold War setting and the reversals of 1948–50.

I was also persuaded *The Nation* had a special role to play in such an effort. Founded in 1865 in large part to protect the rights of the recently emancipated blacks, it had been closely identified with their struggle to achieve full civil rights for nearly a century. With an eye on the upcoming presidential election in 1952, I undertook, as one of my first projects after joining the staff in New York, to project a special issue, "The Southern Negro" (September 17, 1952), which called attention to the significance of what was happening in the South and stressed the theme that the time had finally come to demand federal legislation aimed at ending all forms of legally sanctioned discrimination. But the issue was premature; it might better have been published after the Supreme Court's decision in *Brown v. Board of Education* of May 17, 1954, for only then did the civil-rights issue begin to assume truly national significance.

Following the setbacks in Congress, Eisenhower's election had seemed to write quietus to the issue, but, ironically, it was the new Chief Justice, Earl Warren, an Eisenhower appointee, who wrote the Court's unanimous decision in the Brown case. The decision, of course, gave massive impetus to the civil-rights movement and invested it with a new national significance: Congress and the Executive were then faced with the problem of enforcement. In reversing the "separate but equal" doctrine of *Plessy v. Ferguson* (1896), the Court recommitted the national government to the task of achieving the universal civil freedom which the Thirteenth, Fourteenth, and Fifteenth Amendments were supposed to have guaranteed. Someday it may be possible to trace in detail the evolution of Warren's thinking on racial issues between the controversy over the West Coast Japanese, when he served as attorney general and governor of California, and his appointment as Chief Justice. Of one thing I am sure: the Warren of the earlier period would not have written the decision in the Brown case. But what really matters, of course, is that he was moved to write it in 1954.

One of the major events of the decade, the *Brown* decision set the stage for the civil-rights movement which began in 1955; in a sense the movement was a response to the decision. It reminded the nation of the need to fulfill a promise much too long deferred. It projected a national purpose when one was badly needed. It refocused attention on a great historic goal and gave the highest legal sanction to the struggle to achieve it. Of the decision, I wrote at the time that it marked "the end of an era," namely, the long evasive interlude following adoption of the Civil War amendments when American idealism gave way to moral equivocation and Supreme Court decisions rationalized the post–Civil War paralysis of national will on the racial issue. But, for all its importance, the decision was not greeted with deafening applause, perhaps because it came as something of a surprise and was a step or two ahead of public opinion.

In the South the initial reaction was less vehement than might have been expected. But with the second *Brown* decision in 1955, in which the court used the phrase "with all deliberate speed," the resistance began to mount. That summer a rather shy young man who had studied with C. Wright Mills at Columbia came to see me. His name was Dan Wakefield and he offered to cover the Emmet Till murder case in Mississippi if *The Nation* would buy him a round-trip bus ticket. The reports he sent from Mississippi on the Till case (October 1, 1955) and the rise of the White Citizens Councils (October 22, 1955) were his first writings to be published in a national magazine. Dan was immediately taken on as a regular contributor and became a main reliance in our close and continuous coverage of the emerging civil-rights movement. Most of the material in his books *Revolt in the South* (1960) and *Between the Lines* (1966) first appeared in *The Nation*. Because of his interest and personal involvement, there were few phases of the movement we failed to cover. In addition to his reports we ran pieces by Howard Zinn, Robert Martinson, Alfred Maund, Barbara Deming, Peter de Lissovoy, and many others. And after 1955 we were in close touch with Dr. Martin Luther King, Jr., consulting with him on numerous issues and lending support to his fund-raising activities. Each spring until his death, he sent *The Nation* an annual report on the state of the civil-rights movement.

The Till case was a curtain-raiser for the big action, which began on December 1, 1955, when Mrs. Rosa Parks was arrested for refusing to move back in the bus. The Montgomery, Alabama, bus boycott, conducted by the city's fifty thousand blacks, began on December 5, the day her trial opened. A year later, on December 13, 1956, the Supreme Court struck down the Montgomery ordinance. The year-long bus boycott was perhaps the most important single domestic political development of the decade; historically it would be difficult to exaggerate its significance. It brought Dr. King to national and world attention, prompted formation of the Southern Christian Leadership Conference and the Student Non-Violent Coordinating Committee, and galvanized the civil-rights movement. In an editorial of March 3, 1956, I referred to the boycott as a "miracle," which indeed it was. To be sure, it was skillfully organized by courageous and dedicated individuals, but essentially it was a spontaneous response to a challenge—a situation—which had been a long time in the making. One sensed instantly that it was not merely another protest; this was the big action, with historic overtones, for which the nation had been waiting. Dr. King's brilliant leadership was, of course, a key factor. Without the emphasis on nonviolence, and the singing, hand-clapping, and hallelujahs, the movement might not have captured national attention as quickly as it did. Also, the assistance of such former New Dealers as Clifford Durr, Aubrey Williams, and other white liberals was of major importance; Durr's legal advice was invaluable. But credit the marchers, the black community of Montgomery, with the victory.

From the moment it began, the boycott had a profound impact on national opinion. For a year it played well to a huge national audience; reporters and television newsmen provided admirable coverage. By any standards, it was a great story. In the heart of the Deep South, in the capital of the Confederacy, a miracle had happened; above all, it was the spirit of the movement that captured public and media attention. The demonstrations offered welcome and timely relief to the fear and hostility that McCarthyism had spread. And the spirit was contagious; after a decade of silence and social indifference people began to march, petition, and demonstrate. In its early phases, in what Vernon Jordan has called "that brief, golden moment of history," the civil-rights movement had a religious and emotional fervor about it of the kind that moves mountains.

Later some of the enthusiasm began to abate, but initially the movement generated an authentic sense of fraternity among those, black and white, who participated in it. It came to national attention at a time when many young white Southerners were becoming increasingly restive and impatient with the old order. As a sign of the times, *The Nation* of March 24, 1956, carried an article, "Mississippi Rebel," by Willie Morris—his first contribution to a national publication—which told of his trials and tribulations as the editor of a Southern campus newspaper. To white rebels of his generation, the civil-rights movement offered timely encouragement. A letter by Juliette Morgan, a white librarian, which appeared in a Montgomery newspaper, best sums up the spirit and appeal of the boycott. "It is hard to imagine," she wrote, "a soul so dead, a heart so hard, a vision so blinded and provincial as not to be moved with admiration, at the quiet dignity, discipline and dedication with which the Negroes have conducted their boycott."[10]

The year of the boycott was also the year of the Dixiecrat Manifesto, which touched off the resistance. Issued on March 12, 1956, the manifesto was not so much a response to popular demand as a carefully calculated call to arms by the Dixiecrat leadership. Tactically it was designed to blackmail the liberal Democrats, to make them feel that they had better take a cautious line on civil rights in the upcoming Democratic convention or risk another split of the kind that had taken place in 1948. And the tactic worked: the liberal Democrats, including Adlai Stevenson and Eleanor Roosevelt, suffered an acute "failure of nerve" and decided to appease the Dixiecrats. It was stupid politics; Stevenson would have fared no worse—in fact, he might have done better—if the Democrats had taken a strong line on civil rights. "Gradualism," a fashionable concept that year, was historically off key in view of what was happening in the South. In the summer of 1956, I put together a special *Nation* issue, "Time to Kill Jim Crow" (July 14), with contributions by Clarence Mitchell, Henry Lee Moon, James Baldwin, Richard Long, and E. Franklin Frazier, all blacks, and C. Vann Woodward, a white Southerner, which emphasized the need to strike down all legally sanctioned forms of racial discrimination as a basic precondition to further progress. But "gradualism" and "moderation" triumphed that year, thereby setting the stage for the violence that came later.

Because enforcement had been delayed, the first sharp challenge to the *Brown* decision did not come until 1957. In the meantime, the Dixiecrat Manifesto had flashed a message to Governor Orville Faubus of Arkansas and every demagogue in the region that resistance might be good politics. So when nine black students sought to enroll in Central High School in Little Rock, the issue was promptly joined. On the fringe of the Deep South, Arkansas was ideal terrain on which to stage a dramatic resistance to desegregation. Little Rock was not thought of as a Southern city in quite the same sense, for example, as Jackson, Mississippi, or Mobile, Alabama. As part of their strategy of mobilizing a regionwide opposition to all phases of the civil-rights movement, the Dixiecrats were delighted to see the *Brown* decision challenged in an area peripheral to the Deep South. The brash language of the manifesto, with its use of such words as "nullification" and "interposition," went about as far as it was discreet to go by way of inciting open resistance to a decision of the Supreme Court. Confident of strong regional support and Dixiecrat backing in Congress, Governor Faubus quickly moved from "interposition" to attempted "nullification" by calling out units of the National Guard for the ostensible purpose of maintaining law and order but actually to encourage resistance to the order of the local federal district court.

Up to this point the Eisenhower Administration had been extremely reluctant to act, but once it became clear that local authorities had no intention of protecting the black students, the President put Little Rock under martial law and sent in units of the

101st Airborne Division under the command of Major General Edwin A. Walker. (Later Walker resigned from the service, joined the John Birch Society, and became a hero of the radical right until his bizarre actions became such an acute embarrassment to its leaders that he had to be, in the phrase of William Buckley, "tossed into history's ashcan." He last surfaced in the news on July 8, 1976, when he was arrested in Dallas on a morals charge.) While necessary in the circumstances, given the President's reluctance to lend his personal moral support to the Supreme Court's decision in the Brown case, the dispatch of federal troops to Little Rock was exactly what the Dixiecrats wanted; they knew it would stir memories of "the late rebellion" and set rebel flags flying, and it did. George Wallace and other Southern demagogues were encouraged by the reaction to believe they could ride to power by resisting court-ordered desegregation.[11]

With President Eisenhower the problem was latent bias coupled with massive disinterest. He really did not know what he should have known about the civil-rights movement, from which he was carefully isolated by his top aides. He never seemed to sense that the movement raised issues of major national importance requiring his personal attention and leadership. Either his aides would not let the civil-rights leaders see him or he wanted to keep them at a distance by way of preserving his ties with the Dixiecrats. In either case there was amazingly little contact or communication between the President and the leaders of the civil-rights movement. Vice President Nixon was first introduced to Dr. King at a chance street meeting in Accra during the Ghana independence celebrations, and it was not until late in his second term that President Eisenhower agreed to meet with a group of distinguished black leaders who had been trying to set up an appointment with him since 1952.[12] Chief Justice Warren was convinced the Dixiecrat Manifesto had caused "inestimable damage" and was equally sure much of the subsequent strife might have been avoided if Eisenhower had spoken out in defense of the decision in the Brown case. Administration spokesmen were quoted as saying that the decision had set back improvement in race relations in the South by a quarter of a century. As Warren noted, throughout the Eisenhower years the aphorism dear to the hearts of those who were insensitive to the rights of minority groups, "Discrimination cannot be eliminated by law," was endlessly repeated by White House spokesmen. While the Brown case was pending before the Court, the Chief Justice was invited to a White House dinner along with John W. Davis, counsel for the states involved in the action. Warren did not relish the juxtaposition and, in his memoirs, implies that Eisen-

hower had set up the meeting in an attempt to influence his thinking about the case. Later the President said of his appointment of
Warren that it was "the biggest damn fool thing I ever did."[13]

"Only yesterday" is a poignant phrase in American social and
political history; we remember so little of what happened only
yesterday and the day before. Thus, John W. Gardner was quoted
in a 1969 interview as saying that we had just begun to tackle the
issue of discrimination. But what about the racial ferment of the
war years and the significant if limited gains it achieved? And what
about the eight hundred or more civil-rights demonstrations that
were staged in cities and towns in 1963 alone, culminating in the
march on Washington of August 28, the largest demonstration
ever held in the nation's capital, when Dr. King told of his dream
that "one day . . . this nation will rise up and live out the true meaning of its creed . . . that all men are created equal." By June of that
year, President Kennedy, who had demonstrated a lukewarm attitude toward civil rights, was finally forced to submit a civil-rights
program to the Congress as Eisenhower had done at an earlier
date. Neither program would have been submitted but for the
civil-rights protests. Nor would civil-rights legislation have been
enacted in 1964 and 1965 had it not been for the protests and
marches and demonstrations of the preceding decade.

The *Brown* decision, the Montgomery bus boycott, Little Rock,
the protests of 1963, and the Selma march were but a few of many
signposts on the long march of the civil-rights movement. For me
this march began during World War II and surged to a climax in
1965. John Herbers is right: 1965 was the watershed year. For by
then signs of what he calls "the curious, troubling relationship"
between the war in Vietnam and the civil-rights movement had
become evident. The day after the Selma protests, the first American combat troops arrived in Vietnam. On August 4 President
Johnson signed the Voting Rights Act, but on August 20 headlines
announced B-52 raids on North Vietnam targets. From then on,
protests against the war began to absorb much of the energy that
had previously gone into the civil-rights movement. After the
Watts riots, the movement lost much of its buoyancy and self-confidence and began to be riven by internal dissension.[14]

No doubt Dr. King was right: the first successes of the civil-rights
movement and the massive attention it received caused the leadership to underestimate the intensity of the mounting rage, frustration, and despair that finally exploded in the Watts riots and the
disturbances of the summer of 1967. But we have lost sight of the
fact that the civil-rights movement was not a social revolution: it
began with limited and modest objectives which, by and large, were

attained. No one familiar with the "race problem" ever thought—
I certainly never did—that striking down legally sanctioned discriminations would do more than set the stage for the next round
in the struggle to achieve racial equality. But it was the indispensable first step.

The political power of blacks sharply increased after the Voting
Rights Act was passed in 1965: by 1968 over a million new black
voters had been registered. By 1977 the number of blacks holding
elective office had increased from 1,185 to 4,311. True, this represents a relatively small gain. Blacks still hold less than one percent
of the nation's more than 520,000 elective offices, although they
constitute eleven percent of the population. In 1978 only sixteen
of 435 members of Congress were blacks and only one black served
in the Senate. Even in the South blacks still hold less than three
percent of the region's more than 79,000 elective offices, although
making up twenty percent of the population. But seen in perspective blacks have made remarkable political gains, and these gains
will not be reversed. With a solid base of power in electoral politics,
the minority's political influence will increase as blacks gain political
experience and become more sophisticated about the ways of politics, and as new leadership elements emerge.

And directly and indirectly the civil-rights movement has been
responsible for many additional gains. The number of blacks and
other racial and ethnic minorities enrolled in colleges and universities has increased. Efforts to desegregate public schools have met
with resistance in Northern urban areas, particularly over the issue
of busing; but where proper groundwork has been laid and sound
plans have been prepared, a substantial measure of success has
been achieved despite the reluctance of the courts to cross school
district lines to achieve integration throughout a given metropolitan area. Discrimination in employment has lessened in industry
and business and at every level of government. Restrictive cove-
nants have been ruled unconstitutional, and de facto segregation
in housing is abating, if slowly. Segregation in the armed services
has been virtually eliminated. Most legislated racial discriminations
have been repealed or declared unconstitutional, including statutes
barring interracial marriages. By and large Jim Crow signs in public facilities and places of public accommodation have vanished. In
itself the disappearance of these obnoxious manifestations of racism represents a significant shift in public attitudes, brought about
by organized pressure and political action. Such changes have
more than symbolic importance: they affect attitudes; they reflect
change. Once the formal barriers are lowered, bias begins to abate.
Social intercourse between blacks and whites, between all racial

types, is much freer and more relaxed today than, say, before World War II, although tensions have by no means entirely disappeared.

Culturally an enormous change has occurred. A day's viewing of network television now compared with a day in the middle 1950s would reveal a remarkable change in racial "images," roles, and the symbolism of race, in news programs, commercials, and entertainment features. And content has changed as well as style and casting. The disappearance of cultural taboos and stereotypes cannot be dismissed as mere tokenism; it reflects a change that is taking place in the mores. Today most young people seem massively indifferent to ethnic and racial taboos. And the movement against discrimination continues to gain new recruits: Japanese Americans, Chinese Americans, Indians, Filipinos, and other racial minorities have made their voices heard. The Chicano rebellion—the remarkable emergence of the large Spanish-speaking minority—has added an entirely new dimension to the civil-rights effort.

Of recent years the fervor of the civil-rights movement has largely vanished. "The sweet first flush" of victory, according to A. T. Cooper, mayor of Prichard, Alabama, and chairman of the National Conference of Black Mayors, has given way to a sobering realization that "a lot of drudgery and hard work" lies ahead. Of this there is much painful evidence: high black unemployment rates, particularly among urban teenagers; of 400,000 persons in American jails and prisons 300,000 are "black or brown"—and not because they have any predisposition to criminal conduct; in some big cities, as in New York, the goal of integrated schools has been virtually abandoned; the destruction of the black lower class continues and black–white economic disparities remain about the same. But these stalemates and defeats do not reflect the failure of the civil-rights movement so much as its limitations. It was, in essence, a ground-clearing action, a necessary first step; enactment of civil-rights measures never offered assurance in itself that basic social and economic relationships would be quickly changed. Barriers had to be lowered and basic rights (most particulary the right to vote) secured before further progress was possible. But the gains, if limited, are irreversible and might have been even more significant but for distortions in the economy and the political system caused by thirty years of Cold War. In a sense, the civil-rights movement was a casualty of the war in Vietnam.[15]

Speaking at a race-relations seminar for U.S. troops in Germany on May 28, 1976, Muhammad Ali said, "That race bit is over now. There ain't no color distinction in friendship. We will all one day be brothers." And in the narrowly limited sense in which he used the phrase, the race bit is over—that is, the blatant discriminations, backed by legal sanctions, have been removed and friendship now has a chance to work its miracles. This may seem, and indeed it is, a meager first step, but we hesitated to take it for nearly a century after the end of the Civil War. The inherited historic consequences of racial discrimination have not, of course, been eliminated, nor will they be for years to come, for they are part of the social and economic structure of American society. But with the artificial barriers removed, "the racial problem" can now be seen as primarily an economic or class issue involving the poor and the disadvantaged of all races, and that is a major clarification.

3. THE REVIVAL OF MUCKRAKING

In 1956 James Playsted Wood, the historian of American magazines, announced without qualification that the muckraking tradition was dead, and, indeed, that seemed to be the case. In the years from 1902 to 1912 the original muckrakers—Lincoln Steffens, Ida Tarbell, Ray Stannard Baker, and the rest—had conducted a highly successful postmortem on the excesses of the Gilded Age. But World War I brought this first phase to a close. A revival of a sort took place after the war, with some fine investigative reporting on the scandals of the Harding Administration, but the mood of the 1920s was too buoyant for exposé journalism. One might have expected the 1929 stock market crash to usher in a great decade of investigative reporting, but it did not. With the press so nearly unanimous in its opposition to Roosevelt, most of the muckraking of the 1930s took the form of books based on the superb congressional investigations of those years.

As in World War I, the muckraking impulse was held in abeyance during World War II, and the decade from 1945 to 1955 did not yield much in the way of good investigative journalism. A large section of the press promptly joined Joe McCarthy's cheering section, and the papers that did not were so preoccupied with his antics and fending off his attacks they had little time for exposés. Thus the list of prime subjects that cried aloud for in-depth investigation kept extending; by the middle 1950s it was a mile long. So after I became editor I decided to see what could be done to revive the muckraking tradition, which by then had been dormant for nearly four decades. I knew the timing was right—too many inviting subjects had been too long neglected—but there were some difficult practical problems. *The Nation* lacked the resources to indulge in investigative reporting, which tends to be expensive. Nor did it have the space; exposé articles are often lengthy, and serialization presents special problems for a weekly. Somewhat reluctantly I decided to devote an entire issue now and then to in-depth investigations, even doubling or quadrupling the number of pages if necessary. For an initial project, I thought we might take a fresh look at the Hiss case.

I had met Alger Hiss for the first time in January, 1955, shortly after he had been released from prison. At that time his guilt was generally assumed; there was little apparent interest in the case, and no indication of a willingness or desire to reexamine the evidence, even in the wake of McCarthy's condemnation. That Hiss was guilty had in fact become an article of faith in the "anti-Communist" consensus. For example, as late as 1956 Americans for Democratic Action objected when students at an Eastern college invited Hiss to speak. I never had thought he was guilty, and the better I got to know him the more convinced I became of his innocence. Having accumulated huge files of clippings, documents, articles, and correspondence about the case, I began to look around for a good investigative reporter who might be willing to examine these materials as well as the briefs, the transcripts, and other court records. Bernard Nossiter had first called my attention to Fred Cook's talents when the two of them were working on the New York *World-Telegram and Sun*. On Nossiter's recommendation I had given Fred one or two assignments, and I had been impressed by his ability to sort out, analyze, organize, and make sense of large masses of materials. So I offered him the assignment. But to my surprise I discovered he shared the position of editor-publisher Roy W. Howard that Hiss was guilty. It took some persuading, but he finally agreed to look at the materials. In his book *The Nightmare Decade* (1971), he explains how and why he became convinced that Hiss was innocent. By *Nation* standards, the special issue we devoted to a reexamination of the case (September 21, 1957) was a huge success, and Fred was promptly encouraged to make a book of it: *The Unfinished Case of Alger Hiss* (1958). Of recent years the court of public opinion has begun to tilt in favor of Hiss's innocence, and for this shift in attitude Cook's investigation is primarily responsible. Even more than Earl Jowitt's fine study—a cool scrutiny of the evidence by a brilliant British jurist—Fred's article (and book) set in motion the reexamination of all aspects of the case that is still proceeding.

Encouraged by the response to the issue, I then reprinted a piece Cook wrote for *Saga* magazine on the William Remington prosecution, which, in some respects, was a counterpart of the Hiss case. A graduate of Dartmouth and Columbia (1940), Remington worked for the Tennessee Valley Authority and the War Production Board, served in Navy intelligence, and wound up in 1948 on the staff of the Commerce Department. As a result of Elizabeth Bentley's confessions to the FBI, Remington had been questioned by a grand jury, but no indictment followed. Then, a year later, Bentley testified before a Senate subcommittee that Remington was a Soviet agent, which he promptly denied. The charges, of course, placed his position in jeopardy. But Bentley failed to appear before the Loyalty Review Board—it had no power to subpoena witnesses—on three occasions, and Remington was cleared. Then Bentley repeated the charges over the radio, and Remington, like Hiss, sued for libel, and received ten thousand dollars in an out-of-court settlement. He was then indicted and convicted of perjury in denying the charges—as Hiss had been—but the conviction was reversed. At the second trial he was again convicted, largely on the testimony of his former wife.

Remington, like Hiss, was something of a "square," an All-American Boy; as one reporter observed, he was an "unsinister" type. Like Hiss he was naïve; he never seemed to appreciate the lengths to which the FBI and the Department of Justice were prepared to go to secure convictions in political prosecutions in which the credibility of a key informer—Chambers in the case of Hiss, Bentley in the case of Remington—was at stake. Once out of prison, Alger Hiss was able to carry on a dignified and notably unembittered effort to win ultimate vindication, but Remington was not given this chance. As a trusty, he caught a fellow inmate in an act of petty theft, was stabbed, and bled to death in the early-morning hours at the Lewisburg prison, alone and unattended—a tragic victim of the witch-hunt.

The response to the Hiss and Remington issues having demonstrated that the time had come for a new season of muckraking, I then got Cook to prepare a special issue on the FBI (October 18, 1958), based on a small library of materials I had gathered. It sold even better than the Hiss and Remington issues, won a Page One award from the Newspaper Guild of New York, and was promptly published as a book, *The FBI Nobody Knows*, which also sold briskly for a long time. The only previous serious attempt to focus critical attention on the FBI had been Max Lowenthal's book which J. Edgar Hoover succeeded in suppressing on publication. From then—1950—until the Cook issue appeared, Hoover and the FBI enjoyed almost complete immunity from criticism, not merely on the score of highly questionable practices but on that of routine law-enforcement efficiency as well. Seldom criticized on any count, Hoover and the agency he had fashioned were consistently glorified. When *The Nation* was not instantly incinerated by Hoover's wrath—he ranted and blustered a bit and favorite spokesmen and columnists worked us over, but with no serious damage—the press was emboldened to ask a few questions, but very gingerly and in a most respectful manner. Although we broke the taboo, it was not until Hoover's death in 1972 that the press and Congress began to show a lively critical interest in the FBI and its operations. In general the press had been inattentive and slothful as well as timid. There was nothing particularly new or startling about what Cook had to report; his findings were based on the trunkload of materials I had given him. Most of the facts had been reported, here and there, in a random way, but no one had previously put the parts together in an orderly fashion. A prime function of good investigative reporting, as the original muckrakers demonstrated, is to make known what is already known but to do it in a way that makes sense and leaves a lasting impact.

That *The Nation* was willing to take a somewhat irreverent view of J. Edgar Hoover and the FBI prompted a number of disaffected agents to visit the office. One day Jack Levine, who had been attached to the special unit that kept the Communist Party leadership under surveillance, came to see me. A highly intelligent young man with a cultivated sense of humor, he had recently resigned from the FBI out of disgust for some of the methods it used. Among other things, he explained how the FBI actually helped finance the Communist Party, in the sense that perhaps a fourth of the members of the party's local central committees were agents or informers who regularly listed party dues on their expense accounts. At first he was most reluctant to write a piece based on his experiences; he was about to launch a new career as an attorney in Phoenix and was convinced the publicity would not be helpful (I had insisted the piece would have to carry his byline). But he finally agreed. The article turned out to be quite funny (*The Nation,* October 20, 1962). At least Art Buchwald thought so; he did a column about it. And Jack Paar thought Buchwald's column was funny, for he made use of it on his popular network program. So the Jack Levine story was brought to the attention of an audience running into the millions. The publicity the piece received brought other ex-agents to our offices; we ran articles, for example, by such former agents as William Turner and Arthur Murtagh. These articles appeared, of course, quite some time before Hoover and the FBI became favorite targets of the press in the post-Watergate period.

Following the FBI issue, I asked Cook and Gene Gleason to prepare a special issue on a timeless subject: political corruption in New York City. "The Shame of New York"—October 31, 1959—

was an instant success, in part because of the hubbub that resulted when Cook and Gleason were discharged by the *World-Telegram and Sun,* ostensibly because of a minor indiscretion on Gleason's part. I would have felt badly about the discharges but for the fact that Cook was finally liberated from an irksome relationship—his *Nation* articles had kept him in Roy Howard's doghouse—and launched on a successful career as a free-lance journalist. Nor did Gleason fare too badly; he became a top investigator for a committee of the U.S. Senate. Given a Page One Award by the New York Newspaper Guild, "The Shame of New York" prompted the *Herald-Tribune*—with generous credits to *The Nation*—to undertake a fine series on the same theme. Our issue and this series helped set the stage for John V. Lindsay's election as mayor. As late as June 11, 1977, Samuel Kaplan, assistant editor of the New York *Post*'s editorial page, gave "The Shame of New York" high marks as one of the sharpest, "most unforgiving" documents about misrule in New York. The following year Fred did still another special muckraking issue, on the connection between organized crime and all forms of gambling, the legalized as well as the illegal. Captioned "Gambling Inc.," the special issue—October 22, 1960—sold well and was later published as a book.

In 1956 *The Nation* published a three-part feature by Matthew Josephson, in the best muckraking tradition, on large-scale arms spending; the articles were later reprinted and widely distributed as a pamphlet captioned *The Big Guns.* But when I read Eisenhower's farewell address of January 17, 1961, "We must guard against the acquisition of unwarranted influence, whether sought or unsought, by the military-industrial complex," I realized that an excellent opportunity had been created for a longer and more detailed probe. So once again I assembled a cartload of materials for Cook, from which he fashioned yet another special issue: "Juggernaut: The Warfare State." Bertrand Russell wrote to say it was "one of the most important articles since the end of the war." It broke all previous records for sales of special issues, and the book based on it, *The Warfare State,* also sold impressively. Since 1961, literally dozens of books have been written on the same theme, from much the same point of view, but Josephson and Cook were the first journalists to take a hard look at "the military-industrial complex."

The following summer, again using materials I had accumulated over a period of years, Cook prepared a special issue on the CIA (June 24, 1962), which sold so well that it had to be reprinted several times. Hard to believe but true: this was the first serious attempt to focus critical attention on the record and the performance of the CIA which had been very much a taboo subject since the agency was set up in 1947. In 1962 the CIA enjoyed nearly total immunity from critical scrutiny; only in the aftermath of Watergate did the press and Congress begin to make up for past neglect by launching all sorts of probes, investigations, and exposés of the agency's far-ranging and often incredibly stupid covert operations. Since then we have learned of such bizarre CIA projects as the funding of expensive research on the effect of circumcision on emotional attitudes, the use of prostitutes in studies of sexual aberrations, exotic mind-control experiments, and the effect of hard drugs on the behavior of unwitting subjects. In 1962 even our special issue failed to arouse much curiosity on the part of the general press in the CIA and its operations. But we continued to keep a spotlight focused on the agency with such feature pieces as "Lovestone Diplomacy," by Sidney Lens (July 5, 1965), which broke new ground, and an article by Victor Marchetti, "CIA: The President's Loyal Tool," April 3, 1972, which was the curtain-raiser for the important subsequent disclosures in his book, portions of which the CIA did its best to suppress. After 1972 *The Nation* bowed out of the competition; beating up on the CIA had by then become a media pastime. Yet to this day I am puzzled why an article I solicited from Sir Compton MacKenzie,"The Spy Circus," December 5, 1959, failed to attract the attention it deserved; it should be required reading by all those interested in intelligence agencies.

As often as opportunities arose, I kept wrapping up materials and turning them over to Fred Cook, accompanied by outlines and suggestions on how they might be shaped up as special issues. One, "The Ultras," June 30, 1962, was devoted to the emergence of the radical right; another, "The Corrupt Society," June 1, 1963, to corruption in business and government; both were later published in book form. The latter is still one of the best journalistic accounts of the major scandals of the period. Another special issue, "The Hoffa Trial," May 6, 1964, was one of Cook's more important pieces of investigative reporting, if only because the general press, reacting to Hoffa's bad "image" (and he was certainly no saint), was reluctant to examine the hateful and shabby methods Attorney General Robert Kennedy had approved in order to secure his conviction.

Leonard Downie, Jr., in his book *The New Muckrakers* (1976), credits *The Nation* with keeping the muckraking tradition alive in the decade from 1955 to 1965. Whether we did or not, that is what we tried to do. It was not really our beat. *The Nation* is a journal of opinion and ideas, not a news magazine; but the need, and the opportunity, were obvious. A spotlight was kept on the inquisitorial committees and their antics in such pieces as Bruce Catton's account of the persecution of Harry Dexter White; several fine articles by Waldo Frank on the Oppenheimer case and the "anti-Communist" peril; and former Congressman Byron Scott's devastating analysis of the tall tales Elizabeth Bentley told about W. H. Taylor ("The Letter Nobody Wrote," January 5, 1957). We ran articles on the Rosenberg and Sobell cases by Arthur Garfield Hayes, Stephen Love, and others. We published a fine piece by Bernard Nossiter—one of the few instances in which I permitted a pen name on an article of this kind ("Bud" was still on the staff of the *World-Telegram and Sun*)—about William Perl, a classmate of Julius Rosenberg who had been railroaded to jail on a phony perjury rap. We published Dalton Trumbo on the blacklist ("Blacklist: Black Market," May 4, 1957). Back in 1953 we ran the first article on cigarette smoking and lung cancer to be written by an acknowledged expert, Dr. Alton Ochsner. We kept advancing the wicked notion that a tax should be levied on advertising—still a taboo subject with the media. I was in touch with Ralph Nader when he was still a student. *The Nation* published his first articles, including a famous piece, "The Safe Car You Can't Buy," April 11, 1959, which marked the opening phase of his celebrated encounter with the auto industry. We published the first articles by Richard Cloward and Frances Fox Piven on what is wrong with the welfare system, which later grew into several books on the subject by the two authors. We published a much-publicized article, "The Moynihan Report," by William Ryan (November 2, 1965), which prompted publication of Ryan's interesting book *Blame the Victim*. We kept a critical eye on AT&T and the major insurance companies—institutions systematically neglected by the mass media. We exposed vile jail and prison conditions in articles by Gresham Sykes, Robert Pearman, Bruce Jackson, Tom Murton, Thomas Gaddis, and, yes, Patrick Buchanan, later one of Nixon's aides. The Arkansas prison-farm system was a favorite target. We published countless articles in an unrelenting campaign against the death penalty. We published articles on factory conditions, such as Harvey Swados' famous piece "The Myth of the Happy Worker." A special issue on the "giveaway" programs of the Eisenhower Administration won a University of Illinois journalism award. Another special issue, devoted to Robert Theobald's "Abundance: Threat or Promise?" (May 11, 1963), made his *Free Men, Free Markets* a best seller. A special issue by Ralph Lee Smith first brought the problems of cable television to national attention; later published in book form as *The Wired Nation*, it won the National Magazine Award for Public Service and special awards from the Columbia and Missouri schools of journalism. A grant we obtained for Larry Agran enabled him to do the series of reports on occupationally caused cancer later published as *The Cancer Connection.* We published Alfred Lindesmith's fine articles on narcotic addiction long before the drug scene became a media obsession. The fact is that several anthologies of excellent muckraking articles could be compiled of *Nation* articles by Robert Sherrill, Gene Marine, Stanley Meisler, Kenneth Reich, Stanley Walker, Ralph O'Leary, Desmond Smith, A. G. Mowbray, Jennifer Cross (her articles on supermarkets resulted in a timely book, *The Supermarket Trap,* which went through several printings), Edward Zeigler, Joseph J. Seldin, Joseph Goulden (another National Magazine Award winner), and many others.

The Nation had of course run muckraking articles long before I became editor, but the new emphasis on special-issue journalism in the years from 1955 to 1965 reflected, first, the obvious need and opportunity which then existed and, second, my personal preference. Many of the articles I had written for the magazine in the 1940s would be characterized today as investigative journalism. For example, I wrote the first piece to appear in the national press about Arthur Samish, California's famous legislative boss and lobbyist: "The Guy Who Gets Things Done" (July 9, 1949). Six weeks later, Samish was the subject of a two-part feature in *Collier's* by Lester Velie, "The Secret Boss of California," which resulted in his being convicted of income tax evasion and sent off to McNeil Island to serve a jail term. This distressed me no end. I had not sought to finger Artie but merely to explain how he acquired the awesome power he exercised over the state legislature; most of his corporate clients were probably guilty of much graver infractions of the income tax laws. In any case, he was magnanimous and we exchanged several letters after he was released from prison.[16] And I did other articles of the same kind for *The Nation,* including a much-anthologized three-part feature (April 14, April 21, and May 21, 1951) on the famous California political-public-relations team of Whitaker and Baxter, the first of the professional campaign management firms that have since become a feature of American politics. So to some extent the increased emphasis on muckraking journalism in the years after 1955 reflected my personal interest in this type of reporting.

But by the late 1960s, after *Newsday* and the Associated Press had set up the first teams of investigative reporters, the revival of muckraking was well under way and *The Nation* was rapidly outdistanced. We could not compete once muckraking had become the new radical chic in American journalism, nor was there any reason why we should. During a long arid season we had kept the tradition alive by demonstrating the need for investigative journalism and the interest in it. At the same time we had lifted taboos on subjects long regarded as sacrosanct and called attention to a wealth of new subjects in urgent need of critical media attention.

4. THE PEACE MOVEMENT: FIRST PHASE

The peace movement that began to emerge at the end of World War II did not long survive; it was nipped in the bud by the Cold War freeze. Initially there had been strong support for the United Nations and kindred "one world" concepts, including world federalism. But Truman's upset victory in 1948 and the red-baiting that accompanied it put a hex on these efforts. Two years later the Korean War and the rise of McCarthyism completed the rout of the incipient peace movement. In Lawrence S. Wittner's phrase, "the Cold War had acquired legitimacy."[17]

At the outset, spokesmen for the peace movement failed to recognize that McCarthyism was the domestic counterpart of the Cold War; hence to oppose the one it was necessary to oppose the other. This proved to be a serious mistake, as the brief sad history of the United World Federalists attests. Formed in the late 1940s, the organization got off to a brisk start and soon had a membership of forty thousand and a sizable treasury. An intellectually stylish movement, it avoided the faded rhetoric of the old-line peace groups and managed for a time to escape the taint of "leftism" that attached to them. But by 1950 it too was being viciously red-baited. To deflect and if possible quash these attacks, spokesmen for the organization vied with demagogues in denouncing Communists and radicals, but the slanders persisted. Barring Communists from membership was of no help; it was promptly dismissed as an obvious ruse. Nor did presentation of "peace" awards to Senator Dirksen and Robert McNamara appease its critics or soften their attacks. Membership sharply declined. Legislatures began to rescind world federalist resolutions previously adopted with enthusiasm. Congressional backers withdrew their endorsements. In the space of a few years, United World Federalists had joined the Wallace movement as a casualty of the Cold War.

The career of Cord Meyer, Jr., the organization's "boy wonder," epitomizes the history of the United World Federalists. Meyer had once said that the existence of a secret police was the most damning indictment of the Soviet state, but when he resigned from the federalist movement (after it began to be red-baited) he became a top official with the CIA, and he served in this capacity for sixteen years. It was Meyer who helped arrange a covert subsidy to the National Student Association, the subsequent disclosure of which seriously impaired the organization's credibility and nearly destroyed it. Back in 1949, Meyer had said, "Moscow radio spent some time attacking us, and it attacked me personally not so long ago, as the fig leaf of American imperialism; I think that was the nice phrase they used." A nice phrase it was not, but it proved to be quite apt.

By the middle 1950s the peace movement barely managed to survive; its influence was minimal. But a turning point came in 1955. The condemnation of McCarthy, the cease-fire in Korea, the death of Stalin, and the first "thaw" in Soviet-American relations—illusory as it proved to be—created a somewhat more favorable environment, and the nearly moribund peace movement began to revive. In 1955 the Quakers issued their influential statement *Speak Truth to Power,* which struck a strong affirmative note. *Liberation,* founded in 1956, provided radical pacifists with a forum that had been lacking since Dwight Macdonald's *Politics* suspended publication in 1949. The Montgomery bus boycott and Dr. King's strong advocacy of nonviolence began to generate new currents of interest and support. But it was not until 1957—twelve years after the end of World War II—that the peace movement began to exert much influence.

A precipitating factor in the movement's revival was the rather sudden onset of "the missile era." Just before the Korean War, less than one percent of the defense budget had been devoted to missiles: by 1956 the figure had risen to twenty-one percent. Popular apprehensions, stimulated by the talk of nuclear missiles, suddenly escalated once the Russian sputniks were launched. And this mounting concern was buttressed by a growing skepticism about the arms race; Cold War programs and defense expenditures began to be questioned with a new sharpness and insistence. Writing in *The Nation* of December 14, 1957, Walter Millis voiced a sentiment that could no longer be rejected out of hand: "Our security measures have failed to bring any promise of security. Comparative military strengths, even comparative capacities to release nuclear firepower, have become meaningless. . . . The hydrogen arsenal has not helped; it has disconnected our military power from practical policy in the uncommitted world."

Of this shift in attitudes there were many manifestations. The first of the Pugwash Conferences, which fed a steady stream of sound ideas and fresh initiatives to the peace movement, was held in July, 1957. Formed that same year, the National Committee for a Sane Nuclear Policy soon had 130 chapters out across the country. "Nuclear pacifism," centering on the dangers of tests and radioactive fallout, brought many new adherents to the movement. At the same time, minor splits emerged in the ranks of the intellectual Cold Warriors, some of whom began to have second thoughts about the hazards of a third world war. The pronouncements of the peace groups became less defensive and their protests bolder and more emphatic. In June, 1957, a group of radical pacifists formed Non-Violent Action Against Nuclear Weapons, which later became the Committee for Non-Violent Action, and staged the first of a series of dramatic acts of civil disobedience to protest the continued testing of nuclear weapons. The voyages of the *Golden Rule* and the *Phoenix* in 1958, which focused national attention on the same issue, deeply stirred public opinion.

As the decade drew to a close, the peace movement had to be taken seriously for the first time since 1945. True, it continued to be harassed by rearguard red-baiting and ideological sniping, witness the internal problems that beset SANE[18] and Senator Thomas Dodd's unsuccessful attempt to silence Dr. Linus Pauling, but there was no general retreat. On the contrary, the years from 1957 to 1963 saw a larger proliferation of peace groups than at any time since the 1930s. So much attention has been centered on the movement to halt the war in Vietnam, with its armies of marching protesters and huge demonstrations, that the rebirth of the peace movement that began in the late 1950s has been largely forgotten.

In the first decade of the Cold War (1945–55), the peace movement had been kept alive by the traditional pacifist organizations: the American Friends Service Committee, the Fellowship of Reconciliation, the War Resisters, the Women's International League for Peace and Freedom, and similar groups whose opposition to war in any form had never wavered. Savagely buffeted by the red-baiters, they had somehow managed to survive. *The Nation* had consistently supported these groups; they were long-time friends and allies. After 1955 we gave added coverage to their activities, cooperated with them in lining up special features and articles, and strongly endorsed their efforts. In 1959 alone I projected two special peace issues: "If We Want Peace" (February 21), with contributions by William Appleman Williams, Stewart Meacham, D. F. Fleming, Cecil V. Crabb, Jr., and Urban Whitaker, and "The Economic Hazards of Arms Reduction: What We Must Pay for a Normal Economy in a Stable World" (March 28), with contributions by Paul Baran, Lorie Tarshis, and A. L. Goldberger, all of the economics department at Stanford, Paul Sweezy, co-editor of *Monthly Review,* and others. Both issues bore down heavily on the need for new economic priorities and alternative programs as a means of offsetting continued pressure for heavy arms spending. Even earlier, in the spring of 1957, we ran a series of articles by O. E. Clubb, W. Macmahon Ball, Claudio Veliz, and Paul Johnson on this country's rapid expansion of arms sales overseas which reads today like the first installments of a twenty-year serial. As the 1960 presidential campaign got under way, *The Nation* carried an article on some aspect of the peace movement in almost every other issue. In 1961 alone we published sixteen such articles and many editorials.

Few more powerful peace tracts were published in those years than the articles I was able to induce C. Wright Mills to contribute to *The Nation*. Thousands of reprints of such articles of his as "A Pagan Sermon to the Christian Clergy," March 8, 1955, "A Program for Peace," December 7, 1957, and "The Balance of Blame," June 18, 1960, were distributed by peace groups and church organizations supporting peace candidates. A delightful man, warm, friendly, responsive, outgoing, Mills was an even better polemicist than he was a sociologist; in tone and manner he was just right for *The Nation*, and his untimely death was a severe blow to us and to the peace movement. We also made good use of the talents of Seymour Melman, William S. Royce, Walter Millis, Harold Berman (on Soviet-American trade possibilities), Barbara Deming, who gave us, among other fine pieces, an account (December 23, 1961) of her experiences in the San Francisco to Moscow peace march, and many others. Some years later, Sheed and Ward brought out a collection, edited by Henry Christman, of *Nation* articles of this period devoted to nearly every aspect of the peace movement; published in 1964, it was titled *Peace and Arms: Reports from The Nation*. In its announcement, the publishers said: "Over the years, *The Nation* has been among the very few journals to question the assumptions and analyze the implications of our encompassing military milieu. No journal has reported the issues of peace and arms more regularly or more responsibly."

"Peace" politics, particularly at the congressional level, was another major editorial preoccupation. We devoted close attention to the various peace candidates in the 1958 election, which saw William H. Meyer and Byron Johnson, both *Nation* contributors, elected to Congress: Meyer from Vermont, the first Democrat to be elected from that state, and Johnson from Colorado. In the same way we kept a spotlight on the thirty-two peace candidates who ran for Congress in 1962 and gave special attention to the senatorial candidacy of H. Stuart Hughes in Massachusetts. Politically, peace sentiment was diffuse and lacked national integration. Peace candidacies, for the most part, were restricted to locally sponsored candidates in selected congressional districts in a few states. Even so, this activity was a source of grave concern to the Cold War Establishment.

In those same years *The Nation* conducted an unremitting campaign against the shelter mania, which was at its worst in the summer and fall of 1961. The "sophisticated" rationale offered to justify this insane and costly program was that shelters were necessary to lend credibility to the strategy of nuclear deterrence; otherwise the Russians would not take our threats seriously. But ironically the practical effect of the shelter program was to spread fear and panic which gave added momentum to the peace movement. Defense officials argued that the construction of fallout shelters was "the Christian thing to do, the Godlike thing," even if it meant that neighbors who sought entry to your shelter might have to be treated as aggressors and repelled with whatever force was necessary, as one distinguished theologian reluctantly conceded.[19] In the same spirit, the Civilian Defense coordinator in Riverside, California, urged all local residents to arm themselves so that they could repel the thousands of homeless refugees who might seek shelter there should Los Angeles be bombed. At the same time, Nevada officials announced that measures had been taken to seal off the northeast escape route if Angelenos fled in that direction, while Kern County authorities adopted emergency plans to divert any possible flow of refugees to the Mojave Desert!

In columns which paralleled reports of these grim strategies, Herman Kahn and the editors of *Life* offered cheerful assurances that although millions would certainly perish in a nuclear attack, a minority would survive. So cozy shelters were hastily constructed in the back yards of suburban homes, stocked with supermarket goodies, rock candies, and medical supplies and equipped with TV sets and other gadgets and amenities. Agencies of the federal government spent uncounted millions in stocking rented basements in office buildings, caves, tunnels, and abandoned mine shafts with similar supplies, enough, so we were told, to keep 63 million Americans alive for two weeks. Fifteen years later tons of shelter biscuits, which had been stashed away in underground storage points for nearly two decades, were found to be so rancid even pigs would not touch them, and they had to be destroyed. But during the life of the program local agencies of government were strictly forbidden to tap these supplies even to meet emergency needs during natural disasters; congressional restrictions prohibited such use.

No one will ever know how much this bizarre shelter episode cost American taxpayers, but it would have built thousands of schools, homes, and hospitals. Under any conceivable circumstances, shelters would have been of only minor importance in the strategic-arms balance, since small increases in the power of offensive weapons could easily offset any advantage they offered. As an alternative to shelters, *The Nation* endorsed Dr. E. U. Condon's proposal for the exchange of a large number of Russian and American students as hostages; it would have cost no more and might have had an interesting potential in terms of educational and cultural exchange. But of course this and similar suggestions were dismissed as frivolous by editorial pundits who took quite seriously the "crackpot realism" of Herman Kahn.

After the 1962 election, I managed to secure a foundation grant for Roger Hagan, then at Harvard, which enabled him to undertake a coast-to-coast study of how matters stood with the peace movement. His report (February 2, 1963) pointed out that it was still largely made up of middle-class elements, that relatively few blacks were involved despite Dr. King's emphasis on nonviolence, and that it was not sufficiently concerned with social, economic, and political realities. There seemed to be "no politics in the movement"; it was "more a mood than a movement." Abstract, moralistic, exhortatory, it had few ties with organized interest groups such as small businessmen and farmers, and its support in the unions was narrow and marginal. Election returns clearly demonstrated that communities would invariably vote to retain local defense facilities in the absence of alternative means of providing jobs and income to residents. Peace advocates seemed unwilling to believe that long periods of sustained production approaching full employment had been achieved only during wars or periods of heavy defense spending. And most of them failed to see a connection between Cold War policies and the remarkable expansion of American capitalism overseas.

Both Hagan and Charles Bolton, in a similar *Nation* survey, called attention to the division in the peace movement between confirmed pacifists—the moralists—and the moderates who were too eager to settle for too little. In part because of the tension between these factions, the reborn peace movement made the mistake of overemphasizing the importance of a ban on nuclear tests in the atmosphere. The effect was to cast the peace movement in the role of a single-issue constituency divorced from any permanent concern with underlying causes for ever-increasing arms spending. After the Nuclear Test Ban Treaty was signed, much of the steam seemed to go out of the movement; the peace groups were so relieved—so pleased with their "victory"—that they were slow to note that military expenditures continued to rise sharply and that the number of underground nuclear tests actually increased. Moreover, the signing of the test ban treaty diverted attention from Washington's new reliance on counterinsurgency tactics and other indications that the Cold War was beginning to heat up. With the dramatic escalation of the war in Vietnam that began in 1965, a new or second phase in the history of the peace movement got under way. But then the movement had a definite national objective of broad appeal: to stop the war which the counterinsurgency enthusiasts had escalated.

5. *THE BAY OF PIGS*

John Kennedy's Administration was blighted by the Bay of Pigs invasion almost before the cheering and excitement of his stylish and triumphant inauguration had subsided. Few Presidents have been confronted so early in their first term with a fiasco of this magnitude. It put the Administration immediately on the defensive. It led directly to the Cuban missile crisis. It gave right-wing ultras an issue which they were quick to exploit. Stupidly conceived and amateurishly executed, it revealed a startling failure of the intelligence agencies. Badly reported as it was, it brought to light a pattern of lies, deceptions, betrayals, and attempted cover-ups that foreshadowed the Watergate trickeries. Indeed, there was a direct connection. The Cubans who participated in the Watergate break-in were veterans of the ill-starred invasion, recruited and directed—later lied to and abandoned—by their former CIA sponsors. A series of preinvasion memos which Arthur M. Schlesinger, Jr., then a top aide, prepared for President Kennedy clearly anticipated the Watergate ethic. Fancy scenarios or cover stories were outlined, and alternative answers to possibly embarrassing press conference questions were submitted, but the President was advised to leave most of the explaining to subordinate officials. Beguiled by this and similar briefings, the President went along with plans for the invasion on the assumption that U.S. involvement could be concealed or successfully denied. But once concealment proved to be a fantasy, he quickly realized the folly of the action and canceled the air raids that were supposed to have provided cover and protection, and the invading units were then "dumped," i.e., abandoned. To his credit, he did take full responsibility for the national humiliation and major disaster the Bay of Pigs proved to be.[20]

If the press over the years had not abandoned its adversary role in reporting "sensitive" Cold War issues, the Bay of Pigs debacle might have been avoided. Any careful reading of news stories in the year that preceded the invasion would have suggested the likelihood of some such action; not only was it implicit in past Cuban-American relations, but the press was put on notice that such plans existed. In the 1920s Villard had once cabled Carleton Beals a hundred dollars so that he might proceed by burro into the jungles of Nicaragua to interview the bandit leader Sandino, an assignment that resulted in a major scoop for *The Nation.* In the spring of 1960, Carleton asked me for an advance of substantially the same amount so that he might visit Cuba to find out what was really going on. Few American reporters knew more about Cuba, but neither the wire services nor the newspapers would send him there, because he was known to be critical of U.S. policy. In his first article (July 23, 1960), he reported that tensions between this country and Cuba were mounting in a dangerous fashion, and a later report from Havana—"Cuba's Invasion Jitters," November 12—clearly fore-shadowed what was to happen the following spring. When Castro visited this country that fall, there were numerous rumors of a buildup of anti-Castro guerrilla forces. Later there were stories of "a mighty armada" of U.S. warships cruising about in the Caribbean with no apparent mission. In *The Nation* of October 15, 1960, we pointed out in an editorial captioned "Not Guatemala Again" that it looked as though plans were being prepared to invade Cuba in the guise of protecting Guatemala against a Cuban attack. In this same editorial we suggested it might be somewhat more difficult to knock over the Castro regime, which was reported to have an army of 25,000 and a militia force of 200,000, using Russian equipment and supplies, than it had been to oust the Arbenz regime in Guatemala. Given past U.S. actions and predispositions and with Allen Dulles directing the CIA, it was almost a foregone conclusion that an invasion of Cuba would be staged. As Herbert L. Matthews pointed out in *The Cuban Story* (1961): "It should have been crystal clear that Cuba was not Guatemala, that the Cubans were not Guatemalans and that Fidel Castro was not Jácobo Arbenz. If the CIA was looking at anything crystal it was a crystal ball. Fidel Castro and the others knew that elements in the United States would want to repeat the Guatemalan experience."

Then, one day in November, Paul Baran, a contributor and close personal friend, phoned from Stanford to say that Ronald Hilton, director of the university's Institute of Hispanic-American Studies, had just returned from Guatemala with reports that it was common knowledge—indeed, it had been reported in *La Hora,* a leading newspaper, on October 30—that the CIA was training a guerrilla force at a secret base for an early invasion of Cuba. I promptly got in touch with Hilton, who confirmed what Baran had said, added some details and agreed I might quote him. So I wrote an editorial

which appeared in our issue of November 19, 1960, setting forth
the facts he had given me, including the location of the base near
the mountain town of Retalhuleu and citing him as our source. If
the reports were true, I wrote, "then public pressure should be
brought to bear upon the administration to abandon this dangerous and hare-brained project"; in the meantime the facts should be
checked out immediately "by all U.S. news media with correspondents in Guatemala." A special press release was prepared to which
copies of the editorial were attached, but the wire services ignored
the story and only one or two papers mentioned it. Yet this was *the
first report to appear in the American press of the preparations then being
made for the Bay of Pigs invasion*—by any reckoning a major news
story.

The existence of the "secret" base at Retalhuleu was common
knowledge in Guatemala, so we had not alerted Castro to its existence. Nine days after our editorial appeared, the New York *Times*
carried a report in which President Ydigoras of Guatemala
branded the information about the base as "false . . . a pack of lies."
That seemed to satisfy the *Times*—for the moment. But the St.
Louis *Post-Dispatch* decided to send Richard Dudman to Guatemala, and he had little difficulty in confirming the existence of "a
secret 1,200-foot airstrip" that had been cut in a jungle area and a
nearby barracks with a capacity for housing five hundred men.
Early in January, the Los Angeles *Times* sent its aviation editor,
Don Dwiggins, to check on the facts, and he too confirmed the
report. So I got him to summarize his findings by way of backing
up our first report (*The Nation*, January 7, 1961). In the meantime,
Washington had broken off relations with the Castro regime on
January 3, which prompted *Time* to comment: "What snapped U.S.
patience was a new propaganda offensive from Havana charging
the United States was plotting an 'imminent invasion' of Cuba"!
Then, finally, on January 10, the New York *Times,* in a follow-up
story, guardedly acknowledged the existence of a base at Retalhuleu but said it was apparently being used to train forces to defend
Guatemala against a possible Cuban invasion.

A week or two after the Bay of Pigs disaster, a group of press
executives met with President Kennedy at the White House. At this
session the President complained of premature disclosure of security information in the press and cited Paul Kennedy's story in the
New York *Times* of January 10 as a case in point. Turner Catledge
then reminded him that reports about the base had previously
appeared in *La Hora* and *The Nation*. "But it was not news until it
appeared in *The Times,*" the President replied. On another occasion
he said to Catledge, "If you had printed more about the operation,

you would have saved us from a colossal mistake." And more than a year later he told Orvil Dryfoos, "I wish you had run everything on Cuba . . . I am just sorry you didn't tell it at the time." President Kennedy was correct: timely disclosure of the facts might have prevented what was truly a "colossal mistake"; but the press elected not to pursue the lead *The Nation* had provided.[21]

In the wake of the invasion, I decided to let Ronald Hilton have the last word. In an article captioned "The Cuban Trap"—April 29, 1961—he demonstrated that the press had deliberately remained silent after being charged with notice of the invasion plans; it was, he concluded, a case of self-censorship. And he closed his article by predicting that the stupid invasion scheme, so recklessly conceived, so swathed in lies and deceptions, would sour relations between the United States and Cuba for a generation, which turned out to be a fairly accurate forecast.

But of course there was more—and worse—to come. The Kennedys were determined to settle scores with Castro by any means short of another "secret" invasion. A ransom of $53 million was paid to secure the release of Cubans captured at the Bay of Pigs. Then a secret army of terrorists was organized by the CIA in what proved to be the largest single covert operation it had ever conducted. Trained, directed, and financed by the agency, exile forces launched hundreds of commando raids against Cuba from a string of bases stretching from Miami to Key West, poisoning crops, sabotaging factories, killing civilians. A staff of more than six hundred CIA agents organized the force of perhaps two thousand Cuban exiles that participated in these raids, with shellings of selected targets, incendiary fires, the bombing of Cuban embassies in Latin America and Europe, and other acts of terrorism. Even as President Kennedy spoke at the University of Washington on November 16, 1961, and seemed to adopt a more cautious and conciliatory line, these clandestine raids were being carried out. At the same time, Washington attempted, and with considerable success, to enforce a worldwide embargo against Cuba. Predictably the effect of all this activity was to increase Castro's dependence on the U.S.S.R., although he did not want or request Soviet missiles; that was Khrushchev's idea. But Castro was convinced—and with reason— that the commando raids might well be the prelude to another and larger invasion which would possibly have direct American backing. This "secret army" phase of the Kennedy vendetta culminated, of course, in the missile crisis of October 22, 1962, which was, in the context of events, a crisis of our making and one that might easily have triggered a world war.

In the aftermath of the missile crisis, the Kennedys still pursued their vendetta against Castro. Apparently Washington had agreed not to launch another invasion of Cuba, as part of the understanding by which the missiles were withdrawn. But that did not rule out clandestine operations conducted by Cuban exiles. So the plottings then assumed even more bizarre forms. Castro contends that twenty-four attempts were made on his life; the Church Committee—the Select Committee to Study Governmental Activities with Respect to Intelligence Activities—documented at least eight such attempts. Nutty James Bond schemes were hatched, such as efforts to put LSD into Castro's cigars so he would appear to be drunk when he spoke in public, and attempts to place a powder in his boots which would damage his beard, thereby reducing his charismatic appeal! The assassination plots were carried out by a division of the CIA called Executive Action with the clearly implied approval of the White House. Terrorists were brought from Miami as guests of Robert Kennedy to Hickory Hill, his Virginia residence, to receive his personal assurance of this country's continued support for their criminal activities. At an earlier stage, Mafia elements were enlisted by the CIA in the assassination plots, again with the implied approval of the highest authorities. Well-paid senior American officials, grown men, presumably sane, approved these grotesque schemes.

Apparently the CIA-sponsored commando raids ceased shortly after President Kennedy's assassination, but the Cuban exiles carried on, more or less on their own, with the guidance and help of "retired" CIA personnel and the knowledge of the FBI and the Florida police. On October 6, 1976, fifteen years after the Bay of Pigs fiasco, an Air Cubana plane was bombed, with the loss of seventy-three lives—an action for which the Miami Cuban exiles claimed full credit. And when "Eduardo"—E. Howard Hunt—was authorized to recruit a commando squad to carry out highly dubious "missions" for the Nixon Administration, he had little difficulty in recruiting a force of 120 or more loyal Bay of Pigs veterans. In the end, of course, these and other Cuban exiles originally recruited by the CIA were "dumped" much as were their counterparts in Vietnam. But as late as June 10, 1977, exile terrorists were still carrying on clandestine operations and boasting about it on national television. It was, in fact, not until August of that year that federal and state agents for the first time took the initiative against Cuban terrorists by seizing three boats, an antitank cannon and other weapons to prevent what was to have been another of many hit-and-run raids somewhere on the Cuban coast. On that same day, August 15, CBS announced that the Administration had begun to exchange intelligence with Cuban officials about the

Miami exiles and their activities; one Cuban, a former CIA agent, was actually arrested.[22]

I had suspected, of course, but could not find hard evidence to prove much of what we now know happened after the Bay of Pigs; it was, in fact, implicit in the pattern of the original action. Even so I felt like retching when I watched *The CIA's Secret Army*, the CBS documentary, with its detailed revelation of the manifold lies, deceits, crimes, stupidities, and betrayals that characterized American policy toward Cuba both before and after the Bay of Pigs. All in the name of "national security"; all in the guise of "fighting Communism." Of our various Cuban fantasies none seemed more weird to me than the suggestion that Castro might have plotted the assassination of President Kennedy. As he himself said—and convincingly—on an NBC program, it would have been an act of sheer lunacy; if the slightest evidence of complicity in such a plot had been disclosed, we would have stormed into Cuba with all guns blazing.

In retrospect, I have often wondered how much the pre– and post–Bay of Pigs operations cost, including the millions paid out in concealed and untraceable ways. It would be a tidy sum. But far more significant has been the loss of prestige, the bad faith, and the ultimate humiliation implicit in American policy toward the Castro regime under both the Eisenhower and Kennedy Administrations. From first to last, the Bay of Pigs was one of the least glorious chapters in the history of the Cold War.

6. *SPEAKING OF SCOOPS*

Although not primarily a news magazine, *The Nation* has scored its share of major scoops. The story of the Bay of Pigs invasion was one; Henrique Galvao's account of the seizure of the Portuguese luxury liner *Santa María* was another. Ours was the first published report by the chief participant of the most audacious act of "piracy" on the high seas in modern times. For a week or more, the story commanded headlines in the world press. But it was more than a great news story: in Galvao's words, the seizure of the *Santa María* struck a hard blow at the Salazar dictatorship by "breaching the ramparts of fear" and thereby setting in motion a series of events which eventually led to the undoing of that hateful regime. "How I Seized the *Santa María*," in *The Nation* of April 15, 1961, was the result of a long shot that paid off handsomely.

Henrique Galvao, a former Portuguese Army captain, had been highly critical of Salazar's colonial policies during his term as inspector general of the Portuguese colony of Angola. When his reports continued to be ignored, he returned to Lisbon, denounced Salazar before the National Assembly, and was promptly arrested. Tried by a military tribunal, he was convicted and sentenced to three years at hard labor, but somehow he managed to escape and sought refuge in South America. Through a contact of Del Vayo's, I was able to get his address and induced him to send us an article, "Salazar: Man and Mask," which appeared in *The Nation* of January 9, 1960. A year later the world was electrified by the startling intelligence that Galvao, disguised as a paralytic, and twenty-four Spanish and Portuguese rebels had boarded the *Santa María* at Curaçao as passengers and, once it was on the high seas, had disarmed the crew and taken possession. From January 23 to February 2, the *Santa María* insouciantly circled and zigzagged about in the South Atlantic, with a British cruiser and two American destroyers following in its wake. Galvao was careful to emphasize that the seizure was not an act of piracy in the conventional sense but the rightful retaking of possession by Portuguese rebels of a floating piece of Portuguese "territory" as part of a national political rebellion. After cruising about for more than a week, Captain Galvao allowed the 607 passengers to land at Recife, Brazil, where the next day he formally surrendered the liner to an admiral of the Brazilian Navy and came ashore with his crew, all of them having been granted asylum. The entire action was carried out with high skill, great daring, and extraordinary finesse; there was, as I recall, only one casualty, the result of an accident. The derring-do manner in which the action was staged not only humiliated the Salazar regime but won nearly universal admiration and applause.

As soon as I learned that it was Galvao who had seized the liner, I radioed a message to the *Santa María* urging him to send us an article. On February 28 I had a note from him in São Paulo in which he said he was writing, for our exclusive use, "a narrative of the complete story." When the article appeared it was reprinted in dozens of newspapers and magazines—Sunday *Times* (London), *Observateur* (Paris), Toronto *Star,* St. Louis *Post-Dispatch,* Washington *Post,* New York *Times* and many other publications; an expanded version later appeared in book form: *My Crusade for Portugal* (1961). The seizure of the *Santa María* aroused particularly intense interest and excitement in Luanda, where it was thought Galvao might bring the liner. With this in mind, Angolan rebels, forces of the MPLA—the People's Movement for the Liberation of Angola—attacked the prison at dawn on February 4, 1961, as a first step toward freeing the city in anticipation of Galvao's arrival.

Of this incident, Antonio de Figueiredo writes in *Portugal: Fifty Years of Dictatorship* (1976) that it marked "the first major explosion of African nationalism in Angola in nearly four decades of repression."

Later in 1961 *The Nation* published an article by Galvao, "A Revolutionary Program for Portugal," which makes interesting reading in light of what subsequently happened. And the next year I was delighted to receive from him a manuscript in which he told how, with the aid of a few fellow rebels, he had hijacked an airliner flying from Casablanca and flown it over Lisbon, showering residents with revolutionary leaflets, an action which further humiliated and embarrassed the Salazar regime ("Sky Pilots Over Lisbon," *The Nation*, February 3, 1962). The last article of his we were privileged to publish, "The Price of the Azores," December 21, 1963, contained some advice Washington should have heeded but didn't.

That same month the State Department denied Galvao a visa, but a tacit agreement was finally worked out which permitted him to visit New York for thirty-six hours so that he might address a group of United Nations delegates, at their request, on the state of the Portuguese colonies. No one was quite certain at the time just what would happen. Salazar was, of course, demanding Galvao's arrest: he had been sentenced, in absentia, to twenty-two years in prison for the seizure of the *Santa María*. Once in New York, Galvao sent word he would like to see me, so, accompanied by George Kirstein, I met with him in the basement apartment of a Portuguese refugee who was the building's janitor. The place was swarming with FBI agents and city police and besieged by reporters and cameramen trying to interview Galvao. But despite the noise and confusion, we managed to have a good visit.

Galvao was as I had imagined him to be: a merry man, with a twinkle in his eye, extremely intelligent, friendly, and supremely confident that Salazar's regime would be overthrown and soon. The last note I had from him, written in his rather quaint English, is dated December 16, 1963. In wishing me a Merry Christmas he said: "I have also a great pleasure to meet you and hope de next visit can be more extended." But there was to be no next visit. On June 25, 1970, word came of his death in São Paulo, after a long illness, at age seventy-five. "We are pirates," he wrote of the *Santa María* action, "who are attempting to recover from other pirates the liberty and dignity which they have stolen from an entire people." Just as Del Vayo did not live to return to Spain after Franco's death, so Galvao died in exile before the Salazar regime was toppled. But as much as any one person, he helped bring it down.

7. NOTES ON CONTRIBUTORS

During the years she edited *The Nation,* Freda Kirchwey relied heavily on regular staff contributors, as Villard had done when he was editor. There is much to be said for such a policy. It is easier to plan issues and to maintain editorial standards and is probably less expensive than making individual assignments. But it limits the range of interest and makes for predictability. As editor I thought the magazine should constantly be seeking new talent and fresh subject matter. So I placed less reliance on regular staff contributors, with exceptions noted for back-of-the-book columnists and a Washington correspondent to bother at all hours of the day and night with queries.

The trick, of course, was to stimulate a sufficient flow of material so that one had a fairly wide range of choice. Random queries were routinely sent out in large volume, as well as specific inquiries and suggestions. The number of acceptances based on random queries was never large; in one six-month period we published seven articles submitted in response to seventy-odd queries of this sort. But now and then good manuscripts came in more than a year after the author had received an unacknowledged query. And of course I kept up a steady flow of letters suggesting specific assignments, often accompanied with batches of material by way of piquing curiosity and interest, a technique that proved quite successful. Over the years an impressive number of books developed out of articles *The Nation* had suggested or assigned. I made it a practice to look at all manuscripts submitted, to acknowledge queries, and to accept or reject material as quickly as possible—a practice I had come to admire in H. L. Mencken. Also I learned, early on, the psychological importance of a timely telephone call. If I queried the right person at the right time on a subject of special interest to that person, the chances of acceptance were better if I used the phone, and there was less delay. Amazingly few assignments were rejected because of the meager rates we could offer; indeed, rates were rarely discussed.

But I had no reason to feel apologetic about *The Nation*'s rates, for I knew how many young writers we had helped launch on successful careers. As merely one of many similar examples, consider the case of Hunter Thompson. In 1965 Hunter was living in San Francisco. He had recently quit the *National Observer,* having decided, as he put it in a *Playboy* interview (November, 1974), "to fuck journalism" and was dead broke at the time. Then one day he got a query from me enclosing a report of the California Attorney General's office on motorcycle gangs and an offer of a hundred dollars for an article. I had known Hunter before he went to live in San Francisco and felt sure the subject would intrigue him. "That was the rent," he says in the interview, "and I was about ready to get back into journalism, so I said, 'Of course, I'd do *anything* for a hundred dollars.' " It took him a month to write the piece, and he was viciously worked over by one of the gangs, but he seemed to enjoy the assignment. After the article appeared— *The Nation,* May 17, 1965—his mailbox piled high with offers of magazine assignments and book contracts; he couldn't believe it. It was, he said, "one of the biggest magazine gigs since Burton and Taylor"; he received offers of assignments from *Playboy, Cavalier, Esquire, The Saturday Evening Post* and other magazines and a contract for the publication of *Hell's Angels,* which became one of the liveliest best sellers of the season. But as might be expected his success soon moved him out of our price range; the last piece I was able to wangle out of him was a report on "The Non-Student Left" at Berkeley (September 17, 1965). But when he came to New York he usually dropped by the office for a chat, carting a six-pack of beer. *Hell's Angels* makes a good but by no means exceptional *Nation* story; we also published, for example, James Baldwin's first published piece. Again and again we were able to help launch young writers on successful careers by publishing their first writings and guiding them to promising material. That they soon moved on to more lucrative assignments was only as it should be; it kept the pages open for other young writers.

On rare occasions, *The Nation* would fall heir to a contributor, which is how we acquired Robert Sherrill. Bob was pleased as punch to have gotten the first interview that H. L. Hunt, the Texas tycoon, had granted in more than seven years, and even more delighted when Hunt talked freely and at great length about many topics. But the editors at *Harper's,* including his old Texas friend Willie Morris, were fearful of libel and insisted on deep cuts and changes, so he sent the manuscript to me. Despite the fact that *The Nation* had just spent five or six thousand dollars in the successful defense of a libel action that should never have been filed, I decided to use the Hunt piece as it stood ("H. L. Hunt: Portrait of a Super-Patriot," February 24, 1964). Incidentally, no libel judgments were entered against *The Nation* during my editorship, which was more a matter of luck than of judgment: it is often difficult to spot libel in a manuscript.

After the Hunt interview appeared, I needled Sherrill into doing other portraits for us, of "Jungle Jim" Eastland, George Smathers,

George Wallace, John Connally, and Wright Patman, as well as articles about whatever the two of us found interesting. (The Southern portraits appear in *Gothic Politics in the Deep South,* published in 1968.) Southern political types had an irresistible fascination for him, and he had an intimate knowledge of the region's politics; the son of a Texas editor, he had served as a State House reporter in Tallahassee and Austin. A product of the native American radical or "populist" tradition, Sherrill proved to be a real find: a tough-minded, curious, hard-to-fool, perceptive journalist who was notably free of ideological hang-ups. Early in 1965, I talked him into moving from Austin to Washington to become *The Nation*'s correspondent; although we were never able to pay him a regular salary or retainer, the assignment made it possible for him to establish a reputation as one of the country's top political reporters. The timing was providential. With political power shifting to the Sun Belt, and Southern politics in a state of flux, he was an ideal choice, the more so since he was named correspondent not long after Johnson was sworn in as President. A quintessential Texan himself, Sherrill was an expert on Lyndon Baines Johnson long before Johnson became President. He was, in fact, so perceptive about LBJ that I kept nagging him to do a book about the President, which he finally wrote, after much prodding and many arguments. Naturally I was pleased to discover that *The Accidental President* was dedicated to "Carey and Peter," but just who in hell was Peter? Peter, it turned out, was Sherrill's pet cat, who before he departed this life was named as co-dedicatee of two subsequent Sherrill books.

Down the years, *The Nation* was fortunate to have fine Washington correspondents, including, in addition to Sherrill, Paul Y. Anderson and I. F. Stone. Izzy, an old friend, had left *The Nation* some years before I came east. After *The Compass* suspended publication, I strongly urged Freda to restore his name to the masthead and station him in Washington, but she thought otherwise, much to my disappointment and Izzy's. Years later, in a *Wall Street Journal* interview, Izzy was quoted as saying that *The Nation* would not take him back because of his politics. But in this respect he was mistaken; politics had nothing to do with Freda's decision. She admired Izzy immensely, liked him personally, and in general shared his political point of view. But she was convinced, on the basis of past experience, that no sooner would he be reestablished in Washington as *The Nation*'s correspondent than he would want to take off on a special mission or project; it had happened before. But he proved how mistaken she was by moving to Washington, where he has remained these many years.

Over the years I had the privilege of working with more fine foreign correspondents—Basil Davidson, Carleton Beals, Mark Gayn, Frederick Kuh, Anthony Sampson, Desmond Steward, Edgar Snow, et al.—than I can remember. Of these Alexander Werth ranked at the top of the list. By any reckoning he was one of the finest European correspondents from the early 1930s until his death on March 2, 1969. Alex was born in St. Petersburg, the son of a wealthy banker and industrialist who lost his fortune in the revolution, which his son, whose English mother died when he was quite young, witnessed as a schoolboy and found "very exciting." Educated at the select Reformation School, he learned to speak four languages fluently: English, Russian, German and French. In 1918 father and son left Russia. Alex attended Glasgow University, began his journalistic career with the Glasgow *Bulletin,* and later wrote for the Glasgow *Herald,* the *Manchester Guardian,* the London *Times, New Statesman,* and other papers. He began writing for *The Nation* around 1934 and, with brief interruptions, remained its European correspondent until his death. Alex witnessed Hitler's rise to power, covered the Reichstag fire, and was in Madrid at the height of the Spanish Civil War. Few correspondents could rival his expert knowledge of French politics: *France: 1940–1945, The De Gaulle Revolution,* and *The Strange History of Pierre Mendès-France and the Great Conflict over French North Africa* are still prime sources. He managed to leave Paris two days before the Germans arrived, and his diary, *The Last Days of Paris,* became a best seller in England, where he spent the dramatic years 1940–41 and was three times "bombed out."

Shortly after the Nazis invaded the Soviet Union, Alex lined up some assignments and left for Moscow, where he remained throughout the war. He and Henry Shapiro were the only foreign journalists allowed to enter Leningrad during the blockade. No correspondent reported the war years in Russia with greater insight or knowledge, and his BBC broadcasts were a popular feature of those years. *Moscow War Diary, Leningard,* and *The Year of Stalingrad* were vivid eyewitness accounts of the war on the eastern front. Of his fifteen or more books, *Russia at War: 1941–1945* is perhaps the finest. Alex had an expert knowledge of Russian art, literature, and music; a gifted pianist and musicologist, he knew Prokofiev quite well. In 1946 he had a famous interview with Stalin: "There will be no war, and we shall soon have an atom bomb." But he didn't like the Cold War atmosphere in Russia any better than he liked it elsewhere, so he left the Soviet Union in May, 1948, annoyed and disgusted by the purges and the political arrests and by Soviet policies toward artists and intellectuals. His book *Musical*

Uproar in Moscow (1949) did not improve his standing in the eyes of Soviet authorities.

The next two years he spent in Eastern Europe, principally in Yugoslavia, Czechoslovakia and Poland. Predictably his dispatches were savaged in Eastern Europe and the Soviet Union—where he was even denounced as an English spy—while his resistance to Cold War hysteria made him, for a time, *persona non grata* with the British and American press. For some years *The Nation* was his only outlet aside from one or two French publications. In 1950 he took up permanent residence in France, but he made a last long visit to the Soviet Union in 1959–60 which resulted in two books: *Russia under Khrushchev* and *Russia: Hopes and Fears.* Previously he had spent a year at Ohio State University, of all places, as a visiting professor of modern history, a project arranged by Harvey Goldberg, another *Nation* contributor, with some assistance that we were able to furnish. The year was 1957, and the first Russian sputniks had aroused much concern and anxiety in this country. Alex's book *America in Doubt* (1958), published in Britain but never here, is a striking example of his ability, even in an unfamiliar setting, to read public attitudes with sensitivity and rare insight.

Werth and Claude Bourdet, who succeeded him as *The Nation*'s European correspondent, were superb contributors and a delight to work with. Alex and I had such close rapport we could indulge in a kind of telepathic communication: he knew what we would want about the same time we did and often got the piece to us before we could query him. I have never seen copy as messy as his seemed to be at first glance, but once you got the knack of it, with all the tiny interlineations and delicate marginal notes, it was quite easy to read and required virtually no editing. It would be hard to name a correspondent who had a more intimate knowledge of major European developments in the years from 1930 to the late 1960s. Werth was more than a great journalist: he was part of the history of the times and the events he reported.

Presenting Jacob Bronowski

World War II gave an enormous impetus to the scientific revolution, but the consequences were not widely noted in the press until the middle 1950s. When C. P. Snow's famous essay "The Two Cultures" first appeared—*New Statesman,* October 6, 1956—it was received as a major revelation. As he saw it, the industrial society of electronics, atomic energy, and automation would "in cardinal respects" be different in kind from any previously known and would "change the world much more." In fact, the changes which the scientific revolution had already initiated were responsible, in his view, for the sharp conflict between the older traditional culture and the new scientific culture. But he did not deal with perhaps the most important aspect of the conflict: the impact of science and technology on human values—an issue brilliantly presented in Jacob Bronowski's equally famous essay "Science and Human Values," which appeared in *The Nation* of December 28, 1956.

I had previously recruited Bronowski as a contributor because of his remarkable gifts as an expositor of ideas and concepts in the field of science. His first *Nation* article, "Dilemma of the Scientists," August 14, 1954, discussed the new responsibilities which the scientific revolution had imposed on scientists. A bit later (January 20, 1955) we published "The Face of Violence"—"vice is a personal disfigurement, but violence is an impulse we all share"; "Violence is the sphinx by the fireside, and she has a human face"—which was followed by "Einstein's Influence," "The Abacus and the Rose," and other manuscripts. Then one day in 1956 I happened to be thumbing through an issue of *Universities Quarterly* and came across "Science and Human Values," the text of lectures delivered at MIT in March of 1953 which Bronowski had not submitted to us because of their length. I found it hard to believe that this brilliant book-length statement had not been published until three years after the lectures were delivered and only then in a relatively obscure academic journal, and even harder to believe that the manuscript had never been published in this country. Naturally I lost little time in securing Bronowski's permission to use it.

The special issue we devoted to the manuscript was greeted with extraordinary enthusiasm and drew waves of favorable comment. The new role of science in human affairs was just beginning to receive the attention it deserved, so the timing was excellent. Julian Messner, Inc., promptly brought out a hard-cover edition; later, in 1959, it was included in the Harper Torchbook series and became a best seller. Then, to complete the circle, it was finally published in London by Hutchinson & Company in 1961, nearly a decade after the lectures had been delivered at MIT—a rather remarkable case history of the delayed and more or less accidental discovery of a seminal work. Of *Science and Human Values* C. P. Snow said that if asked to select six works to explain to an intelligent nonscientist something of the meaning of science, he would include it on his list, while to Norbert Wiener it was "a great and courageous statement."

Shortly after our special issue appeared, Saul Bass, the Hollywood designer, phoned to say he was so impressed with it that he proposed to fly to London in an effort to persuade Bronowski to address the 1957 International Design Conference at Aspen and asked if I would arrange an appointment, which I did. When Bronowski arrived in New York that summer en route to Colorado I met him for the first time, and I saw him frequently on subsequent visits. In a roundabout way, his appearance at Aspen led to his being named a fellow of the Salk Institute for Biological Studies at La Jolla, of which he later became deputy director. He himself said that *The Nation*'s publication of "Science and Human Values" was responsible for his coming to this country. After reading it, Leo Szilard had recommended Bronowski to the Salk Foundation as a scientist and science administrator who understood the ethical and human issues in biological research which the Institute proposed to explore.

Bronowski was born in Poland in 1908, the son of Polish-Jewish parents. Polish-speaking, he was taken at the age of three to Germany, where he learned German, and then at age twelve to England, where he learned English. Trained as a mathematician, he received his Ph.D. at Cambridge in 1933 and taught for some years at the University of Hull. On the outbreak of World War II, he left the university to head a number of research projects that had been set up to study the statistical and economic effects of large-scale bombing raids, an assignment that made him one of the pioneers in what came to be known as operational research. P. M. S. Blackett credited Bronowski's theoretical work with the success of Operation Monte Carlo, which disrupted the German submarine offensive operating from bases in the Bay of Biscay. In 1945 he was sent to Japan as scientific deputy to the British Chiefs of Staff mission to study the impact of the Allied air raids. His report, "The Effects of the Atomic Bombs at Hiroshima and Nagasaki," is the classic statement on the subject. It was this experience that prompted Bronowski to write "Science and Human Values." It had made him conscious, he later said, of the gap that exists between the practice of science and the demands to which we allow it to be a servant. Back in Britain, he became director of the Coal Research Establishment of the National Coal Board, directing the work of a large research staff until in 1964 he joined the Salk Institute, where he remained until his death in late August, 1974. For some years he conducted an immensely popular lecture-interview program on the BBC, which was interrupted and never resumed because of serious injuries he sustained in an automobile accident.

Three qualities made Bronowski a most remarkable artist in ideas and an invaluable contributor. He had the ethical passion—the passion for truth—that East European Jewish intellectuals managed to sustain for generations. He was also an artist, with a

poet's interest in poetry and a vivid pictorial imagination. A leading
authority on Blake, he wrote knowledgeably of British poets from
Sidney to Yeats. He was also a brilliantly trained mathematician
with an active interest in many fields of science and technology.
None of these qualities predominated, because they had been
fused in his experience in a way that made for a special unity. He
was not a philosopher, although he had profound philosophical
insights. He was not a great critic, yet his feeling for literature and
the arts colored every aspect of his thinking; he was, in fact, a
unique kind of artist. He was not a great scientist—he had no
single major scientific achievement to his credit. He was not a fellow of the Royal Society, but he understood science as well perhaps
as any scientist of his time and had an extraordinary facility in
explaining science—its methods, its spirit, its ideas—to large audiences of well-informed but not scientifically trained readers and
television viewers. He was also politically astute and knew the kind
of world in which he lived. Much admired as a top science administrator, he had an excellent grasp of public issues and the way
institutions operate. This combination of qualities, and his atypical
background, seemed to set him apart from his peers; he was very
much a part of the scientific-intellectual establishment but could
not be fitted into any particular niche, which is precisely what made
him a superb commentator on science and the work of scientists.

A short, stocky man with black hair and heavy black eyebrows,
slightly swarthy, Bronowski had a square head that sat solidly on
his compact body. A delightful companion and marvelous conver-
sationalist, he often seemed to be enjoying a very special private
joke; the eyes usually had a merry twinkle; his soft-spoken sen-
tences curled out effortlessly in delightful patterns. He was a man
of rare charm and wit, and women were much attracted to him, as
he was to them. He spoke with a very slight lisp which was oddly at
variance with his manner. Although he had not learned English
until twelve years of age, he spoke without a trace of foreign accent.
Yet his speech was not pure Oxbridge either; there was enough
difference to make it distinctive. The marks of a superior British
education were there, but he was not the typical well-bred upper-
class British intellectual; here too there were variations. He was a
superb lecturer and, as this implies, a fine actor. Those who had
the good fortune to hear him deliver the inaugural "Man and
Nature" lectures at the American Museum of Natural History in
New York will attest to his unrivaled gifts as an expositor of profound and complex ideas, talents brilliantly demonstrated and sustained throughout the thirteen-part television production *The Ascent of Man,* a virtuoso performance from first to last, viewed by a

huge audience (700,000 in the New York metropolitan area alone). Bronowski was prompted to do the television series because Lord Clark's famous BBC lectures *Civilization* had scarcely mentioned the word "science." The ideas in *Science and Human Values* were, so to speak, amplified in *The Ascent of Man,* the book on which the TV series was based, which also enjoyed a huge success. Bronowski let us publish the concluding chapter with its eloquent summing up:

> Knowledge is not a loose-leaf notebook of facts. Above all, it is a responsibility for the integrity of what we are as ethical creatures. You cannot possibly maintain that informed integrity if you let other people run the world for you while you yourself continue to live out of a rag bag of morals that come from past beliefs. . . . We are nature's unique experiment to make the rational intelligence prove itself sounder than the reflex. Knowledge is our destiny.

Introducing the Revisionists

History was an early casualty of the Cold War. As Howard Zinn put it, we emerged from World War II—"the most just of wars"— under the spell of an illusion of self-righteousness coupled with an illusion of omnipotence. In such a setting, the official view, strongly reinforced by Cold War pressures, quickly became the generally accepted view; it became history. "The historian's facts and conclusions," writes Lloyd C. Gardner,

> had already been chosen for him, before he began. Scholars personally involved in the Cold War devoted themselves to producing 'White Papers' on Russian violations of their agreements with the West. The object was to see how big a list of these misdeeds one could put together. If the President said that the Soviet Union had violated forty-seven pacts and treaties, the State Department scurried around to draw up a list to conform to the accusation, and Cold War historians all too often came following after.[23]

From 1945 on, *The Nation* made a special point of seeking out scholars who were not irrevocably committed to the official view; fortunately there were a few—but not many—whose insights we could tap. In the early phases of the Cold War, we relied heavily on D. F. Fleming and Frederick L. Schuman. At the time, mainstream journals showed little interest in their views. Even later, when tensions were less severe, Fleming had difficulty in finding an American publisher for his two-volume ritique of American policy, *The Cold War and Its Origins*. Written without benefit of latter-day research and disclosures, it was a pioneer effort to get at the facts and proved to be an enormously useful reference. Both of them experts on international relations and diplomacy, Fleming and Schuman belonged to a prewar generation of scholars. Neither was a "revisionist": both had been writing about the Cold War since the day it began, which proved to be an advantage for us, since their reactions were usually quick and sharp. Thus, when *Collier's* came out with a lurid special issue on how this country won World War III hands down and going away, Fleming promptly took it apart in a scholarly analysis that attracted wide attention here and abroad. *Collier's* promptly backed off, and, for a time, the enthusiasm for flame-throwing journalism abated.

After 1955 the stream of revisionist histories began, with William Appleman Williams' *The Tragedy of American Diplomacy* (1959) and his other books. Of the revisionists, Williams has been perhaps the most influential. For a historian of the Cold War, his background was unique but appropriate. A graduate of Kemper Military School and the United States Naval Academy, he was hospitalized for serious injuries received in the Pacific and ultimately retired from the Navy in 1947. During a protracted period of hospitalization, he decided to become a historian and went on to receive his Ph.D. at Wisconsin in 1950.

In a sense, Bill was a *Nation* discovery; we published his first pieces. Some time before his first book was published, mutual friends he had consulted in the course of his research on Raymond Robins and Russian-American relations had brought his work to my attention. In a series of *Nation* pieces in the late 1950s, most of which have been reprinted in his books, Williams charted a course for other revisionists and acquired a remarkable following among graduate students on many campuses. In one of the best of these pieces, he examined the fruits of Henry Luce's high-noon fantasy, the "American Century." To Williams "the black and white austere certainty" of that grandiose conception had prompted such decisions as one announced by the State Department in 1957, namely, that the projected visit of forty-seven American students to Communist China "would be subversive of United States foreign policy" (New York *Times*, August 13, 1957). Announcements of this sort confirmed the view of those who said that the Soviets appeared to have conquered America without firing a shot; it was the kind of decision that prompted one diplomat to remark, "It is the West which is destroying the West." None of the revisionists had a keener awareness of the bipartisan imperialism underlying American policy than Williams. In a *Nation* piece of November 2, 1957, he summed up his criticism of U.S. Cold War policies in this way:

> America is neither the last best hope of the world nor the agent of civilization destined to destroy the barbarians. We have much to offer, but also much to learn. And the basic lesson is that we have misconceived leadership among equals as the exercise of predominance over others. Such an outlook is neither idealism nor realism; it is either self-righteousness or sophistry. Either is an indulgence which democracy cannot afford.

But while Williams was a prime discovery, there were few American revisionist historians whose first writings did not appear in *The Nation.* The list would include David Horowitz, Walter La Feber, Gabriel Kolko, Barton Bernstein, Lloyd C. Gardner, Christopher Lasch, Howard Zinn, Carl Oglesby, Thomas G. Paterson, Ronald Radosh, H. Stuart Hughes, Fred Warner Neal, Richard J. Walton, and many more. In general I tried to use scholarly commentary and criticism to lend depth and insight to reports from our regular correspondents. In the later 1950s, we first brought Geoffrey Barraclough's work to the attention of American magazine readers. One of the shrewdest critics of Cold War humbug and pretense, he wrote articles that offered valuable insights into the rising tide of unrest in Africa, Asia, and the Middle East quite some years before the Third World theme began to reverberate in the American press. Isaac Deutscher, E. J. Hobsbawm, David Thomson, E. H. Carr, and Raymond Williams also helped keep Cold War developments in proper perspective. Having admired Williams' work for years, I induced him to become *The Nation*'s London correspondent.

As the views of the revisionist historians became better known, and the reporting from Vietnam began to improve, historians and journalists who had long slavishly adhered to the official Washington line began to revise their views retroactively, as by graciously admitting a few minor misjudgments, "clarifying" earlier statements, and hedging on current commitments. Thus, in October, 1967, Richard Rovere felt compelled to admit that the Vietnam War represented "an application of established policy that has miscarried so dreadfully that we must begin re-examining not just the case at hand but the whole works." By then, "the whole works" was, indeed, in deep trouble.[24]

But the revisionist perspective did more than unsettle Establishment dogmas: it contributed significantly to the rising tide of antiwar ferment and agitation. If the Vietnam War was to be opposed effectively, it had to be seen not as an isolated aberration but as the logical consequence of Cold War policies formulated on the basis of false assumptions. It also had to be seen from a Vietnamese perspective, but, as usual, it was our history, not theirs, that mattered. As Alexander Woodside pointed out (*The Nation*, December 13, 1975), we are "the contemporary world's purest example of a society which is perpetually trying to abolish history, to avoid thinking in historical terms, to associate dynamism with amnesia. . . . The American pretense that other people's history doesn't count is unfortunately one of the things that isolates America from the rest of the world."

If the Cold War theoreticians—those "architects of illusion"— had bothered to familiarize themselves with the thousand-year struggle of the Vietnamese to achieve independent nationhood, they might have hesitated before sending in Colonel Edward Lansdale and his associates to win their hearts and minds by the use of counterinsurgency tactics. Perhaps the debacle in Vietnam has finally taught us to respect other people's history. Lloyd C. Gardner thinks it has: "The Cold War ended American history, as distinct from world history, and became the central event in a unique perception of the universe. The illusion was shattered only when other people asserted a claim to determine their share of world history."[25]

Reporting the Counterculture

The much-discussed new radicalism of the 1960s was, as Jack Newfield has noted, "a somewhat amorphous and multilayered movement." As a symbol the young President Kennedy may have helped bring it along—it dated from 1960 or thereabouts—but he was not its spokesman, nor did he represent it. Politically it did not derive from the bankrupt liberalism of the 1950s and it had few ties with the old left, which had been fragmented, isolated, and nearly red-baited out of existence. The brief flurry of interest which the Beat Generation aroused was a premonition of things to come, but the Beats were basically apolitical.

Initially the new radicals exhibited some interest in theory, ideology, and program, but as the Cold War heated up—in Cuba, in Vietnam—they opted for the politics of protest. Very much aware of television, they soon learned how to attract media attention with sit-ins, marches, and demonstrations, as the civil-rights and peace movement activists had done in the late 1950s. In general the new radicalism, so called, represented a revulsion against the complacency, stuffiness and conformity of an "affluent" society. It also reflected the discontents such a society fosters. It was more a product of irritation, resentment, and boredom than a reaction to social inequalities and injustices personally experienced or observed at first hand. After all, many of the young radicals came from white middle-class backgrounds. But their resentments were real. They were justifiably annoyed by fatuous assurances that the major social problems of American society had been solved when this was patently not true. They had had more than enough of direct and indirect pressures for conformity; there had been little movement in American politics for nearly a generation. And they had good reason for wanting to break out of the claustrophobic atmosphere generated by a balance-of-terror diplomacy. But in the absence of leadership in either major party capable of appreciating the extent or understanding the causes of their profound if often vaguely stated dissatisfactions, they had to strike out on their own.

The conflict of generations is, of course, a constant factor in politics, but in the late 1950s it assumed a uniquely sharp form. The young radicals were eager to break, not merely with the bipartisan Cold War consensus, but with the "liberalism" of their parents, to which they initially responded but later came to regard as unreal and pretentious. Theirs was in part a personal revolt; they sought to "liberate" themselves by repudiating conventions and attitudes that had grown irksome. In a sense, they were more concerned with finding where they stood, who they were, and what it was they found so hateful in the society than they were in defining political positions or drafting action programs or organizing at the grass roots. In addition to this existential dimension, stimulated by such writers as Albert Camus and Paul Goodman, their radicalism reflected a strong aversion to the increasingly hierarchial form that most large organizations had assumed.

Convinced that a new radical movement was shaping up quite unlike any we had known in the past, I did what I usually did when a new movement or major social trend seemed to be emerging—i.e., gather materials about it while looking around for the right person to examine them and report what was happening. The files on the new radicalism I turned over to Jack Newfield, whose reporting for *The Village Voice* I had come to admire. Jack was familiar with the Beat Generation, "the first trickle of the angry flood," as he put it. He had been an active participant in the early civil-rights demonstrations and peace marches and did not need to be briefed on "left" movements in American politics. And the offices of the *Voice* were then close by, which made it easy for us to confer from time to time. I had good reason to be pleased with the use Jack made of the materials I turned over to him and kept feeding

him, both in pieces he did for the *Voice* and in those that appeared
in *The Nation*. Most of the pieces he did for us were reprinted, in a
somewhat different form, in his books *A Prophetic Minority* (1966)
and *Bread and Roses Too* (1971). With his help, I was able to initiate
an ongoing dialogue on the new radicalism, its strengths and weaknesses, that continued throughout the 1960s and into the 1970s. In
fact, one could easily compile several thick anthologies of *Nation*
articles dealing with various aspects of "the movement," including
some of the first articles on the new feminism.

But there was, I strongly felt, an acute need for a study of the
cultural background of the new radicalism. What I had in mind
was a long essay or series of articles that would provide a guide or
frame of reference in much the same way that Christopher Lasch
had spelled out the meaning of the "Cultural Cold War." I wanted
an analysis of what it was about the changing cultural scene that
seemed to nag at the times and demand recognition. The wealth
of materials I had assembled, from many sources, on this particular
phase of "the movement" convinced me that another important
subject was in search of the right author.

Previously I had enlisted Theodore Roszak as a contributor while
he was still teaching at Stanford, and the more I had seen of his
work the more I was impressed with his insistent curiosity, his
sensitivity to new values and changing attitudes, and his keen interest in the cultural aspects of modern science and technology. He
had the rare faculty of being able to examine new social and cultural developments in an unbiased, reasonably sympathetic, and
profoundly curious way; new life styles and defiant attitudes, for
example, did not arouse his antipathy; he wanted to find out what
it was about them that interested him. Somewhat bored with academic life, Ted had spent a year in London as the first American
editor of *Peace News,* a position he had secured, incidentally,
through a classified ad in *The Nation*. I kept in touch with him
during his fruitful year in London and had several long talks with
him on his return, so I had reason to know that his rather odd,
offbeat "sabbatical" had given him some original insights into aspects of the new radicalism. On my urging, he agreed to examine
the materials I had assembled on the "counterculture" and see
what sense if any could be made of them.

Four of the eight chapters of *The Making of a Counter Culture*
were first published in *The Nation*. Before the last had appeared,
Ted had signed a contract to expand the articles into a book. The
book, of course, was a huge success, as it deserved to be, for it
caught, in a perceptive and sensitive way, the new "cultural constellation": the psychology of alienation, the interest in Oriental

mysticism, psychedelic drugs, visionary perceptions and intuitions, communitarian experiments, and other aspects of what promptly came to be known as the counterculture. C. P. Snow and Jacob Bronowski had been concerned with the impact of science and technology on the traditional culture and human values. Roszak was preoccupied with the way in which what he called "technocracy" had been used to organize, control, and manipulate people, with its blighting effects on the "visionary" side of politics, and the manner in which it "denatured" the imagination. He had come to see technocracy as representing the peak of the integrating force of an industrial society. To understand the social effects it had produced, he suggested that we explore the "counterculture" it had spawned. Such a culture had begun to emerge in the late 1950s, but prior to the appearance of *The Making of a Counter Culture* neither its origins nor its significance had been carefully examined.

Alienated by consensus politics and repeated assurances that no new "visions" or ideals or utopias were needed or even thinkable, since with a little tinkering here and there and a few minor adjustments it would be easy to usher in a technological paradise of perpetual prosperity, vanguard elements of the new generation had revolted. Above all it was the way society ignored their feelings—indeed, constantly affronted them—that these elements most resented. They did not relish the idea of being locked into a future about which they had not been consulted. Roszak conceded that the counterculture had not matured and that its future was problematical, but he insisted that "the alienated young" were giving shape to "something that looks like the saving vision our endangered civilization requires." To him the emergence of a counterculture pointed to the need of "altering the total cultural context within which our daily politics takes place." And since adherents of the new counterculture were far more numerous than the new radical activists, his study had major political implications. Written at the time, as part of the "cultural constellation" it described, *The Making of a Counter Culture* remains the classic statement on the subject.

In retrospect I am astounded by the number of contributors I recruited for *The Nation* and those I came to know in person or by correspondence. The fruits of my editorship can be inspected in fifty bound volumes. Thumbing through these husky tomes stirs a flood of memories. Nearly every issue reminds me how a particular article was acquired or the reaction it provoked or the problems it presented. Over more than a quarter of a century, I dealt with an army of contributors: reporters and journalists in every state and from all points on the compass; with novelists, critics, poets, playwrights, historians, and philosophers; with academicians in many disciplines on many campuses; with scientists, Nobel Prize winners, heads of state, industrialists, ministers, ambassadors, senators and governors by the score, Washington political reporters, bureaucrats and officials, columnists, members of not one but several parliaments. And also with drug addicts, ex-convicts, tugboat pilots; with blacks, Mexican Americans, Indians; with feminists, lesbians, gays and hippies; with a prince (Sihanouk) and a pirate (Henrique Galvao), with dignitaries, revolutionists, and the nondescript. A parade of contributors trooped through the office in that quarter century, to say hello, to gossip, to argue, to offer editorial proposals. Also on lecture trips I kept meeting contributors wherever I went. Contributors formed a community with *The Nation* as its center, its village post office, its meeting place. Contributors from overseas made it their headquarters on visits to New York.

No task I had to learn as an editor was more taxing than the care, nurture, and handling of contributors. I never mastered it, but I did get better at it. Some contributors can be a pain in the neck, egocentric, demanding, persistent, unreasonable, and quarrelsome. The editor–contributor relationship is not necessarily adversary—quite the contrary—but it has a high potential for conflict and misunderstanding. Contributors are preoccupied with their manuscripts, their masterpieces, while editors must think constantly about last week's, this week's, and next week's issues. But I learned how to avoid some of the pitfalls and had relatively few serious quarrels even with the few contributors I heartily disliked. And no part of the task of editing *The Nation* was more satisfying than unearthing new talent, watching the rows of bound volumes expand, and observing the list of books that grew out of *The Nation* steadily lengthen year by year.

8. THE PERSISTENT RIGHT

Again and again the demise of the far right has been prematurely celebrated: in 1954 with the condemnation of McCarthy, in 1960 with Kennedy's defeat of Nixon, in 1964 with Johnson's victory over Goldwater, and still later with Nixon's departure from the White House. But each time the right has bounced back, sometimes in a new guise, but with essentially the same objectives.

On March 12, 1960, *The Economist* reported, with some surprise, that McCarthyism was still a major force in American politics—six years after condemnation had been voted and three years after the Senator's death. But there was no occasion for surprise. The inception of what came to be known as "the radical right" dated almost from the moment condemnation was voted; it began, so to speak, when and where McCarthyism left off. William F. Buckley's polemic *McCarthy and His Enemies* was published in 1954, and the first issue of *National Review* appeared in November, 1955. The American Security Council, the CIA of the far right, made its debut in 1955. And Robert H. W. Welch, Jr., left the family candy business in 1957, at the time of McCarthy's death, to found the John Birch Society, which twenty years later is still active.

Responding to renewed pressure from the radical right and disturbed by the reborn peace movement of the late 1950s, President Eisenhower decided that extraordinary methods had to be invoked to strengthen popular support for Cold War policies and programs. In 1958 the National Security Council issued a directive that military personnel and facilities were to be used to whip up Cold War sentiment, a brazen attempt to involve the military in domestic politics which, at the time, drew virtually no criticism. For the next several years, this crassly propagandistic program continued in the form of seminars, special briefings, conferences, and public meetings, some financed directly by the military, some by such organizations as the Institute for American Strategy (funded by the Richardson Foundation, which was probably the beneficiary of covert subsidies from the CIA). The program clearly violated the age-old tradition, if not the actual practice, that the military must stay out of politics, a principle Eisenhower had carefully observed in the past. That it functioned as long as it did, with his backing, was a measure of the unabated power of the right even after the condemnation and the death of McCarthy.[26]

But the radical-right movement differed from McCarthyism in two major respects. In launching *National Review,* Buckley had quite shrewdly turned for ideological support to such ex-radical intellectuals as Max Eastman, Will Herberg, James Burnham, and John Dos Passos. Aided by other intellectuals of similar background and persuasion, they succeeded in investing the radical right with an aura of intellectual cachet and sophistication which McCarthyism sorely lacked. Right-winging antiradicalism became the new ideological fashion. An added difference was this: McCarthyism was never a well-organized movement, whereas the radical right was skillfully organized and lavishly financed. By 1961 it had brought into being a network of several hundred well-organized, well-financed, and extremely active right-wing groups and organizations. Most of them had close ties with defense contractors, oil-and-gas tycoons in the Sun Belt, and other big-business interests. For example, the Christian Anti-Communist Crusade was funded initially by the Allen-Bradley Company of Milwaukee, and Harding College, a beehive of right-wing activities, received important support from General Electric. It was GE that launched Ronald Reagan on his political career with its eight-year sponsorship of his appearances on the luncheon-club circuit and before meetings of GE employees, an experience that enabled him to perfect "the speech," which electrified the 1964 Republican convention and made him a leading spokesman for the far right. (Repeated with minor variations for more than a decade, the speech still draws warm applause.) But nouveau-riche elements—manufacturers of razor blades and dog foods—also contributed large sums to the radical right. For some of these types, financing "anti-Communist" fronts was a status trip, more a means of enhancing their social position than of acquiring political influence.

After 1960, with a Democrat once again in the White House after an eight-year hiatus, the radical right quickly assumed a new national prominence; 1961 and 1962 were years of maximum activity and media coverage. The Bay of Pigs fiasco provided a marvelous opportunity to pressure Kennedy to assume a tougher Cold War stance, and the right made the most of it. In the spring of 1961, Hans Engh, a Santa Barbara reporter, provided *The Nation* with one of the first reports on the John Birch Society after it had decided to "go public" (March 29, 1961). And that fall Eugene V. Schneider, in a special feature on the far right (*The Nation*, September 30, 1961), summed up by saying that "in spite of optimistic predictions the voice of the rightwing radical is heard loud and clear in our land once more."

It was heard loud and clear on October 16, 1961, when C. D. Jackson, publisher of *Life,* appeared at a huge rally in Hollywood Bowl staged by the Reverend Fred Schwartz's Christian Anti-Communist Crusade to offer an abject apology for some unkind references to the organization and its sponsors, some of whom spent a lot of money on national advertising. While the radical-right intellectuals exhibited a veneer of sophistication, the grass-roots elements outdid McCarthy in their rabid denunciations. In guerrilla-like forays against individuals, organizations, and institutions suspect of heresies, they indulged in reckless scatter-gun tactics as vicious as any that McCarthy had used. But as the 1964 campaign drew near, the "new conservatives" of the far right concentrated their energies on a major political objective: the nomination of

Barry Goldwater, which gave them control of the national apparatus of the Republican Party—quite a triumph for a movement
that had been pronounced dead in 1954.[27]

At the Cow Palace convention I spent a great deal of time with
the Alabama, South Carolina, Louisiana, and Texas delegations.
Many of these delegates were attending their first national convention and had only recently joined the Republican Party. I found
only a few "Ole Boy" Southern types among the delegates I interviewed. Most of them were young, fairly well educated hustlers
and go-getters, full of drive and energy, who seemed more concerned with their private careers and business interests than with
ideology. Quite a number were recent migrants from the North
who had been drawn to the South and the Southwest by the lure of
better jobs and finer homes in the rapidly expanding centers of
power in the region. Many appeared to have opportunistically
adopted the rhetoric of Goldwater "conservatism" as a means of
winning influence and favor with the dominant interests in these
centers. By and large they were personable, well-mannered and
quite conventional in their attitudes, in contrast with their political
rhetoric, which had harsh and violent overtones. I found it hard to
associate the abuse these and other Goldwater delegates heaped on
Senator Mark Hatfield, Nelson Rockefeller, John Lindsay, and
William Scranton with conventional conservatism. And indeed it
was not "conservatism" that had triumphed in San Francisco but
the radicalism of the right. Conservatism, like liberalism, had become a casualty of the Cold War.

I left the convention feeling that a rising new regional middle
class, aggressive, cocky, and rambunctious, had invaded the Republican Party disguised as "new conservatives" and would not be
easily or quickly dislodged. "This new middle class," I reported in
The Nation (August 24, 1964),

> with its auxiliaries and retainers, has been spawned by the af-
> fluence of the cold-war years. It reflects, in rigid form, the
> cumulative acquisitiveness and arrogance of the period. Many
> of the young pushers and shovers in the movement expect to
> "make it big" by the time they are 40; they cannot conceive—
> and will not concede—that there is any likelihood whatever
> that the long-continued boom of the federally favored regions
> they inhabit could ever end. To some extent, their counter-
> parts may be found in the Middle West and the East, but there
> they are neither so numerous nor so vocal; in the Goldwater
> belt they are loud, numerous, and chesty. As Nixon shrewdly
> observed in a recent interview, these new-money types often

seem to be undergoing "some kind of personal rebellion." They harbor a variety of resentments—against their own antecedents, against those pushing up from below, against those on the next rung above them. Hostility to what they regard as the snobbish ruling elite of the Eastern establishment accounts for part of their belligerence and ebullience. With them "Ivy League," in any context, carries poisonous connotations. Self-satisfied and socially insensitive, their general attitude can be summarized in a phrase: "to hell with you, Jack." This general attitude reflects, of course, great underlying tension and insecurity. Like any new rising middle class, this one has a superabundance of energy and drive.

Earlier in the year, I had obtained a foundation grant for William S. Ellis so that he might visit the then emerging Space Crescent states stretching from Florida through Louisiana and Texas to Arizona and Southern California and report what was happening there. His three-part series (October 12, 19, and 26, 1964) was the first serious journalistic attempt to assess the impact of continued heavy defense and aerospace spending in the region and the changes it had set in motion. To Ellis, who discovered the Sun Belt more than a decade before it became a major media topic, the region was "a pork barrel" that vibrated with the thundering energy of young people. As might be expected, no politician was more aware of the significance of this development than Richard Nixon. The Republican Party, he pointed out in a 1964 interview, had moved well to the right, and the significance of the changes was not to be understood "without a knowledge of what has happened in the West for this conservative surge is to a very great extent a Western surge." True, but he might better have said that the Republican Party had been *moved* to the right by raiding contingents who represented the growing power of new regional interests with a heavy stake in the continuance of Cold War policies.

Over a period of years the political power of the right had been enhanced by the steadily increasing share of defense and aerospace funds spent in the Sun Belt states. It meant, of course, more jobs, more new subdivisions, more new residents, a boom for banks and insurance companies, soaring markets for local merchants, and lowered social costs. The region became a kind of "new frontier" in which a boom-town atmosphere prevailed. A strong consensus supported every effort to increase defense and aerospace appropriations and the region's share in these funds. The same consensus, of course, opposed other types of federal spending. From the region's perspective, deteriorating social services, urban blight, and mounting welfare costs in Northern and Middle Western states were not national problems. Yet the "crisis of the cities" really dates from the end of World War II; again and again needed urban programs had been shelved because of national "emergencies," as in Korea and Vietnam. Urban affairs did not receive Cabinet status until 1965; a mass-transportation act was not passed until 1964. In 1968 one-third of American Negroes—two-thirds of those living outside the South—resided in the twelve largest cities, and of these perhaps twenty percent lived in urban ghettoes. Naturally the Sun Belt states opposed attempts to equalize welfare costs or to tackle the problem of urban blight. As Ralph Ellison told a Senate committee, "We very often get the impression that what is wrong with the American city is the Negro, when the reverse is true. What is wrong with the Negro is what we Americans have done to the city." And what we had done or permitted to happen to the cities was in large part a consequence of the Cold War.

At the San Francisco convention the Goldwaterites seemed to be more interested in settling scores with the Eastern Seaboard "Ivy League" Republicans than in laying the foundation for a strong campaign. I thought at the time that many delegates realized that the Goldwater-Miller ticket could not win the election but were well satisfied to have captured control of the national Republican organization. Nixon would have known how to control the "new conservatives" and keep them in line, but Goldwater constantly cheered them on. Instead of moving toward the center after securing the nomination, he continued to appeal to the right. No doubt President Kennedy would have defeated Goldwater handily, but the combination of his assassination, Johnson's aggressive support of civil-rights and "Great Society" programs, and widespread apprehension aroused by Goldwater's belligerent Cold War pronouncements gave Johnson a landslide victory.

After the election there was a feeling, as in 1960, that the right had been turned back; that "moderation" had prevailed. But while it had lost the election, the right's power had actually been enhanced. It had control of the national apparatus of the Republican Party, and the liberal Republicans had been savagely pummeled. The right was now in a position to exert greater political leverage than at any time since 1952. The returns had hardly been counted before it began to pressure Johnson as it had President Kennedy to adopt more aggressive Cold War policies, and with no countervailing pressure from liberal Republicans and liberal Democrats the pressure brought results. By escalating the war in Vietnam, Johnson managed to keep the right fairly quiescent for a time, but by 1967 it was again demanding more militant action abroad and a crackdown on domestic dissent. As Fred J. Cook pointed out in a *Nation* piece of March 13, 1967, the right had demonstrated that it had nine lives. A captive of Cold War pressures and past decisions and commitments, and besieged by a surging antiwar movement, Johnson finally bowed out, thereby insuring the election of Nixon. So the right finally got what it wanted: Nixon in the White House. Of course it felt betrayed later when he went traipsing off to Moscow and Peking, but it should have been forewarned. As far back as May 2, 1959, *The Nation* had noted that Nixon was acting as though he thought detente might be good politics in 1960, but he later backed off when Goldwater denounced him for roaming too far to the left.[28]

Again after Watergate, nearly a decade later, there were audible sighs of relief: the right had suffered, it seemed, a decisive setback. There was even a feeling that we had narrowly escaped a kind of right-wing *coup d'état*. But it soon became clear that the right was still in business. In no way revolted by Nixon's tactics—the dirty tricks, the counterintelligence capers, the break-ins, the shakedowns and the corruption—the right quickly rallied to his defense despite the Moscow and Peking initiatives. Its spokesmen, including "new conservative" intellectuals, soft-pedaled their criticism, offered apologies for his behavior, and defended him until, near the end, a few of them felt compelled to pull back a step or two in self-protection. With Watergate still a fresh and painful memory, Ronald Reagan, a Nixon loyalist, made a strong bid for the Republican nomination in 1976, and his defeat did not demoralize the right.

Obviously the right has not been routed; it persists.

9. THE CAMOUFLAGE WAR

At the Democratic convention in Los Angeles in 1960, I liked the spirit and tone of Eugene McCarthy's speech nominating Stevenson but found little else there to applaud. Specifically I did not like the steamroller tactics used to secure Lyndon Johnson's nomination as Vice President, by way of appeasing the Dixiecrats, and found Kennedy's "New Frontier" rhetoric empty, pretentious, and imitative. The precise phrase and theme had been borrowed from Harry Hopkins, who had made much better use of both in the 1930s.[29] But in November *The Nation*, while not overcome with enthusiasm, managed "two cheers" for Kennedy.

Hence I was disappointed but not surprised by the failure of the new Administration to fulfill the extravagant hopes it had aroused. From the moment J. Edgar Hoover and Allen Dulles were asked to stay on, I had a dreary feeling we could expect only more of the same: consensus politics, corporate liberalism, token social reform, increased defense spending, a grandiose space program with military implications, and new tensions in the Cold War. There were many new faces in Washington—and some familiar ones—but most of the New Frontiersmen were Cold War types, old before their time. In general the liberals Kennedy attracted to Washington were more aggressively "anti-Communist" than the bureaucrats they replaced. By 1962 the defense budget topped the last one Eisenhower had submitted by $10 billion. The promise implicit in the Peace Corps was never fully realized; the Alliance for Progress was soon put to uses inconsistent with the President's rhetoric. On the domestic side, the Administration refused repeated requests to provide protection for Freedom Riders and civil-rights demonstrators and authorized a wiretap on the Reverend Martin Luther King, Jr. One of Attorney General Robert Kennedy's top aides solemnly assured me that no such tap had been ordered. Not until well into 1963, and only then in response to mounting protests and demonstrations, did the Administration urge adoption of civil-rights legislation. Despite the bold rhetoric about a New Frontier, little if any important social legislation was enacted during President Kennedy's years in the White House.

Almost from the moment it took power the Kennedy Administration began to step up U.S. military involvement in Vietnam. But initially it was difficult to get at the facts: the Administration was less than frank, and the reporting from Saigon was inadequate and often misleading. But from the spring of 1961 on, *The Nation* could point to many signs that American military intervention had taken a more direct form and that counterinsurgency theories and tactics were to be given a major test. On March 18 we warned that it was "late, very late," in Vietnam and that the Administration was initiating military actions which domestic Cold War political pressures would almost certainly force it to expand. In the issue of July 28 we noted: "This dirty war may not be lost by the United States but neither will it be won. At the expense of mounting American casualties it will drag on." Throughout the balance of the year we kept insisting that disaster was coming in installments, and early in January, 1963, we summed up by saying: "Despite our arsenal of weapons we do not have the power to 'win' this war." By then twelve thousand or more U.S. troops were stationed in Vietnam, and the number kept edging up. In a lengthy editorial, "The Booby Trap in Vietnam" (September 14, 1963), *The Nation* repeated what it had been saying about the war since the beginning of this country's involvement:

The cardinal fallacy of American policy has been the idea that "victory" could be achieved by methods as evil as any the Communists have employed, and that democracy can use tyranny as its shield. The situation will deteriorate as long as these grotesque notions prevail in Washington. . . . The odds are that the Communists will eventually win in South Vietnam, their patience is more durable than America's enthusiasm for an expensive, futile war. Nevertheless, Vietnam is important and historic. It is the steamy battleground where the cold war of the past decade was buried; it is the birthplace of the "camouflage" war of the nuclear age.

Up to that time, the camouflage character of U.S. military intervention had combined with other factors to keep opposition at a low level; Americans were not pleased with the war, but significant opposition had been slow in forming. With astronauts circling the globe, exploring "the new oceans of space," and the Great American Barbecue continuing with few signs of abatement, the Vietnam War seemed like a minor irritant or fever, a far-off annoyance that presented no serious threat to our "prosperity" or prestige or sense of national well-being.

The assassination of President Kennedy shattered these illusions. Measured in terms of political impact, the rifle shots fired at Dallas had the explosive force of a nuclear blast. The initial reaction was a combination of shock, sorrow, dismay, fear, rage, panic, and deep national concern. Overnight the popular mood changed from exuberance to paranoia; social and political tensions acquired a new edge; the emotional impact was immeasurable. At the time I felt that the President's assassination marked the beginning of a revolution—in attitudes, outlook, national perspectives—but one I could not define. Suddenly the violence had struck home; the Republic seemed threatened from within by forces which had been building up since the inception of the Cold War. With the subsequent assassinations of Dr. King and Robert Kennedy, the sense of outrage, frenzy, and frustration built to a climax in 1968, when the nation suffered what might be described as a kind of moral, ideological, and political breakdown. But the long-deferred crack-up of the Cold War consensus began with the assassination of President Kennedy.

Like other publications, *The Nation* was inundated with manuscripts about the assassinations; first about the assassination of President Kennedy, then about the Warren Commission report, then about the assassinations of Dr. King and Robert Kennedy. In the excitement following the assassinations, rumors, false reports, and misstatements of fact multiplied in a way that defied verification or timely refutation; before a specific rumor could be disposed of, dozens of facsimiles had appeared which in turn spawned fresh rumors and speculation. There were those, even among our readers, who roundly abused us for refusing to publish transparently wild scenarios about the assassinations devoid of verifiable facts or supporting evidence. I respected the staff of the Warren Commission—Norman Redlich, its chief executive officer, had been a frequent contributor—and had no desire to add to their problems. But *The Nation* was quite willing to test the findings of the Warren Report and did so in a number of articles, including one that prompted the chairman to summon a special meeting of the commission to consider its implications (the article is discussed in Gerald Ford's book on the commission). But it was not interested in hyped-up sensational scripts, nor did it publish speculative pieces unless they were clearly labeled as such and raised issues that seemed to merit investigation.

The furor over the assassinations had an odd twofold political effect, part negative, part positive. To the degree that the assassinations became the major focus of national interest and concern, attention was diverted from the Vietnam War in a way that enabled Johnson to proceed with his unannounced plans to escalate the fighting. On the other hand, there is no doubt that the assassinations—notably President Kennedy's—marked a turning point in Cold War attitudes and expectations; in this respect the political atmosphere was transformed. A profound uneasiness spread throughout the society at all levels; rigid Cold War dogmas were shaken; a surging sense of outrage could no longer be quieted with platitudes or put down by strictures. Confrontation replaced consensus as demonstrators took to the streets and angry armies began to march and protest.

In the fall of 1955, when I had induced George Kirstein to become publisher of *The Nation,* there was some reason to believe that Cold War tensions might be lessening, and the first successes of the civil-rights and peace movements had lent encouragement to these hopes. But the Kirstein Years ended on a note of uncertainty. A succession of crises and abortive summits, capped by the national tragedy in Dallas, had ushered in a new chapter in the Cold War. At the end of 1965 I had no notion what precise form the politics of the next decade might assume, but I knew that an explosion of some sort was in the making. The complacency had vanished; the fear of subversion had subsided; the contagion of dissent was spreading; and the illusion that we could continue to run the world the way we thought it should be run had been badly shaken. Our "prosperity" began to look a bit dubious; our social gains negligible; our technological marvels impressive but not directly relevant to the everyday needs of most people; and the Cold War was heating up. The future seemed even more uncertain than it had in 1955 (it is always uncertain) but, in a curious way, less intimidating and more hopeful. Beneath the surface new forces were roiling.

CHAPTER IX

THE STORROW YEARS

After ten hectic years as publisher of *The Nation,* George Kirstein began to show signs not of fatigue or boredom but of a desire to pursue his own special intellectual interests. In a sense I was responsible, if unintentionally, for his decision to step down. For a long time I had been needling him to write a book about the American rich. He had, I kept telling him, exactly the right credentials and background for the task. He was rich but not too rich. Of Jewish background, he stood outside both the Jewish and the non-Jewish preserves of the rich. He knew the world of inherited wealth and had enjoyed its privileges, yet perhaps he had never felt really a part of it. Soon the idea began to appeal to him, and before I fully realized what I had done in my breezy lunchtime chatter, I had talked *The Nation* out of a fine publisher. Early in 1965 George decided to withdraw at the end of the year in order to write *The Rich: Are They Different?* A gallant man, George. Fully aware of the magazine's problems, he had assumed responsibility for its continuance at a critical moment. The two of us had shared some searing experiences during the years he was publisher but managed somehow to escape unscathed, in good spirits, and, in the process, to become the best of friends. I hated to see him leave, but I had to respect his wishes.

If it had to be, 1965 was a logical year to change publishers. It rounded out a decade of service for George and marked a century of publication for the magazine, the first issue having appeared on

July 7, 1865. With this in mind, we had begun, early in 1965, to make plans for an ambitiously conceived centennial issue. But it soon became evident that a special task force would be needed to carry out the project, since the added burden could not be borne by our minuscule staff. Within a week or so of the time we reached this decision, Kirstein happened to meet James J. Storrow, Jr., of Boston, and decided he would be an ideal person to assume responsibility for the anniversary issue. Like Kirstein, Storrow was a man of inherited wealth, a long-time *Nation* reader, and an expert in microfilm and print technology. Both were Harvard graduates and both had served in the South Pacific in World War II, Kirstein as a naval officer, Storrow with the Seabees. After a few sessions, the two of them worked out the arrangements whereby Storrow undertook the role of publisher for the centennial issue and selected David Boroff to edit it. When Boroff died quite suddenly, Victor Bernstein, our former managing editor, agreed to complete the assignment.

The special 335-page issue was dated September 20, 1965—it had not seemed advisable to bring it out in midsummer—and most of the material was later included in a volume entitled *The State of The Nation* (1965). Among the contributors were Leon Edel, Ralph Ellison, Harvey Swados, Dalton Trumbo, Mark Van Doren, C. Vann Woodward, Howard Zinn, Alfred Kazin, and Louis Kronenberger. The issue also included a valuable history of the magazine for the early decades by Richard Clark Sterne, which I supplemented with some notes on the more recent years. For the occasion, also, Henry M. Christman edited a 378-page centennial anthology, *One Hundred Years of The Nation*, for which I wrote an introduction. Christman had previously edited two other anthologies of *Nation* articles: *A View of The Nation*, 1960, and *Peace and Arms: Reports from The Nation*, 1964. For the centennial, Christman also brought out a collection of John Richard Dennett's classic reports on seven Southern states at the end of the Civil War which had first appeared in *The Nation*, in the summer of 1865. Reissued a hundred years later, under the title *The South as It Is*, they provided pertinent and timely background for the civil-rights movement.

While the centennial issue was being prepared, the transition from Kirstein to Storrow was agreed upon. Kirstein could not have found a successor more sensitive to the values of *The Nation* than Storrow, whose devotion to the magazine is reflected on every page of the handsome anniversary issue. James had an intimate knowledge of *The Nation*'s early ties with Boston and Harvard and had inherited a lively interest in reform politics. The Storrows are proper Bostonians, Brahmin Bostonians. James represents the fifth generation of his family to graduate from Harvard. His grandfather, James Jackson Storrow, was a patrician Boston investment banker. Described by Justin Kaplan in his biography of Lincoln Steffens as a man of "chilling rectitude," he was tapped to run for mayor of Boston by the reform movement headed by Edward Filene which had been organized to carry out the recommendations of Lincoln Steffens' famous report on corruption and misgovernment. But, for all his sterling qualities, Storrow was not a good candidate; he was a Protestant, he could not warm an audience, and he was not notably convivial. So the old-guard elements rallied around John F. Fitzgerald as their candidate—he had just returned from political exile—and "Honey Fitz" won the 1909 election, but not by a wide margin. Much later Storrow chaired a citizens' committee which described the real role Calvin Coolidge had played during the Boston police strike—a report that won high commendation from Oswald Garrison Villard of *The Nation*. As a footnote, Fitzgerald's grandson, John F. Kennedy, and James Jackson Storrow, Jr., were classmates at Harvard, Class of '40, as was Blair Clark, who edited the Harvard *Crimson* and succeeded me as editor of *The Nation*. Some time after the Kirstein-to-Storrow succession was arranged, Linda Storrow, the wife of James, became associate publisher.[1]

A condition of Storrow's acceptance of the role of publisher was that I would agree to stay on as editor. So I found myself in the position of working with a publisher whom I really knew no better than I had known Kirstein when he became publisher. It would be difficult to imagine backgrounds and temperaments more dissimilar than mine and James Storrow's, or, for that matter, than mine and Freda Kirchwey's or George Kirstein's. Getting out a weekly like *The Nation* involves endless opportunities for disagreements between publisher and editor over issues, policies, and emphasis. One might think that compatible backgrounds would be a prime consideration for a sound working relationship between publisher and editor, but it did not prove to be so in my experience with three *Nation* publishers over a period of thirty years. I had many disagreements with Kirchwey, Kirstein, and Storrow, but no major quarrels. One reason, perhaps, is that we had an equal devotion to *The Nation* and concern for its survival. So far as I was concerned, the publisher-editor relationship could have hardly been more casual; in the years I spent at *The Nation*, I never had a formal contract, never requested one, and never felt that one was necessary. When, for example, Kirstein succeeded Kirchwey as publisher, I said, "George, this relationship will either work or it won't and no amount of legal fine print will make any difference." So we skipped the fine print and dealt with each other on an informal, noncontractual, person-to-person basis, and it worked.

The end of *The Nation*'s centennial year was, of course, the appropriate time to effect the transition in publishers. In making the announcement in our issue of January 3, 1966, Kirstein quoted a sentence from an article I had written for the anniversary issue: "No one has ever 'owned' *The Nation;* it is impossible to own or possess it or bequeath it or sell it or mortgage it." This, of course, was not literally true; nevertheless the history of the magazine confirms the general thrust of the statement. Without exception every publisher has regarded the responsibility as a public trust. Any publisher who thought of the magazine as a possible profit-making venture could not have been familiar with its history. When the circulation reached five thousand copies with the third issue, E. L. Godkin was elated. "We have got so much money," he wrote to one of his associates, Frederick Law Olmsted, "that I don't think we can fail, unless by stupendous mismanagement, $100,000 *paid up*" (his emphasis). But by October, 1865, the annual subscription price had been hiked from three dollars to six dollars, and by the end of that first year the initial capital had been exhausted. Nor did *The Nation* ever make money, with the exception of a few years, roughly from 1938 to 1942, when it operated in the black, probably because majority sentiment, for once, aligned with the positions it took. Yet few American magazines have survived so long or preserved their character with greater consistency. When George Kirstein withdrew as publisher at the end of 1965, it was free of debt, its pulse beat was stronger than it had been at any time since the early 1940s, and it had won more than its usual share of journalism prizes and awards during the years he had served as publisher.

1. THE VIETNAM DECADE

The miraculous conclusion of a century of publication for *The Nation* coincided with the escalation of the war in Vietnam, which in turn marked the beginning of the third decade of the Cold War. From 1965 until I resigned as editor at the end of 1975, Vietnam dominated the headlines in one form or another. It was the great ongoing story, with far-ranging social, political, and cultural implications. It distorted the economy, accelerated inflationary trends, diverted attention from social problems neglected since World War II, warped the party system, and poisoned the political atmosphere. It also affected America's self-image, its morale, its position in world affairs, accounted for most of the domestic turbulence of the decade 1965–75, and marked a climactic phase in the Cold War. For it finally brought to the surface, in the most dramatic fashion, many of the false assumptions, the illusions, and the deceptions on which American policy had been based in the "postwar" period. In Vietnam, the chickens came home to roost.

From my editor's desk at *The Nation*, these were exciting, hectic, and ghastly years: an unending succession of crises, riots, protests, demonstrations, violence (including personal violence: I was mugged and robbed by four young thugs one afternoon in the office elevator and suffered a fractured cheekbone, and my wife was mugged in the elevator of our apartment house), bombings, mass arrests, political trials; of disunity, massive corruption, and, at times, total confusion. They were also years of some notable national achievements, but Vietnam cast a dark shadow on the entire decade. It was a period in which most Americans, eventually perhaps a majority, came to feel they had been lied to not once but many times by Presidents Johnson and Nixon; in which disaffection spread to sections of the armed forces; in which bombs were dropped on peasant villages; a decade of brutal "pacification" programs, "intrusions," palace coups, My Lai massacres, assassinations, "Vietnamization" and dirty tricks galore. Vietnam, as Irwin Unger has pointed out, was "a searing experience for the American people and would do more to shake the power structure of the nation than any event since the Great Depression."[2] It was, indeed, the integrative disaster, as the Depression had been for the 1930s, the trauma which tied the major events of the decade together.

From 1946 on (after Ho Chi Minh's repeated appeals to Washington urging support of Vietnamese independence had gone unacknowledged and unanswered), Vietnam was a familiar story to *Nation* readers. But for the first two decades of the conflict national attention had been focused on other aspects of the Cold War, so that once Vietnam became a burning issue in 1965, *The Nation*'s early reports were often forgotten. Thus, Lawrence S. Wittner, in one of the better histories of the Cold War, remarks that by 1970 *The Nation*, along with *The New Republic* and *The Progressive*, "had long ago joined their more radical competitors, *Ramparts* and the *New York Review*, in criticism of the Cold War belligerency that once had been standard fare for liberals." Speaking only for *The Nation*, I can say that we were critical of Cold War belligerency and American intervention in Vietnam in particular years before the first issues of the *New York Review* (1963) and *Ramparts* (1966) had appeared. Perhaps we should have advertised the stand we had taken on Vietnam long before it became a dominant issue, or kept reminding others of what we had said about it, but as usual we were too preoccupied with the present and the future to dote on the past. China presented exactly the same problem. A count I once made indicated that in an eight-year period (1950–58) *The Nation* had published nearly a hundred articles and editorials critical of American policy toward China, many of which had urged recognition of China and its admission to the United Nations. For us China's entry to the UN in 1971 was a ho-hum happening, an anticlimax; by then we had been at the issue so long it was difficult to muster a cheer. And so it was when the end finally came to the war in Vietnam.

The fact is that the conflict in Indochina was a twice-told tale for *Nation* readers long before it began to dominate the headlines. I would be embarrassed to report the total of articles and editorials we devoted to aspects of the Vietnam issue between 1946 and 1975; one count I made indicated sixty-six such items between January 1, 1954, and June 1, 1966, but there were many more before and after those years. Contributors such as Claude Bourdet and Alexander Werth had said about all that ever needed saying on the Vietnam problem long before the escalation of the war began. Two articles by Werth, "The Heart of the French Problem," February 5, 1952, and "Story of an Unknown War," September 12, 1952, along with Victor Purcell's "France's Lost Cause," June 12, 1952, summed up the issues admirably. And what Edgar Snow had to say (April 24, 1954) about the Geneva Conference holds good to this day.

Of the various new talents we turned up in the course of trying to cover the Vietnam conflict without an editorial budget that would permit us to send correspondents there, none was more important than Bernard B. Fall. In a very real sense, Fall was a *Nation* discovery. Shortly after he returned to this country from his 1953 visit to Indochina, we published his article "Solution in Vietnam: Cease-Fire, Negotiate" (March 6, 1954). Nothing more pertinent was said about the "Vietnam problem" in the years that followed. Fall was a scholar, not a partisan; he was not a reporter, but he had the talents of one. His first piece for *The Nation*, incidentally, came about as a result of a tip I had received that this remarkable young scholar might have some important things to say about Vietnam. From then until his untimely death—he was killed by a land-mine explosion in Vietnam in 1967—we published him as often as we could, which was not often enough. After 1953 he was quickly recognized as a major American intellectual resource on Indochina, and his two books on Vietnam provided invaluable guidance and background for American journalists and reporters.

Even with our meager budget it was not too difficult, with a little scrounging around, to get excellent firsthand reports from Vietnam by reporters whose sizable expense tabs were being paid by the wire services, the newspapers, and the networks. That magic word "contacts" provided one key to the problem; another was our ability, now and then, to secure foundation grants or publishers' advances for writers anxious to visit Vietnam. Constant improvising yielded some fine stories by Ernest Zaugg, Jack Foisie, Raymond R. Coffey, Peter Worthington, Karl Purnell, Jonathan Kapstein, and other reporters, including network newsmen such as Desmond Smith, Ted Koppel, and Mike Wallace. At one point I managed to finagle a foundation grant for Daniel Ford, a young novelist who wanted to visit Vietnam, and he sent us a series of vivid eyewitness reports which appeared in the summer of 1964. Novelists, I had reason to discover, were often the best, the most perceptive reporters, in part because they were more interested in people and had a sharper eye for detail. Later I gave a press credential to William Eastlake, who spent three months in Vietnam in 1966 and sent us some fine pieces, most of which were included in his book *The Bamboo Bed* (1969); some of these reports were the most savagely satirical writing the war produced. It may seem an odd way to recruit a future Vietnam correspondent, but I had originally enrolled Eastlake as a contributor because of my admiration for what he had written about cattle, horses, cowhands, Indians, and native New Mexicans.

For critical analysis and background we turned to such contributors as Isaac Deutscher, Werth, Bourdet, O. E. Clubb, Edgar Snow, W. Macmahon Ball, H. Stuart Hughes, C. P. Fitzgerald (one of his pieces, "The Fallacy of the Dominoes," June 28, 1965, had a wide impact), Owen Lattimore, Jules Henry, John Gittings, Eqbal Ahmad ("How to Tell When the Rebels Have Won," a notably fine piece, August 30, 1965), John McDermott ("Welfare Imperialism in Vietnam," July 25, 1966), Barrington Moore, Jr. ("Why We Fear Peasants in Revolt," September 26, 1966), and Howard Zinn, whose long article "Vietnam: Setting the Moral Equation," January 17, 1966, along with other *Nation* pieces, is to be found in *Vietnam: The Logic of Withdrawal* (1967), which I characterized on publication as "the best statement of the case for American withdrawal that has appeared to date."

In retrospect, I regret that I did not have the wit to induce Henry Christman to edit a collection of the best of the pieces we ran about Vietnam, if only to make the continuity and consistency of *The Nation*'s position better known. But I didn't, and once Johnson began to escalate the war what had been written about it in the past did not seem to be important; by then the din was deafening and there was little interest in who had first said what, where, and when about Vietnam.

2. *JOHNSON'S DIRTY WAR*

In its issue of December 21, 1963, *The Nation* observed that Vietnam would be President Johnson's first major test and would determine the success or failure of his Administration. Either he would proceed, and swiftly, to negotiate a settlement or the futile American involvement would inexorably expand. At the time, I thought there was at least a chance that Johnson, with an eye on the November, 1964, election, would see the wisdom of seeking a settlement. But it now seems clear that he never seriously considered such a course, in part, no doubt, because his advisers, blinded by Cold War dogmas, myths, and illusions, were so consistently wrong. In any case as early as February covert raids were launched against the North Vietnamese and plans laid to step up the fighting in the South. In an editorial of February 28, *The Nation* urged the opposition to become more vocal and soon or it would be too late. But the protests were still minimal. On March 10, 1964, Senator Ernest Gruening, a onetime *Nation* editor, delivered a remarkable seven-thousand-word speech to a nearly empty Senate in which he sharply criticized American policy, but it was ignored by the press, including the Washington *Post* and the New York *Times*. Senator Wayne Morse was so indignant he went to the press gallery to complain, but nothing happened; there was as yet little interest in what either Morse or Gruening had to say about the war.

One reason for the seeming public indifference was that Johnson's spectacular performance on domestic issues in the first months of 1964 provided excellent cover for his plans to escalate the war. Taking advantage of the surge of national sentiment that came with Kennedy's assassination, he presented his civil-rights program and declared war on poverty in a forceful and impressive State of the Union Message. By July the Civil Rights Act was on the books: a notable victory. The sense of movement and achievement this flurry of activity aroused diverted public attention from Vietnam. Nevertheless it was evident even then that the war was being quietly, covertly escalated. In an editorial of May 24, 1964, "Mr. Johnson's War," *The Nation* called attention once again to the ways in which American military involvement was increasing. In the meantime, of course, Johnson was waiting for an incident which could be used to wangle an authorization from Congress broad enough to cover past, present, and future actions. By deceitfully manipulating the Gulf of Tonkin incident in August, he was able to secure a resolution which, as he interpreted it, gave him blanket authority to take all measures necessary "to repel armed attacks in order to prevent further aggression." Even from the editorial sidelines, it was obvious that the facts about the incident had been misrepresented by the President; *The Nation* said so at the time. But in the House only Representative George Brown opposed the resolution, and in the Senate Gruening and Morse cast the two no votes (all three, I might point out, were contributors and had close ties with *The Nation*). Not only did Johnson secure adoption of the resolution he had been carrying around in his pocket looking for an opportunity to present, but the Tonkin incident came sufficiently close to the election to muffle the hawkish criticism of Goldwater and the far right. In fact, the election was really no contest: the President won a landslide victory with 61.1 percent of the popular vote.

Despite his handling of the Gulf of Tonkin incident, *The Nation* had not entirely given up on Johnson. We admired his leadership on civil rights, and there had been some language in his Manchester, New Hampshire, speech of September 26 that sounded mildly dovish despite a few disquieting lines in small print. I kept thinking Johnson might have acted as he did in 1964 in order to keep Goldwater off balance. Then, once elected by a wide margin, which seemed certain, he could claim a mandate and open negotiations for a settlement. But of course he never had any intention, as he put it, of "losing the war." Like Kennedy he was a captive of the Cold War consensus he had helped form, and there were as yet no significant countervailing pressures. Even as the votes were counted in November, he was busy with secret plans for bigger bombing raids and stepped-up military operations of the kind he had been quietly preparing since he took office. While piously proclaiming, "We seek no wider war," he had opted for escalation and a larger and more dangerous American involvement.

In February, U.S. planes carried out the first major raids against North Vietnamese targets, and one began to hear talk of projects with such blood-curdling names as "Flaming Dart" and "Rolling Thunder." McGeorge Bundy, a key adviser, darted out to Vietnam, listened to the thunder of the generals, and came back to urge a policy of "graduated continuing reprisal." On February 22, two weeks after the Vietcong attack on the barracks at Pleiku, General Westmoreland requested U.S. combat troops, and on March 8 two Marine battalions landed at DaNang. The double-talk, for a time, was ingenious. Combat troops were to be used to "protect bases," then to "man enclaves," and only somewhat later to engage in "search and destroy" missions. On more than one occasion, the President tried to conceal the real facts from the press and the public. Nor did the public seem aware that the decision to send in combat troops had been taken with no clear or direct request from the Saigon regime. Top presidential aides, including the intelligence agencies, were convinced that Russia or China or both were responsible for prolonging the war. Slight attention was paid to the prior history of the Indochina conflict, including the shifting of the Catholic population from north to south and the Buddhist reaction to this migration. No lessons had been learned, no fresh assessments made. At a July 28 press conference, President Johnson insisted that "the lessons of history" proved that "surrender in Vietnam would not bring peace." He had thereby, as Godfrey Hodgson perceptively notes, "in one breath wrapped together the Munich myth and the domino theory" and in the next announced that the number of troops in Vietnam would be increased from 75,000 to 125,000.[3]

In April, 1965, Students for a Democratic Society staged an antiwar protest in Washington which attracted a much larger attendance than had been anticipated. Up to that point, SDS had hesitated to concentrate its energies on opposition to the war for fear it might suddenly end and leave the organization without an issue. Perhaps as much as any single event, this protest signaled the beginning of widespread popular opposition to the war, although of course there had been earlier protests. One of the speakers at the rally was Senator Gruening, who by then was regarded as a veteran of the opposition even though he had not begun to speak out against the war until the spring of 1964.

As the bombing raids continued and the domestic protests mounted, it soon became apparent that Johnson was caught in a trap of his own making. Each escalation of the fighting provoked more and larger demonstrations and invested the opposition with a significance it had previously lacked. Unable to escape from this trap, the President became increasingly frantic. That spring his splashy intervention in the Dominican Republic—a grotesque overreaction—betrayed his jumpiness. Here too he lied and misrepresented the facts, and on television he seemed hysterical and perhaps slightly intoxicated. The President, Ted Lewis reported in *The Nation,* was deeply worried since "nothing seemed to be going right from early morning until late at night." So he lashed out at "enemies" in the Caribbean and continued to step up the war in Vietnam while insisting he sought only peace with honor. (Incidentally, I had been pleased to get Ted Lewis, the immensely knowledgeable Washington Bureau chief of the New York *Daily News,* and Jerry Greene, its Pentagon expert, to write for *The Nation* at rates of seventy-five or a hundred dollars for two-thousand-word pieces. When Ted first queried their New York office about possible objections to their writing for us, word came back: "Do those guys *really* want the two of you to write for them? If so, fine, we'd like it.")

One source of Johnson's growing anxiety and frustration was the remarkable improvement in the quality, range, and depth of news coverage from Vietnam in both the print and the electronic media. From 1965 on, the coverage got steadily better; a growing skepticism and a new critical tone could be detected. Some of the first good books about the war by American journalists began to appear. Gradually the public became aware, for the first time, that this country was actually engaged in a war in Vietnam which had begun nearly twenty years before. The rapid increase in the number of American combat troops was, of course, another major factor in stimulating public interest and concern. As this new awareness spread, sections of the public began to show some curiosity about the origins of the war and to ask questions; previously American involvement had been glibly rationalized in terms of unexamined Cold War dogmas and doctrines.

This new critical attitude first emerged on the campuses and prompted a most creative innovation: the teach-in. Within a matter of weeks after the National Teach-in of May 15, 1965, teach-ins became a political phenomenon for which it would be difficult to find a precedent. The academic setting was ideal; the cast of scholars impressive; the nonpolitical atmosphere provided a shield against red-baiters and demagogues; and the novelty attracted instant media attention. A real dialogue ensued; this was not partisan pleading but mass political education at a high level. For the first time the issues got a thorough airing. The teach-ins armed the antiwar movement with ideas and arguments and facts, gave it intellectual sanction, and, most importantly, forced the government to respond in a setting in which officials could be questioned. Although the teach-ins were short-lived, they provided an invaluable adjunct to the antiwar movement. From first to last, *The Nation* kept a spotlight on the teach-ins, with reports by Webster Schott, Arnold Kauffman, Christopher Lasch, and other contributors. As much as any single activity, the teach-ins of the spring, summer, and fall of 1965 sowed the seeds of resistance and protest. The big teach-in at Michigan in September, 1965, "Alternative Perspectives on Vietnam," marked the crest of this particular activity.

A year after he had won a "great victory" at the polls, President

Johnson was clearly on the defensive. The Voting Rights Act of 1965, which roughly coincided with the escalation of the war, was perhaps his last significant legislative achievement. By then the Great Society programs were stalled or beginning to sour. "On January 12, 1966," to quote from Lawrence S. Wittner's *Cold War in America,*[4]

> Johnson admitted: "because of Vietnam, we cannot do all that we should, or all that we would like to do." The administration cut back its domestic agenda, paring some projects and dropping others. "I watched the [anti-poverty] program broken and eviscerated," recalled Dr. King, "as if it were some idle political plaything of a society gone mad with war." That September an unhappy Arthur Schlesinger, Jr., reported: "The Great Society is now, except for token gestures, dead."

Nor had progress been made in "winning the war." The tonnage of bombs dropped quadrupled in 1966, but with little apparent effect; the total tonnage, in fact, exceeded that of all bombs dropped in the Pacific Theater in World War II. By then, 1966, the U.S. had 470,000 troops in Vietnam. Yet in November, Defense Secretary Robert McNamara advised the President that the air raids against North Vietnam were without "significant impact," and there was no reason to believe that sending in more combat troops would change matters.

As early as March 28 *The Nation* had noted that opinion was beginning to be deeply troubled and incipiently resentful. Indeed, in an earlier editorial of March 3, 1962, commenting on a "Pause for Peace" demonstration at the University of Iowa, we had suggested that the nation could be witnessing the beginning of a schism so profound that it might determine the politics of the 1960s. By 1966 embittered blacks were in an almost mutinous mood, enraged by our failure to win the other war, the one against poverty and squalor. Violence in Vietnam had begun to breed violence in the ghettoes. "Slums" suddenly became "ghettoes" in news stories, and the substitution reflected a change in attitude and a new intensity in racial feeling. Even so, as Sanford Gottlieb of SANE reported in *The Nation* (November 28, 1966), the war seemed to have "little direct effect on the 1966 election." It had still not bitten deeply enough into the American consciousness—and conscience—to produce clear voting patterns. More to the point, there was no organized political pressure from the left that might have forced the Democrats to reconsider their position; indeed, there was no "left"—it had been smashed fifteen years before, and a "new left" was only beginning to emerge. "Peace movements," while useful and impressive, did not provide a substitute for sustained political action on a national scale. With the liberal Republicans tied in with the bipartisan Cold War consensus, opposition could arise only within the Democratic Party, and in 1966 that opposition consisted of the lonely if prophetic voices of Morse and Gruening and a few others. But sentiment was building up against the war and more rapidly than the politicians realized.

By the end of 1966, Johnson probably knew the war could not be won at the price he was prepared to pay. But by then he was securely locked into policies he had initiated and positions he had taken; the American investment in resources, prestige, and lives had become so enormous he was afraid to confess failure. Nor did he know which way to turn or what to do next. As a group his advisers, both civilian and military, as Hodgson notes, were so "bizarrely unreal" in their perceptions, their judgments so "wildly wrong," that he was left to fume and curse in frustration. Again and again he was told Vietnam was another Munich: a test of America's willingness to lead a worldwide counterrevolutionary alliance; if we failed to hold the line in Indochina we would have lost the Cold War. The pity of it is that he had a magnificent opportunity to end the war on a fairly decent note when he succeeded Kennedy. He had gotten off to a fine start; he seemed to have united the Democratic Party in a renewed pursuit of unfulfilled New Deal objectives; and he might well have interpreted his massive defeat of Goldwater as a mandate, if somewhat ambiguous, to end the war or at least not to escalate it. But he was reluctant to break out of the Cold War trap and too proud to concede that the war could not be won.

3. THE EMERGENCE OF A CHALLENGE

As 1966 drew to a close it was apparent that President Johnson— "Old Cornpone," as the poet Lawrence Ferlinghetti called him— was in deep trouble. President Kennedy had kept up the pretense that Vietnam was "their war," meaning the Vietnamese; Johnson made it unmistakably ours. No longer a "police action," it had become a major conflict to which we were a party. The year 1966 was to have marked the "win phase," but of course it didn't. Late that fall influential reports by Neil Sheehan, Harrison Salisbury and other correspondents reflected a growing skepticism about the way the war was going. Attempts to whip up prowar sentiment by parades and rallies—one was staged in Atlanta, another in New York—drew meager crowds and revealed a distinct lack of enthusiasm. Protests kept mounting, domestic discontent was increasing, disaffection was spreading in academic and intellectual circles, and the war was wildly unpopular even with those who thought we should carry on. But politically antiwar sentiment still lacked a clear national focus. And a challenge would have to surface in 1967 to have much impact on the 1968 presidential election. At year's end there were few signs that such a challenge might emerge.

In the fall of 1966, the California liberal monthly *Frontier* decided to merge with *The Nation*. Patterned after *The Nation, Frontier* had been published in Los Angeles for nearly twenty years. The publisher, Gifford Phillips, and the editor, Phil Kerby (now a Pulitzer Prize–winning member of the editorial staff of the Los Angeles *Times*), were close friends of mine; the three of us were ex-Coloradoans.[5] Once the merger was carried out, Phillips became an associate publisher of *The Nation* and Kerby an associate editor. It was agreed that the merger should be announced in Los Angeles, and to this end I prepared plans for a *Nation* conference there similar to the one that had been staged in 1946. I decided that the theme should be the imperative need to mobilize *national political* opposition to the war in Vietnam and to reorder and redirect American priorities. I then recruited a roster of speakers, including Senators Eugene McCarthy, George McGovern, Ernest Gruening, and Mark Hatfield, along with Dr. Martin Luther King, Jr., Malcolm Browne, who had just returned from a five-year news assignment in Vietnam, Cecil Brown, the popular Los Angeles television commentator, and Seymour Melman. It turned out that we had chosen the right theme and the right place and time to present it; antiwar sentiment was on the rise and notably in California. The conference was held at the Beverly Hilton Hotel, February 25, 1967, and attracted overflow crowds and excellent media coverage. It was at this conference that Dr. King for the first time came out unequivocally against the war, in one of the most eloquent speeches of his career. True, he had denounced the war in moralistic pacifist terms in his column in the Chicago *Defender* on New Year's Day, 1966, but his Los Angeles speech was charged with political significance. It is generally said that his first firm commitment to the antiwar opposition came in his sermon at Riverside Church in New York on April 4, 1967, but this speech, of course, came after the meeting in Los Angeles. Here are a few excerpts from that speech:

> We are certainly all aware of the nightmarish physical casualties of the war. We see them in our living rooms in all of their tragic dimensions on television screens, and we read about them on our subway and bus rides in daily newspaper

accounts. We see the rice fields of a small Asian country being trampled at will and burned at whim. We see grief-stricken mothers with crying babies clutched tightly in their arms as they watch their little huts burst forth into flames. We see the fields and valleys of battle being painted with humankind's blood. We see the broken bodies left prostrate in countless fields. Most tragic of all is the casualty list among children. . . .

But the physical casualties of the war in Vietnam are not alone the catastrophe. The casualties of principles and values are equally disastrous and injurious . . . By entering a war that is little more than a domestic civil war, America has ended up supporting a new form of colonialism covered up by certain niceties of complexity. Whether we realize it or not, our partic-ipation in the war in Vietnam is an ominous expression of our lack of sympathy for the oppressed, our paranoid anti-Com-munism, our failure to feel the ache and anguish of the have-nots . . . We have well over three hundred thousand American servicemen fighting in that unhappy country. American planes are bombing the territory of another country, and we are com-mitting atrocities equal to any perpetrated by the Vietcong. This is the third largest war in American history. All of this reveals that we are in an unthinkable position morally and politically. We are left standing before the world glutted by our own barbarity. We are engaged in a war that seeks to turn the clock of history back and perpetuate white colonialism. The greatest irony and tragedy of it all is that our nation, which initiated much of the revolutionary spirit of the modern world, is now cast in the mold of being an arch-antirevolutionary.

I have always felt that the enthusiasm exhibited at the *Nation* conference helped set the stage for Eugene McCarthy's candidacy. Throughout the sessions the audience seemed eager for the speak-ers to be even more forthright than they were in voicing opposition to the war. McCarthy gave an excellent, if cool, talk on "The Moral Aspects of the War in Vietnam" which stopped short of presenting a direct political challenge. After he and the others had spoken, I said to him that the audience's reactions throughout the confer-ence convinced me that the time had come for some nationally known and respected political figure, preferably a senator not up for reelection, to test antiwar sentiment by entering the 1968 pri-maries in a few key states. McGovern, of course, was up for reelec-tion; McCarthy was not. With no hesitation whatever, he agreed, and the way in which he responded made me feel that he just might be a candidate.

As the bombings began to be stepped up in February, full-page antiwar advertisements appeared in the New York *Times* and other papers, and huge demonstrations were staged; one at United Nations Plaza in New York in late April drew a crowd of 100,000. But still nothing had been done by way of offering a political option in the 1968 election. As "the Vietnam summer" approached, the American Friends Service Committee quietly assembled a small group in Philadelphia for a weekend conference to discuss how best to mobilize opposition to the war. Among those who took part, as I recall, were John Kenneth Galbraith, Father Philip Berrigan, Dr. John C. Bennett, James McNair, Philip Huff (then governor of Vermont), and Arnold Kauffman of the University of Michigan, a leader in the teach-in movement; perhaps a dozen in all. After two days of talk, we reached an understated Quakerlike consensus that somehow, by some means, a direct political challenge had to be projected. But all we could agree on was the need; the means eluded us. Politically the liberal Republicans were in a better position than the liberal Democrats to launch an attack on Johnson's conduct of the war. Some of them—Senators John Sherman Cooper, Mark Hatfield, and Thruston Morton—had voiced their misgivings. Senator Morton had said, for example, that we were "hung up" on Cold War dogmas, as indeed we were, but about all I could get him to say was that he had serious doubts about the war. In general the liberal Republicans were looking over their shoulders at the conservative right-wing elements of the party. Forthright opposition by Morton, a politician of the center, would have been important, but he would not take a strong stand against the war. General Eisenhower's blistering statement from retirement that opposition to the war verged on treason probably kept the antiwar liberal Republicans from voicing their misgivings. As for the liberal Democrats, most of them were still part of the Cold War consensus and the few who were not hesitated to challenge an incumbent Democratic President with a national election in the offing.

The violent race riots in the summer of 1967—in Detroit, Newark, East Harlem, Los Angeles—momentarily diverted attention from the war and also divided the opposition to it. In general the "new left" had become disenchanted with politics; a deep-seated feeling of powerlessness had produced, as it usually does, a preoccupation with power as such. "Anti-politics" and "anti-movements" became the new thing, the radical chic; instead of building grass-roots coalitions to oppose the war, based on social and economic needs, the antiwar activists seemed inclined to dismiss political action as meaningless and a waste of time. In *The Nation* of January

15, 1968, I noted that discussion had been superseded by uproar, debate by demonstrations, dialogue by confrontations, civil disobedience by overt resistance. Much of this activity angered and annoyed thoughtful critics of the war and made it difficult to launch a serious political opposition.

But although there was no consensus on how best to end the war, it became impossible after "the summer of the crack-up" to maintain the bipartisan consensus which until then had kept us bogged down in Vietnam. Not only was the war going badly but domestic discontents were mounting. Ted Lewis reported in *The Nation* that massive anti-Johnson sentiment was building up in many states. In the 1966 elections, Vietnam had not been made an issue in more than forty congressional districts in twenty states, but by 1967 local uncoordinated "antiwar" activities began to mushroom even in small towns, rural areas, and such unlikely states as Wyoming. Some communities, in the absence of a clear political option, had begun to conduct polls on the war or to stage referenda on it. In November, an important Labor-for-Peace conference was held in Chicago, one of the first signs of disaffection in the ranks of organized labor.[6] In September I spoke along with others at a "Dump Johnson" meeting in New York's Community Church, one of a series of such meetings which Allard Lowenstein had organized out across the country in a gallant effort to flush out a candidate who would oppose Johnson on the issue of the war.

Throughout the year *The Nation* kept insisting that popular pressures and protests, no matter how numerous and vocal, would never bring the war to an end; before that could happen the President's leadership would have to be challenged in the first primaries, since it was apparent the Republicans would not make an issue of the war. But where was the candidate? McGovern was committed to seek reelection to the Senate and, besides, he was eying Bobby Kennedy. Kennedy was torn by ambition, doubts, a vestigial loyalty to Johnson (who had been responsible for his confirmation as Attorney General, having been hand-picked for the Vice Presidency by his brother) and a feeling that he could not win as an antiwar candidate. Although he had made a speech in the Senate on March 2, 1967, in which he called for a halt in the bombings, he kept saying as late as November and December that he would not be a candidate. Then on November 30, 1967, Eugene McCarthy announced he would enter the primaries in four states. *The Nation*, of course, promptly endorsed his candidacy. Thus after years of political frustration in which a sense of powerlessness had led to violence and disorder and repressive countermeasures, the issue of the war was finally to be presented, for the first time, to voters in a national election. There is no doubt, as Jack Newfield has pointed out, that McCarthy's announcement is "what dynamited the logjam"; it gave the opposition a credibility and unity which it would not otherwise have been able to achieve and made all the subsequent events possible.[7]

McCarthy's announcement was well timed. By the end of 1967, Johnson's bag of tricks was about empty. Representative George Brown, in a savage open letter to the President, published in *The Nation* of December 11, 1967, and captioned "I'm Tired of Your Gimmicks!," gave blunt expression to a growing national senti- ment. By then Robert McNamara had been eased out. But before leaving he had come up with yet another of his whiz-kid ideas: we should "draw a line" or "build a wall" across Vietnam which would keep the "enemy" on one side and our "friends" on the other—a clear indication that he finally, belatedly, realized the war could not be won as it was being waged. His gimmicky idea—as though ideas and national sentiments could be contained by "lines" and "walls"— was of a piece with one advanced by Herman Kahn, who proposed construction of a death-belt barrier around Saigon and along the Cambodian border, earth-dredged, as high as a fifteen-story build- ing, behind which our wards, the South Vietnamese, could cower. Better proof than these two superbly nutty ideas could hardly be conceived that the Cold Warriors had finally run out of tricks and gimmicks.

In the wake of the 1966 congressional elections, I had suggested in a November 28 editorial that Johnson might not be a candidate in 1968 if he felt uncertain about his chances. Ted Lewis, in a *Nation* article, reached much the same conclusion about the same time. Then in editorials of January 29, 1968, and March 11 and 25, I argued that the logic of the situation would compel Johnson to withdraw and I flatly predicted that he would not be a candidate. *The Nation* was, in fact, *the first publication,* and the only one so far as I know, to take this position. When he finally announced on March 31 that he would not be a candidate, my initial reaction was one of elation and vast relief. But then, almost immediately, I began to have second thoughts and to wonder if this might not turn out to be another of those perverse situations in which the "solution" becomes part of the problem.

On the mornings of January 30 and 31, 1968, during the Lunar New Year holiday of Tet, Vietcong and North Vietnamese forces launched an attack on thirty-five population centers in South Viet- nam, and a team of nineteen sappers—demolition troops—occu- pied the garden of the U.S. Embassy and held it for five hours. Westmoreland and others have tried to make it appear that the press erroneously reported the consequences of the Tet offensive, since in the end, after a month of fighting, the invaders were driven back. But more than any single event, perhaps, Tet destroyed the consensus which had made it possible for Johnson to continue the war. It severely weakened if it did not destroy the Cold War dogma that it was in the national interest to let Presidents run wars and stage military interventions without the concurrence of Congress or the public. And it brought into question, for the first time, the related dogma that the existence of a Socialist or Communist regime, anywhere in the world, somehow threatened this country's national security.

But Tet did more: it destroyed or gravely weakened world confidence in the American dollar. One of the events it set in motion was the so-called gold rush of '68, which threatened chaos in world money markets. No longer could American dollar deficits be ignored. As one observer said, it "cracked the keystone of the world financial system," which collapsed three years later. The effects were still being felt after the lapse of ten years. The Great American Barbecue was over, to be succeeded by a condition bordering on national bankruptcy. On March 10, the central bankers announced they would continue to sell gold to speculators rather than risk the upheaval that might otherwise result. But just then— worse luck—Westmoreland requested 206,000 more troops, which precipitated further panic. Inflation was already rising, accelerated in part by Johnson's delay in seeking, just a few months earlier, a tax surcharge on the war. As political opposition to the war mounted here and abroad, the demand for gold on London markets reached a new high. This was also the tumultuous week in which McCarthy won forty percent of the vote in the New Hampshire Democratic primary. The gold pool was then losing well over $100 million a day. On March 14 the British issued a proclamation closing the gold markets, and by then, of course, Johnson was about ready to call it quits. The stockholders, so to speak, had decided that the chairman of the board should step down. So was it, really, the military situation that induced us finally to reexamine our untenable position in Vietnam? Or was it the threat to American capitalism and the financial system? The famous "domino effect" which had been cited so often to justify our continued presence in Vietnam turned out to be the reverse of what it had been presented to be. It was the "domino effect" of the folly of American Cold War policies on the world's money markets that finally forced us to call a halt to the Vietnam enterprise.[8]

The reaction to the Tet offensive marked the beginning of the end of the postwar Cold War boom which had lasted for thirty years. Just what had this splurge of American military, industrial, and financial power cost? No one, of course, will ever know. And of course much of the money which was voted by representatives of American taxpayers was spent in this country to provide jobs, profits, and economic expansion. But at a frightful cost. Ernest Herman Hahne and Martin Bronfenbrenner, in an article in 1969, estimated the total expenditures for World War I at $211 billion and for World War II at $1,167 billion. The U.S. estimated total for World War II was $387 billion. But Frederick L. Schuman, the distinguished American historian, has made a rough calculation that the cost of the Cold War from its inception to the end of the fighting in Vietnam, including Korea and Vietnam, would be almost three times what World War II cost the United States and only slightly less than the Hahne-Bronfenbrenner total for what *all* belligerents had spent in World War II.[9] And this total would not include all of what was spent for "foreign military aid," and gifts and sales of arms overseas which are still in excess of $10 billion a year. Sooner or later this obscene outpouring of American dollars, spent in pursuit of tragically misconceived Cold War policies, was bound to produce not merely damaging distortions in the economy and a disastrous misuse of resources, but a serious weakening of this country's economic position in world affairs. Indeed, it had the effect of undermining American capitalism, which it was supposed to strengthen and expand. Of course certain American interests profited enormously; certain industries expanded; vast fortunes, measured in depreciated dollars, were created. But the Cold War accented inequalities, created enormous imbalances and distortions in the economy, stimulated inflation, and imposed a truly oppressive long-term burden on the American people.

McCarthy's strong showing in the New Hampshire primary in the wake of the Tet offensive demonstrated Johnson's personal vulnerability even more clearly than it measured antiwar sentiment. That Johnson, an incumbent, had only managed to outpoll McCarthy by less than one percent of the vote in conservative New Hampshire was a sign of major weakness. And Wisconsin, where the President's prospects were never bright, was the next primary on the list. In the meantime, of course, the politically astute Clark Clifford had become Secretary of Defense. So at his bidding the "Wise Men" of the Cold War Establishment were summoned to the White House for a secret strategy session on March 25. It was, as Godfrey Hodgson notes, "a sort of Round Table of the sedentary chivalry of the Cold War . . . a board meeting of the most powerful enterprise on earth. It was also the last occasion on which so many leading members of the Establishment ever found themselves in agreement, and so perhaps in effect the last plenary session of that mythical but once potent body."[10] The hearts of these Wise Men had not melted, but their heads had cleared. The New Hampshire returns, battlefield reports from Vietnam, and charts on the state of the world economy conveyed a clear message: the time had come to call a halt. And they were right: a few days later Johnson's Gallup rating had fallen to thirty-five percent.

Robert Kennedy had no difficulty in reading the New Hampshire returns. He had delayed until February 8, 1968, in speaking out against the war. In this fine speech he said that the history of conflict among nations "does not record another such lengthy and consistent chronicle of error as that brought about by first the French with our aid and then the United States in Vietnam. . . . It is time for the truth; it is time to face the reality that a military victory is not in sight and that it probably will never come." In this same speech he got to the root of the problem: "We have misconceived the nature of the war . . . we have sought to resolve by military might a conflict whose issue depends upon the will and conviction of the South Vietnamese people. It is like sending a lion to halt an epidemic of jungle rot." But he continued to say he was not a candidate. Then at 3 A.M. and before the final New Hampshire count was announced he decided to become a candidate, although his formal announcement was not made until four days later. Editorially *The Nation* welcomed Kennedy's open opposition to Johnson but not his candidacy. If he had endorsed McCarthy, McGovern would probably have followed suit and their endorsements and support might have made quite a difference. I should say that *The Nation* had never been wildly enthusiastic about Robert Kennedy; we had not admired his early support of Joe McCarthy or the unfair tactics he used as Attorney General in his efforts to "get Hoffa" or his role in the Bay of Pigs episode although he did, to his credit, recommend against a retaliatory air strike. When he decided to run for the Senate in 1964, we endorsed Kenneth Keating, the Republican, not because we were all that fond of Keating but as a protest against the way in which Kennedy by barging into New York politics had kept Robert Wagner from being elected to the Senate seat his father had once held. In our view Wagner would have made the better senator.

As the 1968 campaign got under way, I became increasingly troubled over the effect of Johnson's withdrawal. One of the reasons McCarthy had fared so well in New Hampshire was that he had wisely made Johnson the issue. True, Johnson had pushed through civil-rights legislation and Medicare and other domestic reforms, but he made a splendid target because he had escalated the war and lied to the people about his actions. In some respects Vice President Hubert Humphrey was less vulnerable. A Cold War liberal, he had an image that was not as hawkish as Johnson's. He was also acceptable to Chicago Mayor Richard Daley and the other city bosses and party regulars even though Daley had held out to the end in the hope that Senator Edward Kennedy would be a candidate. Humphrey was even more of a favorite with black voters than Johnson because of his long and impressive civil-rights record, and he had strong support from organized labor. He was also a much better campaigner than Johnson. But he was still an undesirable nominee, for he was or appeared to be Johnson's man, a kind of puppet or stand-in for the President, which he was to some extent, although he later claimed to have been a closet dove. The combined forces of Kennedy and McCarthy might have been able to deny Humphrey the nomination even if neither of them had been named, and conceivably one or the other might have been nominated. For example, at the time Kennedy announced his candidacy, the Gallup Poll indicated a substantially equal division: Johnson forty-five percent, Kennedy forty-four percent (March 17, 1968).

But with Robert Kennedy's assassination the antiwar opposition suffered an irreparable blow. I sat staring at the tube on the night of June 4, as did millions of other Americans, in a state of total shock, with apprehension and dismay. Coming as it did in the wake of Martin Luther King's assassination on April 4, it was too much to assimilate or accept. Dr. King's assassination affected me in a deeply personal way. I do not remember ever having been so shaken by the death of someone not a member of my family or close circle of friends. I felt somehow that history had set Dr. King up as a martyr; that the entire nation, in a sense, shared responsibility for his death. But it did not have for me the sickening, numbing, enervating impact of Robert Kennedy's assassination. Those wild scenes in the Ambassador Hotel had a surreal quality that, for the moment, made politics seem meaningless and the campaign an irrelevance, all sound and fury signifying very little. One might have thought the two assassinations would enhance McCarthy's prospects, but the opposite was true. The antiwar opposition suddenly seemed anticlimactic. At the Chicago convention, I found McCarthy to be a curiously uninvolved and rather detached candidate, almost a spectator at an event which he knew from the start would turn out as it did.

And just what had the Republicans been doing in those early months of 1968 when the Democratic Party was being shaken by dissension, assassinations, demonstrations, and bitter strife? After making some vague antiwar noises, George Romney had bowed out of the race on February 28; his candidacy had been hopelessly mishandled from the start. This cleared the way for Rockefeller to again become a candidate, but he also had bowed out (on March 21), which left Nixon virtually without opposition, the residual heir to the nomination. He had the support of the Goldwater faction and most of the state and local leaders, and the liberal Republicans had forfeited whatever credibility they had once possessed.

So what, in the wake of the conventions, had the unprecedented turmoil and excitement of the preceding months netted the opponents of the war? Not a choice, but three candidates, Nixon, Wallace, and Humphrey, who echoed much the same views on the war with some variations in emphasis. This was, in effect, Johnson's bitter legacy, his revenge.

If anything was needed to insure Nixon's election it was the disaster of the Chicago Democratic convention. Chicago, of course, was the worst possible choice, but Johnson had insisted the convention be held there, although Daley had not wanted it. The riots that Dr. King's assassination had triggered in Chicago had prompted Daley to issue his famous "Shoot to kill" directive to the police. This directive, and the way in which the Chicago police had handled the April antiwar demonstrations, prompted *The Nation* to point out that if similarly savage methods were used at the upcoming Democratic convention it might touch off a reaction that even Daley would regret. But his performance exceeded our goriest anticipations. Television coverage of the wild street scenes and bitter feuding at the convention only underscored the impression the Republican gathering at Miami had made—carefully guarded as it had been against possible disturbances—as the acme of dignified deliberation and political good manners, if excessively dull.

I covered the Chicago convention and witnessed some of the violence. At one of the entrances to the Conrad Hilton Hotel, Miles McMillin of the Madison *Capitol-Times* and I tried to remonstrate, in a mild way, with some Chicago police—where, I wondered, had Daley recruited these big, bruising, brawling bullies?—who were clubbing some young demonstrators, and we were lucky to escape without having our skulls cracked, too. But most of the time I spent with the Ohio delegation, courtesy of my friend Edward Lamb of Toledo. From previous experiences, I had learned the wisdom of sticking close to one particular delegation in order to observe the action as the delegates see it. The Ohio delegates were not fully aware of the violence in the streets and along the lakefront; they caught only echoes and glimpses of it. Most of their time was spent in closed sessions, assessing the impact of the platform, issues, and possible nominees on upcoming local elections in Ohio. When not in closed sessions or enjoying a little night life they were being herded into chartered buses and driven from the Sherman Hotel to the convention center and back again, captives of a process they did not fully understand but seemed to enjoy. Had these particular delegates really known what was going on in Chicago, I am not sure they would have reacted any differently, but the fact is they knew very little about it.

In the end, the Chicago convention, which had loomed so importantly as a critical test on the issue of the war, turned out to be a cross between farce, tragedy, and wild confusion. McCarthy's challenge was not so much voted down as it was shouted down: aborted, derailed, sidetracked. The failure of the political process was the ultimate humiliation. Circumstances over which the delegates had little control intervened to rob the convention of whatever meaning it might have had if it had been held in another city, in a different setting. As it was, the confrontation between Cold War and antiwar factions turned out to be a disaster for both. The gavel and the steamroller and police clubs prevailed. Daley's rough handling of the convention made Humphrey seem even more of a puppet than when Johnson pulled the strings. And it was all there, on the tube, for the entire nation to view: the street violence, the clubbings, the mass arrests, along with Daley's arrogance and obscene gestures. What happened seemed to confirm much that the new left had been saying about American politics, although the antics of the antiwar activists had provoked no small amount of the violence. But at least the issue of the war had been raised and some of the state delegation meetings were extremely interesting, notably the sessions of the California delegation under Jess Unruh's leadership, where McGovern made one of his best speeches and McCarthy one of his worst. But I could perceive scarcely any salvage in the convention. I arrived in Chicago with little hope and left with less. There was some excited talk, briefly, about a fourth party, but nothing came of it. An independent "antiwar" ticket might have fared well in 1968 in a four-way split and would not have injured Humphrey's chances, since he lost anyway, as he was fated to lose. But McCarthy, perhaps dreaming of 1972, would not run as an independent candidate, and, besides, there was not enough time to organize such an effort and little enthusiasm for it. So I left Chicago with the feeling of having been royally screwed. For the moment, Chicago wrote *finis* to the brave talk, the long marches, the fervent teach-ins, and the violent agitations that had preceded the convention. Chicago was a bad scene, one of the worst in my political experience.

With the Wallace–Le May ticket siphoning off Democratic votes and contributing to the general disaffection and malaise, Nixon simply coasted to victory. All he needed to do was to take an occasional poke at Humphrey (taking care not to poke too hard), while ignoring Wallace and now and then having nice things to say about Johnson. The polls showed that Vietnam was a major issue, but Nixon managed to say very little about it; he hinted that he had a plan to end the war, but he kept it to himself. He did not have to meet the issues—aside from Vietnam there were none that really mattered—nor did he have to resort to "anti-Communist" demagoguery. He won through massive default of the political process. In September, Walter Lippmann endorsed him; by then it was clear he was a shoo-in. Humphrey did come up a bit in the last weeks of the campaign, but what he had to say about a possible halt in the bombings came too late and had to be discounted as opportunism. During the prior four years Humphrey had gone along with Johnson's policies to the degree that it was difficult to take seriously anything he had to say about the war. McCarthy's endorsement on October 24 came too late to help Humphrey but late enough not to upset the antiwar contingent, most of whom by then didn't give a damn anyway. In fact, it was so perfunctory in tone that it seemed more like a reproof than an endorsement, which may have been part of the intention. It was, however, primarily designed, I feel, to insure McCarthy's standing as a Democrat, which it did but to no purpose.

A sad postscript to Campaign '68 was the failure of Ernest Gruening to win renomination for his Senate seat and the defeat of Wayne Morse in the November election. How often those names Morse and Gruening had been linked in lonely opposition to the Vietnam War. After Gruening lost his Senate seat, *The Nation* promptly restored his name to its masthead, where it remained until his death in 1974. Wayne Morse died that same year.

4. NIXON'S WAR

By the time Richard Nixon was sworn in as President, Vietnam had become the longest war in American history. Our involvement can be dated from August, 1946, when President Truman elected to ignore Ho Chi Minh's appeals on behalf of Vietnamese independence. In December of that year fighting broke out between the French and the Viet Minh, and we backed the French, cautiously at first, openly a bit later. On May 1, 1950, after the Russians and the new Chinese regime had recognized the Democratic Republic of Vietnam led by Ho Chi Minh, Truman approved a $10-million military-assistance loan to the French. As Edgar Snow pointed out, France could not have held out for a year of the ten it tried to stay on in Indochina without our aid; yet in the end it was the French who left, the natives who stayed, and the Americans who paid. By 1954 we had supplied $3 billion in military aid to the French, and by 1958 we were underwriting all the military and most of the civilian costs of the South Vietnamese regime. From 1955 to 1961, the Eisenhower Administration poured in something like $200 million annually but limited the number of American military personnel to 685. Kennedy stepped up the camouflaged war and increased our commitment in funds and personnel; some 16,000 American troops were stationed in Vietnam at the time of his death. The number stood in excess of 500,000 when Nixon took office.

Since no formal declaration of war was ever made, it is impossible to fix a precise date to mark the point at which we became an active belligerent. But 1954 is as good a date as any, for it was then that the French withdrew and the Geneva conferees, French, Chinese, Russian, with Viet Minh and Bao Dai's representatives and Washington observers, established the two zones in Vietnam. Joe McCarthy was condemned that year, but McCarthyism had triumphed, so it was hardly surprising that we elected not to abide by the accords which, if observed, might have brought the war to a close. Eisenhower was convinced that eighty percent of the Vietnamese would have voted for Ho Chi Minh in a nationwide election. Even earlier, at a closed-door committee session on June 8, 1950, Dean Rusk conceded that the problem in Indochina was not entirely or "even largely" military in character and that if the French had pulled out "right away," after World War II, the Viet Minh forces would have prevailed. The first years of the Indochina conflict are usually designated "the colonial phase," 1946 to 1954; the years from 1954 to 1975 as "the civil-war phase"—more accurately, the period of active American intervention. But it was one war to which we were a party from its inception, a thirty-year war in which we suffered an ignominious defeat.

By the time Nixon took office the war had been waged for twenty-three years—nearly the span of a generation—and it was to continue for another six years. Just these six years make "Nixon's War" the longest in American history. By 1969, some 31,000 Americans had been killed in action, we had over 500,000 troops in Vietnam, and the war had cost, by one expert's calculation, more than $300 billion. But the real costs can never be reckoned; the bills are still coming in and the indirect and "psychic" costs cannot be calculated. By January, 1969, the nation was exhausted from the bitter feuding, frustrations, and disappointments of the 1968 campaign and the antiwar agitations, which had steadily mounted after 1963. But the end was not in sight; the war would drag on for another six years.

For me, the Vietnam War was a constant editorial preoccupation from its inception until the last U.S. troops left Saigon on April 30, 1975, but increasingly so after 1954. Not only had it become a central objective of American foreign policy, but after 1965 it became a national obsession. And the longer the war lasted, the more editorial attention it demanded. The side effects, the riots, demonstrations, political prosecutions, the violence, as well as the cultural, economic, social, and political ramifications, were prodigious. Not only that, but the aftereffects were certain to be far-ranging; we were losing a war for the first time in our history and being forced to face realities in our national life and experience that we had long ignored. From 1965 on it was obvious the war was building toward a climax. None of the issues with which I had to deal as editor of *The Nation* in the decade from 1965 to 1975 were more demanding, difficult, and unremitting than the closely interrelated issues of Vietnam and Watergate. In those years, Vietnam was a weekly, almost a daily, preoccupation, in one way or another.

With Nixon's election the problem of keeping an editorial spotlight on Vietnam took on a new complexity. William F. Buckley, Jr., is quite right in stating that Nixon should be viewed as "the central figure in American postwar politics," meaning the period from 1945 to 1975. The instant dislike and distrust which I felt for him in 1946, when he made his political debut in California, had grown with the years, but I had learned not to discount his special brand of political cunning, his basic opportunism, or his often canny reading of American political attitudes. One of his secret strengths was his total lack of any sense of political values or commitments. As one character observes to another in a celebrated *New Yorker* cartoon, "Look, Nixon's no dope. If people wanted moral leadership he'd give them moral leadership." One of his speech writers, Richard Whalen, made this same discovery early in his assignment. He could not find phrases to express Nixon, "because I could not find him. . . . None of us could say what if anything Nixon felt passionate about." In an editorial of July 28, 1956, I summed up my impressions: he was without principles and beyond scruples; he was also without enthusiasms, loyalties, or deep attachments. "You don't need to know him to dislike him: he invites it." In fact, he was not really popular with the constituencies that supported him. In six hundred interviews in twenty-two states in the spring of 1956, a correspondent for one of the wire services found few Republicans who were keen about him for Vice President, and one got the feeling that Eisenhower would have been relieved if Nixon had stepped aside. As James Reston, Jr., is quoted as saying: "That such a figure without belief, for whom 'winning' was everything, could for a quarter of a century so dominate the political life of a country that prides itself as the greatest democracy in the world, is a stunning phenomenon of the twentieth century."[11]

Trying to cope with the war news was difficult enough, but attempting to follow Nixon's management of the war presented a special editorial problem. One never knew what he might do next, for he was capable of almost any action. Johnson was reckless, but I never thought he would risk escalation of the war beyond a certain point; I had no such feeling about Nixon. At the same time I assumed he was much too shrewd to believe the war could be won and well aware that if he could somehow end it his reelection would be assured. On the eve of the 1960 campaign he had recognized, as I had pointed out in *The Nation,* the political dividends that might be reaped by reaching or appearing to reach an understanding with China. By 1969 the Vietnam War had nearly wrecked the Democratic Party and was thoroughly unpopular with Republicans, including those who opposed the withdrawal of American troops. But there was the constant danger Nixon might miscalculate and use tactics that would enlarge the conflict or lead to a major confrontation with China or Russia or both. Always the opportunist, the "operator," he would, I assumed, concentrate on the politics of the problem, not the problem. This implied that he would try to wind down the war without appearing to lose it. "I've come to the conclusion," he told Richard Whalen, "that there's no way to win the war. But we can't say that, of course. In fact, we have to seem to say the opposite, just to keep some degree of bargaining leverage." I never thought he cared a hoot about what might happen in South Vietnam. The total political animal, he would be guided by what seemed to be the course most likely to yield personal political dividends. So it was necessary to concentrate on his every word and action and, at the same time, to provide maximum coverage of the war and to keep hammering away at the imperative need to end it. By 1969 the Vietnam War, in all its ramifications, rated the highest journalistic priority; it had become the centerpiece of the Cold War design and the dominant national concern. But one had to spend as much time watching Nixon as reporting the war. Ironically, Nixon's manner and character, his reputation and record, invited the lack of confidence in his leadership of which he constantly complained. How could anyone who knew Nixon really trust him? That famous line under his photograph, "Would you buy a used car from this man?," said it all. The fact is, of course, that Nixon made it easy at times to be unfair to Nixon; he invited misinterpretation.

By the spring of 1969, the general outline of the "game plan" for winding down the war began to emerge. The cunning Defense Secretary Melvin Laird gave the plan its name: "Vietnamization." Never, it has been said, was more ambiguity crowded into six syllables. U.S. troops would be gradually withdrawn, which would, hopefully, minimize the domestic political protests. At the same time we would beef up the South Vietnamese forces and stage protective air strikes, "intrusions," and similar actions designed to keep the other side off balance and thus prevent or forestall an all-out attack on Saigon. Eventually a settlement might be negotiated or, if not, the Saigon regime could probably hold out for quite a time with American backing and in any case until after the 1972 election. If in the end it collapsed, all or most of the U.S. troops would be out and we could say that the South Vietnamese had "lost" the war which we had so long waged in their name. In part the strategy was designed to saddle the South Vietnamese with responsibility for the bankruptcy of American policy. The first U.S. troop withdrawals were announced on June 8, and the "Nixon Doctrine" of July 25, which made it "perfectly clear" we did not intend to get bogged down in any more such "police actions" or limited wars, invested "Vietnamization" with a degree of credibility.

But there was an inherent weakness in this strategy. It trapped the President in a vicious circle. The slow pace of troop withdrawals simply stimulated the demand in this country for larger and more rapid withdrawals. At the same time, troop withdrawals did little to induce a greater willingness on the part of the North Vietnamese to make further concessions; in fact, it may have had the opposite effect. Yet once the process had started, it was difficult to halt and politically impossible to reverse. Sending more troops back to Vietnam would have raised the volume of protests by several decibels.

By early fall it was evident that the game plan was not proceeding on schedule. Preoccupied as always with crises, Nixon overreacted to the October 15 Moratorium with its huge protests and demonstrations. What bothered him, of course, was the fact that the young activists had now been joined by larger constituencies drawn from academic and intellectual circles. When, for example, seventy-nine presidents of privately endowed colleges joined in an appeal for stepped-up troop withdrawals, the antiwar movement was invested with a respectability it had previously lacked. But even before October 15, the Administration had given top priority to the need to contain domestic protests; the use of covert means began early in 1969. In reacting as he did to the protests, Nixon created the "crisis" he sought to avoid; thereafter, as Ted Lewis reported in *The Nation*, "a political motivation was read into every presidential move." Years later, in the David Frost interviews, Nixon said he had been primarily concerned with the effect domestic demonstrations might have on the North Vietnamese, but he greatly heightened the impact by the panicky countermeasures he took to discredit or suppress them. And in any case, it was a dangerous fallacy to believe, as Walter Lippmann had pointed out earlier, that an apparent domestic consensus would convince the North Vietnamese that we were invincible.

The next major sequence in what might be called the "Seventh Crisis" in Nixon's career came the following spring. On April 20, 1970, in a nationally televised report on the war, Nixon had sounded both optimistic and conciliatory and had announced the withdrawal of 150,000 troops. Then, ten days later, apparently disturbed by reports of a North Vietnamese buildup, he launched the ghastly raids on the Cambodian "sanctuaries." These raids were strictly his idea; the National Security Council had not recommended them. Measured in terms of lives, property damage, and wanton devastation, the destruction was catastrophic. The tonnage was twice that which had been dropped in North Vietnam, and the loss of Cambodian lives was estimated at half a million. "Of all the high crimes for which Richard Nixon must be held to account by history," writes James Thompson, an East Asian policy aide at the State Department and the White House in the years 1961–66, "none can be higher than the senseless destruction of Khmer civilization."[12] Representative Paul McCloskey, who visited Cambodia in 1975, described the wreckage as "greater evil than we have done to any country in the world." The raids, which Nixon described as "defensive action for peace," were utterly lacking in military rationale; they destroyed a peaceful society and brought on the Communist takeover which we sought to prevent. Robert Keatley summed up the raids in the *Wall Street Journal* of April 11, 1975, as "a total policy failure." Some day perhaps we may know more about the circumstances that led to Lon Nol's ouster of Prince Sihanouk in late March. *The Nation* admired the Prince's skill in maintaining as long as he did a tightrope neutrality which, even if it involved a little trickery, kept the country out of war. Unlike Johnson, the President had not contrived a Gulf of Tonkin resolution to cover his actions: he simply ordered the military to destroy the "sanctuaries," and in the process the countryside and its peasant villages were nearly obliterated.

The domestic reaction was predictable: half of the nation's colleges closed down. Thousands of student moderates who had not previously participated joined with faculty and student activists in protesting not merely a monstrous action but the rank deception that had been practiced on them. Quite without precedent in American history, these protests were aimed at the national government, not at the universities as so many of the earlier demonstrations had been. On May 1 the President denounced the demonstrators as "bums" who were "blowing up the campuses," and his words were followed shortly by the Kent State shootings of May 4 and the May 14 disturbances at Jackson State. Between these dates, some 75,000 demonstrators assembled in Washington in one of the most impressive protests of the period.

Nixon seemed to be taken aback, momentarily, by the Kent State student deaths and the extraordinary response they evoked. On June 13 he proceeded to steal a page from Johnson's book of tricks by naming a commission to study the violence for which his own actions were responsible. In a somewhat similar situation and for much the same reason, Johnson had set up the National Advisory Commission on Civic Disorders (the Kerner Commission) after the race riots of 1967.[13] When the commission presented its report on February 29, 1968, he received the members politely enough, but, as John V. Lindsay, who was vice-chairman of the commission, notes, "he never mentioned it again. It ended up on the shelf." At the time it was presented, Richard Drinnon commented in *The Nation* on "the sleight of hand whereby President Johnson directed attention away from the task forces waging a war of destruction against Vietnam, and toward the task forces considering the violence of those protesting it or suffering from it."

After naming the Scranton Commission, Nixon adopted a somewhat less belligerent tone for a week or two but then returned to the attack. Released on September 26, 1970, the Scranton Report was sharper and more pertinent than might have been expected. Privately Nixon told Vice President Agnew to "blast hell out of it"; publicly he ignored the report for nearly eleven weeks and then curtly rejected its recommendations. And as the congressional elections got under way that fall, he followed Agnew out across the country, trying to put together the "new majority"—the "silent majority"—that would support his policies. In these personal appearances, he managed to top the verbal violence, snide comments, and crass abuse Agnew had been heaping on critics of the Administration. For example, at San Jose on October 29 and Phoenix on

October 31, he spoke out against "campus thugs and hoodlums."
But all to no purpose, for despite the violence of some of the
protests, his counterattacks and emphasis on the "social issues" did
not catch on. The Democrats increased their representation in the
House by nine seats and captured governorships from Republicans
in twelve states. Word began to make the rounds that Nixon was a
"defeatable President," and commentators, as they had done so
often, speculated about why his personal support should be so
curiously thin. But for all his criticism of the press and media, he
manipulated both very skillfully; it was not exposure he lacked,
exposure was his problem.

After he had had a chance to assess the results of the election,
Nixon did what one might have expected him to do: he took a
more conciliatory line, briefly. Thus, as Richard E. Peterson and
John A. Bilorsky point out in their study *The Campus Aftermath of
Cambodia and Kent State* (1971), "the stance in official Washington
had shifted from harsh criticism of the universities, to ostensible
solicitude, then back to rancor and bitterness, and finally to appeals
for unity and a peaceful 'revolution'—all within a most memorable
nine-months period." But of course there had been no real change
in his position or policies; the shifts were purely tactical. In fact,
the February "incursion" into Laos had been planned during the
brief period when he appeared to be making overtures to his
critics. But these overtures had little effect; they came too late.
Nothing quite like the tumultuous protests of the period from
Kent State to the end of the year had ever occurred in our history;
the effects, obviously, could not be expunged with a few conciliatory words and phrases, which, in fact, were inconsistent with the
course of action Nixon continued to pursue.

Nixon's problem, in part, was that by the spring of 1970 the
"peace movement" had been supplanted by a militant antiwar in-
surgency. While keeping the editorial focus on the war and the
congressional elections, *The Nation* reported—thoroughly and
fairly, I believe—the often violent protests, including the bombings
and other actions, of antiwar elements whom Kingman Brewster
characterized as "enraged destructionists." But the fact that we
would not go all out in support of the insurgents, largely because
of their tactics, did not win us many plaudits from their more vocal
spokesmen. Tactically the violence was counterproductive; so, too,
was much of the gaudy sophomoric rhetoric with the mindless
repetition of such words as "pig," "bullshit," and "motherfucker."[14]
And so, too, was the inexcusable mistake of permitting the hard-
hats to monopolize the symbols of patriotism, and the failure of
the activists to relate the war to the issues of most immediate con-

cern to blue-collar workers and other elements of the middle and lower-middle class who might have been won over by more intelligent tactics.

But it was easy to understand the character that antiwar protests often assumed even if the tactics were shortsighted. "When the decorum is repression," Abbie Hoffman said, "the only duty free men have is to speak out. We don't respond to authority we regard as illegitimate." Politically some of the tactics used were self-defeating, but the noise and violence and rough language did voice a justifiable sense of outrage. In *The Nation* of May 18, 1970, we quoted a Yale student as saying: "A couple of weeks ago I crossed over . . . I got the feeling that the whole world was insane." Many "enraged destructionists" were embittered idealists who acted in desperation and despair; they were neither "bums" nor "hoodlums," nor could they be dismissed as a lunatic fringe. Issues deeper than the war motivated some of them. Of the reaction to the bombings in Madison, Wisconsin, Peter Weiss wrote (*The Nation;* October 5, 1970): "This is middle class rage against the offspring of its neglect—shouting across the chasm in reply to its own echo—and Old Glory everywhere displayed to ward off a mistake in God's judgment." The Vietnam War had precipitated a generational crisis as well as a crisis in national identity and a sharp conflict in values and attitudes and expectations.

Throughout this turgid period *The Nation* tried to report the antiwar protests and demonstrations in a context that explained the uproar and confusion and occasional violence. Not only did we report the long succession of "incidents" as they occurred, but we managed to cover, with few if any exceptions, the major political trials of the period. And at the same time we kept a spotlight riveted on the twists and turns in the policies Nixon pursued while he continued to incite the protests of which he complained so bitterly. We also reported, without benefit of recent congressional inquiries, the dirty tricks and often illegal counterinsurgency tactics the Administration was using to curb the protests. It was all part of "the Vietnam Story": all part of that strange revolution which the war had finally set in motion, not a social or political revolution so much as a cultural revolution, a nationwide generational upheaval, a belated reckoning with ourselves, a protest against attitudes, values and outlook brought on by years of Cold War; a revulsion against corruption grown chronic, intolerable complacency on social issues, national self-satisfaction and self-righteousness, executive arrogance, the unconstitutional usurpation of power, false pieties, hypocritical postures, Cold War dogmas and assumptions; a confused revolution without ideology or program and with but one clear objective: to end the war. It was, as Michael Harrington noted in an interview, "a mass movement on an uncharted social frontier" which disappeared—or seemed to disappear—as quickly as it had emerged once its immediate objective was achieved, leaving many of the larger issues of Pax Americana unexplored and unresolved. But whatever else it accomplished, or failed to accomplish, the antiwar movement significantly changed social perspectives.

An eerie calm seemed to settle over the campus in the early weeks of 1971, a reaction no doubt to nine months of political turbulence and demonstrations. But I knew—everyone knew—it would not last long, and it didn't. In February, Nixon, apparently responding to military pressure, approved plans to cut the Ho Chi Minh Trail, and the "incursion" into Laos got under way. Once again he acted without congressional authorization or approval, but in this round only air power was used. By February 20 it was apparent, despite misleading official reports, that incessant heavy bombing could not stop the movement of supplies and troops along infiltration routes. Even so the President thought that the South Vietnamese could "hack it" and that they were doing very well. Two weeks later, after uncounted helicopter sorties against an enemy without air power had failed to accomplish the objective of cutting supply routes, he was less confident, perhaps because his approval ratings in the polls had dropped sharply. In mid-April, Stewart Alsop concluded in *Newsweek* that the incursion effort had been a military failure in Laos and a disaster in the United States. The President should realize, he added, that it was simply "not practical to continue to fight a war that has no popular support at all."

On May 5 a huge demonstration was staged in Washington, with many arrests. The Calley case, publication of the Pentagon Papers, and the usual steady barrage of reports of corruption and incompetence in Saigon led to speculation that perhaps the President couldn't "hack it" much longer. In fact, there was some talk, quite a bit of it, that Nixon might suffer the same loss of confidence that had forced Johnson to withdraw. But in an editorial of October 25 *The Nation* pointed out that Nixon was not as vulnerable as some of his critics assumed; he was never a popular politician, but that did not mean he might not win reelection. Indeed, by then he had set the stage for his victory of the following year. For on April 30, 1971, at the year's low point for him, *Life* carried a report by Edgar Snow in which Mao Tse-tung was quoted as saying that he was of a mind to invite the President to China or agreeable to the idea. (Earlier feelers for such a visit had been put out through the Pakistanis.) For Nixon the suggestion could not have come at a more opportune time. On July 9, 1971, Henry Kissinger was en route to Peking.

The moment it was announced that Nixon would go to Peking, I felt sure he would win reelection; merely to have broken the twenty-year impasse in relations with China would carry him to victory. In a sense, China was always the crux of the Vietnam problem. Speaking at Stanford in the spring of 1965, Alfred Grosser, the French historian, raised the key question: "Does the United States consider China a country or not? The question comes down to that." For years Washington had accepted the answer Dean Rusk had given to the same question in 1951. "The Peking regime," he had said, "may be a colonial Russian government—a Slavonic Man-chukuo on a larger scale. It is not the government of China. It does not pass the first test. It is not Chinese." The insistence that the regime was not Chinese was based on the dogma, despite clear evidence to the contrary, that the Russians controlled it. For twenty years that had been one of the prime assumptions underlying Cold War policies in Asia. And now Richard Nixon, one of the authors and most vocal advocates of our disastrously mistaken China policy, had finally reached the revolutionary conclusion that the Chinese regime met the first test of legitimacy: it was Chinese, not Russian.

But by the time the President returned from Peking, he was confronted with still another "crisis." With the Paris peace talks stalled, the North Vietnamese had launched a savage offensive and the South Vietnamese were in deep trouble. So on May 8 he "made the call," as he put it: Haiphong harbor would be mined, road and rail connections with China would be smashed, and the bombing raids against North Vietnam stepped up. The "call" was made, of course, without any real consultation with other branches of government. It was made, moreover, on the eve of his departure for the Moscow summit. He had risked a similar gamble when the Air Force had made one thousand or so massive strikes against North Vietnam targets between December 26 and 30 before he left for Peking. The Chinese had expressed their indignation but had nevertheless received him with full honors in February. That both "calls" had provoked only protests from Moscow and Peking was no doubt carefully pondered in Hanoi. Small wonder, then, that William Safire should regard the summits of the early months of 1972 as the apex of Nixon's years in the White House. Both were perfectly timed: close enough to the November election to be vividly remembered, far enough removed not to appear to be blatantly political. I was grateful that the Peking and Moscow summit meetings had been held but could muster no enthusiasm for the action that preceded them; the risks were too great, and the same results might have been achieved years earlier had any President sought to initiate a policy of detente.

When Senator George McGovern first began to be mentioned for the Democratic nomination, I wrote an editorial captioned "Can a Good Man Win?" (*The Nation*, January 25, 1971), and my answer was that much as I liked and admired McGovern I did not think he could be elected. Given his fine personal qualities, I felt he would be at a distinct disadvantage in a race with Nixon, but *The Nation*, of course, supported his candidacy. I thought McGovern ran a rather remarkable campaign in the primaries, but mistakes made at the convention, and later, kept him on the defensive throughout the last months of the campaign. But even if he had waged a flawless campaign, it would not have mattered: Nixon would have won. The missions to Moscow and Peking—important first steps in lifting the Cold War iron curtain—and the troop withdrawals assured his reelection. McGovern's final television address on Vietnam was a courageous and irrefutable summation, but Nixon had preempted the key positions. The coldest of Cold Warriors had reversed his field, crossed up his opposition, left his right-wing supporters sputtering with rage, and walked off with the prize.

If the press had been more alert in pressing the investigation of the Watergate break-in after June, 1972, the disclosures might have shaped up as a major issue in the campaign, but this did not happen. "The real scandal of the Watergate caper," I wrote in *The Nation* of September 4, 1972, "is that the Administration may succeed in keeping the lid on the facts until after November 7th," which of course it did. Even the Washington *Post* began to lay off Watergate as the election neared. Later Ben Bagdikian estimated that only fourteen of 2,200 reporters in Washington had done substantial work on Watergate in the early months of the scandal. However, the 1972 election was a "negative landslide." Nixon got 60.7 percent of the popular vote, but this percentage was less than Johnson had received in 1964. Nor was his victory quite as impressive as it appeared to be: some forty-five percent of those eligible to vote didn't bother to cast ballots—the lowest turnout since the 1948 campaign. And there was no general swing to the right. The last-minute histrionics of Kissinger's announcement of October 26 that "peace is at hand" provided the final touch: perfectly timed for maximum effect.

In 1968 Nixon had won by default; in 1972 he won because he had skillfully engineered a situation which really made it no contest. Seldom in political history have a politician's personal qualities as a candidate had so little to do with his victories at the polls. In a piece in *The Spectator,* written a week before the 1972 election, Henry Fairlie pointed out that Nixon was "about to win an all-but-friendless victory. Never to my knowledge in the history of the great democracies has it seemed a political leader was about to receive so large a majority for such negative reasons. . . . The man was neither liked nor admired." It was as if the people had come to distinguish between the man and the President "and were willing to vote against the first without condemning the second." Nixon's "disembodied voice"—his preference for radio in an age of television—had "an eerie effect. Every image of faceless men, of Big Brother, of 1984, seems to have come true. There is no Richard Nixon who can be put out of office or turned out of it. There is only this impersonal power, speaking without any presence, inaccessible to restraint or protest." As a matter of fact, the margin of Nixon's victory in 1972 was in part enhanced by his decision to campaign from the wings and to minimize personal appearances, confident that the summits and the apparent winding down of the war would carry him to victory.*

In *The Nation* of November 6, 1972, I pointed to the hard-to-believe fact that Nixon's War had by then lasted 1,400 days after he had first announced a plan to end it: a period of approximately the same time span as that between Pearl Harbor and V-J Day. Yet despite campaign preelection assurances that peace was at hand, the war continued, for the negotiations kept breaking down. Then came the Christmas bombings of North Vietnam in which, for a period of eleven days, American B-52s and other planes carried out two thousand air strikes on Hanoi and Haiphong. Again these raids were planned in secret, in part to appease South Vietnamese President Thieu, and carried out with no serious explanation to Congress or the public or this country's allies. Apparently there was no consultation with the Joint Chiefs or the Secretary of Defense, and Kissinger may or may not have had some doubts about the wisdom of the action. The raids were carried out at an esti-

---

* In *Man in the Modern Age,* first published in 1931 but not issued in an English edition until 1951, Karl Jaspers had foreseen the emergence of "faceless" types in a technological mass society in which individuals tend to merge in the functions they perform. "It is as if the man," he wrote, "thus deracinated to the level of a thing, had lost the essence of humanity. Nothing appeals to him with the verity of substantial being. Whether in enjoyment or discomfort, whether strenuous or fatigued, he is still nothing more than the function of his daily task. As he lives on from day to day, the only desire that may stir him from beyond that of performing this task is the desire to occupy the best obtainable place in the apparatus." That Nixon meets Jasper's specification so neatly is perhaps what made him, in a sense, a "representative" man for many Americans in the Cold War decades, for they too had been "deracinated" to the same level and therefore could identify with him even if they didn't like him.

mated cost of $500 million. In a bitter piece in *The Nation* (January 22, 1973), William L. Shirer pointed out that the Germans had dropped only 80,000 tons of bombs on Britain in more than five years; we had dropped 100,000 tons on the North Vietnamese in a single month. As a postscript, I remember feeling there was a curious historical symbolism in the fact that President Truman was buried at Independence, Missouri, as these raids were being carried out. And I had a similar feeling when President Johnson died, just as Nixon was about to announce that a cease-fire had at long last been ordered. But since Vietnam had been "an exceptionally untidy war," Frank Snepp's CIA boss assured him, "so the peace has got to be untidy too." In truth there never was a "peace"; many issues remained unresolved. And by early April it was clear that the cease-fire was *kaput*.[15] Congress finally felt compelled to impose restraints—the War Powers Act was adopted on August 15, 1973— and the final curtain then began to descend on the least glorious military adventure this country has ever engaged in.

Even so, would the fighting have ended but for Watergate? Ironically, Watergate finally overtook Nixon at almost the precise moment the so-called Paris Accords were signed. William Safire is right: in the period from the summit triumphs of 1972 until the second inaugural, Nixon and crew, without being aware of the fact, were "on board the steepest fastest roller-coaster in American political history"—from the summits to subbasement levels in less than a year's time. And there is a sense in which Safire is also right in concluding that "Nixon consciously presided over the end of the 'postwar' period."[16] But he wisely put "postwar" in quotes. What Nixon did was to create a situation which, in the context of Watergate, made it possible for President Ford to let the Vietnamese War finally lapse and thereby usher in a "postwar" period after thirty years of Cold War.

Nixon and his apologists would have us believe it was his gutsy "calls," his gambles in ordering the bombing raids at critical points in the war, which finally made it possible to secure a cease-fire. But the argument has a hollow ring to it. The raids on the Cambodian sanctuaries very nearly destroyed Cambodia. Did Nixon end the war as early as it might have been ended or did he prolong it for nearly seven years? What, in essence, was "Vietnamization" but a clever device for quieting antiwar protests while, at the same time, leading the hawks to believe we were still "hanging in there," tough as ever. No one can prove, of course, that a serious effort to end the war at an earlier date, on the frankly acknowledged premise that American intervention was a tragic mistake, would have succeeded. But by the same token it cannot be proven that Nixon ended the war. The South Vietnam regime collapsed because it was fated to collapse, and the end result was precisely what Nixon said he would never accept. Nothing could be more cynical than the way Ford and Kissinger kept up the pleas for further military appropriations to aid the South Vietnamese, knowing that the jig was up but determined, if possible, to establish a record which would show they had done all that they could to save a regime that we had kept in power for nearly twenty years. In the same vein, "Vietnamization" may have made it psychologically and politically possible for diehard elements to accept American withdrawal; it may also have lessened the guilt feelings of other elements by inducing them to believe we had done all that we could to sustain a commitment that should never have been made. Thus it could be said that we were not humiliated and had proven to be anything but a "pitiful helpless giant"; but the fact is we were humiliated and in the end we did prove to be a giant that if not pitiful was helpless to prevent a disaster of our own making.

Did withdrawal of American troops and the end of the fighting have the dreadful consequences so long predicted? Our allies seemed vastly relieved that circumstances—specifically Watergate —had finally made it possible for us to extricate ourselves from a monumental mess that was an embarrassment to them. And there was no "blood bath" in Vietnam, as had been predicted, although we left $5 billion in military equipment and a $1-billion investment in South Vietnam's infrastructure, roads, ports, airfields, and the like, which would have made it easy for the North Vietnamese to conduct a swift and bloody purge if they had so desired. But by then no one really cared about South Vietnam including those South Vietnamese who had served us; nor were we concerned about the costs, or the equipment we had left there; it was enough that the war had ended. Nixon, Safire writes, "hung tough, on Vietnam, hung tough once again on Watergate, and hung himself."[17] In the process of hanging himself, he made it possible to end the war, but he did not end it. Measured in terms of the final end result, what had the long years of the Nixon War accomplished? And the war would not have ended when it did but for Watergate.

5. COVERING UP THE COVER-UP

From the Watergate break-in to the November election, Nixon and his key aides were able to keep enough of a lid on the scandals to minimize the political impact. The Moscow and Peking summits helped; so, too, did the fact that a national election was under way.

Most of the press seemed reluctant to dig into the scandals, in part for fear of being charged with "smearing" the President. The press had good reason to know that Nixon had a long memory and could be vindictive, so it kept waiting, with a few notable exceptions, for proof positive of his guilt. After Nixon's victory in November, he and his aides must have concluded that they could keep the scandals under wraps. Between the election and his second inaugural address, Nixon acted as though he were the monarch of the universe. The barbarous Christmas bombings—he was enough of a Quaker to order that there should be no raids on Christmas Day—were merely one measure of his imperial self-confidence.

But almost from the moment he was sworn in for a second term, he found himself enmeshed in the proliferating Watergate scandals. Until then, he and his aides had been preoccupied with the cover-up; now their attention and energies shifted to covering up the cover-up. Each day brought new disclosures, new sensations, new headlines; by early spring the elaborate cover-up began to fall apart. The substitutions he made to placate public opinion—Elliot Richardson to replace Richard Kleindienst as Attorney General was a case in point—only added to his difficulties. Richardson would not be pushed around, beyond a point. Agnew's difficulties and ultimate resignation momentarily diverted some of the pressure, but in the end the effect was to weaken the President's position. The notion of impeaching Nixon or forcing his resignation had less support among Republicans as long as Agnew was Vice President. No doubt Nixon thought that appointment of the colorless Gerald Ford as Vice President would discourage pressures for impeachment or resignation—would Republicans want to run with Ford at the head of the ticket?—but if so it proved to be a miscalculation. Looking ahead to 1974 and beyond to the Bicentennial election of 1976, Republicans began to be deeply worried about their chances if Nixon managed to remain in the White House. Loyal Republican support began to evaporate; Senator James Buckley suggested Nixon should resign, and Senators Tower and Goldwater and Representative John Rhodes showed signs of mounting concern. Cold War intellectuals, including Sidney Hook and Irving Kristol, who had enjoyed White House hospitality, and Daniel Patrick Moynihan, who had held high office in the Administration and had once thought that Nixon might become an American Disraeli, now began to distance themselves as far as possible from him. It did not take long, in fact, for the resignation clamor to reach a climax, but Nixon, like Agnew, wanted to plea-bargain; he would not resign until he had some assurance of a pardon or felt confident a pardon would follow resignation.

Someday perhaps historians will tell us precisely what happened during Nixon's final hours in the White House. In *The Nation* of November 9, 1974, Bill Nigut examined very closely the final sequence of events that led to the resignation. Impeachment was imminent, there was no doubt of that; the Republicans wanted, if possible, to avoid the embarrassment of campaigning in November with an incumbent Republican President facing impeachment charges. But Congress could not grant immunity, and Nixon was not about to resign unless he was sure he would not be prosecuted and could retain the various perquisites ex-Presidents normally receive. If one examines Ford's statements closely, as Nigut did, it is hard to escape the conclusion that he was not entirely candid about what he had said in those final talks with Haig and Nixon. But it does not really matter whether an explicit commitment for a pardon was made; a pardon was implicit in the situation. It may not have been promised Nixon in so many words, but he had every reason to believe it would be forthcoming, as it was on September 6.

The movement which finally resulted in adoption of articles of impeachment by the House Judiciary Committee has a history portions of which have been forgotten. Outraged by continued State Department sophistries, a group of New York lawyers—Joseph Crown, William Standard, Victor Rabinowitz, Harold Cammer and others—had formed the Lawyers Committee on American Policy Toward Vietnam in 1965. Most were members of the National Lawyers Guild. Initially Robert W. Kenny, of California, served as chairman, Joe Crown as secretary, while I was named vice-chairman along with William Standard. The committee promptly challenged the assumptions on which the "undeclared" war was being waged. Among other steps, it commissioned Marvin E. Gettleman to prepare a study—*Vietnam: History, Documents and Opinions on a Major World Crisis*—which quickly became a major resource for groups opposing the war. The committee's first formal brief on the legality of the war was placed in the *Congressional Record* on September 23, 1965, by Senators Morse and Gruening. Thousands of copies were distributed. After a time the State Department finally and most reluctantly agreed to participate in debates on the issues raised by the brief, including an NBC-TV debate between Arthur Goldberg and Joe Crown. It is a measure of the hypnotic effect of Cold War propaganda that the legal and constitutional issues had been so long ignored or obscured. Once they had been raised, the antiwar groups began to stress these issues, a tactic which had the effect of bypassing ideological fixations and zeroing in on the fundamental question of authorization.

Early in 1972 the Lawyers Committee decided that impeachment charges should be pressed. But even then impeachment struck many opponents of the war as being farfetched and impractical. Shaking some dust from the history texts, the committee had little difficulty in proving that impeachment was not merely an appropriate remedy but the only one available. A memorandum to this effect, which appeared in the *Congressional Record,* was the first public proposal urging impeachment. On May 18, 1972, H.R. 989, a resolution calling for impeachment and based on the committee's brief, was introduced by a group of representatives. It should be emphasized that this action took place *a month before* the Watergate break-in. Later a new committee—Citizens Committee for Constitutional Government—headed by William Meyers, Peter Weiss, and Joe Crown, renewed the demand for impeachment and kept pressing the issue at meetings and in full-page ads in the press.[18] This same group of lawyers then prepared a bill of impeachment which, in a somewhat modified form, became H.R. 976 (Ninety-second Congress), introduced by Representative John Conyers. Like the earlier resolution, this one was bottled up in committee, but it should not be forgotten that two years before formal articles of impeachment were finally adopted and Watergate had provided the necessary impetus, a small group of lawyers, mostly of the so-called "old left," had offered the first legal challenge to the legitimacy of a war that had been waged for nearly three decades in defiance of the UN Charter and the Constitution.

By the time Nixon delivered his State of the Union address in 1973 it was clear his days in the White House were numbered. "Operation Candor," launched in November, had proven to be no more convincing than the various tactics of deception. Murray Chotiner's death on the day the message was delivered served as a reminder of the famous Checkers speech of 1952, echoes of which could be caught in its half-apologetic, defensive tone (Chotiner had helped draft the Checkers speech). Nixon had good reason to feel defensive: his approval rating in the polls had by then dropped to twenty-six percent. New tensions in the Middle East momentarily diverted attention from Watergate, as did the President's extensively televised visit to Cairo with fireworks on the Nile and throngs of cheering Egyptians along the parade routes. But inexorably the pressures kept closing in. Once the impeachment proceedings got under way the end was clearly in sight. For nearly two years the nation had been preoccupied with Watergate in one way or another and had watched with mounting interest as Nixon twisted, squirmed, lied, double-talked, retreated, counterattacked and, in the end, finally convicted himself. His statement on the June 23,

1972, tape was in effect a plea of guilty to Articles I and II of the impeachment resolution. By then virtually the entire press had turned against him, and even his close associates in the White House realized he would help none of them at any risk to himself. How many careers and reputations had he destroyed along with his own? In Conrad's phrase, he had left "a mound of skulls" from California to Washington. And in the end even his partisans on the House Judiciary Committee began to put pressure on him to resign, if only to get themselves off the hook.

The finale to the long and painful ordeal came almost overnight. Suddenly Nixon was limping across the White House lawn to the helicopter, having bid a tearful adieu to his aides and attendants. At long last he was out of the White House and on his way back, in disgrace, to a self-imposed exile at San Clemente. His "farewell" was itself a kind of maudlin plea bargain couched in familiar Checkers rhetoric: "I have always tried to do what was best . . . I felt my duty was to persevere. . . . No matter what the personal agony . . . ," etc.

Why, one asks, did it take so long for the Watergate scandals to catch up with Nixon, or, stated another way, why did it take so long for the people to catch on to him? His past record indicated he was quite capable of using illegal tactics to win an election. In the 1962 gubernatorial campaign in California, he and his top assistants had staged a plan to snare votes that not only was unethical but violated the law. Under the letterhead of something called "The Committee for the Preservation of the Democratic Party," Nixon and his aides had sent out a loaded questionnaire to *conservative* Democratic voters and had then misrepresented the results of the survey. This was done at considerable expense, and the funds were laundered so as to make it appear that the committee was what it purported to be. A California court issued an injunction against the scheme in 1962. Yet curiously enough this earlier Watergate, and the court decision which set forth the facts in detail, had been forgotten; it was not even mentioned in the best Nixon biographies. Nor did the general press call attention to it even after Watergate became headline news.[19]

Indeed, for a time it seemed as though Nixon might "stonewall" Watergate as he had successfully stonewalled earlier unpleasant episodes in his career including the 1962 caper in California. He had come to feel, and not without reason, that his consistent and highly publicized "anti-Communism" had invested him with immunity against political scandals and slimy tactics. Also, of course, he had no hesitancy about using the enormous powers of the Presidency to cover up the cover-up. Neither he nor his aides had any scruples about using dirty tricks, pressure tactics, surveillance, patronage, and intimidation to cover their tracks. In addition they had huge resources in the form of slush funds, loose cash, leftover campaign contributions, many of which were illegal, and packs of bills stashed in safes. With such resources it was easy to hire mercenaries to carry out hazardous assignments, most of which were executed, however, with inexplicable incompetence. From first to last the cover-up of the cover-up was the work of amateurs. Ruthless and cunning, Nixon was also stupid about some things, as, for example, his failure to destroy the tapes. Yet he managed to stay one jump ahead of his pursuers for nearly two years during which the encirclement and eventual "capture" of Richard Nixon was a top news story.

Once Nixon had left the White House, a mood of relief and self-congratulation swept the nation. The press was pleased with the role it had played in forcing his ouster, although only a handful of reporters and newspapers really deserved much credit for exposing the facts. Congress was pleased with its role, as well it might be, for the Ervin Committee and the House Judiciary Committee had demonstrated Nixon's guilt to nationwide audiences. The role of the judiciary was extolled. Individual citizens and officials were honored for contributions they had made to the disclosures. In general it was agreed that "the system" had worked, and so it had, after a fashion. Even so, the nation had come closer to a *coup d'état* than many cared to admit then or later, a conclusion that finds well-documented support in *Agency of Fear* (1977), by Edward Jay Epstein. Several contributors to *The Nation* had, in fact, warned of the danger of a *coup d'état*. Actually there was little reason to be pleased with the way "the system" had functioned; it certainly had not worked well in the months immediately following the first Watergate disclosures. The fact is that Nixon was responsible for his own undoing; in the end it was his weaknesses, as much as the strength of "the system," that resulted in his ouster. If he had destroyed the tapes, if he had granted a general pardon, if he had really "stonewalled" it, who knows what might have happened? A set of lucky circumstances is what made "the system" work as well as it did.

Again and again I asked myself why it was that so many Americans either found it difficult to take Nixon's measure or were prepared to give him the benefit of the doubt. Nixon was not that hard to read. Over the years I came to feel that many people knew or sensed what he was like as a person long before they were prepared to acknowledge it to themselves or to others. It was, in a way, a well-kept national secret. A section of the public apparently felt that the times called for a bastard and that Nixon met the specification. As they saw it, the politician could be divorced from the man; it didn't matter what kind of person he was as long as he did what they wanted done. Stewart Alsop once referred to Nixon as our "first professional president"; the man was so perfectly fused with his function that there was little left of him as a person and that little he did not understand, nor did anyone else. Leone Baxter, of the famous California political public-relations firm of Whitaker and Baxter, once told me that about the only person who really understood Nixon was his friend Robert Finch. Fragments of a portrait emerged in many pieces that *The Nation* had published about Nixon since he first ran for public office. For example, in the issue of July 6, 1974, René J. Muller shrewdly said of Nixon that he was not a self-made man: he had made a career, not a self. And in a piece captioned "Nixon: A Type to Remember"—August 31, 1974—Mark Harris pointed out that the most disturbing aspect of the evidence against Nixon was its power to suggest that everything anyone had ever suspected about him was true, with or without evidence. As Harris wrote:

> We don't have Nixon to kick around any more. He produced his own last crisis. The danger has always been that he would take the rest of us down with him. I feared that, especially after the 1972 election, which left him bereft of further offices to run for. His world was at an end, would he then demolish ours, yours and mine and the children's, and the United States he loved so much (he said)? We have escaped by the skin of our teeth.

When it came, Nixon's pardon momentarily created a major rumpus, but President Ford managed to ride out the storm without too much discomfort. Most people were vastly relieved to have Nixon out of the White House; in fact, they were so relieved they failed to realize that the fighting in Vietnam had entered its final phase. President Ford and Kissinger kept requesting more funds from Congress for the South Vietnamese, but more for the record than in the expectation that the requests would be granted. Both the North and the South Vietnamese could read the headlines from Washington. The fall of Nixon meant the end of the war. What he might have done had he remained in office no one knows, but his ouster came at the right moment. Watergate and Vietnam had become linked in such a way that Nixon's debacle made it politically possible to end the war or, stated another way, politically impossible to continue it.

There was never any doubt how the final climactic burst of fighting would end. By mid-March the news from Vietnam was almost too painful to read or to view on television. As Thieu abandoned the central highlands, refugees surged south by the thousands: women and children, the old, the lame, the sick, the blind, in an endless procession. A cargo plane crashed near Saigon, killing more than two hundred children. Each evening the television shots became more agonizing; chaos and confusion grew by the hour. Millions of Americans sat in comfortable living rooms and watched network news scenes of South Vietnamese struggling to board the last plane, boat, cart, tank or truck that was heading south. When Chiang Kai-shek died on April 6, 1975, it was as though his death were timed to coincide with the debacle his policies had helped stage; but his death went largely unnoticed in the confusion of the news. For three or four days in April, as the fighting reached a climax, President Ford played golf in Palm Springs, apparently to demonstrate his lack of concern. Mercifully the end came soon. We were treated to the painful scene of Ambassador Graham Martin leaving the besieged embassy compound with the American flag folded under his arm. On April 21, Thieu issued a denunciation of Kissinger, Ford and Nixon which, from his point of view, was justified; he and his faction had been used, manipulated, lied to, and then abandoned. But the statement received little notice.

The final petulant flareup took place with the *Mayaguez* incident, in which a dozen or more Americans needlessly lost their lives because Kissinger and Ford felt it necessary to prove that this country was not "a pitiful helpless giant," even in defeat. Network shots of the President and his Secretary of State in a mutually self-congratulatory scene at the White House, wreathed in smiles, immensely pleased over the way the incident had been handled, flashed one of the last images of the Vietnam disaster to the American public. Still another came when Ford entered the Cabinet Room to inform assembled congressional leaders of the reasons for his decision to use force to free the *Mayaguez*. Veterans of similar supportive sessions with Johnson and Nixon, well rehearsed in their role, these carefully selected legislators knew how to act: they rose to their feet and greeted the President with prolonged applause before he had said a word. As James Weighart reported in *The Nation* of May 31, 1975, they were "like the goose of the barnyard, honking at the rising sun, lacking memories and foresight." Machismo diplomacy at its most absurd, it was as if yesterday had never happened and tomorrow might never come. With these scenes, the war in Vietnam which had climaxed thirty years of Cold War belligerence—there had been some 215 U.S. military interventions between 1945 and 1975—came to an end, not with a nuclear bombardment, fortunately, but with a growl of rage and frustration.

In fact, the Vietnam experience proved to be much too painful to assimilate. James M. Perry, writing in *National Observer*, April 12, 1975, quoted Eugene V. Rostow, Yale Law School professor and former State Department official, as saying that Vietnam was "a gone goose, and we're just going to have to swallow it. . . . But it's so hard to get it down. We choke and gasp, and it sticks in our craw. Vietnam has been our national obsession, more than a nightmare. . . . Now all our mistakes, all our misjudgments, all our self-righteous, self-satisfied self-delusions have come down to what is really the very last toss of the dice. And our loss is brutal and humiliating. It is the worst defeat, politically and militarily, we have ever known . . . we can't hide from it." Which prompted Perry to observe: "Funny, though, Rostow and all the rest—the best and brightest—kept telling us for years we were winning the war. Most of them even believed it."

But neither then nor later was the nation in a mood to conduct a postmortem on the Vietnam War, much less on the first thirty years of the Cold War. As Anthony Lewis pointed out in one of a series of thoughtful columns in the New York *Times:* "In this forgetful country, the necessity to remember is a lesson in itself." But even this lesson went unheeded. Postmortems of any kind were too painful; too many Americans had too many reasons to want to forget what had happened.

In the eagerness to forget about Vietnam—to pretend that it had never happened—the interaction between the war and Watergate was largely ignored. The ease with which the Vietnam War had been waged illegally, in defiance of constitutional restrictions, encouraged similar abuses of executive power. Vietnam and the Cold War were responsible for much of the abuse of power that came with the Imperial Presidency. Both Johnson and Nixon sought to check popular resistance to the war by improper and illegal means. The tactics which the Nixon Administration began to use in 1969 to silence antiwar demonstrators were later used to ferret out "unreliable" officials suspected of leaking documents and information to the press and also to harass political "enemies" in general. And the influence operated in reverse. If a genuine cease-fire and agreement had been achieved early in the negotiations with the South Vietnamese, Nixon might have been able to ride out the Watergate storm. Then, too, the inability of the South

Vietnamese to "hack it" helped turn opinion against him. And if Congress, reacting to Watergate as well as the antiwar demonstrations, had not finally prohibited further American military activities on August 15, 1973, the fighting might have continued with unforeseeable consequences. As it worked out, Nixon's departure from the White House and the cumulative effects of the Watergate disclosures made it politically possible for Ford and Kissinger to accept the fact that the enormous gamble of "Vietnamization" had failed. In a sense, therefore, Nixon is right in saying that he was "the last casualty in Vietnam."

With the collapse of the Saigon regime and Nixon's resignation, domestic perspectives suddenly clarified as though a post–Cold War period had finally arrived. To cite merely one example, New York City's fiscal crisis, which has a long history, became a top news story for the first time in late May, 1975. In much the same fashion the misuse of corporate funds to bribe officials and party leaders of foreign nations—a practice long encouraged and frequently instigated by the CIA—began to receive media attention even though it had never been much of a secret. And the excesses of the FBI and the CIA—well known for at least two decades—began to be investigated by congressional committees and the general press.

And once Vietnam and Watergate had ceased to dominate the headlines, other major domestic problems suddenly assumed a new visibility. The large-scale misuse of corporate funds for procurement bribes, illegal campaign contributions, outright misappropriations, expensive "perks" for executives, and rip-offs of one kind or another became a major ongoing news story. Stories of abject domestic poverty began to appear in parallel columns with reports of the abandonment of $5 billion of military equipment in Vietnam. After the spring of 1975 inflation quickly became a major national concern, but, as Seymour Melman pointed out, between 1946 and 1975 the United States spent $1.6 trillion for economically unproductive military goods and services which had exerted a steadily upward pressure on prices. The productivity of American industry, it was ruefully conceded, had declined relative to some of our allies in no small measure because of the concentration on military production. It was noted, with something of a shock, that the number of poor people rose by 2.5 million in 1975—the largest increase in a single year since government began to keep poverty statistics. The prison population was acknowledged to be at an all-time high, and most of the inmates, it was noted, had black or brown skins. Reports of expanding overseas sales of military equipment had a rather jarring impact when juxtaposed with stories of overseas famines and food shortages. After thirty years of

Cold War, goodwill toward this country was at the lowest level in the twenty-two-year history of U.S. Information Agency surveys. Not that there was anything new in these and similar disclosures, but previously they had been obscured by Cold War excitements and preoccupation with Watergate scandals. In a post–Watergate-Vietnam atmosphere it became possible to see, with a degree of clarity, aspects of the Cold War that had been long neglected or ignored.

And a few amends were belatedly offered for past injustices. In the fall of 1975, CBS presented *Fear on Trial,* in which it sought to make amends to John Henry Faulk and other victims of the network blacklist. But would the program have been presented but for Nixon's ouster and the death of J. Edgar Hoover? And in February, 1977, NBC presented *Tail Gunner Joe*—twenty years after McCarthy's death—which stirred painful memories and aroused strenuous protests. The death of Will Geer in 1978 was mourned by millions of Americans and their children for whom he had become a much-beloved grandfather figure because of his role in the CBS soap opera *The Waltons*; but this vast audience was not reminded that for twelve years "Grandpa" had been blacklisted.

But other signs suggested that Cold War tensions still survived. The attacks directed against Lillian Hellman's *Scoundrel Time* and the concerted efforts to re-try and re-convict Alger Hiss were merely two of numerous indications that the ideological feuds of an earlier period survived in a muted form. Most of the attacks against the Hellman book made the point that the "antifascists" had discriminated against right-wing writers and artists in the 1930s and therefore had no basis to complain if they had been blacklisted in the 1950s. But Granville Hicks, an ardent anti-Communist ex-Communist, had been able to think of only one or two books that had been suppressed in the heyday of antifascism when anti-Communist books, tracts, and articles were published without the slightest harassment by inquisitorial committees and other government agencies.[20] The Hellman, Hiss and similar incidents lent credence to Senator George McGovern's remark when Theodore Sorensen was forced to withdraw as President Carter's nominee to head the CIA: "The ghost of Joe McCarthy still stalks the land."

Luckily the liquidation of the Vietnam and Watergate crises made it possible to observe the Bicentennial without too much embarrassment but with less exuberance and self-confidence than might otherwise have been the case. Oddly enough there were similarities in the settings for the Centennial and the Bicentennial. The year 1876 had also marked the beginning of a deferred postwar period; only then had the nation begun to recover from the

trauma of the Civil War. It had also marked the end of a decade of
violent domestic turbulence and unrest, as did 1976. The year
1876 opened with the first of a year-long series of scandals involving the Grant Administration and closed with Grant's Farewell
Address in which he abjectly apologized for "errors of judgment,
not intent," much as Nixon did in his farewell remarks. The election of 1876 had been characterized by violence and fraud, the
election of 1972 by fraud and deceit. Responsible scholars have
spoken of the 1972 election as a kind of *coup d'état* not unlike the
way in which Republicans stole the 1876 election through a recount
of votes in the Electoral College. But there was this difference in
the two celebrations: the Centennial closed on a note of excitement
about the future which loomed bright and splendid, whereas the
Bicentennial opened and closed with widespread awareness that
the future was clouded and uncertain. But the reassuring decency
of President Ford, which resembled that of President Hayes, made
it possible to observe the Bicentennial in fairly good spirits even
though an opportunity was lost to reflect on the history which had
preceded the celebration.[21]

6. THE COLD WAR TRAP

Why had it proven so difficult to raise the Vietnam War as a
major issue in national politics? Specifically, how did it happen that
six American Presidents, three Democrats and three Republicans,
supported this country's involvement in Vietnam? "Already in
1961," Michael Rogin wrote in *The Listener* of February 22, 1968,
"Kennedy . . . 'had to support' Diem unconditionally because Eisenhower had sent in 800 advisors. Johnson tells the American
people he has to keep an 'agreement.' . . . Yet no one, apparently,
is responsible for any decisions which created America's commitment. Asserting the power to transform and destroy the world we
inhabit, the makers of American policy claim at the same time to
be hemmed in, powerless, committed by others." What hemmed
them in? What were those commitments? Who made them?

The Cold Warriors would have us believe that the military threat
of the U.S.S.R. was so quickly and instinctively sensed by the overwhelming majority that no propagandistic or coercive measures
were necessary to produce and maintain a massive "anti-Communist" consensus. But a glance at the two postwar witch-hunts casts
doubt on this theory.

The Russian Revolution was only in its infancy in the wake of
World War I; it certainly did not present a military threat of any
kind, and the American Communist Party was then merely a small

if noisy minority within the left. The "red scare" of 1919–20 was not brought about by spontaneous popular clamor so much as it was engineered by a combination of business, industrial, veteran, trade-association, and superpatriotic groups. These groups had the support of powerful agencies of government, federal, state, and local, and the nearly unanimous backing of the press, which reneged on its obligation to speak out on behalf of civil liberties and enthusiastically joined in the witch-hunt. What the Establishment of that time feared was a rising tide of postwar labor unrest. Strikes were called by the building trades, miners, longshoremen, shipworkers, stockyard workers, carpenters, policemen, shoe and steel workers, and other groups. In 1919 some 3,600 strikes were called, involving more than four million workers. Moreover, business was disturbed by what appeared to be a leftward trend in American labor; there was talk, for example, about nationalizing the steel industry and the railroads.[22] The response to this engineered "red scare," with its mass raids and arrests, deportations, and political prosecutions, was sensational; but the campaign itself was contrived. Many of the "scare" stories were pure inventions. For all its fraudulence, however, the "red scare" was effective. By 1923 organized labor had lost something like a million members, and 240 open-shop movements had spread to forty-four states. In fact, the labor movement did not stage a comeback until the mid-1930s, with the enactment of the NLRA.

After World War II, the situation was similar in some respects but different in others. The Russian Revolution was by then firmly established. But the Stalin regime, an ally in the war, had suffered catastrophic losses; in 1945 it could not be regarded as a military threat, and top planners in the State and Defense Departments did not see it in this light. Nevertheless the possibility of revolutionary or socialist regimes coming to power was regarded as sufficiently imminent so that policy-makers felt it imperative to launch a worldwide ideological crusade against "Communism" under cover of which American capitalism might expand to the far corners of the earth. Such a strategy required massive support on a bipartisan basis. But because New Deal objectives had aroused immense appeal, the public had to be whipped into line by measures far more repressive and ingenious than those used in the "red scare" after World War I. By comparison, the repression that came after 1945 was incomparably more severe, systematic and persistent. Whatever justification there was for the tough—often venomous—line we took against the Soviets after 1945, the domestic witch-hunt was inexcusable. David Caute, in *The Great Fear,* his study of the anti-Communist purge under Truman and Eisenhower, could find no evidence that the American Communist Party had engaged in espionage or sabotage. But the Communist Party was never the primary target; the purge was aimed at silencing potential criticism and dissent of the kind that had been expressed in the late 1940s. And it accomplished this purpose; after 1950, American policymakers were given a free hand to wage Cold War as they saw fit.

In general American policy throughout the first decades of the Cold War consistently confused ideological with military competition and dealt with the inevitable confrontations and tensions in military rather than political terms. Of course the Soviet Union often acted provocatively in the early postwar period. But under Truman this country, with its vastly superior military resources, was the more intransigent of the two great powers. Predictably the aggressive policies it pursued stimulated a strenuous Soviet response. Even so, as late as the missile crisis of 1961, American military superiority was incontestable; but since then the margin has narrowed. Ironically, Cold War policies have brought about Soviet military parity in some fields and superiority in others, which was exactly what these policies were supposed to preclude. The Soviets might have rushed ahead with a vast armament program in any case, but American policies and actions provided a goad if one were needed. Now, of course, the two great powers are the leading arms merchants of the world, with the United States accounting for thirty-eight percent of world arms sales and the U.S.S.R. running a close second with thirty-four percent. Between them the two great powers accounted for more than half of the $400-billion worldwide arms expenditures in 1978: twice the gross domestic product of the whole of Africa—a total that has doubled in the last twenty years.

Politically American policy-makers found themselves trapped by the assumption they had propagated—namely, that national security was inseparable from the freedom of American capitalism to expand throughout the world. Every socialist regime was seen, therefore, as an implied threat to national security. Right-wing dictatorships were never sensed as a menace; they did not threaten capitalist expansion. Nations that went socialist were "lost" to the free world; those that set up right-wing regimes remained part of it. Little thought was given to the possibility that someday trade might flourish between Socialist and capitalist nations. Or that socialist-Communist regimes might evolve in a way that would bring them a bit closer to the capitalist model. Or that nations in the Communist bloc might develop sharp internal differences. Containment was aimed at preventing the spread of socialist-Communist regimes whether or not they had Russian backing and support.

Such a policy involved an incalculable extension of American commitments. Doubtful nations were placed under close surveillance; interventions in their internal affairs became a common practice, bribing their top officials and party leaders an accepted strategy. Spending billions to prop up regimes that lacked popular support was approved by both major parties as an eminently sound strategy. In Greece, as Lawrence Stern demonstrates in *The Wrong Horse* (1978), it committed Washington to supporting a succession of repressive, undemocratic, and incompetent regimes for a quarter of a century. Many of the regimes Washington sought to keep in the capitalist orbit may yet end up in the Socialist camp, as a few already have done. And in more than one case, U.S. funds have been used to weaken American prestige and authority. The military dictatorship in South Korea, for example, has used funds, some of which were doubtless siphoned off from American aid, to bribe and influence American congressmen. Ironically, it never seems to have occurred to American policy-makers that in waging Cold War around the globe for three decades they might be changing the structure of American capitalism. Who today thinks that ours is any longer a capitalist economy in the textbook sense?

Yet so firmly had national security become identified with the dogma that socialist regimes were a menace to national security that successive Presidents assumed that any waffling on this issue might cost them or their party the next election. Arthur Krock, of the New York *Times,* in a moment of intense exasperation, let the cat out of the bag. "Vietnam," he wrote, "is vital to national security or the greatest blunder on earth." Vietnam was not necessary to national security but it proved to be "the greatest blunder" of the postwar period. Few American spokesmen were as candid as Eisenhower in stressing the real importance Cold War planners attached to Vietnam. In an address of April 4, 1956, he pointed out that by strengthening the South Vietnam regime and securing the sea lanes off its coast, we could safeguard Southeast Asia and gradually develop "the great trade potential between this region . . . and highly industrialized Japan to the benefit of both." And in a *Nation* piece of April 25, 1956, Jules Henry of Washington University was even more explicit. Being primarily a capital-exporting nation, the United States needed "markets for investment," he wrote.

> Since 1939, the gross national product of the United States has risen steeply, in large part because of the demand for armaments to wage cold war and to maintain the universal gendarmerie. A main purpose of this activity has been to keep socialism at bay, and the prime reason for doing so is that the

socialists' economies are useless to a country relying heavily on
capital export . . . part of the corporate profits must always be
invested in expansion. Capitalism is a sorcerer's mill, and nobody knows the magic word that will stop its grinding out the
surplus.

Of course there are many reasons for the success with which a
bipartisan Cold War consensus was achieved and maintained; there
is certainly no one explanation. But the fact that socialism has
always been an inadmissible heresy in American eyes helps account
for the massive support that Cold War policy-makers were able to
enlist. This country has been the one major industrial nation in the
world without a viable socialist movement. Not only does the taboo
against socialism help explain the American susceptibility to "red
scares" and witch-hunts, but it illuminates U.S. policy toward the
Soviet Union. Since its inception the U.S.S.R. has been regarded
not as another great power but as the embodiment of an ideology
we detest. More than most nations, Russia has been influenced by
its history, and that history has been obscured by the American
fixation on Soviet ideology. Russia's borders invite invasion and
have been violated more than once. Today it is faced in the west by
an alliance of European nations backed by the United States and
in the east by a hostile China and a potentially dangerous Japan.
In the south it faces a hostile Iran, one of the most heavily armed
nations in the world, and a group of unfriendly nations in the
Middle East. With long borders difficult to defend, east, west, and
south, the Russians have some reason to be slightly paranoid. But
this "historic" Russia hardly exists for the American public. For us
Russia is not Russia but a "Communist" power and therefore an
"enemy." And in Russian eyes the United States, China, Iran, and
the nations of the NATO alliance are placed in a similar "enemy"
category.

If the idea of socialism had ever been domesticated—if it had
ever been made a live issue in American politics—then the majority
might have been less susceptible to "red scares" and less prone to
view the revolutions and social upheavals that came after World
War II as Soviet-inspired and therefore a threat to national security. But as Theodore Roszak has pointed out, "the left-wing of our
political spectrum has always been pathetically fore-shortened." As
a result, the rejection of socialism has become an article of faith,
part of the American ideology. In the absence of a widely aired
and freely debated socialist perspective, the mainstream of the
American political tradition, as the British journalist Michael Davie
once suggested, "flows between firm banks . . . and features a

steady belief in the sanctity of private property, the importance of economic individualism, and the unifying effect of greed. . . . Marx has had less influence in the United States than on any country in the western world. . . . The wretched victims of the American system . . . are convinced that only luck or geography, never the system, stands between them and all-American prosperity."[23] Yet ironically, the more effort and resources the United States has devoted to preventing the spread of socialist regimes, the more the American economy has assumed a curiously ambiguous form and the more confused both socialist and capitalist models have become. Since neither model has worked out quite as its partisans predicted, the degree of ideological confusion has steadily increased, which is an odd outcome after thirty years of Cold War.

Given the national confidence in "free enterprise," this country should in theory have nothing to fear from socialism or from competition with socialist regimes; yet the fear continues to haunt American politics and to influence American policy. The effect has been to build massive uncritical support for Cold War policies and to make it extremely difficult to cope with domestic problems that require national planning and controls. In the absence of a socialist perspective, capitalism has had a free ride; no one has thought much about it. It is not seen or recognized *as a system,* for there is no alternative theory or model. "The economy," "the market," and "business" are discussed as though they were mechanisms quite divorced from capitalism. "Business," writes Robert Heilbroner, "creates a special landscape and envelops us completely." Business is everywhere; it permeates every aspect of society. Yet "business" is only a facade for the workings of a capitalist economy in an age of conglomerates and multinational corporations. "Rather than seeking to discover the invisible structure of capital within the goings on of the business world, economists look for the invisible relationships of something called 'the economy.' The difference is that whereas capitalism is inextricably mixed up with the dirty stuff of history, the economy can be considered *sub specie aeternitatus.*"[24] Since its structure is more or less invisible and therefore seldom discussed, most Americans have consistently failed to see how capitalism has been inextricably mixed up with the dirty stuff of the Cold War.

After 1880 a socialist movement struggled to find a place for itself in American politics. But this movement really came to an end with the "red scare" of 1919–20. Later the radicalism of the 1930s—which was more "populist" and Keynesian than socialist or Communist—was largely destroyed by the postwar purge. "In the past," as Saul Alinsky once pointed out, "the radicals of each generation passed the torch of experience to the next generation. But the late Senator Joe McCarthy's political inquisition destroyed most of the radicals of that generation," or silenced them. This "breach in the radical continuum" occurred at a critical time not merely in terms of changes that were taking place in the economy and in the direction of American foreign policy, but because a new generation was coming along that had not experienced the rigors of Mc-Carthyism or the ideological feuding of the early Cold War years. If "the hereditary left" had not been largely vanquished, it might have been able to transmit a sense of political realities, based on past experience, to "the new left," but this did not happen; With the result, as Alinsky (a typical radical of the 1930s) observed (in *American Report,* Jan. 15, 1971), that "the present generation was aborted into a world without radical parents or guides. Is it any wonder that they cooped themselves into a chronological cage rejecting anything over 30 years of age, from persons to history?"

Although the radical impulse of the 1930s did reemerge in the 1950s, it found expression in a few publications, not in movements or political parties. Leo Huberman and Paul Sweezy founded *Monthly Review* in 1949, and Irving Howe began to publish *Dissent* in 1954. Huberman and Sweezy and their associates Paul Baran and Harry Magdoff were old friends; at my initiative *Monthly Review* shared offices with *The Nation* from November 1, 1959, to June, 23, 1966. The influence of *Monthly Review* and *Dissent* was far-ranging but did not result in a revived or modernized socialist party or movement. In the post-1945 period, in fact, the influence of the Socialist Party was minimal. One could, however, see the influence of *Monthly Review* in *Studies on the Left,* which came along in 1959, and in one or two similar publications, but, in general, "movement" radicals of the 1960s were ideological orphans who fashioned their own doctrines, struck out in a variety of directions, and exhibited only a limited confidence in political action. *New Left Review,* which began publication in Britain in 1960, was influential but never succeeded in voicing "movement" concerns and interests.

Just as the "old left" had been endlessly harassed, so the "new left" was also the target of break-ins, dirty tricks of all kinds, elaborate surveillance, incessant police activity, and the large-scale use of informers and provocateurs. Not surprisingly it was riven by internal divisions and dissension. These tensions came to the surface at the ill-fated "New Politics Conference" in Chicago in 1967.[25] Called to discuss the need for a new politics, the conference revealed a wild divergence of points of view. Black delegates were deferred to in a way that suggested a kind of racism in reverse. The importance of community organization was stressed, but little attention was focused on the need for political action. Instead of laying the groundwork for a grass-roots opposition to the Vietnam War that might have appealed to blue-collar workers and the middle class, theoretical issues were discussed on which there could be little agreement. For most of the 2,100 delegates too much had happened too soon and with too little guidance; they were simply not prepared to fuse the key issues in a way that might have made political sense. In fact, the conference provided a preview of what was to happen at the Democratic convention the following summer. And in the wake of that disaster, a later breed of radicals— the Weathermen and the SLA—were even further removed from political realities.

Even so, the political impact of the new left was extremely significant. The young radicals of the 1960s were a distinct minority of their generation; only some three percent of the college students considered themselves radicals. In 1966 Jack Newfield estimated the new left at probably not more than 250,000, mostly young people between the ages of fifteen and thirty. It was never more than a fraction of a generation in which 5.2 million students were enrolled in colleges and universities. But it was, in Newfield's phrase, "a prophetic minority," intellectually gifted, spirited, idealistic, and capable of exerting considerable influence on its contemporaries. It was their activities, widely covered by television, that released the new currents of feeling and energy that brought the Cold War "freeze" to an end. If they failed to see the importance of relating Vietnam and racism to basic questions of power, they did succeed in lifting both issues to a new level of national awareness.

Johnson's Commission on Violence reported that in the five years from 1963 to May, 1968, two million Americans participated in civil-rights and antiwar demonstrations; the civil-rights demonstrations alone mobilized 1.1 million. Some 75,000 arrests and two hundred casualties resulted, with blacks being the principal victims. Youth and students, the commission noted, had never figured significantly in opposition to any previous war; in this instance their opposition was of decisive importance. But because it was not based on a thoroughgoing critique of the society and its power structure, it failed to create a new "left" or socialist movement. When the war ended, there was still no socialist or radical opposition of any significance despite the immense energies and resources that had been devoted to the antiwar and civil-rights demonstrations.

During the climactic phases of the Watergate-Vietnam debacle—
1972 to the spring of 1975—I had been compelled to follow both
political dramas with a closeness and intensity that began to take its
toll. Each script kept unfolding, week after week, so swiftly that I
had to write most of the editorials myself, usually at the last moment, as well as get out the magazine. The experience made me
feel that I was writing a frenzied, never-ending political serial on
The Last Days of Richard Nixon with alternating notes on This
Week in Vietnam. The incessant editorial grind began to get to me,
but at the time there was no escape; I was a prisoner of events, of
headlines. However, I began to feel that just as the political drama
was obviously building toward a climax, so a thirty-year phase in
my "education" was coming to a close. When Nixon finally left the
White House and the fighting ceased in Vietnam, I was convinced
that for me another "world" had ended and that it was time to
move on.

Also I felt intuitively that the post–Watergate-Vietnam scene
would emerge rather slowly and would be quite different from the
"worlds" I had known and in which I had been an active participant. This new world would represent a turning point, a "crunch
point," as one UN official put it, in the history of industrial societies, socialist, Communist, and capitalist; less a new chapter than
a new book. I could never hope to live long enough to see it take
shape, and whatever editorial insights I had acquired would be
only marginally relevant. The scene had changed; the cast was
different. Nixon was not there to "kick around" anymore, Hoover
was dead, the FBI and the CIA were fending off critics, and the
treasury was depleted or nearly so; it would be a long and painful
process for the American people to adjust to realities obscured by
thirty years of Cold War folly and extravagance.

This was indeed a "crunch point" in history. "With a neatness
history seldom offers," wrote economic historian John E. Sawyer in
the New York *Times* of December 30, 1974, "the era now ending
can be said to have begun five centuries ago with the great geographical explorations that opened the way to the outpouring of
energies, ideas, and institutions of Western Europe." Seen in this
light, the American Dream was an episode in a long historical
process; now, at last, we would face a confrontation with our history, with ourselves. What Sheldon Wolin calls "the culture of increase," of endless growth and expansion, had been shaken by the
realization that the potentialities of science and modern technology
and communications may not be realizable within "the limits imposed by the realities, political and ecological, of this world." As he
writes: "The prospects of managing a cooled-down society, accus-

tomed to the intoxication of endless growth," is bound to have a sobering effect on the dominant elites with their "take-off" mentality; they cannot help but feel "suffocated and hemmed in," while the middle class feels surprised, disappointed, and apprehensive.[26]

I felt, therefore, that it was a logical time for me to leave *The Nation;* another phase of my "education" had ended. So at lunch on June 17, 1975, I told James Storrow I was resigning as of the end of that year. Politically and historically, the timing was "neat"; by the spring of 1975 it was clear that a thirty-year phase of the Cold War was coming to an end and a new chapter was being written. The closely interrelated issues of most concern to me—the Cold War, McCarthyism, civil rights—would now assume a different form; not that they had been resolved, but the pattern, the setting had changed. No one as closely associated for many years with the civil-rights phase of "the racial problem" as I had been could doubt that a corner had been turned. Much remained to be done—the inequalities were still glaring and obdurate—but the civil-rights chapter had been concluded. And while I was convinced that the last had not been heard or seen of McCarthyism and witch-hunts, I felt sure future recurrences would assume a different form. The cultural revolution of the 1960s had changed the setting in a way that would make it difficult to launch witch-hunts of the kind that followed World Wars I and II. In the context of Eurocommunism and the global spread of American capitalism it would be difficult to whip up "anti-Communist" hysteria; even *Time,* in an eight-page report of March 13, 1978, had conceded that socialism is currently the world's dominant political and economic ideology. And with a study of the Joint Economic Committee in late 1974 estimating the amount of federal subsidies to the private sector at $95.1 billion, it had become difficult to determine where the public sector ends and the private sector begins. The Cold War, of course, continues, but the "freeze" has moderated significantly since 1946 and new factors have come into play. For one thing, resources have been depleted to the point that Pax Americana is no longer feasible; our accounts are overdrawn. Interventions on the grand and reckless scale of the 1950s would be difficult to execute; the public wants no more Vietnams. And the emergence of the Third World nations has created new problems for the industrially developed world.

In terms of personal history, I had experienced five "worlds": the pre–World War I world with its aura of innocence; the world of the 1920s; the fervent years of the 1930s; the exciting years of World War II with their high hopes and expectations; and the thirty years of Cold War that began in 1945 and finally phased out in the spring of 1975. Despite crosscurrents and diversions, this thirty-year period was for me a "world" in the sense that the Cold War was the dominant theme; it tied these years together; it was the major obsession. One sensed this the moment Nixon left the White House and the fighting ceased in Vietnam. The Cold War had been the major force not merely in American politics and diplomacy but in the way it distorted the economy, bloated the state, played havoc with older values, generated endemic inflation, wasted resources without thought of present or future conse- quences, and ended with the disaster in Vietnam and the embar- rassment of Watergate. Only in 1975—on the eve of the Bicenten- nial—did I feel that a post–Cold War period, or at least the end of a long phase of the Cold War, had finally arrived.

My "education" had consisted essentially of immersion in these five "worlds," each of which had a beginning, a development, and a finale. Once they had passed into history—and only then—could I see that they had a certain unity or at least could be thought of as entities of a sort. The contours of each had been determined, to a large extent, by the "world" that had preceded it. Over the years I came to give much more weight to the historical factors than when I set out to explore the first of these "worlds." But I never lost a feeling for the importance of idealism in keeping alive the belief that injustices can be corrected and inequalities lessened. At the same time, however, I learned early on that idealists cannot create the kind of future of which they dream if only because they cannot agree on the form it should assume. Even if they could agree, they would find that in the shaping their new world had assumed as- pects which were not part of the original plan or vision. No future can be fully anticipated; the contingent, the unforeseeable, play hob with utopian blueprints. So I have learned to be wary of uto- pian projections based on rigid models. But I have also learned that some sense of ideology, or the logic of economic systems, is a prerequisite for restructuring power relationships, a task that im- plies an awareness that the existing economy functions as a system and that changes should be made with some alternative model in mind. The problem is to avoid becoming so imprisoned in a partic- ular ideology that changing realities are ignored. The past is con- stantly being reinterpreted and there are no infallible charts for the future; only the present is real, immediate, inescapable. No doubt this is why I have been accused of being present-oriented: I have always been much more concerned with what is happening here and now than with what happened yesterday or might happen tomorrow.

In the 1920s I was a rebel; in the 1930s I became, and I have remained, an unreconstructed, unapologetic radical. But Western radicalism is not like its Eastern counterpart in all respects. In the East, and notably in the New York City area, leftists of all persuasions are preoccupied with the theoretical correctness of their positions; with them the style factor is important. In the West, radicals concentrate on issues. In the East more attention is devoted to scrutinizing the political backgrounds of one's associates; in the West, agreement on issues and objectives is the prime consideration. In California, I got used to being called a variety of names: fellow traveler, socialist, Communist, softheaded liberal. I was a fellow traveler in the sense that I sponsored some committees that took positions I thought were important even though I did not always agree with the politics of the other sponsors. Some of these committees were no doubt Communist-inspired or contained names of Communist Party members on their letterheads; but at the time no other groups were raising these issues, and I have never thought it necessary or practical to screen associates when taking a political position on a specific issue of immediate importance. In a sense I have been a socialist for many years, but the fact is that I have never known a socialist party or movement with which I could identify; I have had differences with all of them. And I have never been a member of the Communist Party, although I have known individual Communists whom I respected and whose courage I admired. I would also agree with what Edmund Wilson said in a letter to John Dos Passos in 1935: that Communists, for all their shortcomings, should be given credit for having played a valuable role as agitators; they did raise some fundamental questions and worried people into trying to find answers. But had I been accused of being a radical (Western style), I would readily have pleaded guilty.

I am unable, however, to offer a pat definition of what it means to be an American radical. The radical tradition has been discontinuous, surfacing at some periods, seeming to disappear at others; it has been not so much a movement as an attitude, a tradition. In Michael Harrington's phrase, it is "part of the secret history of the United States." By which he means that there has never been a well-organized coherent identifiable radical movement that has persisted over any considerable period of time in the same place. The impulse has been intermittent but persistent and has been stronger in the West than elsewhere. It has found expression, at different times, in tracts, publications, manifestos, support for political underdogs—Sacco and Vanzetti, Mooney and Billings, strikers, immigrants, minorities—and in a variety of political initiatives. It has also found expression in court decisions, novels,

speeches, sermons, biographies, autobiographies, editorials, histories, and critical studies. At different times in their lives, individuals
have voiced radical sentiments only to disavow them at a later date;
Tom Watson, the Georgia demagogue, might be cited as a case in
point. And there have been a few—a very few—demagogues who
ended up being radicals. One could find, I am sure, individual
Socialists, Communists, Trotskyites, Republicans (a few), Democrats, and independents who could fairly be called radicals. But
radicals have always been a minority within the minority of the left.
Unlike liberals, they never feel part of the existing order and are
invariably critical of it.

Hannah Arendt once wrote that the radical is engaged in the
unbiased search for those facts in everyday affairs that contain the
roots for future development. She defined "radical" in the sense of
"going back and reviving much that belongs to the very roots of
the American radical tradition as well as much that belongs to the
radical tradition everywhere—the tradition of nay-saying and independence, of cheerful 'negativism' when confronted with the
temptation of *Realpolitik,* and of self-confidence: pride and trust in
one's own judgment. These qualities distinguish the radical who
always remains true to reality in his search for the root of the
matter, from the extremist, who single-mindedly follows the logic
of whatever 'cause' he may espouse at the moment."[27] The radical
is the perpetual outsider, the odd man (or woman) out, constantly
critical of the power structure and of things as they are.

But I am also a socialist in the sense that I share the socialist
critique of capitalism. But this critique does not tell us all that we
need to know about socialism, precisely what it would do and how
it would do it. And socialism in practice, while varied and feasible,
has shown limitations that have disappointed its most enthusiastic
advocates. It is easy to talk about "democratic socialism," but just
how would an American socialist regime safeguard civil liberties?
How could it prevent a slavish dependence on state power? How
would it go about changing the structure of economic power?
Could it avoid bureaucratic sloth? How would it stimulate social
incentives? Could it achieve efficient management? How would it
revive and sustain a sense of pride in work performed? Would it
make for a more genuine public—as distinguished from bureaucratic—control of productive capacity? Would it be able to breathe
new life into the constitutional concept of government of, by, and
for the people?

Despite these and other unanswered questions, the socialist perspective does make it possible to see that the growth of corporate
power constitutes a threat to democracy, since it focuses attention

on the "bottom-line" capitalist imperatives of profits and expansion. Much as apologists prate about "corporate responsibility" and the rise of a new managerial class sensitive to public needs, the concentration of economic power can no longer, if it ever could, be adequately controlled by regulatory measures and executive directives. For one thing, the political power of the people has become increasingly diffuse and atomized with the rise of media politics. True, the people continue to elect officials, but the power remains in the board rooms, and changes in national administrations produce at best only marginal modifications in the structure of power. Nowadays even academic economists—Charles E. Lindblom of Yale is one—are disturbed by the uneasy relationship between corporate enterprise and democracy; between corporate power and democratic principles.

Over the years I have come to believe that radicals should be primarily concerned with values. If they could achieve substantial agreement on the kinds of values society should encourage, it might then be possible to proceed experimentally, tentatively, to invent new forms and institutional arrangements which would best safeguard and extend these values. Values, in a word, should take precedence over programs. This way the risks of the remedy becoming part of the problem could be minimized. This is what Henry Adams had in mind when he said of Theodore Roosevelt's trust-busting activities that the problem was "not so much to control the trusts as to create the society that could manage the trusts." But since agreement on values is unlikely and the task of altering the structure of power so formidable, the role of the radical as goad, critic, and dissenter will be needed for a long time; in fact, I cannot conceive of a society in which this function could safely be dispensed with. In the 1840s, Dostoevski believed in radicalism, basic Christian values, and the autonomy of art. My loyalties, after a rough, informal "education" in five "worlds" of politics and experience, are to radicalism, socialism (a more rational economy with a more equal distribution of power and responsibility and a more sensible use of resources), democratic principles, the kind of "Christian" humanism F. O. Matthiessen emphasized, and the autonomy of art, ideas, and values.

What it comes down to is that I am the rebel-radical I have always been (for reasons I have never fully understood) and that I still take a generous view of the future and remain basically an optimist despite much evidence that I could be wrong. On balance, however, my brand of indigenous radicalism and idealism has stood the test of time as well as or better than some of the apocalyptic ideologies of the right and the left. As a journalist I have learned to take all ideological projections with a grain of salt. What my "education" has given me, in brief, is some understanding of the realities of the different "worlds" I have known and what it has meant to be part of the action. Exploring these "worlds" has been my life. The past I do not purport to understand, the future I cannot fathom. But I have managed to escape the blight of boredom by exploring these five "worlds" and noting how they affected me.

Education ended for Henry Adams in 1905, the year I was born. Only beyond some remoter horizon, as he saw it, could society's values be fixed and renewed. The new forces would educate, of that he was certain, for the mind would continue to react. And the next great influx of new forces seemed near at hand. Perhaps at some point in the future—and he selected the year 1938, the centenary of his birth as a target date—he might be allowed to return with his friends to "see the mistakes of their own lives made clear in the light of the mistakes of their successors; and perhaps then, for the first time since man began his education among the carnivores," they would find a world that "sensitive and timid natures could regard without a shudder." But by 1938 the world was on the verge of war, and he and his friends, had they been allowed to return, would have had good reason to shudder at the consequences.

The centenary of my birth would be the year 2005, and I have no notion whether "sensitive and timid natures" will then be able to regard the world without a shudder. But I agree with what Oscar Ameringer, an American radical, once said to a small gathering of Socialists at one of the movement's bleaker moments. "The rank and file," he said, "is like the grass in the fields. The rains and snows beat upon it; winds and flame devour it; but one day in the early spring there is a secret stirring in the earth and behold the grass has sprung up again—green and very beautiful under a golden sun. So with you, dear brothers. You will rise again even as the grass of the field, though all men's hands be set against you, though you feel yourselves isolated and abandoned, you, the rank and file, will surely rise to spread the green mantle of democracy over this ravished American soil."

NOTES

PREFACE

1. *Centennial Review,* Vol. XVIII, pp. 288–305.

CHAPTER I

1. Kansas City *Star,* Aug. 17, 1975.
2. "Commitment to the Modern," by Lionel Trilling, Teachers College *Record,* February, 1963.

CHAPTER II

1. *Where the Old West Stayed Young,* by John Rolfe Burroughs, p. 4. See also, by the same author, *Steamboat in the Rockies* and *Guardian of the Grasslands: The First Hundred Years of the Wyoming Stock Growers Association.*
2. *Ibid.,* p. 259.

CHAPTER III

1. In "A Generation in Politics: A Definition," by Marvin Rintala, *Review of Politics,* October, 1963.
2. F. Scott Fitzgerald, *The Crack-Up,* ed. Edmund Wilson, p. 70.
3. From introduction to *The Culture of The Twenties,* ed. Loren Baritz, p. xvi.
4. *The Economic Consequences of the Peace,* by John Maynard Keynes, pp. 297–98.
5. See *A Mask for Privilege: Anti-Semitism in America* (1948), pp. 56–68, where I discuss the fashionable racist theorists and myth-makers of the period.
6. See *The Aspirin Age: 1919–1941,* ed. Isabel Leighton, Simon & Schus-

ter, which carries a chapter, pp. 50–81, that I wrote about Aimee Semple McPherson.

7. *The American 1890s,* by Larzer Ziff.
8. See "Letters of George Sterling to Carey McWilliams," ed. John R. Dunbar, *California Historical Society Quarterly,* September, 1967, and also the sketch of Sterling's life I contributed to *The Dictionary of American Biography.*
9. See *The Legend of John Brown,* by Richard O. Boyer, p. 560.
10. *The Summit Beacon,* Akron, Ohio, Dec. 7, 1859.
11. *Michigan Academician,* Winter, 1969.
12. See *The Brand Book* (Denver Westerners' Monthly Brand Book, December, 1952. Since renamed *The Roundup*), December, 1952; also see *Ambrose Bierce and the Black Hills,* by Paul Fatout.
13. *Robinson Jeffers: A Portrait,* by Louis Adamic, and "Robinson Jeffers: An Antitoxin," a piece of mine, *Saturday Night,* Aug. 3, 1929.

CHAPTER IV

1. See *Letters on Literature and Politics,* ed. Elena Wilson, pp. 175–76, 194–95.
2. See *The New Republic,* July 18, Aug. 22, Nov. 7, 1934; also the Baltimore *Sun,* Oct. 7, 14, 21, 1934.
3. See *A Companion to The Grapes of Wrath,* by Warren French, where the controversy is discussed in detail.
4. *California and the Dust Bowl Migration,* by Walter J. Stein, p. 191.
5. *Labor and Liberty,* by Jerold S. Auerbach, p. 180.
6. See Stein, *supra;* Auerbach, *supra;* and *Olson's New Deal for California,* by Robert E. Burke.
7. Stein, *supra,* p. 136.
8. See *A History of the Los Angeles Labor Movement, 1911–1941,* by Louis B. Perry and Richard S. Perry, pp. 476–80.
9. "Mirror of the Dream," by T. H. Watkins and R. R. Olmsted, *California Living Magazine,* May 2, 1976, pp. 33–35.
10. See *Thinking Big: The Story of the Los Angeles Times . . . ,* by Robert Gottlieb and Irene Wolt, for a discussion of the case.
11. See *The Legacy of Al Capone,* by George Murray, pp. 229–95; *The Extortionists,* by Herbert Aller; and *The Green Felt Jungle,* by Ed Reid and Ovid Demaris, pp. 46–49. Also *Hollywood Labor Dispute: A Study in Immorality,* by Father George H. Dunne; and "You Don't Choose Your Friends," by Herbert Knott Sorrell, UCLA Oral History Project, 1963, and the Nitto tax hearings, Sept. 27 to Oct. 4, 1958, IRS Dockets #8840, 8841, and 8842.
12. See H. R. Philbrick, *Legislative Investigation Report,* Sacramento, Dec. 28, 1938.
13. See *The Devil's Decade: The Thirties,* by Claud Cockburn, an invaluable source on the antifascist politics of the 1930s.

CHAPTER V

1. *Racial Tensions in Chicago,* by Robert C. Weaver, reprinted from *Social Service Year Book,* Chicago, 1943.

2. *While You Were Gone,* ed. Jack Goodman, p. 94.
3. See Goodman, *supra,* Chapter IV, pp. 89–111, in which I reported on wartime changes in the racial pattern.
4. See my article "Race Discrimination and the Law," *Science and Society,* Vol. IX (1945), No. 1.
5. *Hawaii Under Army Rule,* by J. Garner Anthony.
6. From a report by Robert C. Toth, Los Angeles *Times,* Oct. 17, 1977.
7. See "The Not-Always-Accurate Memoirs of Earl Warren," by Richard Rodda, *California Journal,* November, 1977, pp. 378–79.
8. "The Default of Leadership," paper read by Dr. George I. Sanchez, Fourth Regional Conference, Southwest Council on the Education of Spanish-Speaking People, Albuquerque, NM, Jan. 23–25, 1950.
9. A chapter is devoted to the case in my book *North from Mexico;* it is also discussed in Anthony Quinn's *The Original Sin,* in a pamphlet by Guy Endore, in a number of monographs and dissertations, and in a forthcoming book by Mark Day. Luis Valdez' play *Zoot Suit,* based on the case, was produced at the Mark Taper Playhouse in Los Angeles in April and again in August, 1978.
10. My testimony appears in *Viva La Raza!,* ed. Julian Nava, pp. 151–56.
11. *Negro Labor: A National Problem,* by Robert C. Weaver, p. 78.
12. The riots are described in Chapter XIII of *North from Mexico,* in reports I wrote for *PM* and *The New Republic* and in a number of special studies, including one by Patricia Rae Adler which appears in *The Awakening Minority: The Mexican-Americans,* ed. Manuel P. Servin, pp. 142–58; books by Ruth Tuck and Beatrice Griffith also provide interesting background and insights.
13. *To Stem This Tide,* by Charles S. Johnson and his associates, provides a good contemporary report on these wartime activities.

CHAPTER VI

1. *Hiroshima and Nagasaki Reconsidered,* by Barton Bernstein; *V Was for Victory,* by John Morton Blum, p. 320; *Meeting at Potsdam,* by Charles F. Mee, Jr.; and P. M. S. Blackett in *The Nation,* March 23, 1963.

2. See "With Whom Is the Alliance Allied?," a paper I presented at a conference in Hollywood chaired by John Cromwell, later published in *The Film and the Actor,* published by the Hollywood Arts, Sciences and Professions Council, Progressive Citizens of America, (1947); also my reports in *PM* of Oct. 6 and 20, 1946.
3. *Crisis and Conflict: The Presidency of Harry S. Truman, 1945–1948,* by Robert J. Donovan, pp. 188, 197.
4. *The Rise and Fall of the People's Century,* by Norman D. Markowitz, p. 193.
5. Donovan, *supra,* p. 285.
6. See *The Press and the Cold War,* by James Aronson.
7. *America in Our Time,* by Godfrey Hodgson, p. 32.
8. *Men Against McCarthy,* by Richard M. Fried, p. 169.
9. See *The Origins of the Marshall Plan,* by John Gimbel.
10. See comments, Daniel Yergin, New York *Times,* Oct. 24, 1976.

11. Markowitz, *supra*, p. 297. See also *Henry Wallace, Harry Truman and the Cold War*, by Richard J. Walton.
12. Jan. 17, 1978, Op-Ed Page.
13. See *Commentary*, May, 1948, for a special analysis I prepared of social discrimination as practiced by exclusive clubs and similar institutions.

14. See my article "Once a Well-Kept Secret," *Pacific Historical Review*, August, 1973, for an account of the circumstances that prompted me to write *North from Mexico*. See also article by Arthur M. Corwin in the same issue.
15. See *Violence in Peekskill*, a report of the American Civil Liberties Union, December, 1949.
16. See *Un-American Activities in the State of Washington: The Work of the Canwell Committee*, by Vern Countryman.
17. See also *False Witness*, by Melvin Rader; *The Year of the Oath*, by George R. Stewart, Jr.; and *The California Oath Controversy*, by David P. Gardner.

CHAPTER VII

1. *Beyond the New Deal: Harry S. Truman and American Liberalism*, by Alonzo L. Hamby, Jr., p. 471.
2. *Ibid.*, p. 473.
3. *Shame and Glory of the Intellectuals*, by Peter Viereck, p. 178.
4. Hamby, *supra*, p. 479.
5. *Fighting Years: Memoirs of a Liberal Editor*, by Oswald Garrison Villard, p. 461.
6. For O'Brien's comments, see *New York Review*, May 12, 1977, p. 28.
7. *The New Yorker*, Nov. 8, 1958, pp. 171–72.
8. *New Statesman*, Feb. 24, 1967, p. 249. Quoted by Lasch, *The Agony of the American Left*, p. 111.
9. Viereck, *supra*, p. 150.
10. *Shattered Peace: The Origins of the Cold War and the National Security State*, by Daniel Yergin, p. 408.
11. *The Truman Doctrine and the Origins of McCarthyism*, by Richard M. Freeland, p. 360; also see a review by Gaddis Smith, *New York Times Book Review*, Sept. 12, 1976.
12. *Men Against McCarthy*, by Richard M. Fried, p. 33.
13. See a piece I wrote for *The Chicago Jewish Forum*, Winter, 1951–52, pp. 136–40.
14. See *Can We Afford Academic Freedom?*, a report of a radio debate broadcast from the Harvard Law School in which I participated along with Allen Zoll and McGeorge Bundy, Dec. 7, 1951.
15. See *Crisis on the Left: Cold War Politics and American Liberalism, 1947–1954*, by Mary Sperling McAuliffe, for an excellent account of the impact of McCarthyism on liberal intellectuals.
16. Quoted in *The Politics of Fear*, by Robert Griffith, p. 292.
17. See *A Fine Old Conflict*, by Jessica Mitford, p. 205; also *Anatomy of Anti-Communism*, report of the American Friends Service Committee, p. 37.

18. See "The Letter Nobody Wrote," by Byron Scott, *The Nation*, Jan. 5, 1957.

19. *The Nation*, Dec. 1, 1956.

20. New York *Times*, April 1, 1977.

21. *New York Teachers News*, April 30, 1950, and in general see *The Time of the Toad: A Study of the Inquisition in America*, by Dalton Trumbo.

22. See "The Congressional Testing of Linus Pauling," by Harry Kalven, Jr., *Bulletin of the Atomic Scientists*, Vol. XVI, December, 1960, pp. 383–90, and Vol. XVII, January, 1961, pp. 12–19.

23. See *The Times*, London, Nov. 3, 1958.

24. *America in Our Time*, by Godfrey Hodgson, p. 45.

25. *Ibid.*

26. See "The McCarthy Era," *The Nation*, Aug. 27, 1955, an editorial I wrote.

27. From a special issue of *Monthly Review*, October, 1950, dedicated to the memory of Matthiessen.

28. *Ibid.*

29. *Ibid.*

30. *New York Review*, May 12, 1977.

31. See *The Nation*, Sept. 22, 1951, for further details on this meeting.

32. Quoted in *A Journal of the Plague Years*, by Stefan Kanfer, p. 177.

33. Quoted by Lois Snow in *A Death with Dignity*, p. 130.

34. See a column by William F. Buckley, New York *Post*, March 5, 1977.

35. For full details see *No Lamb for Slaughter*, by Edward Lamb.

36. For full details on the Siegel and Solow involvements see a long editorial I wrote in *The Nation*, July 28, 1955.

37. See "Classics of Free Thought: Freda Kirchwey and *The Nation* Magazine on Religious Censorship," by Paul Blanshard, *The Humanist*, July/August, 1976.

38. For details on *The Reporter*, see *Concerned About the Planet*, by Martin K. Doudna.

CHAPTER VIII

1. See "The Airpower Lobby," by Al Toffler, and a piece I did, "Small Business and the Cold War," which appear in *A View of The Nation, 1955–59*, ed. Henry M. Christman.

2. *The Nation*, Oct. 23, 1954.

3. Sept. 8, 1956.

4. New York *Post*, Nov. 19, 1977.

5. *The Nation*, Feb. 14, 1966.

6. The Elliott piece and Kenneth Burke's article appear in Christman, *supra;* see also a piece I did for *Christian Century:* "Ethics in an Affluent Society," June 22, 1966.

7. *The Sin of Henry R. Luce*, by David Cort.

8. *The Nation*, Dec. 12, 1953, and Dec. 11, 1954.

9. The issue was later reprinted in *The 1950s: America's "Placid" Decade*, ed. Joseph Satin.

10. Quoted by Nicholas C. Chriss in an article on the boycott "twenty years later," Los Angeles *Times*, Dec. 1, 1975.

11. "Little Rock," by Robert McKay, *The Nation,* Sept. 28, 1957.
12. See *Black Man in the White House,* by E. Frederick Morrow, the first black presidential aide; a most perceptive volume.
13. *The Memoirs of Earl Warren,* p. 289.
14. *The Lost Priority,* by John Herbers, p. 18; also see my editorial "Watts: The Forgotten Slum," *The Nation,* Aug. 30, 1965.
15. For a reexamination of the civil-rights movement see "The Legacy of Martin Luther King," two articles in the New York *Times,* April 2, 3, 1978; also a series of articles captioned "A Decade After the Kerner Report," by John Herbers, Paul Delaney, and Michael Sterne, New York *Times,* Feb. 26, 27, 28, and March 1, 1978.
16. See *The Secret Boss of California: The Life and High Times of Art Samish,* by Arthur Samish and Bob Thomas, a book that should be used as a text in the art of managing legislatures.
17. *Rebels Against War,* by Lawrence S. Wittner, p. 198.
18. See "The Ordeal of SANE," by Barbara Deming, *The Nation,* March 11, 1961.
19. See *The Nation,* Nov. 4, 1961, p. 347; also *America in Hiding: The Shelter Mania,* by Arthur I. Waskow and Stanley Newman, 1962.
20. See an exchange of letters between Arthur M. Schlesinger, Jr., and William Moyers, *Wall Street Journal,* July 5, 20, and 27, 1977.
21. "The Press and the Bay of Pigs," by Victor Bernstein and Jesse Gordon, Columbia University *Forum,* Fall, 1967; see also Charles Collingwood's CBS commentary of April 23, 1961, devoted to *The Nation*'s handling of the Bay of Pigs incident.
22. See an article by Robert Fink, Center for National Security Studies, Los Angeles *Times,* Nov. 6, 1977; also three feature articles in the New York *Times,* Dec. 25, 26, 27, 1977, on the CIA's secret operations to shape public opinion.
23. *Architects of Illusion,* by Lloyd C. Gardner, p. 301.
24. In general see "The Cold War Revisionists," by W. A. Williams, *The Nation,* Nov. 13, 1967, reprinted in his book *History as a Way of Learning,* pp. 369–79, which also contains some of his other *Nation* pieces.
25. Gardner, *supra,* p. 320.
26. See the New York *Times,* June 17, 1961, for a report on this program.
27. See "The Ultras," by Fred J. Cook, in a special *Nation* issue of June 30, 1962, devoted to the radical right.
28. *The Nation,* March 29, 1960.
29. See *Harry Hopkins: A Biography,* by Henry Adams, p. 136.

CHAPTER IX

1. For Storrow's background see *Son of New England: James Jackson Storrow, 1864–1926,* by Henry Greenleaf Pearson (Boston: privately printed, 1932).
2. *The Movement,* by Irwin Unger, p. 85.
3. *America in Our Time,* by Godfrey Hodgson, p. 233.
4. P. 266.
5. See a piece I wrote about Phillips in *The Nation,* Dec. 24, 1949.
6. See *The Nation,* Nov. 27, 1967.

7. *Robert Kennedy: A Memoir,* by Jack Newfield, p. 196.
8. See John M. Lee, New York *Times,* March 12, 1978.
9. Letter to the author, dated Aug. 9, 1976.
10. Hodgson, *supra,* p. 359.
11. Quoted in *"I Gave Them a Sword,"* by David Frost, p. 70; see also "The Cardboard Hero," by Gene Marine, *The Nation,* Aug. 18, 1956.
12. New York *Times,* April 10, 1975.
13. See *The Politics of Riot Commissions,* by Anthony Platt.
14. See "The Rhetoric of Violence," by Eugene Goodheart, *The Nation,* April 6, 1970.
15. See *Decent Interval,* by Frank Snepp, pp. 48 and 51.
16. *Before the Fall,* by William Safire, p. 691.
17. *Ibid.,* p. 664.
18. New York *Times,* May 20, 1973.
19. See "Warming Up for Watergate," by Joseph C. Goulden, *The Nation,* May 28, 1973; also *Congressional Record,* May 7, 1973, pp. S-8373–77.
20. See *The Radical Right,* ed. Daniel Bell, p. 53.
21. See a piece I wrote, "Thoughts on the Bicentennial," *The Nation,* April 12, 1975.
22. *Political Hysteria in America,* by Murray B. Levin, pp. 66 and 109.
23. *The Nation,* Jan. 15, 1968, p. 75.
24. See *New York Review,* Feb. 9, 1978.
25. See Paul Blumenthal's report, *The Nation,* Sept. 25, 1967.
26. *New York Review,* May 18, 1978. See also "Waking from the American Dream," by George P. Elliott, *The Nation,* Nov. 16, 1974.
27. See *The American Radical Press, 1880–1960,* ed. Joseph R. Conlin, Vol. II, p. 615.

SELECTED BIBLIOGRAPHY

Books

Adamic, Louis, *Robinson Jeffers: A Portrait.* University of Washington Press, 1929.

Adams, Henry H., *Harry Hopkins: A Biography.* G. P. Putnam's Sons, 1977.

Allen, Charles R., Jr., *Concentration Camps USA.* Marzani & Munsell, Inc., 1966.

Alperovitz, Gar, *Cold War Essays;* introduction by Christopher Lasch. Doubleday & Co., 1970.

Andrews, Bert, and Peter Andrews, *A Tragedy of History.* Robert B. Luce, 1962.

Anthony, J. Garner, *Hawaii Under Army Rule.* University Press of Hawaii, 1955.

Aronson, James, *The Press and the Cold War.* Bobbs-Merrill Co., 1970.

Auerbach, Jerold S., *Labor and Liberty: The La Follette Committee and the New Deal.* Bobbs-Merrill Co., 1966.

Aya, Robert, and Norman Miller (eds.), *The New American Revolution;* epilogue by Christopher Lasch. The Free Press, 1971.

Baritz, Loren (ed.), *The American Left: Radical Political Thought in the Twentieth Century.* Basic Books, 1971.

———, *The Culture of the Twenties.* Bobbs-Merrill Co., 1970.

Barnard, Harry, *Eagle Forgotten: The Life of John Peter Altgeld.* Bobbs-Merrill Co., 1938.

Barnet, Richard J., *The Economy of Death.* Atheneum, 1969.

———, *Intervention and Revolution: The United States in the Third World.* World Publishing Co., 1968.

———, and Marcus G. Raskin, *An American Manifesto.* New American Library, 1970.

Barrett, Edward L., Jr., *The Tenney Committee: Legislative Investigation of Subversive Activities in California.* Cornell University Press, 1951.

Bazelon, David T., *Power in America: The Politics of the New Class.* New American Library, 1967.

Belfrage, Cedric, *The American Inquisition, 1945–1960.* Bobbs-Merrill Co., 1973.

Bell, Daniel (ed.), *The Radical Right.* Doubleday & Co., 1963.

Bendiner, Robert, *Just Around the Corner: A Highly Selective History of the Thirties.* Harper & Row, 1967.

Benson, Frederick R., *Writers in Arms: The Literary Impact of the Spanish Civil War.* New York University Press, 1967.

Bentley, Eric, *Are You Now or Have You Ever Been? The Investigation of Show Business by the Un-American Activities Committee, 1947–1958.* Harper & Row, 1972.

———, *Thirty Years of Treason: Excerpts from Hearings Before the House Committee on Un-American Activities.* Viking Press, 1971.

Bernstein, Barton, *Hiroshima and Nagasaki Reconsidered: The Atomic Bombings of Japan and the Origins of the Cold War, 1941–1945.*

Bessie, Alvah, *Inquisition in Eden.* Macmillan Co., 1965.

Bierce, Lucius Verus, *Travels in the Southland (1822–1823)*; introduction by George W. Knepper. Ohio State University Press, 1966.

Blanshard, Paul, *The Right to Read: The Battle Against Censorship.* Beacon Press, 1955.

Blum, John Morton, *V Was for Victory: Politics and American Culture During World War II.* Harcourt Brace Jovanovich, 1976.

Bondurant, Joan V., *Conquest of Violence: The Gandhian Philosophy of Conflict.* University of California Press, 1965.

Bosworth, Allan R., *America's Concentration Camps.* W. W. Norton & Co., 1967.

Boyer, Richard O., *The Legend of John Brown: A Biography and a History.* Alfred A. Knopf, 1973. See p. 560.

Bronowski, J., *The Ascent of Man.* Little, Brown and Co., 1973.

———, *The Common Sense of Science.* Harvard University Press, 1953.

———, *The Face of Violence*, revised edition. World Publishing Co., 1967.

———, *Science and Human Values*, revised and enlarged edition with *The Abacus and the Rose.* Harper & Row, 1965.

Brookhouser, Frank, *These Were Our Years: A Panoramic and Nostalgic Look at American Life Between the Two World Wars.* Doubleday & Co., 1959.

Brown, Ralph S., Jr., *Loyalty and Security: Employment Tests in the United States.* Yale University Press, 1958.

Burke, Robert E., *Olson's New Deal for California.* University of California Press, 1953.

Burns, James MacGregor, *John Kennedy: A Political Profile.* Harcourt Brace and Co., 1959, 1960.

Burroughs, John Rolfe, *Guardians of the Grasslands: The First Hundred Years of the Wyoming Stock Growers Association,* 1971.

———, *Steamboat in the Rockies,* 1974.

———, *Where the Old West Stayed Young.* William Morrow, 1962.

Carr, Robert K., *The House Committee on Un-American Activities, 1945–1950.* Cornell University Press, 1952.

Carter, Dan T., *Scottsboro: A Tragedy of the American South.* Louisiana State University Press, 1969.

Cattell, David T., *Soviet Diplomacy and the Spanish Civil War.* University of California Press, 1957.

Caughey, John M., *Their Majesties the Mob.* University of Chicago Press, 1960.

Caute, David, *The Great Fear: The Anti-Communist Purges Under Truman and Eisenhower.* Simon and Schuster, 1978.

Chambers, Clarke A., *California Farm Organization.* University of California Press, 1952.

Chatfield, Charles (ed.), *Peace Movements in America.* Schocken Books, 1973.

Chevalier, Haakon, *Oppenheimer: The Story of a Friendship.* George Braziller, 1965.

Christian, Henry A., *Louis Adamic: A Checklist.* Kent State University Press, 1971.

Christman, Henry M., *A View of the Nation, 1955–59.* Grove, 1960.

—— (ed.), *Peace and Arms: Reports from the Nation.* Sheed and Ward, 1964.

Christoffel, Tom, *et al., Up Against the American Myth.* Holt, Rinehart & Winston, 1970.

Clecak, Peter, *Radical Paradoxes: Dilemmas of the American Left, 1945–1970.* Harper & Row, 1973.

Clubb, O. Edmund, *The Witness and I.* Columbia University Press, 1975.

Cockburn, Claud, *The Devil's Decade: The Thirties.* Mason & Lipscomb, 1973.

Collier, John, *From Every Zenith: A Memoir.* Sage Books, 1963.

Colodny, Robert G., *Spain: The Glory and the Tragedy.* Humanities Press, 1970.

Commager, Henry Steele, *Freedom Loyalty Dissent.* Oxford University Press, 1954.

Congdon, Don (ed.), *The '30s: A Time to Remember.* Simon and Schuster, 1962.

Conlin, Joseph R. (ed.), *The American Radical Press, 1880–1960.* Greenwood Press, 1974.

Cook, Bruce, *Dalton Trumbo: A Biography of the Oscar-Winning Screenwriter Who Broke the Hollywood Blacklist.* Charles Scribner's Sons, 1977.

Cook, Fred J., *The Nightmare Decade: The Life and Times of Senator Joe McCarthy.* Random House, 1971.

Cort, David, *The Sin of Henry R. Luce.* Lyle Stuart, Inc., 1974.

Countryman, Vern, *Un-American Activities in the State of Washington: The Work of the Canwell Committee.* Cornell University Press, 1951.

Crankshaw, Edward, *The New Cold War: Moscow v. Peking.* Penguin Books, 1963.

Crown, James Tracy, *Kennedy in Power.* Ballantine Books, 1961.

Cushman, Robert E., *Civil Liberties in the United States: A Guide to Current Problems and Experience.* Cornell University Press, 1956.

Davie, Michael, *California: The Vanishing Dream.* Dodd, Mead & Co., 1973.

De Figueiredo, Antonio, *Portugal and Its Empire.* Victor Gollancz, 1961.

Delmatier, Royce D., *et al., The Rumble of California Politics, 1848–1970.* John Wiley & Sons, 1970.

Del Vayo, J. Alvarez, *Freedom's Battle.* Hill & Wang, 1968.

——, *The Last Optimist.* Viking Press, 1950.

Diggins, John P., *Up from Communism: Conservative Odysseys in American Intellectual History.* Harper & Row, 1975.

Donner, Frank J., *The Un-Americans.* Ballantine Books, 1961.

Donovan, Robert J., *Conflict and Crisis: The Presidency of Harry S. Truman, 1945–1948.* W. W. Norton & Co., 1977.

Doudna, Martin K., *Concerned About the Planet: The Reporter Magazine and American Liberalism, 1949–1968.* Greenwood Press, Inc., 1977.

Douglas, William O., *Go East, Young Man: The Early Years. The Autobiography of William O. Douglas.* Random House, 1974.

——, *A Living Bill of Rights.* Doubleday & Co., 1961.

——, *The Right of the People.* Doubleday & Co., 1958.

Downie, Leonard, Jr., *The New Muckrakers.* New Republic Books, 1976.

Du Bois, W. E. B., *Black Reconstruction in America, 1860–1880.* World Publishing Co., 1964.

Dudman, Richard, *Men of the Far Right.* Pyramid Books, 1962.

Dunham, Barrows, *Giant in Chains.* Little, Brown and Co., 1953.

——, *Heroes & Heretics.* Alfred A. Knopf, 1964.

Dunne, John Gregory, *Delano: The Story of the California Grape Strike*. Farrar, Straus & Giroux, 1967.

Ehnmark, Anders, "Rebels in American Literature," *Western Humanities Review*, Autumn, 1958.

Eisinger, Chester E. (ed.), *The 1940's: Profile of a Nation in Crisis*. Doubleday & Co., 1969.

Emerson, Thomas I., *The System of Freedom of Expression*. Random House, 1970.

Fatout, Paul, *Ambrose Bierce and the Black Hills*. University of Oklahoma Press, 1956.

Fecher, Charles A., *H. L. Mencken: A Study of His Thought*. Alfred A. Knopf, 1978.

Fiedler, Leslie A., *An End to Innocence: Essays on Culture and Politics*. Beacon Press, 1955.

Finn, James, *Protest, Pacifism and Politics: Some Passionate Views of War and Non-Violence*. Random House, 1967.

Finney, Guy W., *The 2 Faces of Richard Nixon*. Los Angeles, no date.

Fitzgerald, F. Scott, *The Crack-up*, ed. Edmund Wilson. New Directions, 1956.

Fleming, D. F., *The Cold War and Its Origins, 1950–1960*, 2 vols. Doubleday & Co., 1961.

Forcey, Charles, *The Crossroads of Liberalism, 1900–1925*. Oxford University Press, 1961.

Fraenkel, Osmond K., *The Rights We Have*. Thomas Y. Crowell Co., 1971.

Freeland, Richard M., *The Truman Doctrine and the Origins of McCarthyism*. Alfred A. Knopf, 1972.

French, Warren, *A Companion to The Grapes of Wrath*. Kelley Press, 1963.

Fried, Albert (ed.), *Socialism in America*. Doubleday & Co., 1970.

Fried, Richard M., *Men Against McCarthy*. Columbia University Press, 1976.

Friedrich, Carl J., *The Pathology of Politics*. Harper & Row, 1972.

Fritchman, Stephen H., *Heretic: A Partisan Autobiography*. Beacon Press, 1977.

Frost, David, *"I Gave Them a Sword": Behind the Scenes of the Nixon Interviews*. William Morrow and Co., 1978.

Frost, Richard H., *The Mooney Case*. Stanford University Press, 1968.

Galvao, Henrique, *Santa Maria: My Crusade for Portugal*. World Publishing Co., 1961.

Gardner, David P., *The California Oath Controversy*. University of California Press, 1967.

Gardner, Lloyd C., *Architects of Illusion: Men and Ideas in American Foreign Policy, 1941–1949*. Quadrangle Books, 1970.

Gellerman, William, *Martin Dies*. Da Capo Press, 1972.

Gellhorn, Walter, *American Rights: The Constitution in Action*. Macmillan Co., 1960.

——— (ed.), *The States and Subversion*. Cornell University Press, 1952.

Gertz, Elmer, *Censored: Books and Their Right to Live*. University of Kansas Libraries, 1965.

Gilbert, James Burkhart, *Writers and Partisans: A History of Literary Radicalism in America*. John Wiley and Sons, 1968.

Gillers, Stephen, and Pat Watters (eds.), *Investigating the FBI*. Doubleday & Co., 1973.

Gillmor, Dan, *Fear, the Accuser*. Abelard-Schuman, 1954.

Gimbel, John, *The Origins of the Marshall Plan*. Stanford University Press, 1976.

Ginzburg, Benjamin, *Rededication to Freedom*. Simon and Schuster, 1956.

Glazer, Nathan, *The Social Basis of American Communism.* Harcourt, Brace & World, 1961.

Goldman, Eric F., *The Crucial Decade: America 1945–1955.* Alfred A. Knopf, 1956.

Gomez, David F., *Somos Chicanos: Strangers in Our Own Land.* Beacon Press, 1973.

Goodman, Jack (ed.), *While You Were Gone: A Report on Wartime Life in the United States.* Simon & Schuster, 1946.

Goodman, Paul, *Drawing the Line.* Random House, 1962.

——— (ed.), *Seeds of Liberation.* George Braziller, 1964.

Goodman, Walter, *The Committee: The Extraordinary Career of the House Un-American Activities Committee;* introduction by Richard Rovere. Farrar, Straus & Giroux, 1968.

Gorz, André, *Socialism and Revolution.* Doubleday & Co., 1973.

Gottlieb, Robert, and Irene Wolt, *Thinking Big: The Story of the Los Angeles Times, Its Publishers and Their Influence on Southern California.* G. P. Putnam's Sons, 1977.

Graebner, Norman A., *Cold War Diplomacy 1945–1960.* D. Van Nostrand Co., 1962.

Griffith, Robert, *The Politics of Fear: Joseph R. McCarthy and the Senate.* University Press of Kentucky, 1970.

Grodzins, Martin, *The Loyal and the Disloyal.* University of Chicago Press, 1956.

Gruening, Ernest, *Many Battles: The Autobiography of Ernest Gruening.* Liveright, 1973.

———, and Herbert Walter Beaser, *Vietnam Folly.* National Press, Inc., 1968.

Guttman, Allen, *The Wound in the Heart: America and the Spanish Civil War.* Free Press of Glencoe, 1962.

Hamby, Alonzo L., *Beyond the New Deal: Harry S. Truman and American Liberalism.* Columbia University Press, 1973.

Harris, Leon, *Upton Sinclair: American Rebel.* Thomas Y. Crowell Co., 1975.

Harrison, John M., and Harry H. Stein (eds.), *Muckraking: Past, Present and Future.* Pennsylvania State University Press, 1970. See pp. 118–135.

Hellman, Lillian, *Scoundrel Time;* introduction by Garry Wills. Little, Brown and Co., 1976.

Henderson, Charles P., Jr., *The Nixon Theology.* Harper & Row, 1970. Portions appeared in *The Nation.*

Herbers, John, *The Lost Priority: What Happened to the Civil Rights Movement in America?* Funk and Wagnalls, 1970.

Hodgson, Godfrey, *America in Our Time.* Doubleday & Co., 1976.

Horn, Robert A., *Groups and the Constitution.* Stanford University Press, 1956.

Horowitz, David, *The Free World Colossus: A Critique of American Foreign Policy in the Cold War.* Hill and Wang, 1965.

Hosokawa, Bill, *Nisei: The Quiet Americans.* William Morrow & Co., 1969.

Hoyt, Edwin P., *The Tempering Years* (a portrait of the decade 1929–1939). Charles Scribner's Sons, 1963.

Humes, D. Joy, *Oswald Garrison Villard: Liberal of the 1920s.* Syracuse University Press, 1960.

Hundley, Norris, Jr. (ed.), *The Chicano.* Clio Books, 1975. See pp. 1–41 and 47–57.

Hunt, Howard, *"Give Us This Day."* Arlington House, 1973.

Jackson, Gabriel, *The Spanish Republic and the Civil War 1931–1939.* Princeton University Press, 1965.

Jaffe, Philip J., "The Rise and Fall of Earl Browder," *The Survey: A Journal of East and West Studies,* Spring, 1972.

Johnson, Charles S., *To Stem This Tide: A Survey of Racial Tension Areas in the United States.* Pilgrim Press, 1943.

Johnson, Walter, *1600 Pennsylvania Avenue: Presidents and the People, 1929–1959.* Little, Brown and Co., 1960.

Julian, Joseph, *This Was Radio: A Personal Memoir;* introduction by Harold Clurman. Viking Press, 1975.

Kanfer, Stefan, *A Journal of the Plague Years.* Atheneum, 1973.

Katcher, Leo, *Earl Warren: A Political Biography.* McGraw-Hill Book Co., 1967.

Kelley, Stanley, Jr., *Professional Public Relations and Political Power.* Johns Hopkins Press, 1956. See chapter on Whitaker and Baxter, p. 50 *et seq.*

Kemler, Edgar, *The Irreverent Mr. Mencken.* Little, Brown & Co., 1948.

Keynes, John Maynard, *The Economic Consequences of the Peace.* St. Martin Press, 1920.

Klare, Michael, *War Without End.* Alfred A. Knopf, 1972.

Kluger, Richard, *Simple Justice.* Alfred A. Knopf, 1976.

Koen, Ross Y., *The China Lobby in American Politics.* Octagon Books, 1974.

Kraft, Hy, *On My Way to the Theater.* Macmillan Co., 1971.

Lamar, Howard Roberts, *The Far Southwest: 1846–1912.* W. W. Norton and Co., 1970. See references to David H. Moffat, Jr.

Lamb, Edward, *No Lamb for Slaughter: An Autobiography.* Harcourt Brace Jovanovich, 1963.

Lamont, Corliss (ed.), *The Trial of Elizabeth Gurley Flynn by the American Civil Liberties Union.* Horizon Press, 1968.

Lardner, Ring, Jr., *The Ecstasy of Owen Muir.* Cameron & Kahn, 1954.

Larrowe, Charles P., *Harry Bridges: The Rise and Fall of Radical Labor in the United States.* Lawrence Hill and Co., 1972.

Lasch, Christopher, *The Agony of the American Left.* Alfred A. Knopf, 1969.

———, *The New Radicalism in America, 1889–1963.* Alfred A. Knopf, 1965.

Lawson, R. Alan, *The Failure of Independent Liberalism, 1930–1941.* G. P. Putnam's Sons, 1971.

Leighton, Isabel (ed.), *The Aspirin Age: 1919–1941.* Simon and Schuster, 1946.

Lens, Sidney, *The Futile Crusade: Anti-Communism as an American Credo.* Quadrangle Books, 1964.

Lerche, Charles O., Jr., *The Cold War and After.* Prentice-Hall, 1965.

Levin, Murray B., *Political Hysteria in America: The Democratic Capacity for Repression.* Basic Books, 1971.

Levison, Andrew, *The Working Class Majority.* Coward, McCann and Geoghegan, 1974.

Lindbeck, Assar, *The Political Economy of the New Left: An Outsider's View;* foreword by Paul H. Samuelson. Harper & Row, 1971.

Lippman, Theo, Jr. (ed.), *A Gang of Pecksniffs, and Other Comments on Newspaper Publishers, Editors and Reporters by H. L. Mencken.* Arlington House, 1975.

Loftis, Anne, and Audrie Girdner, *The Great Betrayal: The Evacuation of the Japanese-Americans During World War II.* Macmillan Co., 1969.

Long, Priscilla (ed.), *The New Left.* Porter Sargent, 1964.

Lowenthal, Max, *The Federal Bureau of Investigation.* William Sloane Associates, 1950.

————, *Police Methods in Crime Detection and Counter Espionage.* University of Chicago, March 1951.

Lowi, Theodore, *The End of Liberalism: Ideology, Policy, and the Crisis of Public Authority.* W. W. Norton and Co., 1969.

Lukacs, John, *A History of the Cold War.* Doubleday & Co., 1961.

MacDougall, Curtis D., *Gideon's Army,* 3 vols. A history of the Wallace campaign. Marzani & Munsell, 1965.

Madden, Charles F., *Talks with Social Scientists.* Southern Illinois University Press, 1968. See pp. 133–37.

Manchester, William, *Disturber of the Peace: The Life of H. L. Mencken.* Harper and Brothers, 1950.

Mandelbaum, Seymour J., *The Social Setting of Intolerance: The Know-Nothings, the Red Scare, McCarthyism.* Scott, Foresman and Co., 1964.

Mankiewicz, Frank, *Perfectly Clear: Nixon from Whittier to Watergate.* Quadrangle Books, 1973.

Markowitz, Norman D., *The Rise and Fall of the People's Century: Henry Wallace and American Liberalism, 1941–1948.* Free Press, 1973.

Matthews, Herbert L., *The Cuban Story.* George Braziller, 1961.

Matusow, Harvey, *False Witness.* Cameron & Kahn, 1955.

McAuliffe, Mary Sperling, *Crisis on the Left: Cold War Politics and American Liberalism, 1947–1954.* University of Massachusetts Press, 1978. An excellent survey of the period.

McCarthy, Eugene J., *The Year of the People.* Doubleday & Co., 1969.

McClure, Robert C., *et al., Social Science and Freedom: A Report to the People.* Social Science Research Center, University of Minnesota, 1955.

McConnell, Grant, *The Decline of Agrarian Democracy.* University of California Press, 1953.

McKean, Robert, *et al., The Freedom to Read: Perspective and Program.* R. R. Bowker Co., 1957.

Medvedev, Roy A., *On Socialist Democracy.* Alfred A. Knopf, 1975.

Mee, Charles F., Jr., *Meeting at Potsdam.* Dell Publishing Co., 1975.

Meiklejohn, Alexander, *Political Freedom: The Constitutional Powers of the People.* Harper and Brothers, 1948.

Meister, Dick, and Anne Loftis, *A Long Time Coming: The Struggle to Unionize America's Farm Workers.* Macmillan Co., 1977.

Melman, Seymour, *The Peace Race.* Ballantine Books, 1961.

———— (ed.), *The War Economy of the United States.* St. Martin's Press, 1971.

Meltzer, Milton, *The Right to Remain Silent.* Harcourt Brace Jovanovich, 1972.

Miller, Herman, *Rich Man, Poor Man: The Distribution of Income in America.* Thomas Y. Crowell Co., 1964.

Miller, Loren, *The Petitioners: The Story of the Supreme Court of the United States and the Negro.* Pantheon Books, 1966.

Miller, Merle, *Plain Speaking: An Oral Biography of Harry S. Truman.* Berkeley Publishing Co., 1973.

Mitchell, David, *1919 Red Mirage.* Macmillan Co., 1970.

Mitford, Jessica, *A Fine Old Conflict.* Alfred A. Knopf, 1977.

Moore, Truman E., *The Slaves We Rent.* Random House, 1963.

Morgan, Charles, *Liberties of the Mind.* Macmillan Co., 1951.

Morray, Joseph P., *Pride of State: A Study in Patriotism and American Morality.* Beacon Press, 1959.

Morrow, E. Frederick, *Black Man in the White House.*

Murray, George, *The Legacy of Al Capone.* G. P. Putnam's Sons, 1975. See references to Bioff-and-Browne in Hollywood.

Murray, Robert K., *Red Scare: A Study in National Hysteria, 1919–1920.* University of Minnesota Press, 1955.

Muse, Benjamin, *The American Negro Revolution from Non-Violence to Black Power, 1963–1967.* Indiana University Press, 1968.

Nava, Julian (ed.), *Viva La Raza!* D. Van Nostrand Co., 1973. See pp. 151–55 for testimony of the author before the Los Angeles County grand jury in 1942, one year before the Zoot Suit Riots.

Nelson, Keith L., *The Impact of War on America.* Holt, Rinehart & Winston, 1971.

Nelson, Lowry, *American Farm Life.* Harvard University Press, 1954.

Newfield, Jack, *Bread and Roses Too: Reporting About America.* E. P. Dutton & Co., 1971.

———, *A Prophetic Minority.* New American Library, 1966.

———, *Robert Kennedy: A Memoir.* E. P. Dutton & Co., 1969.

Newman, William J., *Liberalism and the Retreat from Politics.* George Braziller, 1964.

Nieburg, H. L., *In the Name of Science* (on the military-industrial complex). Quadrangle Books, 1969.

Nobile, Philip, *Intellectual Skywriting: Literary Politics and the New York Review of Books.* Charterhouse, 1978.

O'Brian, John Lord, *National Security and Individual Freedom.* Harvard University Press, 1955.

Ogden, August Raymond, *The Dies Committee: A Study of the Special Committee for the Investigation of Un-American Activities, 1938–1944.* Catholic University of America Press, 1945.

Osborne, John, *The Nixon Watch.* Liveright, 1970.

———, *The Last Nixon Watch.* New Republic Book Co., 1975.

Ostrander, Gilman, *The Rights of Man in America.* University of Missouri Press, 1961.

Oxnam, G. Bromley, *I Protest.* Harper and Brothers, 1954.

Packer, Herbert L., *Ex-Communist Witnesses. Four Studies in Fact Finding.* Stanford University Press, 1962.

Perry, Louis B. and Richard S., *A History of the Los Angeles Labor Movement, 1911–1941.* University of California Press, 1963.

Peterson, Richard E., and John A. Bilorusky, *May, 1970: The Campus Aftermath of Cambodia and Kent State.* Carnegie Foundation for the Advancement of Learning, 1971.

Platt, Anthony, *The Politics of Riot Commissions.* Collier Books, 1971.

Powledge, Fred, *The Engineering of Restraint: The Nixon Administration and the Press.* Public Affairs Press, 1971.

Putnam, Jackson K., *Old-Age Politics in California: From Richardson to Reagan.* Stanford University Press, 1970.

Quinn, Anthony, *The Original Sin.* Little, Brown & Co., 1972.

Rader, Melvin, *False Witness.* University of Washington Press, 1969.

Raskin, Marcus, *Notes on the Old System: To Transform American Politics.* David McKay Co., 1974.

Reid, Ed, with Ovid Demaris, *The Green Felt Jungle.* Trident Press, 1963. For references on Bioff-Browne.

Reitman, Alan, *The Price of Liberty.* W. W. Norton and Co., 1968.

————, *The Pulse of Freedom.* W. W. Norton and Co., 1975.

Reuben, William A., *The Honorable Mr. Nixon.* Action Books, 1956.

Richmond, Al, *A Long View from the Left: Memoirs of an American Revolutionary.* Houghton Mifflin Co., 1972.

Robinson, Joan, *Freedom and Necessity: An Introduction to the Study of Society.* Pantheon Books, 1970.

Rogin, Michael P., with John L. Shover, *Political Change in California: Critical Elections and Social Movements, 1890–1969.* Greenwood Publishing Corp., 1970.

Rosenstone, Robert A., *Romantic Revolutionary: A Biography of John Reed.* Alfred A. Knopf, 1975.

Ross, Sherwood, *Gruening of Alaska.* Best Books, Inc., 1968.

Rovere, Richard, *Senator Joe McCarthy.* Harcourt, Brace and Co., 1959.

Rubenstein, Richard E., *Left Turn: Origins of the Next American Revolution.* Little, Brown and Co., 1973.

Safire, William, *Before the Fall: An Inside View of the Pre-Watergate White House.* Doubleday & Co., 1975.

Salzman, Jack, *The Survival Years: An Anthology of the Writings of the 1940's.* Pegasus, 1969.

Samish, Arthur, and Bob Thomas, *The Secret Boss of California: The Life and High Times of Art Samish.* Crown Publishers, 1971.

Sampson, R. V., *The Psychology of Power.* Pantheon, 1966.

Sarton, May, *Faithful Are the Wounds.* Rinehart & Co., 1955.

Satin, Joseph (ed.), *The 1950's: America's "Placid" Decade,* an anthology. Houghton Mifflin Co., 1960.

Schapsmeier, Edward L. and Frederick H., *Prophet in Politics: Henry A. Wallace and the War Years 1940–1965.* Iowa State University Press, 1970.

Schneir, Walter and Miriam, *Invitation to an Inquest: A New Look at the Rosenberg-Sobell Case.* Doubleday & Co., 1965.

Servin, Manuel P. (ed.), *The Mexican-Americans: An Awakening Minority.* Glencoe Press, 1970. See "The Sleepy Lagoon Case and the Grand Jury Investigation," p. 115, and "The Zoot-Suit Riots," p. 116 and again p. 124.

Sharp, Malcolm P., *Was Justice Done? The Rosenberg-Sobell Case.* Monthly Review Press, 1956.

Shirer, William L., *20th Century Journey: A Memoir of the Life and the Time.* Simon and Schuster, 1976.

Simon, Rita James (ed.), *As We Saw the Thirties,* an anthology. University of Illinois Press, 1967.

Simonson, Harold P., *Francis Grierson.* Twayne Publishers, 1966.

Singer, David, *Prelude to Revolution: France in May, 1968.* Hill and Wang, 1970.

Smith, Bradford, *Americans From Japan.* J. B. Lippincott Co., 1948.

Smith, Geoffrey S., *To Save a Nation: American Countersubversives, and the New Deal, and the Coming of World War II.* Basic Books, 1973.

Smith, Robert, *The Economics of the Cold War.* Hudson Rand Corp., 1972.

Snepp, Frank, *Decent Interval.* Random House, 1977.

Snow, Lois Wheeler, *A Death with Dignity.* Random House, 1974.

Solberg, Carl, *Riding High: America in the Cold War.* Mason and Lipscomb, 1973.

Stein, Walter J., *California and the Dust Bowl Migration.* Greenwood Press, 1973.

Stenerson, Douglas C., *H. L. Mencken: Iconoclast from Baltimore.* University of Chicago Press, 1971.

Stern, Philip M., *The Oppenheimer Case.* Harper & Row, 1969.

Stewart, Donald Ogden, *By a Stroke of Luck! An Autobiography.* Paddington Press, 1975.

Stewart, George R., Jr., *The Year of the Oath.* Doubleday & Company, 1950.

Stimson, Grace Heilman, *Rise of the Labor Movement in Los Angeles.* University of California Press, 1955.

Strout, Cushing, *Conscience, Science, and Security: The Case of Dr. J. Robert Oppenheimer.* Rand McNally Co., 1963.

Swanberg, W. A., *Norman Thomas: The Last Idealist.* Charles Scribner's Sons, 1976.

Taylor, F. Jay, *The United States and the Spanish Civil War, 1936–1939.* Bookman Associates, 1956.

Taylor, Ron, *Sweatshops in the Sun.* Beacon Press, 1973.

Thomas, Lately, *When Even Angels Wept: The Senator McCarthy Affair. A Story Without a Hero.* William Morrow Co., 1973.

Trumbo, Dalton, *Additional Dialogue: Letters of Dalton Trumbo, 1942–1962*, edited by Helen Manfull. M. Evans and Co., 1970.

———, *The Devil in the Book.* California Emergency Defense Committee, May, 1956.

———, *The Time of the Toad: A Study of Inquisition in America.* Harper & Row, 1972.

Unger, Irwin, *The Movement: A History of the American Left.* Dodd, Mead & Co., 1974.

Vaughan, Robert, *Only Victims: A Study of the Show Business Blacklisting.* G. P. Putnam's Sons, 1972.

Viereck, Peter, *Shame and Glory of the Intellectuals.* Beacon Press, 1953.

Villard, Oswald Garrison, *Fighting Years: Memoirs of a Liberal Editor.* Harcourt, Brace and Co., 1939.

Viorst, Milton, *Liberalism: A Guide to the Past, Present and Future in American Politics.* Avon Books, 1967.

Voorhis, Jerry, *The Strange Case of Richard Milhous Nixon.* Paul S. Eriksson, Inc., 1972.

Walker, Franklin, *The Seacoast of Bohemia.* Peregrine Smith, Inc., 1973. A fine account of early Carmel.

Walton, Richard J., *Cold War and Counter-Revolution: The Foreign Policy of John F. Kennedy.* Reader's Magazine Press, 1972.

———, *Henry Wallace, Harry Truman and the Cold War.* Viking Press, 1976.

Warren, Earl, *The Memoirs of Earl Warren.* Doubleday & Co., 1977.

Waskow, Arthur, with Stanley Newman, *America in Hiding: The Shelter Mania.* Ballantine Books, 1962.

Watkins, Arthur V., *Enough Rope: The Inside Story of the Censure of Senator Joe McCarthy.* Prentice-Hall, 1969.

Watters, Pat, *Down to Now: Reflections on the Southern Civil Rights Movement.* Pantheon, 1971.

Weaver, John D., *Warren: The Man, the Court, the Era.* Little, Brown & Co., 1967.

Watters, Pat, *Down to Now: Reflections on the Southern Civil Rights Movement.* Pantheon, 1971.

Weaver, John D., *Warren: The Man, the Court, the Era.* Little, Brown & Co., 1967.

Weaver, Robert C., *Negro Labor: A National Problem.* Harcourt Brace and Co., 1946.

———, *Racial Tensions in Chicago.* Social Science Year Book, 1943.

Wechsler, James, *The Age of Treason*. Random House, 1953.

Weglyn, Michi, *Years of Infamy: The Untold Story of America's Concentration Camps*. William Morrow and Co., 1976.

Weinstein, James, and David W. Eakins (eds.), *For a New America: Essays in History and Politics from "Studies on the Left," 1959–1967*. Random House, 1970.

Weintraub, Stanley, *The Last Great Cause: The Intellectuals and the Spanish Civil War*. Weybright and Talley, 1968.

Westin, Alan F. (ed.), *Freedom Now! The Civil Rights Struggle in America*. Basic Books, 1964.

Wexley, John, *The Judgment of Julius and Ethel Rosenberg*. Cameron and Kahn, 1955.

White, Theodore H., *Breach of Faith: The Fall of Richard Nixon*. Atheneum, 1975.

———, *In Search of History: A Personal Adventure*. Harper & Row, 1978.

———, *The Making of the President*. Atheneum, 1968.

Widmer, Kingsley, *The End of Culture: Essays on Sensibility in Contemporary Society*. San Diego State University Press, 1975.

Williams, W. A., *History as a Way of Learning*. New Viewpoints, 1973.

Wills, Garry, *Nixon Agonistes: The Crisis of the Self-Made Man*. Houghton Mifflin Co., 1969.

Wilson, Edmund, *Letters on Literature and Politics, 1912–1972*, edited by Elena Wilson. Farrar, Straus and Giroux, 1977. See pp. 175 and 194.

Wittner, Lawrence S., *Cold War America: From Hiroshima to Watergate*. Praeger Publishers, 1974.

———, *Rebels Against War: The American Peace Movement, 1941–1960*. Columbia University Press, 1969.

Wolfe, Alan, *The Seamy Side of Democracy: Repression in America*. David McKay Co., 1973.

Wolff, Robert Paul, *The Poverty of Liberalism*. Beacon Press, 1968.

———, with Barrington Moore, Jr., and Herbert Marcuse, *A Critique of Pure Tolerance*. Beacon Press, 1968.

Wreszin, Michael, *Oswald Garrison Villard: Pacifist at War*. Indiana University Press, 1965.

Yergin, Daniel, *Shattered Peace: The Origins of the Cold War and the National Security State*. Houghton Mifflin Co., 1977.

Young, Alfred, *Dissent: Explorations in the History of American Radicalism*. Northern Illinois University Press, 1968.

Ziff, Larzer, *The American 1890s: Life and Times of a Lost Generation*. Viking Press, 1966.

Zinn, Howard, *Post-War America: 1945–1971*. Bobbs-Merrill Co., 1973.

———, *SNCC: The New Abolitionists*. Beacon Press, 1964.

———, *The Southern Mystique*. Alfred A. Knopf, 1964.

———, *Vietnam: The Logic of Withdrawal*. Beacon Press, 1967.

Articles, Pamphlets, Periodicals, Reports, and Other Materials

Anatomy of Anti-Communism. Report prepared for the Peace Education Division of the American Friends Service Committee, 1969.

Barr, Stringfellow, *Let's Join the Human Race* (pamphlet). University of Chicago Press, 1950.

Brogan, Denis, "Those Silly 'Twenties,' " *The Spectator*, Sept. 13, 1968.

Can We Afford Academic Freedom? A discussion at the Harvard Law School Forum by Allen A. Zoll, McGeorge Bundy, and Carey McWilliams, Dec. 7, 1951. Beacon Reference Series.

"The Changing Cold War," *Annals of the American Academy of Political and Social Science,* January, 1964.

Dunne, Father George H., *Hollywood Labor Dispute: A Study in Immorality* (pamphlet). Los Angeles: Conference Publishing Co., no date. (For the Bioff-Browne incident.)

Finman, Ted, and Stewart Macauley, "Freedom to Dissent: The Vietnam Protests and the Words of Public Officials," *Wisconsin Law Review,* Summer, 1966.

Freedom Agenda Pamphlets, published by the Carrie Chapman Catt Memorial Fund, Inc., in 1954, including *The Constitution and Loyalty Programs,* by Alan Westin; *Constitutional Liberty and Seditious Activity,* by Jack W. Peltason; *Where Constitutional Liberty Came From,* by Alfred H. Kelly; *Freedom of Speech and Press,* by Zechariah Chafee, Jr.; *The Bill of Rights and Our Individual Liberties,* by T. V. Smith; *The Constitution and Congressional Investigating Committees,* by Robert K. Carr.

Horowitz, Harold W., "Loyalty Tests for Employment in the Motion Picture Industry," *Stanford Law Review,* March, 1954.

In the Matter of J. Robert Oppenheimer. Transcript of hearings before the Personnel Security Board, April 12, 1954, through May 6, 1954.

"Internal Security and Civil Rights," *Annals of the American Academy of Political and Social Science,* July, 1955.

Isaac, Dan, "The Other Scott Fitzgerald," *The Nation,* Sept. 28, 1974.

Journal of Mexican American History, edited by Joseph and Kathleen Navarro, published in Santa Barbara, Calif.

Journal of Social Issues, Vol. XI (1955), No. 3, on Anti-Intellectualism in the United States. See the chapter beginning on p. 18.

Loyalty in a Democracy. Public Affairs Pamphlet No. 179, May 26, 1951.

McWilliams, Carey, "The American Burden," *The Current,* March, 1961.

———, *Carey McWilliams: A Selected Bibliography of His Work, 1924–1954,* by Zoe Anne Feliz. San Jose, Calif.: Department of Librarianship, California State University, 1974.

———, "The Hollywood Gesture," *Panorama,* September, 1934.

———, *Small Farm and Big Farm.* Public Affairs Pamphlet No. 100.

Meiklejohn, Alexander, "What Does the First Amendment Mean?," *University of Chicago Law Review,* Spring, 1953.

Miller, Arthur, "The Year It Came Apart," *New York Times,* Dec. 30, 1974.

Miller, Ross Lincoln, "Henry Adams: Making It Over Again," *Centennial Review,* Summer, 1974.

The Nation. Files from Jan. 1, 1945, to Dec. 1, 1975.

New University Thought. Special issue, "Decisions for America, 66/67." See pp. 133–37.

Paterson, Thomas G., "The Abortive American Loan to Russia and the Origins of the Cold War, 1943–1946," *Journal of American History,* June, 1960.

Philbrick, H. R., *Legislative Investigation Report.* Sacramento, Calif., Dec. 28, 1938.

Report of the President's Commission on Campus Unrest (William Scranton, chairman), Sept. 26, 1970.

Rintala, Marvin, "A Generation in Politics: A Definition," *Review of Politics,* October, 1963.

Sorrell, Herbert Knott, "You Don't Choose Your Friends." Oral History Project, Department of Special Collections, Library, University of California at Los Angeles. (For the Bioff-Browne incident.)

Subversive Infiltration of Radio, Television, and the Entertainment Industry. Hearings before the Senate Subcommittee to Investigate the Administration of the Internal Security Act and Other Internal Security Laws. U.S. Government Printing Office, 1952.

Uncle Sam Is Watching You: Highlights from the Hearings of the Senate Subcommittee on Constitutional Rights; introduction by Alan Barth. Public Affairs Press, 1971.

Vietnam and International Law: An Analysis of the Legality of the United States Military Involvement. Lawyers Committee on American Policy Vis-à-Vis Vietnam, 1967.

Violence in America, 2 vols. Report of the National Commission on the Causes and Prevention of Violence, chaired by Milton Eisenhower, 1969.

Woodside, Alexander, "American Attitudes Toward History," *The Nation,* Dec. 13, 1975.

INDEX

Abbott, Wilbur Cortez, 41
Accidental President, The (Sherrill), 237
Acheson, Dean, 126, 127, 162
Adamic, Louis, 47, 48, 55, 63, 83–84,
    85*fn*., 96
  and *Common Ground*, 134, 179
  life and death of, 173, 176–79
  on Los Angeles, 45
Adamic, Stella, 176, 178, 179
Adams, Brooks, 62
Adams, Charles, 62
Adams, Henry, 27, 323, 324
"affluent society," 195–204, 246
Agency of Fear (Epstein), 304
Agnew, Spiro T., 291, 300
Agony of the American Left, The (Lasch), 151,
  155
Agran, Larry, 220
Ahmad, Eqbal, 267
Aikman, Duncan, 47
Algren, Nelson, 201
Alinsky, Saul, 111, 315–16
Allen, George, 123
Allen, Willis and Lawrence, 72
Allen-Bradley Co., 252
Alliance for Progress, 257
All Quiet on the Western Front (Remarque),
  95
Alsop, Stewart, 294, 305
Ambrose Bierce (McWilliams), 56–58, 64
America in Doubt (Werth), 239
American Civil Liberties Union, 81, 109,
  161, 187
American Committee for Cultural
  Freedom, 151, 152, 154–57
American Council on Race Relations, 115
American Dilemma, An (Myrdal), 115

American Federation of Labor, 98–99
American Friends Service Committee
  (Quakers), 158, 222, 223, 276
American Jitters, The (Wilson), 69
American League Against War and
  Fascism, 92
American Legion, 105, 139
American Mercury, The, 53–55, 56, 177
American Potash and Chemical Co., 82
American Renaissance (Matthiessen), 174
American Report, 316
American Security Council, 251
Americans for Democratic Action, 124–25,
  129, 130, 187, 214
American Theosophical Association, 46
American Tragedy, An (Dreiser), 41
American Vigilante Intelligence
  Federation, 166
Ameringer, Oscar, 324
Anderson, Marian, 98
Anderson, Paul Y., 237
Anglo-German Naval Pact, 94
Angola, 233
Anti-Defamation League, 182
antifascist movement, 92–95
anti-Semitism, 130–34
antiwar movement, 195
  challenges war's legality, 301–2
  demonstrations, 270, 272, 276, 283–84,
    289–94, 307, 317
  early phase, 221–27
  Johnson forced out by, 256, 277*ff*.
  King and, 274–75
  and new left, 276–77
  and teach-ins, 271
Apéritif, 67
Arbenz, Jácobo, 228

Arbuckle, Fatty, 46
Arendt, Hannah, 322
Argonaut, The, 47, 56
Arkies, 75–80, 133
Armitage, Merle, 47
Army-McCarthy hearings, 173
Aronson, James, 190–91
Arrowsmith (Lewis), 41
Ascent of Man, The (TV series), 242–43
Ascoli, Max, 191
Associated Farmers, 74, 77, 79
Associated Press, 220
Atherton, Gertrude, 56
Austin, Mary, 47, 56, 66
Authors' League, 165
Automation (Dreher), 194
Aware, Inc., 166
Ayres, E. Duran, 110

Bagdikian, Ben, 168, 296
Bainbridge, Sherman, 72
Baker, Carlos, 203
Baker, Ray Stannard, 213
Baldwin, James, 208, 236
Ball, W. Macmahon, 185, 224, 267
Balogh, T., 197
Baltimore *Sun,* 67
Bamboo Bed, The (Eastlake), 267
Bancroft, Philip, 79
Bao Dai, 286
Baran, Paul, 198, 223, 228, 316
Baritz, Loren, 39
Barnes, Joseph, 147–48, 190
Barr, Stringfellow, 161
Barraclough, Geoffrey, 195, 245
Bass, Saul, 240
Bassett, Queen Ann, 28
Bassie, V. Lewis, 198
Bates, Ralph, 93
Baxter, Leone, 305
Bay of Pigs, 162, 195, 227–32, 252, 281
Beals, Carleton, 195, 228, 238
Beat Generation, 246, 247
Beckett, Henry, 179
Beichman, Arnold, 157
Belden, Jack, 148
Belfrage, Cedric, 190–91
Bellow, Saul, 66, 200
Bennett, John C., 276
Bennett, Wallace F., 172
Bentley, Elizabeth, 167, 178, 189, 215, 219
Bergamin, José, 93

Berger, Henry, 198
Berkeley "loyalty oath" controversy, 139, 140
Berkove, Lawrence I., 60, 61
Berman, Harold, 224
Bernstein, Barton, 155, 245
Bernstein, Victor, 194, 262
Berrigan, Philip, 276
Berton, Pierre, 24, 25
Besant, Annie, 46
Bessie, Alvah, 135–38
Between the Lines (Wakefield), 206
Bevan, Aneurin, 185
Biberman, Herbert, 135–38
Bicentennial, 309–10
Bierce, Ambrose, 50, 51, 55–62, 64, 66, 97
Bierce, Helen, 57–58
Bierce, Lucius Verus, 58–59
Big Guns, The (Josephson), 217
Billings, Warren, 80, 107, 321
Bill of Rights ceremony, 164
Bilorsky, John A., 292
Bioff, Willie, 86–92
Bissell, Richard, 162
Black, Algernon, 153
Black, Hugo, 167
Blackett, P. M. S., 241
Black, Hammack and McWilliams, 85
Blame the Victim (Ryan), 219
Blanshard, Paul, 189
Blatnik, John, 179
Boas, Franz, 115
Boddy, Manchester, 67, 70, 93
Boilermakers Union, 99
Bolton, Charles, 226
Bongartz, Roy, 201
Boni, Albert, 56
Bookman, The, 66
Borah, William E., 93
Boroff, David, 262
Boudin, Leonard, 168
Bourdet, Claude, 161, 169, 195, 239, 266, 267
Bourgin, Simon, 179
Bowron, Fletcher, 83, 104
Boy Gravely (Dornfeld), 65
Braverman, Harry, 110, 111
Bread and Roses Too (Newfield), 248
Brennan, William J., 164
Brewer, Roy, 181
Brewster, Kingman, 292
Bricker, John W., 122
Bridges, Harry, 70, 84–85, 107, 138, 164
Brogan, Denis, 40
Bronfenbrenner, Martin, 280

Bronowski, Jacob, 239–43, 249
Brooks, Van Wyck, 46, 47, 61–62
Brothers Under the Skin (McWilliams), 21, 112, 114, 115, 130, 134
Brown, Cecil, 274
Brown, Edmund G. "Pat," 121–22
Brown, George, 269, 278
Brown, John, 59
Browne, George, 87–91
Browne, Lewis, 93
Browne, Malcolm, 274
Brownell, Herbert, 167, 172, 186, 187
Brownell, Robert, 70
Brown v. Board of Education, 205–6, 208–10
Buchanan, Patrick, 219
Buchwald, Art, 216
Buckley, James L., 300
Buckley, William F., 209, 251, 287
Budenz, Louis, 167
Buitenhuis, Peter, 53
Bundy, McGeorge, 269
Bureau of Indian Affairs, 108
Burke, Kenneth, 198, 201
Burnham, James, 251
Burns, Arthur, 197
Burroughs, John Rolfe, 28, 37
Burton, Harold H., 164
Business Week, 199
Byrnes, James F., 116–17, 118, 123

Caldwell, Erskine, 48
California Committee on Un-American Activities, 109, 146, 178, 180
California Division of Immigration and Housing, 76–79, 85, 100
California Federation for Civic Unity, 115
California social-protest movements, 66, 67–74
California: The Great Exception (McWilliams), 119, 132
Calley, William, 294
Cambodia, 290–91, 298
Cammer, Harold, 301
Campus Aftermath of Cambodia and Kent State (Peterson/Bilorsky), 292
Camus, Albert, 247
Cancer Connection, The (Agran), 220
Canwell Committee, 139
Capouya, Emile, 194
Cárdenas, Lázaro, 111
Carillo, Leo, 113–14
Carlson, Frank, 172

Carr, E. H., 245
Carter, Jimmy, 309
Cary, John, 30
Case, Francis, 172
Casley, Lottie Oatley, 23–26
Casley, Paul, 22–23, 25
Casley, Vernon, 23, 25–26
Cassidy, Butch, 28
Castongue, Paul, 22
Castro, Fidel, 88, 162, 228–32
Catledge, Turner, 229
Catton, Bruce, 194, 219
Caute, David, 311
Cavalier, 236
CBS, 131–32, 231–32, 309
Centennial, 309–10
Central Intelligence Agency, *see* CIA
Central Pacific R.R., 62
Chafee, Zechariah, Jr., 148
Chamberlain, Neville, 96
Chambers, Whittaker, 129, 154, 186, 200–201, 215
Chandler, Harry, 44
Chap-Book, The, 51
Chaplin, Charles, 46, 168
Chapman, John Jay, 41, 62
Chapman, Oscar, 122
Chavez, Cesar, 109, 112
Chevalier, Haakon, 94
Chiang Kai-shek, 306
Chicago *Daily News,* 163
Chicago *Defender,* 274
Chicano movement, 109, 134, 212
China, 182–85, 266, 285–86, 314
  Nixon and, 183, 288, 294–95, 296
China Fights Back (Smedley), 184
China Lobby in American Politics, The (Koen), 185
China's Red Army Marches (Smedley), 184
Chinatown (film), 42
Chinese Americans, 100, 132, 212
Chinese Destinies (Smedley), 184
Chinese Exclusion Act, 106
Chinese Revolution, 182
Chotiner, Murray, 122, 302
Chou En-lai, 183
Christian, Henry A., 179
Christian Anti-Communist Crusade, 252
Christian Science Monitor, The, 157
Christman, Henry M., 224, 262, 267
Church Committee, 231
Churchill, Winston, 117, 124, 125, 178
CIA, 127, 308, 309, 318
  and Cuba, 88, 162, 227–32
  and media, 157–58

CIA (*cont.*)
  Nation special issue on, 217–18
  subsidies, 115–57, 221–22, 251
Ciardi, John, 200
CIA's Secret Army, The (CBS documentary),
  232
CIO, 98
Circuit Rider, Inc., 166
Citizen 13660 (Okubo), 105
Citizens Committee for Constitutional
  Government, 302
Civilisation (TV series), 243
civil rights
  Johnson and, 210, 255, 268, 272, 281
  movement, 98–100, 114, 195, 204–13,
    257, 317
  Nation and, 195, 204–8, 262
  Stevenson and, 164
  Truman and, 125, 128, 130
  and World War II, 98–115
Civil Rights Act, 268
Civil Rights Congress, 138
Civil Service Commission, 189
Clark, Blair, 263
Clark, John Gee, 81
Clark, Sir Kenneth, 243
Clark, Tom, 104, 164
Clay, Henry, 27
Cleveland, Grover, 20
Clifford, Clark, 129, 280
Cloward, Richard, 198, 219
Clubb, O. E., 185, 195, 224, 267
Clurman, Harold, 92, 194
Cobb, Humphrey, 95–97
Cobb, Lee J., 180
Cody, Wild Bill, 35
Coffey, Raymond R., 267
Coffin, William Sloane, Jr., 203
Cohen, Elliot, 154–55
Cold War and Its Origins (Fleming), 244
Cold War in America (Wittner), 272
Cole, Lester, 135–38
Collected Works of Ambrose Bierce, The, 55, 56
Collier, John, 77
Collier's, 220
Coming Showdown, The (Dreher), 194
Commentary, 151, 152, 154, 156
Commission on Violence, 317
Committee for Non-Violent Action, 223
Common Ground, 105, 131, 134, 179
Communist Party, 69, 93–94, 129, 166,
  167, 204, 216, 310–12
Community Service Organization, 111–12
Compass, The, 190, 191, 237

Condon, Edward U., 168, 226
Conference of Studio Unions, 119
Congress for Cultural Freedom, 154–57
Connally, John, 237
Connell, Will, 47
Conover, Grandin, 194
Contempo, 67
Conyers, John, 302
Cook, Fred J., 192, 198, 214–18, 256
Coolidge, Calvin, 41, 44, 66, 263
Cooper, A. T., 212
Cooper, John Sherman, 276
corruption, 216–17, 218
Cort, David, 200–201
Cort, Joseph H., 168
Cotten, Joseph, 110
Coughlin, Charles, 71, 171
Council Against Intolerance in America,
  139
Council for Civic Unity, 113
Council on Human Relations, 131
Counterattack, 153
counterculture, 246–49
  see also new left
Countryman, Vern, 148
Cowell, Henry, 80–81
Cowley, Malcolm, 64
Crabb, Cecil V., Jr., 223
Crane, Clarkson, 55
Criminal Syndicalism Act prosecutions,
  74–75
Crocker, Charles, 62
Cross, Jennifer, 220
Crown, Joseph, 301, 302
Crum, Bartley, 135, 190, 192
Cuban missile crisis, 227, 230, 312
Cuban Story, The (Matthews), 228
cults, 46–47
Cup of Gold (Steinbeck), 64
Curtis, Mina, 192, 195

Daily Trojan, 50
Daley, Richard, 282, 283, 284
Damnation of Theron Ware, The (Frederic),
  55
Darrow, Clarence, 86*fn.*
Daugherty, "Nigger Jim," 25–26
Daughter of Earth (Smedley), 184
Daughters of the American Revolution,
  98, 201
Davidson, Basil, 195, 238

Davie, Michael, 314
Davies, John Paton, Jr., 168
Davis, John W., 40, 209
Dawson, Yukon Territory, 24–25
Day of the Locust, The (West), 44
De Gaulle Revolution, The (Werth), 238
Dekker, Albert, 173, 180–82
Dekker, Esther, 180
Dell, Robert, 96
Del Vayo, J. Álvarez, 149–51, 193–94, 233, 234
Deming, Barbara, 206, 224
Democratic Party
  in California, 68–69, 70, 73, 85, 121–22, 124–25
  and McCarthyism, 171
  1960 election, 256
  1968 election, 277–85
  and Vietnam War, 273, 288
  and Wallace movement (1948), 128–30
Dennett, John Richard, 262
Denver, Colorado, 35, 36–37, 45
Denver, University of, 37, 40, 41
Denver & Rio Grande R.R., 22, 29
Depression, 65ff.
Desmond, Earl, 79
Deutscher, Isaac, 245, 267
Devil's Dictionary, The (Bierce), 55
de Voto, Bernard, 46
Dewey, Thomas E., 128, 129–30
De Witt, J. L., 102
Díaz, José, 109
Diem, Ngo Dinh, 310
Dies, Martin, 104
Dillard, Irving, 149
Dirksen, Everett M., 221
Dissent (periodical), 316
Dixiecrats, 129, 130, 207–9, 256
Dmytryk, Edward, 135–38
Dodd, Thomas, 223
Dominican Republic, 270
Donner, Frank, 149, 186, 188
Donovan, Robert J., 124, 125, 130
Dornfeld, Iris, 65, 175
Dos Passos, John, 251, 321
Dostoevski, Fëdor, 323
Double Dealer, The, 67
Douglas, Helen Gahagan, 78, 180
Douglas, Paul, 163
Douglas, William O., 19, 163, 165
Downey, Sheridan, 70, 72
Downie, Leonard, Jr., 218
Dreher, Carl, 194
Dreiser, Theodore, 93, 174

Drinnon, Richard, 291
Dryfoos, Orvil, 230
Dudman, Richard, 229
Dulles, Allen, 228, 256
Dulles, John Foster, 172
Dumbook, The, 47
Dunham, Barrows, 175
Durr, Clifford, 207
Dwiggins, Dwight, 229
Dynamite (Adamic), 85–86fn.

Earle, George, 126
Eastlake, William, 267
Eastland, James O., 236
Eastman, Max, 251
Eaton, S. B., 60
Eby, Kermit, 149, 198
Economist, The, 251
Edel, Leon, 262
Edwards, Fred, 76
Egghead's Guide to America (Thompson), 202
Eggleston, Arthur, 79
Eisenhower, Dwight D., 117, 219
  and civil rights, 208–10
  and Cuba, 232
  and domestic Cold War, 251, 311–12
  farewell address, 217
  and Korea, 127, 164
  and McCarthy, 163, 172
  1952 campaign, 163–64
  and Nixon, 288
  and Vietnam, 276, 286, 310, 313
  and Warren, 164–65, 205, 209–10
Eisenhower, Milton, 104
Eisler, Hans, 136
Elliott, George Y., 200
Ellis, William S., 254
Ellison, Ralph, 255, 262
Emergency Civil Liberties Committee, 161
Emerson, Thomas I., 161
Encounter magazine, 155, 156
Engh, Hans, 252
EPIC, 67, 68–70, 71, 73, 74, 122
Epstein, Edward Jay, 304
Ervin, Sam, 172
Ervin Committee, 304
Erskine, Charles, 56
Esquire, 236
Evans, Ernestine, 148
Evening Post, 153

Exurbanites, The (Spectorsky), 202
Eyster, Warren, 95, 97

Factories in the Field (McWilliams), 74–76,
    78, 79, 85
Fairlie, Henry, 297
Faithful Are the Wounds (Sarton), 174
Fall, Bernard B., 266
fallout shelters, 225–26
False Witness (Matusow), 186
Fante, John, 48, 55
farm labor, *see* migrant farm labor
Farm Security Administration, 111
Farm Workers Union, 112
Faubus, Orville, 208
Faulk, John Henry, 309
Faulkner, William, 48
FBI, 148, 161, 215–16, 308, 318
FBI Nobody Knows, The (Cook), 215
Fear on Trial (CBS documentary), 309
Federal Bureau of Investigation, *see* FBI
Federal Communications Commission, 187
Fellowship of Reconciliation, 223
feminist movement, 144
Fenton, Frank, 49
Ferguson, Otis, 96
Ferlinghetti, Lawrence, 273
Fiedler, Leslie, 152
Field, Harold, 145
Field, Marshall, 190
Figueiredo, Antonio de, 234
Filene, Edward, 263
Finch, Robert, 305
Fitzgerald, C. P., 185, 267
Fitzgerald, F. Scott, 39–40, 41, 52
Fitzgerald, John F. "Honey Fitz," 263
Flanders, Ralph, 172
Flanner, Hildegarde, 47
Fleming, D. F., 223, 243–44
Foisie, Jack, 267
Fong, Hiram L., 107
Ford, Daniel, 267
Ford, Gerald R., 107, 170, 259, 300, 310
    Nixon pardon, 301, 305
    and Vietnam, 298–99, 305, 306, 308
Ford, John, 78
Foreman, Clark, 161
Forrestal, James V., 123
Forster, Arnold, 182
Fortune, 199
France: 1940–1945 (Werth), 238

France Observateur, 195, 233
Francis, Owen, 48
Franco, Francisco, 144, 149, 234
Franco-Soviet Pact, 94
Frank, Waldo, 219
Frantz, Laurent, 149
Frazier, E. Franklin, 98, 115, 208
Frederic, Harold, 55
Freed, Judy, 148
Freedom Riders, 257
Freeland, Richard M., 159
Free Men, Free Markets (Theobald), 219
Fried, Richard M., 126
Frink, Maurice, 60
Frontier, 274
Frost, David, 162, 290
Funding Bill (1896), 62

Gaddis, Thomas, 219
Galbraith, John Kenneth, 199, 276
Gale, Zona, 46–47
Galvão, Henrique, 232–34, 250
Game and Gossip, 47
Gardner, John W., 210
Gardner, Lloyd C., 243, 245, 246
Garland, Hamlin, 46
Garrison, William Lloyd, 144
Gayn, Mark, 185, 195, 238
Geer, Will, 309
General Electric Co., 60, 252
Geneva Conference (1954), 266, 286
Gettleman, Marvin E., 301
Girvetz, Harry, 124, 125
Gitt, Jess, 179
Gittings, John, 267
Gleason, Gene, 216–17
Glossy Rats, The (Cort), 201
Godkin, E. L., 62, 264
Goldberg, Arthur, 301
Goldberg, Harvey, 239
Goldberger, A. L., 223
Golden Rule (peace ship), 223
Goldman, Eric, 138
Goldwater, Barry, 90
    defeat of, 250, 269, 273
    and Nixon, 283, 300
    nomination of, 173, 252–53, 255
Gomberg, William, 195
Good Girl, The (O'Sullivan), 55
Goodman, Jack, 147–48
Goodman, Paul, 247

Gothic Politics in the Deep South (Sherrill), 237

Gottlieb, Sanford, 272

Goulden, Joseph, 220

Grandsons (Adamic), 177

Grant, Ulysses S., 310

Grapes of Wrath, The (Steinbeck), 64, 76, 78, 92

Great Fear, The (Caute), 311

Great Gatsby, The (Fitzgerald), 41

Great Society, 255, 272

Greenbaum, Gus, 90

Greenberg, Clement, 149–51, 189

Greene, Jerry, 271

Greenfield, Alice, 110

Grierson, Francis, 46–47

Gross, Beverly, 194

Grosser, Alfred, 295

Gruening, Ernest, 268, 269, 270, 273, 274, 285, 301

Guatemala, 228–29

Guevara, Che, 158

Hagan, Roger, 226

Hahne, Herman, 280

Haig, Alexander M., Jr., 301

Haight, Raymond, 69

Halsey, Margaret, 200

Hamby, Alonzo L., 145, 150, 151, 153

Hammack, Daniel, Jr., 64–65

Ham-'n-Eggs, 67, 71–72, 73

Hanna, Phil Townsend, 47

Harding, Warren G., 44, 53, 213

Harding College, 252

Harlan, John Marshall, 164

Harper's, 105, 236

Harrington, Alan, 202–3

Harrington, Michael, 198, 294, 321

Harris, Harwell, 47

Harris, Mark, 305

Harrison, Gilbert, 190

Hatch, Robert, 194

Hatfield, Mark, 253, 274, 276

Hayes, Arthur Garfield, 219

Hayes, Roland, 98

Hayes, Rutherford B., 310

Hazen, William B., 60

Hearst, William Randolph, 62

Hedrick, E. R., 65

Heilbroner, Robert, 315

Hellman, Lillian, 309

Hell's Angels (Thompson), 236

Hemingway, Ernest, 93

Henry, Jules, 267, 313

Hepburn, Katharine, 128

Herberg, Will, 251

Herbers, John, 210

Hersey, John, 117

Hesperian, 47, 67

Hicks, Granville, 151, 152, 309

Hillman, Sidney, 120, 121

Hilton, Ronald, 228, 230

Hiroshima, 117

Hiss, Alger, 129, 138, 152, 214, 215, 309

Hitler, Adolf, 92, 94–95

Hobsbawm, E. J., 245

Ho Chi Minh, 265, 285–86

Hodgson, Godfrey, 126, 170, 171, 270, 273, 280

Hoffa, James, 218, 281

Hoffman, Abbie, 293

Hollywood *Citizen-News*, 82–83

Hollywood Ten, 119, 132, 135–38, 140

Holmes, Justice Oliver Wendell, 60, 61

Hook, Sidney, 152, 154–55, 157, 300

Hoopes, Townsend W., 185

Hoover, Herbert, 44, 66

Hoover, J. Edgar, 103, 167, 201, 215–16, 256, 309

Hoover Committee, 162

Hopkins, Harry, 256

Hopper, Hedda, 136

Hora, La, 228

Horn, Tom, 28

Horowitz, David, 245

House Committee on Inter-State Migration, 103–4

House Judiciary Committee, 301, 303, 304

House Un-American Activities Committee (HUAC), 92, 104, 118–19, 125, 136, 137, 166–67, 201

Howard, Roy W., 214

Howard, Sidney, 95

Howe, Irving, 316

Howelsen, Carl, 32

Hoy, 111

Huberman, Leo, 316

Huff, Philip, 276

Hughes, H. Stuart, 224, 245, 267

Hughes, Langston, 153

Hughes, Paul, 186–88

Humphrey, Hubert H., 131, 282–85 *passim*

Hunt, E. Howard, 231

Hunt, H. L., 236

Huntington, Collis P., 62

Huntley, Chet, 122
Huston, John, 167
Huxley, Aldous, 48, 58

Ickes, Harold L., 123
Idea of Fraternity in America, The (W. C.
    McWilliams), 65
Iglesias, Helen, 194
Ill Fares the Land (McWilliams), 108
Indians, 101, 106, 132, 212
In Dubious Battle (Steinbeck), 64
Industrial Areas Foundation, 111
Ingersoll, Ralph, 99
Inouye, Daniel K., 107
Institute for American Strategy, 251
Institute of Pacific Relations, 105
International Alliance of Theatrical and
    Stage Employees, 87–89
Isaacs, Harold R., 185
Isaacs, Stanley M., 124
Ivens, Joris, 93
Is There an American in the House? (Cort),
    201

Jackson, Bruce, 219
Jackson, C. D., 252
Jackson State disturbances, 291
James, Daniel, 151, 152, 157–58
James, Henry, 38
Japanese Americans, 21, 100, 107, 112,
    205, 212
Jaspers, Karl, 297*fn.*
Jeeny Ray (Dornfeld), 65
Jeffers, Robinson, 52, 63, 65
Jeffers, Una, 63, 65
Jencks, Clinton, 188
Jenner, William E., 122
John Birch Society, 209, 251, 252
Johnson, Byron, 224
Johnson, Hiram, 62, 70, 77, 102
Johnson, Lyndon B., 127, 237
    and civil rights, 210, 255, 268, 272, 281
    death of, 298
    and dissenters, 170, 307
    downfall of, 128–29, 256, 277–82
    election of (1964), 250, 255, 269, 273
    and McCarthy, 172
    and 1968 election, 283, 285
    and race riots, 291

Tonkin Gulf incident, 269
Vice Presidential nomination, 256
and Vietnam, 210, 255–56, 259, 265,
    267–73, 288, 310
Johnson, Mordecai, 153
Johnson, Paul, 224
Johnson, Roger, 82–83
Johnston, Eric, 136
Joint Economic Committee, 319
Jones, Howard Mumford, 149
Jordan, Vernon, 207
Josephson, Matthew, 148, 198, 217
Jowitt, Earl, 214
Jungle, The (Sinclair), 70

Kahn, Herman, 225, 226, 278
Kalven, Harry, Jr., 170
Kampelman, Max M., 131
Kaplan, Justin, 263
Kaplan, Samuel, 217
Kapstein, Jonathan, 267
Katz, Charles W., 135
Kauffman, Arnold, 271, 276
Kazin, Alfred, 262
Keating, Kenneth, 281
Keatley, Robert, 290
Kemler, Edgar, 194
Kempton, Murray, 53
Kennan, George F., 123
Kennedy, Edward M., 282
Kennedy, John F., 127, 170, 250, 263
    administration of, 256–58
    assassination, 231, 232, 255, 258–59
    and civil rights, 210, 257
    and Cold War, 252, 257
    and Cuba, 227, 229–31
    and Vietnam, 257–58, 273, 286, 310
Kennedy, Paul, 229
Kennedy, Robert F., 257
    assassination of, 258–59, 282
    and Cuba, 230–31, 281
    and Hoffa, 218, 281
    and 1968 campaign, 277, 281–82
Kenny, Robert W., 81, 106, 113–14, 121–
    122, 135, 301
Kent State shootings, 291, 292
Kerby, Phil, 274
Kern, John W., 89
Kerner Commission, 291
Keynes, John Maynard, 40
Khrushchev, Nikita, 230
King, Martin Luther, Jr., 222

and antiwar movement, 226, 274–75
assassination of, 258–59, 282, 283
and bus boycott, 206–7
march on Washington, 210
wiretap on, 257
Kirchwey, Freda, 122, 143–44, 188, 194,
235, 237
and attacks on *Nation*, 151, 153, 190
and Greenberg incident, 149–50
McWilliams and, 140, 143, 145, 190, 263
and N.Y.C. school-library ban, 189
resigns, 191–92
and Wallace movement, 128
Kirchwey, George, 144
Kirstein, George, 191–92, 195, 259, 261–
264
Kirstein, Lincoln, 192
Kissinger, Henry A., 183, 295, 296, 297,
299, 305, 306, 308
Klein, Herbert, 47, 75
Kleindienst, Richard, 300
Klondike Fever, The (Berton), 24
Knepper, George, 59
Knowland, William F., 122
Koen, Ross Y., 185
Kolko, Gabriel, 245
Kopkind, Andrew, 156
Koppel, Ted, 267
Korean War, 159, 164, 190, 196, 221
cease-fire, 173, 193, 222
cost of, 280
Truman and, 127, 140
Kristol, Irving, 152, 154–57, 300
Krock, Arthur, 313
Kronenberger, Louis, 262
Krutch, Joseph Wood, 143
Kubrick, Stanley, 95
Kuh, Frederick, 195, 238
Kunitz, Stanley, 203
Kynette, Earl, 72

La Feber, Walter, 245
La Follette, Robert M., 40–41, 78
La Follette Committee, 78–79, 103, 107
Laird, Melvin, 289
Lamb, Edward, 187, 283
Lamb, Robert, 103
Lamont, Corliss, 161
Lampell, Millard, 148
Lampman, Robert, 198
Landy, Eugene W., 168
Lansdale, Edward, 246

Laos, 292, 294
Lardner, Ring, Jr., 135–38
Lark, The, 51
Lasch, Christopher, 151, 155, 156, 245,
248, 271
Lasky, Melvin, 155, 156
Last Days of Paris, The (Werth), 238
Lattimore, Owen, 152, 184, 185, 267
Lawrence, D. H., 48
Lawyers Committee on American Policy
Toward Vietnam, 301–2
Lawson, John Howard, 135–38
League of Nations, 92
League to Abolish Capital Punishment,
144
Lehmann, Paul, 161
Le May, Curtis, 285
Lemke, William, 71
Leningrad (Werth), 238
Lens, Sidney, 198, 218
Lerner, Max, 123
Levine, Jack, 216
Lewis, Anthony, 307
Lewis, Ted, 270, 277, 278, 290
Leyvas, Henry, 109–11
Liberation, 222
Life, 183, 200, 225, 252, 294
Life in the Crystal Palace (Harrington), 203
Lindblom, Charles E., 323
Lindesmith, Alfred, 220
Lindsay, John V., 217, 253, 291
Lippmann, Walter, 55, 104, 200, 285, 290
Lissovoy, Peter de, 206
Listener, The, 310
Literaturnaya Gazeta, 170
Little Rock, 208–9, 210
Loew, Marcus, 91
London *Times*, 233, 238
Long, Huey, 147, 171
Long, Lulu, 35
Long, Richard, 208
Lon Nol, 290
Los Angeles, 42*ff*.
1920s literary scene, 47–50
Los Angeles *Daily News*, 67, 70
Los Angeles Newspaper Guild, 82–83
Los Angeles *Times*, 42, 43–44, 47, 49, 85–
86*fn*., 229, 275
Louis Adamic and Shadow America
(McWilliams), 177
Love, Stephen, 219
Lovestone, Jay, 181
Lowenstein, Allard, 277
Lowenthal, Max, 148, 215
loyalty program, 126, 138–40

Lubin, Simon J., 77
Luce, Henry, 125–26, 200, 244

Macdonald, Dwight, 222
Mackenzie, Sir Compton, 218
MacLeish, Archibald, 200
Madison, Wisconsin, bombings, 293
Madison *Capitol-Times*, 189
Mafia, 231
Magdoff, Harry, 316
Making of a Counter Culture, The (Roszak),
    248–49
Male Animal, The (film), 167
Malone, George Wilson, 122
Maloy, Tommy, 88
Malraux, André, 135–38
Manchester *Guardian*, 129, 171, 238
Mandell, Maurice, 194
Man in the Modern Age (Jaspers), 297*fn.*
Mann, Thomas, 138, 139, 153
Mansfield, Portia, 32
Mao Tse-tung, 127, 294
Marchetti, Victor, 218
Marine, Gene, 220
Markham, Edwin, 46–47
Markowitz, Norman D., 124, 130
Marquand, David, 171
Marshall, Margaret, 194
Marshall Plan, 126–27
Martin, Graham, 306
Martin, Kingsley, 151
Martinson, Robert, 206
Marx, Leo, 175, 203
Masaryk, Jan, 129
Mask for Privilege, A (McWilliams), 132–34
Matsunaga, Spark M., 107
Matthews, Herbert L., 228
Matthiessen, F. O., 173–76, 178, 179, 323
Matusow, Harvey, 167, 186–89
Maund, Alfred, 191, 206
Mayaguez incident, 306
Mayer, Louis B., 86, 89–90, 91
McAdoo, William Gibbs, 87–88
McCarran, Pat, 138
McCarran Act, 163
McCarthy, Eugene, 256, 274, 275, 277–82,
    284, 285
McCarthy, Joseph R., 122, 146, 148, 151,
    187, 190, 281, 309
    and the Army, 171–73
    "anti-Communism" exploitation by,
        159–60, 162*ff.*

downfall of, 172–73
    and media, 147, 171, 213
    Wheeling speech, 140, 160
McCarthy, Mary, 117
McCarthy and His Enemies (Buckley), 251
McCloskey, Paul, 290
McDermott, John, 267
McGee, Reece, 200
McGovern, George, 274, 275, 277, 281,
    284, 296, 309
McMillin, Miles, 283
McNair, James, 276
McNamara, J. B. and J. J., 85*fn.*
McNamara, Robert, 221, 272, 278
McNickle, D'Arcy, 134
McPherson, Aimee Semple, 45, 46, 69
McWilliams, Carey
    background, 19–31
    childhood, 31–38
    education, 36–37, 41, 42, 50
    California years, 41, 42–140
    newspaper work, 42, 43–44
    early magazine writing, 46–47, 66–67
    in bohemian circle, 47–49
    as lawyer, 48, 64–66, 74, 81–83, 85, 86–
        92, 136
    and Sinclair, 49–50, 69–71, 73–74
    and Mencken, 52, 55, 57
    Bierce biography, 55–58, 64
    marries, 65
    and farm labor, 64, 74–79, 107, 108
    and social-protest movements, 73–74
    as Immigration and Housing head, 76–
        79, 85, 100–101, 103–6, 107, 119
    labor-union involvement, 81–92
    and antifascist movement, 92–95
    and "racial problem," 100*ff.*, 119, 139
    and Japanese Americans, 100–101,
        103–6, 107
    and Mexican Americans, 108–14
    work for *Nation* on West Coast, 116, 119,
        120, 122, 132, 143, 144
    in California progressive politics, 120–
        122, 124–25, 128
    and anti-Semitism, 130–34
    and Hollywood Ten, 135–36, 137–38
    and "loyalty program," 139–40
    at *Nation* under Kirchwey, 145*ff.*
    as editor of *Nation*, 191–319 *passim*
    resigns as editor, 264, 319
    political philosophy of, 319–24
McWilliams, Casley, 19, 26, 27, 29, 32, 33–
    34, 36–37, 41
McWilliams, Dorothy Hedrick, 65
McWilliams, Elizabeth Cleveland, 20

McWilliams, Hattie Casley (mother of Carey), 26, 27, 31, 33, 34, 41
McWilliams, Homer, 19–20, 21–22, 29
McWilliams, Iris Dornfeld, 65, 175
McWilliams, Jeremiah Newby, 20, 21, 26, 27, 28–33, 36–38
McWilliams, John, 20
McWilliams, Nancy McCorkle, 21, 23
McWilliams, "Captain Sam," 20–21, 23, 26
McWilliams, Wilson Carey, 65
Meacham, Stewart, 223
Medicare, 281
Meeker Massacre, 35
Meiklejohn, Alexander, 136, 149
Meisler, Stanley, 198, 220
Melman, Seymour, 198, 224, 274, 308
Mencken, H. L., 50–55, 56, 57, 235
Mental Radio (Sinclair), 47
Merriam, Frank, 69, 73
Mexican Americans, 73, 81, 108–9, 111–114, 134
Meyer, Cord, Jr., 221–22
Meyer, William H., 224
Meyers, William, 302
migrant farm labor, 64, 66, 74–80, 107, 108
Milburn, George, 48
military-industrial complex, 195, 196–98, 217
Miller, Arthur, 116, 138, 140, 148, 174
Miller, Herman P., 198
Miller, Merle, 148
Miller, Warren, 194
Miller, William, 255
Millier, Arthur, 47
Millis, Walter, 198, 222, 224
Mills, C. Wright, 199, 202, 206, 224
Mine, Mill and Smelter Workers Union, 82, 188
Mink, Patsy T., 107
Minneapolis, 131–32
Minton, Sherman, 164
Missouri State Conference of Social Work, 21
Mitchell, Clarence, 208
Mitford, Jessica, 167, 203
M'lle New York, 51
Moffat, David H., 31
Moffat rail line, 28, 31–32
Montgomery bus boycott, 134, 206–7, 208, 210, 222
Monthly Review, 223, 316
Moon, Henry Lee, 208
Mooney, Tom, 80, 97, 107, 321
Moore, Barrington, Jr., 267

Moore, Harry, 204
Morgan, Juliette, 207
Morris, Willie, 207, 236
Morse, Wayne, 268, 269, 273, 285, 301
Morton, Thruston, 276
Moscow Conference (1947), 126
Moscow summit conference (1972), 236, 295–96, 299
Moscow War Diary (Werth), 238
Moses, Robert, 201
Mostel, Zero, 181
Motion Picture Alliance for the Preservation of American Ideals, 119
motion picture industry, 43, 44, 46, 86–92
Moulton, Arthur W., 153
Mowbray, A. G., 220
Moynihan, Daniel Patrick, 300
MPLA, 233
MPLS, 132
muckraking, 62, 195, 213–21
Muhammad Ali, 212
Muhlen, N., 152
Muller, René J., 305
Munich crisis, 94, 96
Munson, Curtis B., 102
Murphy, Frank, 135
Murphy, Gardner, 153
Murphy, George, 180
Murray, George, 86
Murtagh, Arthur, 216
Murton, Tom, 219
Musical Uproar in Moscow (Werth), 238–39
Mussolini, Benito, 92, 94
My Crusade for Portugal (Galvão), 233
Myrdal, Gunnar, 115
Myer, Dillon, 104

Nader, Ralph, 219
Nagasaki, 117
Nathan, George Jean, 52–53
Nation, The, 66, 67, 105
and "affluent society," 195, 198–204
and antiwar movement, 195, 222, 223–227, 276–77, 292–93
attacked by "anti-Communists," 144–45, 148, 151–53, 190
ban on, 189–90
and Bay of Pigs, 195, 228–30, 234
and Cambodia, 290
centennial issue, 262
and China, 182, 185
CIA special issue, 217–18

Nation (cont.)
and CIA-subsidized groups, 155–57
civil-liberties special issues, 145, 148–49
and civil rights, 195, 204–8, 262
Commencement Day special issues, 203–4
conferences, 122, 144, 153, 274–75
correspondents of, 235–50
and Dominican Republic, 270–71
early years of, 143, 153, 205; *see also* Villard, Oswald Garrison
FBI special issue, 215–16
financial problems of, 144, 145, 190, 191, 264
and *Frontier,* 274
Greenberg incident, 149–51, 189
Gruening and, 268, 269, 274, 285
Hiss special issue, 214
and informer system, 185–88
under Kirchwey, *see* Kirchwey, Freda
Kirstein and, 191–93, 195, 259, 261–64
McCarthyism opposed by, 147–49, 151, 160–61, 167, 169, 173
McWilliams' editorship of, 145–46, 191–319 *passim*
McWilliams' West Coast work for, 116, 119, 120, 122, 132, 143, 144
and military-industrial complex, 195, 198, 217
and *Monthly Review,* 316
muckraking by, 195, 213–21
and New York corruption, 216–17
and 1968 election, 281, 283
and 1972 election, 296
and Nixon, 288, 290, 293, 294, 296–98, 301, 304, 305, 318
and Pasternak, 170
and Portugal, 232–34
and poverty, 198
and radical right, 252, 253–54, 256
satire in, 200–203
and Spain, 144, 149
Storrow and, 262–63, 319
and Stevenson, 163–64
and Vietnam War, 195, 257–58, 265–72, 274–78, 281, 287, 291–93, 297–98, 306, 313, 316
and Wallace movement, 128
and Warren Commission Report, 258–259
and Watergate, 287, 296, 318
National Advisory Commission on Civic Disorders, 291
National Association for the Advancement of Colored People, 99

National Citizens Political Action Committee, 120, 175
National Committee for a Sane Nuclear Policy (SANE), 222, 223
National Conference of Black Mayors, 212
National Farm Workers Union, 112
National Guardian, 190, 191
National Industrial Recovery Act, 81
National Labor Relations Act, 81, 311
National Labor Relations Board, 81–82
National Lawyers Guild, 301
National Observer, 235, 307
National Review, 251
National Security Council, 251, 290
National Spiritualists Association, 46
National Student Association, 222
Nation Associates, The, 144
Native Sons of the Golden West, 107
Nazi-Soviet Pact, 93–94, 96
NBC, 309
Neal, Fred Warner, 245
Neblett, William, 87–88, 89
Nehru, Jawaharlal, 170
Neihardt, John G., 55
Neither Free Nor Equal (radio series), 132
Neutra, Richard, 47
New Barbarians, The (Abbott), 41
New Deal, 53, 68, 80, 120–22
Newfield, Jack, 246, 247–48, 278, 317
New Frontier, 256–57
New Leader, The, 148, 149, 151–52, 153, 157, 189
new left, 246–49, 272, 276–77, 316–17
New Left Review, 316
New Muckrakers, The (Downie), 218
New Politics Conference, 316–17
New Regionalism in American Literature, The (McWilliams), 66
New Republic, The, 67, 95, 105, 113, 190, 191, 265
Newsday, 220
New Statesman, 151, 161, 238
Newsweek, 199, 294
New York City, 216–17, 308
New York *Daily News,* 271
New Yorker, The, 117, 166, 167, 287
New York *Herald-Tribune,* 217
New York Newspaper Guild awards, 134, 215, 217
New York Review, 265
New York *Times,* 157–58, 229–30
New York *World-Telegram and Sun,* 153, 214, 217, 219
Nightmare Decade, The (Cook), 192, 214
Nigut, William, 301

Nitti, Frank, 87, 88, 90
Nixon, Richard M., 127, 162, 170, 250, 254
  and antiwar protests, 289–94, 307
  character assessment, 304–5
  Checkers speech, 302, 303
  and China, 183, 256, 288, 294–95, 296
  Christmas bombings, 297–98, 300
  impeachment, 301–3
  and King, 209
  and McCarthy, 172
  1946 campaign, 122, 287
  1952 campaign, 163, 302
  1956 campaign, 164, 288
  1962 campaign, 303
  1968 campaign, 256, 283, 285
  1972 election, 296
  pardon of, 301, 305
  resignation, 303, 306, 309, 310
  and Vietnam War, 265, 285–99, 300
  and Watergate, 296, 298, 299–304
Noble, Robert, 71–72
Non-Violent Action Against Nuclear Weapons, 223
Normand, Mabel, 46
North American Review, 66
Northern Indianan, The, 59
North from Mexico (McWilliams), 134
Nossiter, Bernard, 151, 198, 214, 219
Nuclear Test Ban Treaty, 226

Oatley, Polly, 23–25
O'Brien, Conor Cruise, 154, 156, 176
"Observers, The," 147–48
Ochsner, Alton, 219
O'Connor, Harvey, 194, 198
October 15 Moratorium, 289–90
Oglesby, Carl, 245
Ohio Un-American Activities Committee, 187
Oil (Sinclair), 50
Okies, 75–80, 133
Okubo, Mine, 105
Old-Age Revolving Pensions, Ltd., 71
Older, Fremont, 56
O'Leary, Ralph, 220
Olmsted, Frederick Law, 264
Olson, Culbert L., 104, 107, 147
  administration of, 80
  election of, 70, 72, 73, 85
  and farm labor, 79
  McWilliams appointment, 76–77, 79

One Hundred Years of The Nation (Christman), 262
Opinion magazine, 48
Oppenheimer, J. Robert, 94, 173, 219
Organization Man, The (Whyte), 202
Ornitz, Samuel, 135–38
O'Sullivan, Vincent, 55
Otis, Harrison Gray, 43–44
Our Changing Morality (Kirchwey), 144
Overland Monthly, The, 47

Paar, Jack, 216
Packing House Workers, 112
Pagano, Jo, 48
Palestine, 144
Palmer, Harlan G., 83
Paris Accords, 298
Parker, Carleton, 77
Parks, Rosa, 206
Pasternak, Boris, 170
Paterson, Thomas G., 245
Paths of Glory (Cobb), 95, 97
Patman, Wright, 237
Pauley, Edwin, 123
Pauling, Linus, 128, 169–70, 223
Peace and Arms: Reports from The Nation (Christman), 224, 262
Peace Corps, 257
peace movement, *see* antiwar movement
Peace News, 248
Peale, Norman Vincent, 201
Pearman, Robert, 219
Peekskill riots, 138
Peffer, Nathaniel, 185
Pegler, Westbrook, 88, 103
Peking summit conference, 256, 295–96, 299
Pendergast, Thomas, 118
Pentagon Papers, 294
People's Movement for the Liberation of Angola, 233
People v. Zamora et al., 110
Perl, William, 219
Perry, Charlotte, 32
Perry, James M., 307
Peterson, Richard E., 292
Philbrick, Herbert, 88, 89
Phillips, Clara, 45
Phillips, Gifford, 274
Phipps, Lawrence, 36
Phoenix (peace ship), 223
Piel, Gerard, 148

Piven, Frances Fox, 198, 219
Place in the Sun, A (Fenton), 49
Playboy, 235, 236
Plessy v. Ferguson, 205
PM, 99, 105, 106, 190, 191
Point Counter Point, 58
Political Nursery, The, 62
Politics, 222
Polk, James K., 27
Polonsky, Abe, 139
Portsmouth, Earl of, 108
Portugal: Fifty Years of Dictatorship
    (Figueiredo), 234
Potsdam Conference, 117
Powell, Lawrence Clark, 47
Power Elite, The (Mills), 202
Prejudice (McWilliams), 21, 101, 105, 130,
    134
President's Commission on Civil Rights,
    125, 128, 204
Price, Archie, 72–73
Primavera Press, 48
Progressive, The, 265
Progressive Citizens of America, 124–25,
    128, 175, 178, 180
Progressive Party, 129–30, 144, 175
Prohibition, 35, 41, 53
Prophetic Minority, A (Newfield), 248
Pseudo Ethic, The (Halsey), 199–200
Psycho-Phone Messages (Grierson), 47
Pugwash Conferences, 222
Purcell, Victor, 266
Purnell, Karl, 267

Quinn, Anthony, 110

Rabinowitz, Victor, 301
racial violence, 112–14, 125, 272, 276, 283,
    291
radical right, 218, 250–56, 269
Radin, Max, 107
Radosh, Ronald, 245
Ramparts, 265
Randolph, A. Philip, 99
Rankin, John E., 118–19
Rao, V. K. V. R., 185
Rauh, Joseph L., Jr., 187
Reagan, Ronald, 122, 180, 252, 256
Red Channels, 166

Red Channels, 136
Redding, J. Saunders, 134
Redlich, Norman, 148–49, 259
"red scare" (1919–20), 311, 315
Red Star over China (Snow), 182
Reedy's Mirror, 51
Reich, Kenneth, 220
Reid, Wallace, 45
Reik, Louis, 203
Remarque, Erich Maria, 96
Remington, William, 152, 214–15
Reporter, The, 191
Republican Party
    in California, 70, 85
    1946 victories, 122
    1964 convention, 253–55
    1968 campaign, 282–83, 285
    Reagan and, 256
    and Vietnam War, 288
Reston, James, Jr., 183, 288
revisionists, 243–46
Revolt in the South (Wakefield), 206
Rexroth, Kenneth, 201
Rhodes, John J., 300
Richardson Foundation, 251
Richardson, Elliot, 300
Rich: Are They Different?, The (Kirstein), 261
Ritchie, Ward, 47
Robeson, Paul, 138
Robins, Raymond, 244
Robinson, Joan, 185
Rockefeller, Nelson, 110, 253, 283
Rockettes' strike, 201–2
Rodriguez, José, 47
Rogers, Will, Jr., 121–22
Rogers, William P., 107, 172
Rogin, Michael, 310
Romney, George, 283
Roosevelt, Eleanor, 208
Roosevelt, Franklin D., 69, 93, 130, 182,
    192, 213
    death of, 116, 120–21
    and Japanese Americans, 102–3
    and old-age pensions, 71
    and Sinclair, 70
Roosevelt, Theodore, 323
Rose, Stanley, 48–49
Roselli, John, 88
Rosenberg, Julius and Ethel, 152, 219
Rosenwald, Julius, 191
Ross, Fred, 111–12
Ross, Lillian, 136, 167
Rossen, Robert, 137
Rostow, Eugene V., 307
Roszak, Theodore, 248–49, 314

Rovere, Richard, 148, 152, 154–55, 157, 245
Roybal, Edward, 111
Royce, William S., 224
Rusk, Dean, 183, 286, 295
Russell, Bertrand, 217
Russell, Charles Edward, 62
Russia at War: 1941–1945 (Werth), 238
Russia: Hopes and Fears (Werth), 239
Russian Revolution, 310, 311
Russia Under Khrushchev (Werth), 239
Rutledge, Wiley B., 135
Ryan, William, 219

Sacco, Nicola, 50, 51, 321
Safire, William, 295, 298, 299
St. Louis *Post-Dispatch*, 229, 233
St. Paul, Minnesota, 131–32
Salazar, Antonio de Oliveira, 232–34
Salisbury, Harrison, 273
Salk Institute for Biological Studies, 241
Samish, Arthur, 220
Sampson, Anthony, 238
Sanchez, George, 108
San Diego *Union*, 47
Sandino, Augusto César, 228
SANE, 222, 223
San Francisco *Chronicle*, 79
San Francisco general strike (1934), 69–70, 74
San Francisco *Review*, 47
Santa María, 232–33, 234
Saroyan, William, 48, 55
Sarton, May, 174, 175
Sartre, Jean-Paul, 115, 160
Sasuly, Richard, 198
Saturday Evening Post, The, 236
Saturday Night, 47, 48
Saturday Night and Sunday Morning (Sillitoe), 62–63
Saturday Review of Literature, The, 66
Sawyer, John E., 318
Schapiro, Leonard, 184
Schary, Dore, 136–37
Schenck, Joseph, 88, 89–90, 91
Schenck, Nicholas, 89, 91
Schindler, R. W., 47
Schlesinger, Arthur, Jr., 154–55, 157, 161, 227
Schneider, Eugene V., 252
Schott, Walter, 271
Schuman, Frederick L., 243–44, 280

Schwartz, Fred, 252
Schwarzbart, Elias M., 98
Science and Human Values (Bronowski), 240, 243
Scopes trial, 41
Scott, Adrian, 135–38
Scott, Byron, 219
Scottsboro case, 98
Scoundrel Time (Hellman), 309
Scranton, William, 253
Scranton Commission, 291
Screen Writers Guild, 136
Seager, Allan, 149, 202, 203
Seldes, Timothy, 179
Seldin, Joseph J., 220
Select Committee to Study . . . Intelligence Activities, 231
Seligman, Joseph, 133
Selma, Alabama, march, 210
Senate Judiciary Committee, 170
Sender, Ramon, 93
Service, John S., 168, 183
Shahn, Ben, 148
Shapiro, Carl, 203
Shapiro, Henry, 238
Shaw, Frank, 72, 83
Sheehan, Neil, 273
Shelley, John, 121–22
shelter program, 225–26
Sherrill, Robert, 194, 220, 236–37
Shippey, Lee, 45
Shirer, William L., 136, 148, 298
Shuler, Robert, 45
Shultz, Lillie, 144, 188, 190
Siegel, Lawrence, 187–88
Sihanouk, Prince, 250, 290
Sillitoe, Alan, 62
Simmons, Ernest J., 170, 175
Simon J. Lubin Society, 78
Sinclair, Craig, 71
Sinclair, Upton, 47, 49–50, 73
  EPIC campaign, 67, 68–71, 74, 85
SLA (Symbionese Liberation Army), 317
Sleepy Lagoon case, 108–11
Small Farm and Big Farm (McWilliams), 108
Smart Set, The, 41, 51–53
Smathers, George, 236
Smedley, Agnes, 184
Smith, Desmond, 220, 267
Smith, Gerald L. K., 71, 147
Smith, Howard K., 123, 185
Smith, Paul Jordan, 47
Smith, Ralph Lee, 219
Smith Act prosecutions, 138, 146, 163
Snepp, Frank, 298

Snow, C. P., 239–40, 249
Snow, Edgar, 148, 195–96, 238
 life and death of, 173, 182–85
 and Nixon's China visit, 183, 294
 and Vietnam War, 266, 267, 286
Snow, Lois, 183
Snyder, John W., 123
Sobell case, 219
Social Astonishments (Cort), 201
socialism, 314–16, 319, 321–24
Socialist Party, 69, 73, 316, 324
Social Security Act, 71
Soil Conservation Service, 108
Solow, Martin, 188
Sorensen, Theodore, 309
South as It Is, The (Dennett/Christman), 262
Southern, Terry, 201
Southern California, University of, 42, 50
Southern California Country (McWilliams),
 119, 120, 132
Southern Christian Leadership Council,
 206
Southern Farmer, 191
Southern Pacific R.R., 62
Southern Regional Council, 115
Southwest Review, 66
Soviet-Nazi Pact, 93–94, 96
space program, 254, 258
Spanish-American War, 51–52
Spanish Civil War, 92, 93
Speak Truth to Power, 222
Spectator, The, 297
Spectorsky, A. C., 202
Spencer, Theodore, 46
Spender, Stephen, 156
Spitz, Leo, 89
Sports and Vanities, 47
Stalin, Joseph, 118, 173, 222, 311
Standard, William, 301
Stander, Lionel, 93, 137
Stanford, Leland, 62
Star, The, 190, 191
State of The Nation, The, 262
Steamboat Springs, Colorado, 28, 29–30,
 31, 32, 34, 35
Steffens, Lincoln, 62, 86*fn.*, 213, 263
Stegner, Wallace, 105, 203
Stein, Sol, 151
Stein, Walter J., 78, 79
Steinbeck, John, 64, 78, 200
Steinbeck Committee to Aid Agricultural
 Workers, 78
Stenerson, Douglas C., 53
Stennis, John C., 172

Sterling, George, 56–57, 176
Stern, Lawrence, 313
Sterne, Richard Clark, 262
Stevenson, Adlai, 163–64, 208, 256
Steward, Desmond, 238
Stewart, George R., 203
Stewart, Potter, 164
Stimson, Henry L., 138
Stone, I. F., 161, 173, 191, 237
Storrow, James J., Jr., 262–63, 319
Storrow, James Jackson, 263
Storrow, Linda, 263
Straight, Michael, 190
Strange History of Pierre Mendès-France, The
 (Werth), 238
Strong, Anna Louise, 184
Struik, Richard, 153
Student Non-Violent Coordinating
 Committee, 206
Students for a Democratic Society, 270
Studies on the Left, 316
Supermarket Trap, The (Cross), 220
Supreme Court, 76, 82
 and civil rights, 100, 106, 205–6, 209
 and First Amendment, 136
 and Taft-Hartley, 165–66
Sutherland, Elizabeth, 194
Swados, Harvey, 198, 219, 262
Swanson, Gloria, 188
Sweezy, Paul, 223, 316
Sykes, Gresham, 219
Szilard, Leo, 241

Taft, Robert A., 123, 163
Taft-Hartley Act, 123, 128, 165–66
Tail Gunner Joe (NBC documentary), 309
Takasugi, Robert, 106
Tarbell, Ida, 213
Tarshis, Lorie, 223
Taylor, W. H., 189, 219
Taylor, William Desmond, 45
teach-ins, 271, 276, 284
Teasdale, Sara, 47
Temporary Commission on Employee
 Loyalty, 125
Tenney, Jack, 109, 146–47
Tet offensive, 185, 278–79
Thackrey, Ted, 190
Theobald, Robert, 219
Thieu, Nguyen Van, 297, 306
Thirty-Every-Thursday, *see* Ham-'n-Eggs

This Side of Paradise (Fitzgerald), 40, 41
Thomas, J. Parnell, 125
Thomas, Norman, 73
Thompson, Hunter, 235–36
Thompson, James, 290
Thompson, Wade, 201–2
Thomson, David, 245
Thurber, James, 39
Thurmond, Strom, 130
Till, Emmet, 206
Time, 148, 200, 229, 319
Toffler, Al, 198
Tolan Committee, 103–4
Tonkin, Gulf of, 269
Toronto *Star*, 233
Towards a New Past (Bernstein), 155
Tower, John G., 300
Towne, Robert, 43
Townsend, Francis E., 71
Townsend Plan, 67, 71, 73
Tragedy of American Diplomacy, The
   (Williams), 244
Travels in the Southland (L. V. Bierce), 58
Trevor-Roper, H. R., 157
Trilling, Diana, 154–55
Trilling, Lionel, 26
Trona, California, 82
Truehaft, Jessica Mitford, 167, 203
Truman, Harry, 120
   administration of, 122–23
   and atom bomb, 116–18, 122
   and civil rights, 125, 128, 130
   and Cold War, 118, 125–27, 129, 144,
      311–12
   death of, 298
   and H-bomb, 138
   and Korea, 127
   "loyalty program" of, 126
   McCarthyism and, 126, 159
   1948 election, 128–30, 163
   and Taft-Hartley, 123, 128
   and Vietnam War, 285–86
Truman Doctrine, 125–27
Trumbo, Dalton, 135–38, 169, 219, 262
Tufts, James, 56
Tully, Jim, 48
Turner, William, 216

Unfinished Case of Alger Hiss, The (Cook),
   214
Unger, Irwin, 265

United Auto Workers, 163
United Nations, 144, 149, 266
United Nations Charter, 140
U.S. Information Agency, 309
U.S. Strategic Bombing Survey, 117
United World Federalists, 221
Unruh, Jesse, 284
Utopian Society, 67–68, 73

Valley of Shadows, The (Grierson), 46
Van Doren, Mark, 262
Vanzetti, Bartolomeo, 50, 51, 167, 321
Vardman, James K., Jr., 123
Vaughan, Harry, 123
Velie, Lester, 220
Veliz, Claudio, 224
Viereck, Peter, 151, 152, 154–55, 157
*Vietnam: History, Documents and Opinions on
   a Major World Crisis* (Gettleman), 301
Vietnam: The Logic of Withdrawal (Zinn), 267
Vietnam War, 193, 227, 264–99
   Christmas bombings, 297–98, 300
   and civil-rights movement, 210, 212
   and Cold War, 162, 310, 312
   cost of, 280
   early years of, 265–66, 270, 285–86
   end of, 305–8
   Johnson and, 128, 255, 259, 265, 267–
      273, 307
   Kennedy and, 257–59
   legality question, 301–2
   McCarthyism and, 171
   Nation and, 195, 257–58, 265–72, 274–
      278, 281, 287, 291–93, 297–98, 306,
      313, 316
   Nixon and, 265, 286–99, 300
   protests, *see* antiwar movement
   revisionists and, 245–46
   "Vietnamization" of, 265, 289, 298–99,
      308
   and Watergate, 287, 305–6, 307–8
View of The Nation, A (Christman), 262
Village Voice, The, 247–48
Villard, Mrs. Henry, 144
Villard, Oswald Garrison, 41, 62, 144, 153,
   228, 235, 263
Vincent, John Carter, 168–69
Vinson, Frederick M., 164
Voice of America, 170
Voorhis, H. Jerry, 122
Voting Rights Act, 210, 211, 272

Wagner, Robert F., 281
Wagner, Tennessee Carolee, 35
Wakefield, Dan, 206
Walker, Edwin A., 209
Walker, Stanley, 220
Wallace, George, 209, 237, 283, 285
Wallace, Henry A., 121, 123, 124
    candidacy of, 127–30, 138, 145, 175,
        180, 221
    on Truman Doctrine, 126
Wallace, June, 148
Wallace, Mike, 267
Wall Street Journal, 199, 237, 290
Walpole, Hugh, 48
Walsh, J. Raymond, 128
Walton, Richard J., 245
Warfare State, The (Cook), 217
War Labor Board, 192
Warner, Harry, 90, 91–92
War Powers Act, 298
War Relocation Authority, 104, 106
Warren, Earl, 129
    appointment to Court, 164–65, 173, 210
    Brown decision, 205, 209–10
    and Japanese Americans, 104–7 *passim,*
        205
    McCarthy and, 172
    and McWilliams, 107–8
    and zoot-suit riots, 113–14
Warren Commission, 148–49, 258–59
War Resisters, 223
Washington, University of, 139, 140
Washington *Post,* 187, 233, 296
Wasp, The, 61
Watch and Ward Society, 55
Watergate scandal, 227, 287, 296, 298,
        299–304, 305–8
Watkins, Arthur V., 127, 172
Watson, Tom, 322
Watts riots, 210
Weathermen, 317
Weaver, Robert C., 99, 112
Weber, Kim, 47
Wechsler, James, 187
Weighart, James, 306
Weil, Simon, 176
Weiss, Peter, 293, 302
Welch, Robert H. W., Jr., 251
Welles, Orson, 110
Werner, Bud, 32
Werth, Alexander, 195, 238–39, 266, 267
West, Nathanael, 44, 48
Western Writers Congress, 93
Westmoreland, William C., 269, 278, 279

Weston, Edward, 48
Westways, 119
Whalen, Richard, 287, 288
Wheatland hop pickers' riot, 76–77
Wheeler, Burton K., 40–41
Whitaker, Urban, 223
Whitaker and Baxter, 220, 235
White, E. B., 200
White, Harry Dexter, 152, 219
White Citizens Councils, 206
Whyte, William H., Jr., 202
Widick, B. J., 194, 198
Wiener, Norbert, 240
Wilkins, Roy, 99
Williams, Aubrey, 191, 207
Williams, Raymond, 245
Williams, William Appleman, 223, 244–45
Willkie, Wendell, 114, 120, 134, 192
Wilson, Edmund, 46, 53–54, 61, 69, 321
Wilson, H. H., 161
Wilson, Woodrow, 40
Wired Nation, The (Smith), 219
Witch Hunt: The Revival of Heresy
        (McWilliams), 139, 140, 146
Witness (Chambers), 186
Wittner, Lawrence S., 221, 265, 272
Wolfe Hall Military Academy, 36–37
Wolfe, Thomas, 39
Wolfert, Ira, 148
Wolfram, Harold, 149
Wolin, Sheldon, 318
Woltman, Frederick, 153
Women's International League for Peace
        and Freedom, 223
Wood, James Playsted, 213
Wood, Scott, 56
Woodside, Alexander, 246
Woodward, C. Vann, 208, 262
Wooley v. Maynard, 136
World War I, 38, 40, 63, 95, 280
World War II, 94–95, 96–119, 280
Worthington, Peter, 267
Wright, Frank Lloyd, 47
Wright, Lloyd, 47, 48
Wright, S. MacDonald, 47
Wright, Willard Huntington, 47, 52
Wrong Horse, The (Stern), 313

Ydigoras, Miguel, 229
Year of Stalingrad, The (Werth), 238
Yellow Book, The, 51
Yergin, Daniel, 159

York Gazette and Daily, 179
Yorty, Sam, 147

Zaugg, Ernest, 267
Zeigler, Edward, 220

Zeitlin, Jake, 47, 48
Ziebarth, E. W., 131
Ziff, Larzer, 51
Zinn, Howard, 206, 243, 245, 262, 267
zoot-suit riots, 112–14